The Everyman Companion
to Food and Nutrition

THE EVERYMAN COMPANION TO FOOD AND NUTRITION

Sheila Bingham

J M Dent & Sons Ltd
London Melbourne

First published 1987
© Sheila Bingham 1987

All rights reserved. No part of this publication may
be reproduced, stored in a retrieval system, or transmitted,
in any form or by any means, electronic, mechanical, photocopying,
recording or otherwise, without the prior permission of
J.M. Dent & Sons Ltd.

This book is set in Bembo by Gee Graphics Ltd
Printed in Great Britain by Mackays of Chatham for
J.M. Dent & Sons Ltd
Aldine House, 33 Welbeck Street, London W1M 8LX

British Library Cataloguing in Publication Data

Bingham, Sheila
    The Everyman Companion to food and nutrition.
    1. Nutrition 2. Food-Composition
    I. Title
    641.1 TX551

ISBN 0-460 03038-8

CONTENTS

Contents

Contents

ACKNOWLEDGEMENTS

Data from the following publications has been reproduced with the permission of the Controller, Her Majesty's Stationery Office.

Paul, A.A., Southgate, D.A.T., 1978, McCance and Widdowson's *The Composition of Foods,* Fourth Edition, M.R.C. Special Report No. 297

Paul, A.A., Southgate, D.A.T., Russell, C., 1980, First Supplement to *The Composition of Foods*

Tann, S., Wenlock, S., Buss, D., 1985, Second Supplement to *The Composition of Foods*

Department of Health and Social Security, 1979, *Report on Health and Social Subjects* No 15 (Appendix I)

Ministry of Agriculture, Fisheries and Food, 1984, *Look at the Label* Appendix, Serial Numbers of Food Additives (Appendix II)

INTRODUCTION

The potential for good health through diet is enormous. Hence, this *Everyman Companion* with over 400 entries on food, diet and nutrition.

For a general introduction, a history of the science of nutrition, and a taste of current aspects of research, read first the general sections on **diet**[1] and **nutrition**. Then delve into any one of the 100 or so entries which tell you about nutrients in detail - from **amino acids**, through **cholesterol, fat, fibre, protein, vitamins,** and **trace elements**, to **zinc**. Each of these sections explains exactly what these nutrients do, why some are important to health, where to find them, and how to cook food the right way to preserve them.

There are also 220 separate sections on foods - from **ackee** fruit, **broccoli** and **beef** to **octopus, yoghurt** and **yams**. Find out what is in a **kiwi fruit, kumquat** or **ladies' finger** - each has a full nutritional analysis. Also there is some history of food, from **bread, biscuits, breakfast cereals** and **croissants**, to **honey, oysters** and **venison**. The entries also tell you why eating **cabbage** is good for your health, the difference between **lemons and limes**, and how to spot a fresh **egg**.

Forty other entries are devoted to medical conditions which may be related to the type of food we eat. These range from the classic vitamin deficiency diseases such as **scurvy, pellagra** and **beriberi,** to individual problems such as **allergy, gout, diabetes,** and **coeliac disease**. On a national scale, the role of diet and the effect it may have on the risk of developing **heart disease, stroke** and **cancer** are discussed. The section on **energy** tells you how to work out how much you should be using each day - if **body weight** tells you you are over the limit, turn to **slimming diets** to discover a few home truths and a slimming diet to enjoy.

Lastly, the other aspects of food - **additives** and **poisons in food** (including radiation) are comprehensively discussed, from **antioxidants, emulsifiers, colours** and **preservatives**, through to **organic food, health food** and **macrobiotic diets**. The *Companion* explains clearly what additives are, about **E numbers** (all of which are listed in the Appendix), and tells you about some other aspects of food constituents, such as **histamine, salicylates, alcohol, tryptophan** and **caffeine** which may affect mood or health.

Overall, the purpose of this book is to be a companion to food, nutrition and diet. It is a complete guide to the nutritional facts of food and a healthy diet. The introductions to most entries contain the salient points - those who would like to find out more should read on.

[1] Cross-referenced entries are in bold type.

Acetic acid (E260)

Acetic acid is the main acid in **vinegar**, and is added to pickles, sauces and flavoured foods as a preservative and acidifier. Calcium, sodium and potassium salts (E261, 262, 263) are used as buffers (see **miscellaneous additives**).

Acetic acid is produced in the body in quite large amounts and has a central role in energy **metabolism**. It is also produced by bacteria fermenting dietary **fibre** in the large bowel and absorbed into the blood stream.

Ackee, see also **vegetables**

A tropical fruit of West African origin, widely grown in the West Indies. Parts of the ackee are poisonous and episodes of 'vomiting sickness' in Jamaica have been attributed to a chemical, hypoglycin, contained in it. The yellow part is edible and can be cooked and served as a vegetable, reputedly tasting of scrambled eggs. Ackee is rich in fat, and consequently higher in energy than most **vegetables** (see table). Canned ackee contains added salt.

Average nutrients in 100 grams (3½ oz) Ackee (canned)

Energy kilojoules	625	Iron milligrams	0.7
kilocalories	151	Copper milligrams	0.27
Protein grams	2.9	Zinc milligrams	0.60
Total fat grams	15.2	Vitamin A micrograms	–
Saturated fat grams	–	Vitamin D micrograms	0
Polyunsaturated fat grams	–	Vitamin C milligrams	30
		Vitamin E milligrams	–
Cholesterol milligrams	0	B vitamins:	
Sugars grams	0.8	Thiamin (B_1) milligrams	0.03
Starch grams	0	Riboflavin (B_2) milligrams	0.07
Dietary fibre grams	2.7	Nicotinic acid milligrams	1.1
Sodium milligrams	240	Pyridoxine (B_6) milligrams	0.06
Potassium milligrams	270	Vitamin B_{12} micrograms	0
Calcium milligrams	35	Folic acid micrograms	41
Magnesium milligrams	40	Pantothenic acid milligrams	–
		Biotin micrograms	–

(–) No information available   (0) Contains zero or trace amounts

Additives in food

A diverse number of substances are added to food, particularly **convenience foods**, to increase shelf life, to assist in processing and to improve its palatability. Some occur naturally in food and in the body, such as **citric** and **acetic** acids and present no risks to health in the amounts used. Others however are not naturally occurring.

At present there is much public awareness of additives in food. This is partly because of recent legislation which requires many additives to be specifically declared by name or number (see E number) on food **labels**. The statistics on food additives are also alarming – the number of additives in use is estimated to be between 2000–3500. The average person eats about 10 grams of additives each day – more than the average consumption of many foods – such as fresh oranges. However, 1500–3000 of the total number are **flavours** which account for 20% (2 grams) of the average consumption of 10 grams. Thickeners and stabilisers (such as **modified starch**) account for another 20%, and nutrients and vitamins for 15%.

In some respects there is less cause for concern when food additives are compared with other aspects of diet. They are subject to far greater control than, for example, farm chemicals (see poisons in food) and the evidence suggests that they do much less harm than, for example, diets which contain a lot of **fat, sucrose** or too few **vegetables**. According to one estimate, less than 1% of cancers can be attributed to the use of additives in food, compared with 35% from these other aspects of diet. All food consists of a vast array of different chemicals and in some respects an additive is safer than many 'natural' products because it is a small amount of one known chemical rather than a mixture of a great number of unmeasured chemicals, as in 'natural' products. The risks of food poisoning from bacteria are also offset to an extent by additives used as preservatives in food.

Nevertheless, there is no doubt that some additives are important in **allergy** especially amongst workers in the food industry who handle large amounts. It is also possible that a diet consisting almost entirely of convenience foods containing many additives might incur a greater risk of general ill health and susceptibility to disease, particularly since these foods tend to contain less of the trace elements and vitamins. In addition, the safety and toxicity of some additives in present use has not been fully assessed. Even when safety tests are complete, the effect of an additive on human health cannot always be predicted because safety tests are necessarily restricted to animals and bacteria. Apart from the differences in the way man and animals utilise food and additives, interaction of foods and additives may sometimes occur, causing toxic compounds.

The use of food additives, and the composition of important staple foods, such as milk, meat, and bread, is under the general control of the Food Act 1984. This makes it an offence to prepare or sell food unfit for human consumption and not of the nature, substance and quality demanded, or injurious to health. Among other general provisions it authorises the Minister of Agriculture, Fisheries and Food and the Secretary of State for Social Services jointly to make regulations to control the use of food additives, food labelling, and food composition. In making the regulations, the government is advised by the Food Advisory Committee (FAC) which draws on data from the food industry (mostly responsible for carrying out toxicity tests) and from other reports from, for example, the EEC and the World Health Organisation.

In regulating the use of additives, sometimes a ban may be introduced, as happened with chloroform in 1980, and cyclamate in 1969. Neither of these may now be used in food. The major means of control however is by the use of permitted lists. Additives on the permitted lists may either be considered safe by the FAC, or they may have been given temporary clearance, pending further investigation. There are about 280 additives specifically permitted in food and a full list is given in Appendix II, together with the E number. The regulations covering these specify their purity, and make it an offence to use additives which are not permitted additives. They must also be declared on the labels of foods either by name or number.

Additives are grouped according to their main use by the food industry and there are permitted lists for **Preservatives, Colours, Antioxidants, Emulsifiers and Stabilisers, Sweeteners, Solvents** and **Mineral Hydrocarbons** (see individual entries). In addition there is a large list of **Miscellaneous Additives**. Of these the colours are perhaps the most controversial because they are permitted in most processed foods – and account for about 5% of the total average consumption of additives – but do not contribute to the nutritive value or safety of foods. The great majority of miscellaneous additives are also permitted in all food. Preservatives and antioxidants are more closely controlled because the chemical properties that make them effective as preservatives also make them potentially harmful to health. Hence, these are restricted to certain foods only and the maximum levels are stated. Preservatives and antioxidants account for about 1.5% of the weight of additives eaten by the average person.

Enzymes, modified starches and **flavours** are not yet covered by permitted lists. As already mentioned, the majority (3000) of additives used are in flavours and by sheer weight of numbers they will probably defeat any attempt by the FAC to devise a permitted list. They must be declared on food labels as, for example, 'flavourings' but the specific substance used does not have to be declared.

Adipose tissue

Adipose tissue is an **energy** reserve of **fat** stored as congregations of cells around organs and under the skin. Fat soluble food constituents such as **carotene, antioxidants** and pesticides also accumulate in adipose tissue. Women usually contain about twice as much adipose tissue as men – about 25 and 12% as fat respectively in people of normal **body weight**. Athletes, both men and women, contain less, about 8%, but, individuals vary greatly in the amount of fat they hold in store. The fat cells may become larger and (at least during growth) increase in number. A body containing over 20% in a man (14 kilograms or 2¾ stones for a 70 kilogram (11 stone) man) and 30% in a woman would be considered obese – see **obesity**. Fat stores can be reduced to as little as one kilogram (2¼ lbs) during **starvation**.

The major determinant of basal **metabolic rate** is the amount of active (lean) tissue, whereas adipose tissue is by comparison inactive, at least in the case of the majority – white adipose tissue. However, in rodents, brown adipose tissue is metabolically active, and indeed regulates body temperature in many mammals and human infants by a mechanism called non-shivering thermogenesis, which is stimulated by the hormone noradrenalin. Also in some animals, particularly the rat, brown adipose tissue can be shown to increase energy expenditure on overfeeding and there is much other evidence that the regulatory activities of brown adipose tissue are important in the aetiology of obesity in the rat and some other mammals. In humans, active brown adipose tissue occurs in infants, but in adults its contribution to energy expenditure appears to be small, except in people who have a rare tumour of the adrenal gland. Consequently the possibility that obese people are unable to increase their energy expenditure in response to excess food because they are unfortunate in not having been endowed with brown adipose tissue is debatable.

Agar (E406)

Agar is an extract of red seaweed which dissolves in hot water and sets to a jelly when cooled. It is used as a thickener and stabiliser (see **Emulsifiers**) in many foods such as ice cream, soups and desserts and is used by vegetarians as a jelling agent.

Agar is a **polysaccharide** composed of chains of **galactose**. It is not broken down during **digestion** and contributes to dietary **fibre**.

Alcohol – chemical names ethanol, ethyl alcohol

Alcohol is a drug, which also supplies energy (Calories) to the body. Each gram of alcohol in alcoholic drinks supplies 29 kilojoules (7 kilocalories) and **beers** and **wines** also contain **sugars** – see beers, wines and spirits and liqueurs. Although part of the social life of man, alcohol in excess is damaging to many parts of the body.

About one fifth of the alcohol in a drink is absorbed through the walls of the stomach into the blood stream. Effervescent drinks and spirits are absorbed more quickly, but food or – in some people – fat (for example in milk) taken in advance delays absorption from the stomach. The rest of the alcohol is steadily absorbed into the blood stream from the small intestine (see **digestion**) at a constant rate unaffected by food. Most people will have absorbed all the alcohol in a drink after about two hours.

Once in the blood stream, alcohol diffuses into the water in all cells of the body. Nerve cells are particularly susceptible to its inhibitory effects. Areas of the brain responsible for self control and criticism are depressed first, promoting euphoria and lack of judgment. Later taste, smell, coordination (reaction time), hearing and vision are adversely affected. Symptoms of intoxication are apparent – especially to those unused to alcohol – when the blood contains about 100 milligrams of alcohol in 100 mls. This is equivalent to 50 grams of alcohol (contained in about 3 pints of bitter beer) for a 70 kilogram (11 stone) man. In Britain it is an offence to drive a car when the blood alcohol content is greater than 80 milligrams per 100 mls. This is equivalent to 40 grams of alcohol (contained in about 2½ pints of bitter beer) for a 70 kilogram (11 stone) man, but less for those with a smaller build.

The liver is chiefly responsible for ridding the body of alcohol, converting it to carbon dioxide and water and releasing energy in the process. Most of the energy released is converted to **fat** which is used immediately or stored for later use. A small quantity (5 to 10% of the intake) is passed out of the body unchanged in urine, breath and sweat.

The rate at which alcohol is used by the body varies for each individual: some people have half the average rate, others double. On average a 70 kilogram (11 stone) man would need 1¾ hours to use up 10 grams of alcohol (in just over ½ pint of bitter beer). Women have a slower rate and are generally smaller than men, so that the intoxicant effects for the same dose of alcohol are apparent for longer. They are also more susceptible to the harmful effects of alcohol so that the limit for 'moderate' drinking habits is lower, 30 grams per day, compared with 50 grams for men. This is equivalent respectively to three glasses of wine and 2½ pints of beer (see table).

Measures of drinks containing 10 grams alcohol

Drink	Weight	Measure
Most beers and ciders	300–450 grams	½ pint
Wines, vintage cider	125 grams	small wine glass
Port, sherry, vermouth	65 grams	sherry glass
Liqueurs, spirits	30 grams	one measure (⅙ gill)

Harmful effects of alcohol

In excess, alcohol damages the heart, liver and brain. Pregnant women should not drink any alcohol, as it passes into the developing child's blood stream. Alcohol is also implicated in a number of **cancers**, particularly of the mouth, throat and upper digestive system.

Chronic alcoholics, and some heavy drinkers, are likely to suffer from **malnutrition**. There is evidence that alcohol is also primarily responsible (rather than malnutrition) for liver damage. Initially fat accumulates in liver cells but can be eliminated if the consumption of alcohol is reduced. Several years' excessive alcohol consumption is one cause of liver inflammation (hepatitis) which is usually followed by cirrhosis: a condition in which the liver cells die and are replaced by scars. An extensively cirrhosed liver cannot support life.

Deaths from cirrhosis are associated with the amount of alcohol consumed within any one country. In France for example three times more alcohol is consumed and there are twelve times more deaths from cirrhosis than in the UK. In the UK both deaths from cirrhosis and the amount of alcohol consumed were much greater in the late nineteenth century than present day levels, although a comparatively recent increase in consumption – at least a doubling of intakes from 1950 to 1980 – has been accompanied by an upturn and steady rise in cirrhosis deaths.

Hangovers

Hangovers are due to the dehydrating effect of alcohol – it increases the flow of urine – and to the non-alcoholic congeners in alcoholic drinks which contribute to the flavour. The best way of preventing a hangover is to drink a lot of water, either with alcoholic drinks or before succumbing to sleep, and to avoid the high congener drinks such as brandy and red wine, which may also contain **histamine**. Coffee can make a hangover worse because it contains **caffeine** which also dehydrates the body. Fruit juice is a better alternative because it contains **fructose** which speeds up the rate of alcohol eliminated by the liver.

Other effects of alcohol

Alcohol dilates the blood vessels of the skin, causing a feeling of warmth. However, the warming effects of alcohol are superficial: when blood is diverted to the skin, the body actually loses heat. For this reason it should not be given to persons suffering from exposure. Alcohol is also inadvisable after severe exercise or lack of food because it suppresses the regeneration of **glycogen**, necessary for the maintenance of an acceptable blood **glucose** level. The resultant fall in the blood sugar level has sometimes induced coma and further lowering of the body temperature, with occasional fatal results. Children and diabetics

5

treated by drugs or insulin are more susceptible to the blood sugar lowering effect of a moderate to large dose of alcohol.

Alginates (E400 – E405)

Extracted from kelp seaweed, alginates are used in many foods as **emulsifiers**, thickeners, stabilisers, and jelling agents. Instant puddings, ice cream, salad cream, processed cheese, artificial cream and whipped cream may all contain alginates. Other uses include the manufacture of fruit 'pieces' for pie fillings from comminuted fruit, and artificial cherries.

Alginates are calcium, potassium, sodium, iron, magnesium or ammonium salts of alginic acid (in the same way that sodium chloride, salt, is the sodium salt of hydrochloric acid). They are **polysaccharides** which contribute to dietary **fibre**.

Allergy

The term 'allergy', commonly used with regard to diet, is a misnomer. An allergic response to food is only one of a number of idiosyncratic unpleasant reactions to food or food constituents and perhaps the least common numerically. The recognition that these reactions exist is part of the reason why the incidence of food 'allergy' has seemingly increased suddenly over the past few years. The group of reactions as a whole is called 'food intolerance'. The causes of food intolerance range from allergy to lack of **enzymes** needed for digesting or metabolising food (see **Inborn errors of metabolism**) to the many pharmacological effects of food constituents such as **alcohol, caffeine, salt, monosodium glutamate** and **histamine**.

There are four main types of allergic reactions. The first, the atopic or anaphylactic type, is largely inherited and probably the most common, affecting about 10% of people in Britain and the USA. In atopic people, the most common substances causing the allergy (the allergen) are in the air – such as house dust, pollen, and dandruff, but a proportion, less than 10%, are sensitive to foods. Food allergy is commonest in children – in adulthood food allergies tend to be replaced with other allergies, such as pollen, or animal fur.

With regard to food, allergens are usually **proteins** or glycoproteins (complexes of protein and **carbohydrates**) and the most notorious foods are cows' milk, hens' eggs and fish, partly because they contain a lot of allergens and partly because they are most commonly eaten. The pattern of allergy in a particular country or individual depends as a result on food habits. In Norway, for example, allergy to fish is particularly common, and children who are allergic to cows' milk can become allergic to soya milk when this is used as a substitute. Other foods commonly causing allergy in Britain are tomatoes, oranges, bananas, meat, nuts, chocolates, cereals and peanuts.

Normally, little protein from food reaches the blood stream. It is mostly dismantled to its **amino acids** during **digestion** and part of the immune system – the immunoglobulins A – specifically protects the body by coating large unwanted molecules such as proteins and bacteria, thus preventing intrusion and infection. However, recent research has shown that small amounts of some proteins do enter the blood stream. Immunoglobulin E antibodies are then formed and fix onto cells, particularly the 'mast' cells found in the skin and linings of the lungs, nose, sinuses and digestive system. For reasons not understood, when the allergen next enters the blood stream in allergic individuals the union of allergen and antibodies causes the mast cells to rupture, releasing powerful substances including histamine, serotonin and prostaglandins. Individual symptoms depend on whether the antibodies are fixed in the skin, respiratory system, or digestive system. **Urticaria, eczema**, hay fever, **asthma**, stomach cramps, vomiting or diarrhoea may result.

Potentially allergenic food proteins have been found in the brain, at least in animals. However, although mood is affected in allergic disease, most individuals who are referred to allergy clinics for mental problems alone, such as tiredness without other symptoms of allergic disease like eczema, either require conventional psychiatric care, for, for example, depression or anxiety or, in many cases, should drink less tea and coffee. The **caffeine** in these has been found to cause various mental symptoms, including depression. They also contain **salicylates**. (See also migraine.)

The second type of allergic reaction important to diet is called type IV, cell mediated, or delayed allergy. In this, another part of the immune system called T cells, are involved together with other reactive non-protein materials called haptens. Haptens include metals such as **chromium, nickel** and **cobalt** and particularly reactive parts of some chemicals found naturally in many plants and used in perfumes, cosmetics and as food **additives**. Haptens unite with proteins on the skin after prolonged contact and especially in some cases in that part of the skin exposed to sunlight. On the next exposure, some T cells are able to recognise and bind the hapten–protein complex using specific receptors, and as a result secrete substances called lymphokines which cause redness, swelling, scaling and weeping of the skin. This type of reaction takes about two days to develop and there are a large number of food constituents capable of causing this allergy. The most likely are garlic, lemons, oranges, cinnamon and vanilla, but contact with mangoes, celery, carrots and food additives can also cause problems in individuals. The people most at risk are those who *handle* these substances frequently, especially workers in the food, dye, and cosmetics industries, and cooks. Because the haptens are not necessarily specific to one food or plant, cross-sensitivity is also common, for example to both turpentine and lemon, **salicylates** in foods and **tartrazine** in drinks, drugs and cosmetics. People who have become sensitised to aspirin may also be sensitive to salicylates in foods, others sensitive to penicillin may react to the penicillin in milk from cows treated with it for an infection. A person may also become sensitised to benzoates used as preservatives in cosmetics, medicines and cleaning agents, or to **para amino benzoic acid** used in sunscreen lotions, and later react to benzoic acid used as a **preservative** in pickles, soft drinks and instant coffee.

The other two types of allergic reaction are not commonly involved in food allergy – although some diseases of the large bowel, particularly **coeliac disease** may involve some disorder of the immune system. This may however be a consequence, rather than a cause, of the disease.

Diagnosis of allergy

Some people have only mild allergies, others recover spontaneously. When there is an immediate reaction it is easy to pinpoint and avoid the food concerned, but other allergens may only be established from detailed investigations at specialised clinics. Allergies are particularly difficult to deal with because there is no straightforward and accurate biochemical test for them. The two that are the most reliable are called the skin test and the radioallergosorbent (RAST) test. The skin test relies on the presence of immunoglobulin E on mast cells in the skin to react with a wheal and flare within 20 minutes when drops of the suspect antigen are pricked or scratched in. The RAST also depends on the presence of immunoglobulin E in the blood which is specific for the allergen being tested. Both tests have their limitations especially in the delayed type of allergy. People who think they have an allergy should be particularly careful of results obtained from other blood tests. The cytotoxic food test (based on the assumption that white blood cells of food allergic patients disintegrate in the presence of the suspect substance) is unable to give the correct result, even when tested on blood taken from the same person at the same time of day.

The most reliable – and most time consuming – test for allergy is an elimination diet composed of a few foods known to be unlikely to have allergens in them. This diet usually consists of lamb, pears, rice, water and vegetable oils, since these are the foods least likely to cause a reaction in themselves. The suspect foods are then added back singly, one at a time; most conclusive results are obtained if tests are done under conditions where the patient does not know if the food under test is the suspected allergen or a 'placebo'.

Elimination diets should not be undertaken without expert advice from a qualified dietitian, especially in children. There have been several reports of **malnutrition** in children who have been kept on too narrow choices of food for too long – either for allergy or because parents follow unbalanced diets themselves, for example **macrobiotic diets**.

Once an allergy has been confirmed, doctors should be informed. Severe reactions, anaphylactic shock, can follow injection of the allergen. For instance, people allergic to egg can be made very ill from immunising injections prepared from egg, such as some flu vaccines. Others, allergic to pork, are sensitive to insulins obtained from pigs.

'Total allergy syndrome'

This is a condition that has been reported in the press. Victims suffer a variety of symptoms, from weakness, convulsions, faintness, aches, and increased skin sensitivity. However, true allergic responses are not found and the present explanation is that this is a psychosomatic illness, caused sometimes by overbreathing (which raises the level of carbon dioxide in the blood), or a type of **anorexia nervosa**.

Almonds, see also nuts

Like all nuts, almonds are rich in **fat, protein, zinc** and **fibre**. Almonds are also rich in **vitamin E**. However, nuts need to be well chewed or ground for complete **digestion**. Even so, the high contents of **phytic acid** and **oxalic acid** in almonds result in little of the calcium, magnesium and iron being absorbed into the bloodstream.

Average nutrients in 100 grams (3½ oz) Almonds

Energy kilojoules	2336	Iron milligrams	4.2
kilocalories	565	Copper milligrams	0.14
Protein grams	16.9	Zinc milligrams	3.1
Total fat grams	53.5	Vitamin A micrograms	0
Saturated fat grams	4.3	Vitamin D micrograms	0
Polyunsaturated fat grams	10.0	Vitamin C milligrams	0
		Vitamen E milligrams	20.0
Cholesterol milligrams	0	B vitamins:	
Sugars grams	4.3	Thiamin (B_1) milligrams	0.24[a]
Starch grams	0	Riboflavin (B_2) milligrams	0.92
Dietary fibre grams	14.3	Nicotinic acid milligrams	4.7
Sodium milligrams	6	Pyridoxine (B_6) milligrams	0.10
Potassium milligrams	860	Vitamin B_{12} micrograms	0
Calcium milligrams	250	Folic acid micrograms	96
Magnesium milligrams	260	Pantothenic acid milligrams	0.47[b]
		Biotin micrograms	0.4

(–) No information available   (0) Contains zero or trace amounts

[a]Reduced to 0.05 mg on roasting
[b]Reduced to 0.25 mg on roasting

Aluminium

Aluminium is the third most abundant element and it is found combined with oxygen as bauxite and, with **silicon**, as mica, felspar and kaolin. Alum (containing aluminium, oxygen, sulphur and potassium) is used in many areas to purify water, and aluminium is extensively used for cooking utensils.

Aluminium occurs naturally in foods; rice and lentils contain quite large amounts (30 and 50 milligrams per 100 grams), and tea is a notable source (8 to 20 milligrams per cup). Some aluminium salts are also permitted food **additives** so that cakes made from mixes may contain 5–15 milligrams per serving, and processed cheese about 50 milligrams per slice. The average intake is about 20 milligrams per day. Aluminium is also found in some drugs for example antacids and some brands of aspirin. The aluminium used for cooking pots is usually protected by a film of aluminium oxide which is very stable. However, it is corroded by salty water and by the acids in fruits and vinegar.

Aluminium is not thought to be an essential nutrient but traces from water, food and drugs are absorbed and accumulate in the body, particularly in the brain and in bones. The importance of this to human health is unknown – see Alzheimer's disease. Recently patients have been found to accumulate large amounts of aluminium during treatment with artificial kidney machines connected to municipal supplies of water with a high aluminium content. The brain is particularly sensitive to aluminium and these patients developed dementia before the cause was realised.

Alzheimer's disease

Alzheimer's disease is the most common cause of senile dementia affecting about half of all patients. In about a further one fifth of patients dementia develops following small strokes in the brain. The cause of Alzheimer's disease is unknown but abnormal deposits in the brain tissue are found and defects in the production of an **enzyme** responsible for an important brain transmitter, acetyl choline, are known to occur. Attempts to improve brain function by giving **choline** and **lecithin** which are precursors of acetyl choline have met with little success. Brain tissue from patients with Alzheimer's disease has been found to contain more **aluminium** and a recent report has located this as a complex of aluminium and **silicon** in the abnormal brain deposits. However, these were found also in normal elderly people. The importance of aluminium in Alzheimer's disease is therefore not certain.

Amino acids

Amino acids are the basic units of **proteins**. In living tissue they must be replaced as a consequence of protein turnover, and extra are required for growth. Plants make their own from **nitrogen** in the soil but animals require them preformed from food. At least 200g of amino acids turn over in the adult human body each day – twice as much as is eaten in food and four times the minimum requirement.

Some twenty amino acids are naturally occurring. As a rough analogy, proteins are built up in living cells from individual amino acids just as words are built up from individual letters in the alphabet. In the case of proteins though, the 'word' is several hundreds of 'letters' long. The type of protein is determined by the sequence of amino acids: the protein in hair – keratin – is very different from a protein in milk – casein. The sequence is dictated by the genetic machinery (genes) in each cell and different species of animals and plants make different proteins.

During **digestion**, proteins are split to their constituent amino acids, which are absorbed into the blood stream. Amino acids in the correct proportion, are withdrawn from the blood stream by cells throughout the day, and used to resynthesise new cell (body) protein discarded during **metabolism**. The potentially toxic nitrogen, released from the old amino acids, is eventually converted to urea – a relatively harmless substance later filtered out of the blood stream by the kidney and excreted into the urine. The carbon, hydrogen and oxygen fraction is used to supply **energy**.

Eight of the twenty amino acids are not produced naturally in the human body. For resynthesis of new body protein to continue, these *essential amino acids* methionine, tryptophan, threonine, valine, isoleucine, leucine, phenylalanine, and lysine (see individual entries) must be provided from proteins in the daily diet. Histidine is called semi-essential: adults seem able to manage without it, but growing children cannot. Different quantities of each essential amino acid are needed – for instance adults probably need about ¼ gram of tryptophan and ½ gram of lysine each day. The other amino acids – the non essential amino acids – are present in food proteins and can also be made in the body, provided there is sufficient nitrogen available from the breakdown of unwanted amino acids in food and discarded proteins.

The proportion of essential amino acids in a particular protein determines its 'quality', or the extent to which it can support growth and replacement in the body. If it is relatively lacking by half the required amount of one essential amino acid, only half of the other essential amino acids can be used for synthesis. The amino acids most likely to be 'limiting' are methionine and cysteine (the sulphur containing amino acids) and, in cereals, lysine. In general the proteins derived from animal tissues – in milk, meat, eggs and fish – contain the essential amino acids in their assumed correct proportions and, provided there is sufficient **energy** in the diet, can all be used for protein synthesis. Whilst much has been made of this in the past, by calling animal protein 'first class', different food proteins are able to complement each other when eaten together. Bread for example is limited to about 50% by lysine, but if eaten with cheese, a good source of lysine, the proteins are used with greater efficiency. Another supplementary combination is rice and peas. The average British diet is limited to about 70% by the sulphur containing amino acids and **recommended allowances** for protein in the diet are adjusted accordingly. See also **vegetarianism**.

Anaemia

Anaemia is an insufficiency of the red pigment haemoglobin necessary to transport oxygen in the blood stream from the lungs to all parts of the body. Sufferers from anaemia are tired, breathless and pale, and severe anaemias can be life threatening.

There are many medical causes of anaemia, including inherited defects, kidney failure, **malabsorption**, and excessive blood losses, for instance because of heavy periods or peptic **ulcers**. It can also occur as a result of a faulty **diet** lacking in the **nutrients** necessary for the formation of haemoglobin which is carried in the blood stream as red blood cells. Normal individual red blood cells circulate in the blood stream for about four months, when they are withdrawn and dismantled in the spleen. They are constantly replaced by new red blood cells synthesised in the bone marrow, provided the nutrients iron, protein, vitamin B_{12}, folic acid, pyridoxine (vitamin B_6) copper and vitamin C are available. In anaemia however, too few cells, or cells containing low levels of haemoglobin may be formed depending on the nutrient lacking. Iron deficiency is the most common dietary cause of anaemia – but see individual entries.

Anorexia nervosa, see also starvation

A psychological illness, affecting primarily adolescent girls and young women, usually middle class and of above average intelligence. Males are less commonly affected. The problem is believed to lie in a fear of normal adolescent body weight and difficulties in accepting the biological changes accompanying adult sexuality are important. Body weight is reduced to near danger levels (35 kilograms, i.e. 5 stones or less) and cessation of menstrual periods is usual. Despite severe emaciation, usually disguised by bulky clothes, anorectics commonly believe themselves to be overweight and studies have shown that they overestimate their hip, waist and bust size by about 50%.

Anorectics cannot be treated by diet alone: there is an underlying resistance to gaining weight which can only be overcome by psychiatric care. Sufferers go to great lengths to deceive – for instance they will force themselves to vomit or will conceal food they are thought to have eaten, and undertake vigorous exercises when left alone. Only about half of anorectics make a complete recovery. The 'total **allergy** syndrome' is probably related to anorexia.

Antibiotics

Antibiotics are available for use in veterinary practice and in animal feeds under the Medicines Act 1968, subject to veterinary control. In animal feeds, some act as growth promoters so that feed requirements are reduced. Small amounts, much less than one part per million, are left in the carcase and offal: over one kilogram of meat would have to be eaten to consume one milligram of antibiotic, compared with the daily dose of at least one gram (1000 milligrams) of antibiotic used medicinally.

Since some of the antibiotics used in animals are also used for humans, people who have become allergic to antibiotics used to treat an infection might also react to the small quantities in meat and offal. Some of the antibiotics used to treat cows for infections such as mastitis can also get into milk and for this reason Milk Marketing Board regulations prohibit the use of milk from cows recently treated for infections. A more serious effect is that small pervasive amounts of antibiotic in animal feeds and food result in the multiplication of resistant strains of bacteria which also infect humans. These resistant strains have caused illness themselves, or severe problems following antibiotic treatment for other infections.[1]

Nisin, an antibiotic which occurs naturally in milk and which is not used in medical practice is a permitted **preservative** in all canned foods and in cheese.

[1] Science (1986) 234, 964–969

Antioxidants – see also **additives**

Antioxidants are added to **fats** to prevent rancidity. They prolong shelf life by conserving flavour but – in contrast to **preservatives** – do not retard putrefaction.

Rancid odours are due to compounds formed when fats react with oxygen. Ultra violet light, heat, and minute quantities of **copper**, **nickel** and **molybdenum** initiate rancidity. The impurities can be inactivated by sequestering agents (see Miscellaneous additives) – like **citric acid** but heat (from cooking and a warm storage area) and ultraviolet light (penetrating clear packaging materials) cannot always be avoided.

Several hundred chemicals have antioxidant properties, including **vitamin C** and **E** (E300–309). The Antioxidant in Food Regulations 1978 permit the addition of these vitamins, or their salts, or synthetic equivalents, to any food. Vitamin C for instance is used in sausages and foil packed vegetables.

Six other substances are permitted in specific foods up to specified amounts. All edible fats and oils, dairy products (including butter and cheese) for use as ingredients in food manufacturing, chewing gum, potato powder and walnuts are allowed to contain BHT (E321 – butylated hydroxytoluene) BHA (E320 – butylated hydroxyanisole), or gallic acid esters (E310–312). (See Appendix II.) Apples and pears may contain ethoxyquin: it prevents browning, or 'scald' of the skin and flesh during storage. The other foods which may contain antioxidants are vitamin and flavouring (essential) oils and some **emulsifiers**.

Although the use of antioxidants is apparently restricted, they are carried over in any food in which fat, oil, butter, or flavour is an ingredient. Examples are crisps, frozen fried food, biscuits and cakes. Baby foods are exceptional: no ingredient containing antioxidant (other than Vitamin E and C) is allowed to be used in their preparation.

Antioxidants accumulate in the body fat (adipose tissue). Americans reportedly have accumulated more antioxidant than Britons – a probable reflection of their higher consumption of margarine and **convenience foods**. The significance of this is unknown; studies on the carcinogenicity of BHT are inconclusive, and BHA has been found to inhibit several known carcinogens in animal studies.

Apples, see also fruit

Apples are the most popular fruit in Britain, accounting for about a third of all fresh fruit bought in 1983. About 6.5 oz (200 grams) are bought each week per person. Apples are not a particularly rich source of Vitamin C, most containing about 3 milligrams per 100 grams, although eaten with skin they contain slightly more. The exceptions are Worcester Pearmain (10 milligrams) and Sturmer Pippin (20 milligrams). Because the flesh is white, apples contain little vitamin A.

There are small losses in vitamin C when apples are cooked. If sugar is added, the energy (Calorie) content increases, to 280 kilojoules (66 kilocalories) in a 100 gram portion, with 2 teaspoons (10 grams) added sugar.

Average nutrients in 100 grams (3½ oz) Apples (fresh)

	eating	cooking		eating	cooking
Energy kilojoules	196	159	Iron milligrams	0.3	0.3
kilocalories	46	37	Copper milligrams	0.04	0.09
Protein grams	0.3	0.3	Zinc milligrams	0.1	0.1
Total fat grams	0	0	Vitamin A micrograms	5	5
Saturated fat grams	0	0	Vitamin D micrograms	0	0
Polyunsaturated fat grams	0	0	Vitamin C milligrams	3[b]	15[b]
			Vitamin E milligrams	0	0
Cholesterol milligrams	0	0	B vitamins:	0.2	0.2
Sugars grams	11.9	9.6	Thiamin (B$_1$) milligrams	0.04	0.04
Starch grams	0	0	Riboflavin (B$_2$) milligrams	0.02	0.02
Dietary fibre grams	2.0[a]	2.4[a]	Nicotinic acid milligrams	0.1	0.1
Sodium milligrams	2	2	Pyridoxine (B$_6$) milligrams	0.03	0.03

	eating	cooking		eating	cooking
Potassium milligrams	120	120	Vitamin B$_{12}$ micrograms	0	0
Calcium milligrams	4	4	Folic acid micrograms	5	5
Magnesium milligrams	5	3	Pantothenic acid milligrams	0.10	0.10
			Biotin micrograms	0.3	0.3

(–) No information available (0) Contains zero or trace amounts

[a]More in the peel (3.7 grams) than in the flesh. Eating apples eaten with peel contain about 2.2 grams per 100 grams
[b]More in unpeeled (5–30 milligrams) than in peeled (3-20 milligrams)

Apricots, see also fruit

Apricots were probably first cultivated as early as 2200 BC in China. By AD 50 they were a gourmet food in Italy but only by the fifteenth century were they widespread in Europe.

Apricots are notable for their **vitamin A** content, due to their high content of orange coloured **carotene**. The amount of vitamin A is, however, very variable, the more brightly coloured fruits containing the most (see table). Apricots lose their colour and vitamin A when dried in the sun unless sulphur dioxide, a **preservative** is added. Brown sun-dried apricots are likely to contain little vitamin A as a result. Apricots are also rich in **potassium**, but are not a notable source of vitamin C.

Average nutrients in 100 grams (3½ oz) Apricots

	fresh	stewed, no sugar	dried stewed, no sugar	canned
Energy kilojoules	117	98	288	452
kilocalories	28	23	66	106
Protein grams	0.6	0.4	1.8	0.5
Total fat grams	0	0	0	0
Saturated fat grams	0	0	0	0
Polyunsaturated fat grams	0	0	0	0
Cholesterol milligrams	0	0	0	0
Sugars grams	6.7	5.7	16.1	27.7[c]
Starch grams	0	0	0	0
Dietary fibre grams	2.1	1.7	8.9	1.3
Sodium milligrams	0	0	21	1
Potassium milligrams	320	270	700	260
Calcium milligrams	17	15	34	12
Magnesium milligrams	12	10	24	7
Iron milligrams	0.4	0.3	1.5	0.7
Copper milligrams	0.12	0.10	0.10	0.05
Zinc milligrams	0.1	0.1	0.1	0.1
Vitamin A micrograms	165–400	210[a]	220[b]	165
Vitamin D micrograms	0	0	0	0
Vitamin C milligrams	7	5	0	2
Vitamin E milligrams	–	–	–	–
B vitamins:				
Thiamin (B$_1$) milligrams	0.04	0.03	0	0.02
Riboflavin (B$_2$) milligrams	0.05	0.04	0.06	0.01
Nicotinic acid milligrams	0.6	0.4	1.4	0.4

Pyridoxine (B₆) milligrams	0.07	0.04	0.05	0.05
Vitamin B₁₂ micrograms	0	0	0	0
Folic acid micrograms	5	2	2	5
Pantothenic acid milligrams	0.30	0.23	0.23	0.10
Biotin micrograms	–	–	–	–

(–) No information available   (0) Contains zero or trace amounts

ᵃAverage value
ᵇThe range in dried apricots before cooking is 400 to 750 micrograms
ᶜMostly added sugar (sucrose)

Arginine

Arginine is an **amino acid**, needed for the growth of many young animals, but apparently a non–essential amino acid for children and adults. It occurs in all food **proteins** and, in common with other amino acids, daily excesses are converted to **glucose** and used for **energy**.

Arrowroot

Arrowroot is a refined starch, produced from the roots of a West Indian plant. Sometimes called a **cereal** but it contains no germ, and is of poor nutritive value, providing **energy** but hardly any essential **nutrients**.

Average nutrients in 100 grams (3½ oz) Arrowroot

Energy kilojoules	1515	Iron milligrams	2.0
kilocalories	355	Copper milligrams	0.2
Protein grams	0.4	Zinc milligrams	–
Total fat grams	0.1	Vitamin A micrograms	0
Saturated fat grams	–	Vitamin D micrograms	0
Polyunsaturated fat grams	–	Vitamin C milligrams	0
		Vitamin E milligrams	0
Cholesterol milligrams	0	B vitamins:	
Sugars grams	0	Thiamin (B₁) milligrams	0
Starch grams	94.0	Riboflavin (B₂) milligrams	0
Dietary fibre grams	–	Nicotinic acid milligrams	0
Sodium milligrams	5	Pyridoxine (B₆) milligrams	0
Potassium milligrams	18	Vitamin B₁₂ micrograms	0
Calcium milligrams	7	Folic acid micrograms	0
Magnesium milligrams	8	Pantothenic acid milligrams	0
		Biotin micrograms	0

(–) No information available   (0) Contains zero or trace amounts

Arsenic

Arsenic is a **trace element** found to be essential for growth in some animals. It may be essential for man, but if so its role in **metabolism** is uncertain. Like all trace elements, arsenic is well known to be toxic in excess. See section on trace elements in **poisons in food**.

Arthritis

Arthritis is an important cause of disablement, second only to bronchitis. It may occur in **gout** but the major forms are osteoarthritis and rheumatoid arthritis.

In osteoarthritis, general health is usually good but the loss of cartilage in joints causes pain and eventual stiffness. **Obesity** predisposes to this type of arthritis in the spine, hips and knees, and weight loss is recommended (see **slimming diets**).

Rheumatoid arthritis arises from a disorder of the immune system, when the membrane protecting the joints becomes inflamed and thickened. The onset is slow with a general feeling of ill health, tiredness, stiffness, pain and swelling in many joints. Loss of weight and **anaemia** are common. The major treatment is with drugs to reduce the inflammation and pain, and plenty of rest. Some recent studies have shown a vigorous programme of exercise to be of benefit in people who have a mild form of the disease. When there is a severe loss of movement and pain, surgery to replace the diseased hip and knee joints can help a great deal.

Many unorthodox treatments are used by sufferers of arthritis – partly because conventional treatment cannot cure the disease. Copper bracelets are the most popular and in a recent Australian survey, 60% of patients used them. However only 13% of these found them useful. Acupuncture and avoidance of red meat were used less commonly (by 16% and 11% of those questioned) but 50% found them to be helpful. The avoidance of red meat may be sensible because it is high in saturated **fatty acids** and a recent study has shown that a diet low in saturated fatty acids and supplemented with some of the **essential fatty acids** in evening primrose oil did result in some, albeit small, improvement in joint pain in rheumatoid arthritis. In people with a family history of **allergy**, withdrawal of the sensitising food may be important. There is no reason why acid tasting foods, such as citrus fruits and tomatoes should be avoided in arthritis (unless an allergic reaction is likely). The connection with acidity may have occurred because too much meat should be avoided when gout is the cause of arthritis. Meat is an acid **ash** food.

Artichokes, see also **vegetables**

There are two different types of artichokes. The Jerusalem artichoke is a native of North America, brought to France during the seventeenth century. It is a relative of the sunflower, but cultivated for its edible tubers. These are rich in potassium, but contain little vitamin C and no vitamin A.

The globe artichoke probably originated in the Mediterranean region, where it was unknown to the ancient Greeks and Romans. Globe artichokes are a type of thistle; the young flower head is cooked whole and the fleshy part of the bracts and base (artichoke bottom) eaten.

The nutrient composition of both types of artichoke are similar, and both contain **inulin** in place of **starch**.

Average nutrients in 100 grams (3½ oz) Artichokes (cooked)

	globe[a]	Jerusalem		globe[a]	Jerusalem
Energy kilojoules	62	78	Iron milligrams	0.5	0.4
kilocalories	15	18	Copper milligrams	0.09	0.12
Protein grams	1.1	1.6	Zinc milligrams	–	0.1
Total fat grams	0	0	Vitamin A micrograms	15	0
Saturated fat grams	0	0	Vitamin D micrograms	0	0
Polyunsaturated fat grams	0	0	Vitamin C milligrams	8	2
			Vitamin E milligrams	–	0.2
Cholesterol milligrams	0	0	B vitamins:		
Sugars grams	–	–	Thiamin (B_1) milligrams	0.07	0.10
Starch grams	0[b]	0[b]	Riboflavin (B_2) milligrams	0.03	0
Dietary fibre grams	–	–	Nicotinic acid milligrams	1.1	–
Sodium milligrams	15	3	Pyridoxine (B_6) milligrams	0.07	–
Potassium milligrams	330	420	Vitamin B_{12} micrograms	0	0
Calcium milligrams	44	30	Folic acid micrograms	30	–
Magnesium milligrams	27	11	Pantothenic acid milligrams	0.21	–
			Biotin micrograms	4.1	–

(–) No information available   (0) Contains zero or trace amounts

[a]Edible parts
[b]Contains about 3 grams inulin in place of starch

Ascorbic acid (E300–304)

Ascorbic acid is the chemical name for **vitamin C**. Large quantities of synthetic ascorbic acid are used in processed foods.

Ascorbic acid combines with oxygen and is used as an **antioxidant** in fats and meats, for example sausages, and frozen fish. It is not permitted in fresh and fresh minced meat. It also enhances the effects of **nitrite** allowing less to be used in cured meats like ham. Significant amounts remain in these foods. In vegetables it prevents browning and in fruits, fruit juices and carrots it stabilises the colour and preserves carotene (pro vitamin A). In **flour** ascorbic acid is used as an improver, especially in new **bread** making processes. In beer and wine it preserves colour and flavour, and in condensed milk it preserves flavour and vitamin A.

Ash

Ash is the **mineral** matter left after foods are burnt in oxygen. All other components, **carbohydrate, protein**, etc., are removed as gases.

It may also refer to acidity or alkalinity of urine, which is affected by diet. Diets high in **phosphorus** and **sulphur**, which are excreted in the urine as sulphuric and phosphoric acids, cause the urine to be acid. Diets high in **sodium** and **potassium** have an alkaline effect. Diets high in meat are acid ash: diets high in fruit and vegetables are alkaline ash. A diet high in meat, causing an acid urine, may increase the amount of calcium lost in urine; this may be important in the disease **osteoporosis**.

Asparagus, see also **vegetables**

The name asparagus is of Greek origin and implied originally several tender shoots picked and eaten very young. Today, asparagus is a luxury food but it does contain significant quantities of vitamins A, C, E and folic acid, like all green vegetables. The flavour of asparagus is best conserved by steaming rather than boiling.

Average nutrients in 100 grams (3½ oz) Asparagus(boiled)

Energy kilojoules	75	Iron milligrams	0.9
kilocalories	18	Copper milligrams	0.2
Protein grams	3.4	Zinc milligrams	0.3
Total fat grams	0	Vitamin A micrograms	67–133
Saturated fat grams	0	Vitamin D micrograms	0
Polyunsaturated fat grams	0	Vitamin C milligrams	15–30
		Vitamin E milligrams	2.5
Cholesterol milligrams	0	B vitamins:	
Sugars grams	1.1	Thiamin (B_1) milligrams	0.10
Starch grams	0	Riboflavin (B_2) milligrams	0.08
Dietary fibre grams	1.5	Nicotinic acid milligrams	1.4
Sodium milligrams	2	Pyridoxine (B_6) milligrams	0.04
Potassium milligrams	240	Vitamin B_{12} micrograms	0
Calcium milligrams	26	Folic acid micrograms	30
Magnesium milligrams	10	Pantothenic acid milligrams	0.13
		Biotin micrograms	0.4

(–) No information available   (0) Contains zero or trace amounts

Asthma

Asthma often results from an **allergy**, sometimes, but not always, to food. When food is responsible, eggs, cheese, milk, nuts and seafood are usually the sensitising agents. Treatment is with drugs to improve lung function and, when necessary, avoiding the sensitising food. Some asthmatic attacks are made worse by aspirin and **salicylates**. Aspirin inhibits the formation of substances called prostaglandins and this in turn allows other substances to cause the small airways in the lung to constrict, causing the asthmatic even greater difficulty in breathing. Some food **additives**, notably benzoic acid (see **preservatives**) and food **colours** such as **tartrazine** have also been shown to provoke attacks but the way in which they do so is not known.

Atherosclerosis

Atherosclerosis is the progressive accumulation of deposits of **cholesterol**, other fatty substances (**lipid**), and fibrous tissue in the lining of the arteries, which become thickened and constricted and eventually may ulcerate. Blood tends to stick and form a clot (thrombus) more easily in these areas, obstructing the flow of blood through the artery. These blockages can occur in any large or medium-sized artery in the body, but they have more serious consequences in arteries supplying the heart muscle and the brain, causing ischaemic **heart disease**, and **strokes**.

Aubergine

Aubergine is also called eggplant, or brinjal. It is a tropical plant, said to have originated in India. It was unknown to the Greeks and Romans, and only appeared in Europe in the fourteenth century, probably via Africa. In most recipes, oil is added or the aubergine is fried, considerably increasing its **fat** and energy content. However, whole small aubergines can be 'puffed' by baking them in their skins, without adding fat.

Average nutrients in 100 grams (3½ oz) Aubergine(raw)

Energy kilojoules	62	Iron milligrams	0.4
kilocalories	14	Copper milligrams	0.08
Protein grams	0.7	Zinc milligrams	–
Total fat grams	0	Vitamin A micrograms	0
Saturated fat grams	0	Vitamin D micrograms	0
Polyunsaturated fat grams	0	Vitamin C milligrams	5
		Vitamin E milligrams	–
Cholesterol milligrams	0	B vitamins:	
Sugars grams	2.9	Thiamin (B$_1$) milligrams	0.05
Starch grams	0.2	Riboflavin (B$_2$) milligrams	0.03
Dietary fibre grams	2.5	Nicotinic acid milligrams	0.9
Sodium milligrams	3	Pyridoxine (B$_6$) milligrams	0.08
Potassium milligrams	240	Vitamin B$_{12}$ micrograms	0
Calcium milligrams	10	Folic acid micrograms	20
Magnesium milligrams	10	Pantothenic acid milligrams	0.22
		Biotin micrograms	–

(–) No information available   (0) Contains zero or trace amounts

Avocado pears

Avocado pears are unusual in that they are fruits containing a large amount of **fat**. There is also an (unconfirmed) report that they contain **vitamin D**. When fully ripe they can be spread as an alternative to butter or margarine. Avocados were probably first cultivated in Peru about 9,000 years ago.

Average nutrients in 100 grams (3½ oz) Avocado pears

Energy kilojoules	922	Iron milligrams	1.5
kilocalories	223	Copper milligrams	0.21
Protein grams	4.2	Zinc milligrams	–
Total fat grams	11–39	Vitamin A micrograms	17
Saturated fat grams	2.6	Vitamin D micrograms	a
Polyunsaturated fat grams	1.9	Vitamin C milligrams	5–30
		Vitamin E milligrams	3.2
Cholesterol milligrams	0	B vitamins:	
Sugars grams	1.8	Thiamin (B$_1$) milligrams	0.10
Starch grams	0	Riboflavin (B$_2$) milligrams	0.10
Dietary fibre grams	2.0	Nicotinic acid milligrams	1.8
Sodium milligrams	2	Pyridoxine (B$_6$) milligrams	0.42
Potassium milligrams	400	Vitamin B$_{12}$ micrograms	0
Calcium milligrams	15	Folic acid micrograms	66
Magnesium milligrams	29	Pantothenic acid milligrams	1.1
		Biotin micrograms	3.2

(–) No information available   (0) Contains zero or trace amounts

[a] Avocado pears are reported to contain vitamin D

Bacon, see also meat

Bacon generally is produced from the body of the pig, ham from the leg. Curing consists of treatment in **salt** and **nitrites and nitrates**. Bacon is high in **fat**; cooked bacon (see table) ranging from 20 to 45% fat depending on the cut; for this reason many nutritionists favour **breakfast cereals** rather than the traditional bacon and eggs. Grilling results in slightly less fat, 36% in grilled streaky bacon compared with 45% in fried.

Average nutrients in 100 grams (3½ oz) Bacon rashers (cooked)

	grilled lean	fried streaky		grilled lean	fried streaky
Energy kilojoules	1218	2050	Iron milligrams	1.6	1.2
kilocalories	292	496	Copper milligrams	0.17	0.12
Protein grams	30.5	23.1	Zinc milligrams	3.7	2.4
Total fat grams	18.9	44.8	Vitamin A micrograms	0	0
Saturated fat grams	7.6	18.1	Vitamin D micrograms	0	0
Polyunsaturated fat grams	1.4	3.3	Vitamin C milligrams	0	0
			Vitamin E milligrams	0.04	0.21
Cholesterol milligrams	77	80	B vitamins:		
Sugars grams	0	0	Thiamin (B_1) milligrams	0.59	0.37
Starch grams	0	0	Riboflavin (B_2) milligrams	0.23	0.19
Dietary fibre grams	0	0	Nicotinic acid milligrams	11.9	8.9
Sodium milligrams	2240	1820	Pyridoxine (B_6) milligrams	0.37	0.27
Potassium milligrams	350	290	Vitamin B_{12} micrograms	0	0
Calcium milligrams	13	12	Folic acid micrograms	2	1
Magnesium milligrams	18	19	Pantothenic acid milligrams	0.7	0.3
			Biotin micrograms	3	2

(–) No information available   (0) Contains zero or trace amounts

Baked beans

Canned baked beans are one of the most popular vegetables bought in Britain. In 1983, for example, about 125 grams (4.45 oz) was bought on average per person per week, compared with about 45 grams (1.63 oz) frozen peas. They are high in **fibre**, and low in fat, and like all beans supply useful amounts of **protein**, minerals and **vitamins**. Their calcium, magnesium and iron, however, may be poorly absorbed because they also contain **oxalic** and **phytic** acid. Baked beans also contain added salt (see table).

Average nutrients in 100 grams (3½ oz) Baked beans

Energy kilojoules	270	Iron milligrams	1.4
kilocalories	64	Copper milligrams	0.21
Protein grams	5.1	Zinc milligrams	0.7
Total fat grams	0.5	Vitamin A micrograms	–
Saturated fat grams	0.08	Vitamin D micrograms	0
Polyunsaturated fat grams	0.25	Vitamin C milligrams	0
		Vitamin E milligrams	0.6
Cholesterol milligrams	0	B vitamins:	
Sugars grams	5.2[a]	Thiamin (B_1) milligrams	0.07
Starch grams	5.1	Riboflavin (B_2) milligrams	0.05
Dietary fibre grams	7.3	Nicotinic acid milligrams	1.3

Sodium milligrams	480	Pyridoxine (B_6) milligrams	0.12
Potassium milligrams	300	Vitamin B_{12} micrograms	0
Calcium milligrams	45	Folic acid micrograms	29
Magnesium milligrams	31	Pantothenic acid milligrams	–
		Biotin micrograms	–

(–) No information available   (0) Contains zero or trace amounts

[a] 3.4 grams is added sugar (sucrose)

Bananas, see also fruit

Bananas contain about twice as much carbohydrate (starch and sugars) as other fruit. Cooking bananas contain as much starch as potatoes and are the staple food of populations in East Africa, for example in southern Uganda. The amount of **starch** in dessert bananas varies greatly and inversely with the amount of **sugar**. Thus bananas with green tips contain 16 grams starch and 5 grams sugar, whereas very ripe bananas, with brown flecks on the skin, contain only 2 grams of starch and 18 grams sugars. As the starch in bananas is poorly digested, unless cooked, unripe bananas could cause some abdominal discomfort if eaten in large amounts.

Average nutrients in 100 grams (3½ oz) Bananas

Energy kilojoules	337	Iron milligrams	0.4
kilocalories	79	Copper milligrams	0.16
Protein grams	1.1	Zinc milligrams	0.2
Total fat grams	0.3	Vitamin A micrograms	33
Saturated fat grams	0.1	Vitamin D micrograms	0
Polyunsaturated fat grams	0.1	Vitamin C milligrams	10
		Vitamin E milligrams	0.2
Cholesterol milligrams	0	B vitamins:	
Sugars grams	16.2[ab]	Thiamin (B_1) milligrams	0.04
Starch grams	3.0[a]	Riboflavin (B_2) milligrams	0.07
Dietary fibre (NSP) grams	1.1	Nicotinic acid milligrams	0.8
Sodium milligrams	1	Pyridoxine (B_6) milligrams	0.51
Potassium milligrams	350	Vitamin B_{12} micrograms	0
Calcium milligrams	7	Folic acid micrograms	22
Magnesium milligrams	42	Pantothenic acid milligrams	0.26
		Biotin micrograms	–

(–) No information available   (0) Contains zero or trace amounts

[a] Varies according to ripeness, see text
[b] About ½ sucrose and ½ glucose and fructose

Barley

Barley has a similar nutrient value to other **cereals** with most of the minerals and vitamins in the outer layers. Wholegrain, hulled (Scotch) barley retains all the **nutrients** in the grain, but pearl barley has the outer bran and germ removed, when 60% of **thiamin** (vitamin B_1) is lost.

Barley meal (from hulled barley) and barley flour (from pearl barley) can be made into bread, but wheat is preferred because of its higher content of **gluten**. Barley water is made from pearl barley boiled in water – it contains 2% **starch** but little else (see soft drinks).

Two thirds of the UK grain crop is barley but little is now used for human consumption. Nearly 90% is fed to animals. The rest is used to make malt (see maltose) used in **beer**, vinegar, whisky, malted drinks, malt flour and for malt extract with cod liver oil.

Average nutrients in 100 grams (3½ oz) Barley (uncooked)

	wholegrain	pearl		wholegrain	pearl
Energy kilojoules	1368	1535	Iron milligrams	6.0	0.7
kilocalories	327	360	Copper milligrams	0.2	0.1
Protein grams	10.5	7.9	Zinc milligrams	2.3	2.0
Total fat grams	2.1	1.7	Vitamin A micrograms	0	0
Saturated fat grams	–	0.3	Vitamin D micrograms	0	0
Polyunsaturated fat grams	–	0.8	Vitamin C milligrams	0	0
			Vitamin E milligrams	–	0.2
Cholesterol milligrams	0	0	B vitamins:		
Sugars grams	0	0	Thiamin (B_1) milligrams	0.31	0.12
Starch grams	69.3	83.6	Riboflavin (B_2) milligrams	0.10	0.05
Dietary fibre (NSP) grams	11.3	–	Nicotinic acid milligrams	2.5	2.5
Sodium milligrams	4	3	Pyridoxine (B_6) milligrams	–	0.2
Potassium milligrams	562	120	Vitamin B_{12} micrograms	0	0
Calcium milligrams	50	10	Folic acid micrograms	50	20
Magnesium milligrams	91	20	Pantothenic acid milligrams	–	0.5
			Biotin micrograms	–	–

(–) No information available   (0) Contains zero or trace amounts

Beans, see also **runner** and **broad beans, dahl, soya, baked beans**

Beans are rich sources of **protein, minerals,** and **B vitamins** and like all the pulses have been important foods for man for many thousands of years. Phaseolus vulgaris (kidney beans) for instance are known to have been culti-vated in Peru as early as 5000 BC. Butter and haricot beans also probably originated in South America, black gram and mung beans (green gram) in India. The food composition of the many different varieties of dried beans are similar; four common ones are shown in the table. Broad beans are generally eaten fresh and their food value is similar to **runner beans**. On soaking and cooking, beans take up about two and half times their own weight in water. Nutrient values when cooked are therefore about 40% of the raw value. Beans are also low in fat and high in fibre.

Despite their high content of minerals, beans contain **phytic acid** and some **oxalic acid** which interferes with the absorption of calcium, magnesium, iron, and zinc. They also require thorough chewing for complete **digestion** of other nutrients. Uncooked kidney, haricot, butter and runner beans have recently been found to cause severe vomiting and diarrhoea. This is because they contain toxins called lectins; after soaking for at least five hours, dried beans must be boiled for a minimum of ten minutes to destroy the lectins. Mung beans however have not been found to contain lectins.

Average nutrients in 100 grams (3½ oz) Beans (dried)

	butter	haricot	green gram (mung)	kidney	black gram
Energy kilojoules	1162	1151	981	1159	1452
kilocalories	273	271	231	272	347
Protein grams	19.1	21.4	22.0	22.1	24.0
Total fat grams	1.1	1.6	1.0	1.7	1.4
Saturated fat grams	–	–	–	–	–
Polyunsaturated fat grams	–	–	–	–	–
Cholesterol milligrams	0	0	0	0	0
Sugars grams	3.6	2.8	1.2	3.0	} 59.6
Starch grams	46.2	42.7	34.4	42.0	
Dietary fibre grams	21.6	25.4	22.0	25.0	–
Sodium milligrams	62	43	28	40	40
Potassium milligrams	1700	1160	850	1160	800
Calcium milligrams	85	180	100	140	154
Magnesium milligrams	164	180	170	180	185
Iron milligrams	5.9	6.7	8.0	6.7	9.1
Copper milligrams	1.22	0.61	0.97	0.61	0.72
Zinc milligrams	2.8	2.8	–	2.8	–
Vitamin A micrograms	0	0	4	0	6
Vitamin D micrograms	0	0	0	0	0
Vitamin C milligrams	0	0	0	0	0
Vitamin E milligrams	–	–	–	–	–
B vitamins:					
Thiamin (B₁) milligrams	0.45	0.45	0.45	0.54	0.42
Riboflavin (B₂) milligrams	0.13	0.13	0.20	0.18	0.37
Nicotinic acid milligrams	5.6	7.9	5.5	5.5	–
Pyridoxine (B₆) milligrams	0.58	0.56	0.50	0.44	–
Vitamin B₁₂ micrograms	0	0	0	0	0
Folic acid micrograms	110	–	140	130	132
Pantothenic acid milligrams	1.0	0.7	–	0.5	–
Biotin micrograms	–	–	–	–	–

(–) No information available   (0) Contains zero or trace amounts

Bean sprouts

Dried beans contain no vitamin C, but moistened beans allowed to sprout contain about 30 milligrams **vitamin C** per 100 grams. Canned bean sprouts contain less (see table). Most bean sprouts sold are from the mung bean (see **beans**).

Average nutrients in 100 grams (3½ oz) Bean sprouts (canned)

Energy kilojoules	40	Iron milligrams	1.0
kilocalories	9	Copper milligrams	0.09
Protein grams	1.6	Zinc milligrams	0.8
Total fat grams	0	Vitamin A micrograms	0
Saturated fat grams	0	Vitamin D micrograms	0
Polyunsaturated fat grams	0	Vitamin C milligrams	1
		Vitamin E milligrams	–
Cholesterol milligrams	0	B vitamins:	
Sugars grams	0.4	Thiamin (B₁) milligrams	0.02
Starch grams	0.4	Riboflavin (B₂) milligrams	0.03
Dietary fibre grams	3.0	Nicotinic acid milligrams	0.5

Average nutrients in 100 grams (3½ oz) Bean sprouts (canned) *(continued)*

Sodium milligrams	80	Pyridoxine (B$_6$) milligrams	0.03
Potassium milligrams	36	Vitamin B$_{12}$ micrograms	0
Calcium milligrams	13	Folic acid micrograms	12
Magnesium milligrams	10	Pantothenic acid milligrams	–
		Biotin micrograms	–

(–) No information available   (0) Contains zero or trace amounts

Beef, see also meat

Beef is one of the most highly prized of meats. Beef cattle were probably first domesticated 7000 years ago with the development of settled agriculture. Nutritionally, beef has advantages and disadvantages. It is a good source of most essential nutrients (except vitamins A, D and C) and is a particularly good source of **iron** and **zinc**. Corned beef is an easy to eat, nutritious standby for the elderly. However, the **fat** content of different cuts of beef can vary from 5 to 20% (see table) and western sedentary man probably does well to avoid large helpings of beef, particularly fatty beef, beefburgers etc. High levels of meat (mainly beef) consumption are associated with **cancer** of the large bowel, and the saturated **fatty acids** of beef fat can be expected to raise blood **cholesterol** levels.

Average nutrients in 100 grams (3½ oz) Beef (cooked)

	grilled rump steak	roast sirloin + fat	roast sirloin no fat	corned beef	fried beefburger	lean stewed oxtail
Energy kilojoules	708	1182	806	905	1099	1014
kilocalories	168	284	192	217	264	243
Protein grams	28.6	23.6	27.6	26.9	20.4	30.5
Total fat grams	6.0	21.1	9.1	12.1	17.3	13.4
Saturated fat grams	2.5	8.8	3.8	5.1	7.3	5.6
Polyunsaturated fat grams	0.2	0.8	0.3	0.5	0.7	0.5
Cholesterol milligrams	82	82	82	85	68	110
Sugars grams	0	0	0	0	0	0
Starch grams	0	0	0	0	7.0	0
Dietary fibre grams	0	0	0	0	–	0
Sodium milligrams	56	54	59	950[a]	880[a]	190
Potassium milligrams	400	300	350	140	340	170
Calcium milligrams	7	10	10	14	33	14
Magnesium milligrams	26	19	22	15	23	18
Iron milligrams	3.5	1.9	2.1	2.9	3.1	3.8
Copper milligrams	0.18	0.18	0.19	0.24	0.28	0.27
Zinc milligrams	5.3	4.6	5.5	5.6	4.2	8.8
Vitamin A micrograms	0	0	0	0	0	0
Vitamin D micrograms	0	0	0	0	0	0
Vitamin C milligrams	0	0	0	0	0	0
Vitamin E milligrams	0.29	0.34	0.29	0.78	0.58	0.29
B vitamins:						
Thiamin (B$_1$) milligrams	0.09	0.06	0.07	0	0.02	0.03
Riboflavin (B$_2$) milligrams	0.36	0.25	0.31	0.23	0.23	0.29
Nicotinic acid milligrams	12.5	9.8	11.9	9.0	8.0	8.8
Pyridoxine (B$_6$) milligrams	0.33	0.26	0.33	0.06	0.20	0.14

Vitamin B$_{12}$ micrograms	2	2	2	2	2	2
Folic acid micrograms	17	14	17	2	15	9
Pantothenic acid milligrams	0.9	0.7	0.9	0.4	0.5	0.9
Biotin micrograms	0	0	0	2	2	2

(–) No information available   (0) Contains zero or trace amounts

^{a}Salt added

Beer – see also alcohol

Beer contains alcohol and sugar, both of which supply **energy**. Most beers contain from 300–500 kilojoules (75–120 Calories) per ½ pint; from 6 to 13 grams **alcohol** per ½ pint; and from 4 to 13 grams **carbohydrate** per ½ pint. They are a surprising source of vitamin B$_{12}$, two pints supplying sufficient for daily needs. B$_{12}$ is normally confined to animal foods but it is synthesised by brewer's **yeast**. This however sequesters vitamin B$_1$ so that beer contains none – also it has virtually no protein, and little minerals, except **potassium**.

Beer is amongst the least alcoholic of the alcohol containing beverages – most have 2–4% alcohol by weight – but it is drunk in the greatest quantities in Britain. The average adult consumption is about 4¾ pints per week in the UK. Beer is a general term for ale, stout and lager, but it is also used synonymously today with ale, which was originally brewed in the medieval home from any cereal. Beer eventually became the more popular drink after the introduction of hops from Flanders in the fifteenth century.

The differences in ale, stout and lager are due to modifications of the basic process: fermentation of sugars with yeast. Barley is the common cereal and it is malted by allowing it to sprout when **enzymes** partially convert the starch to **maltose** and **dextrins**. After drying, the sugars are dissolved out of the grain in water, to form wort, boiled with hops and inoculated with a pure culture of brewer's yeast. Resin in the hops flavour and also preserve the beer by inhibiting the growth of acetic acid forming bacteria.

Bitter beers contain the most hops. For stout brewing, the malt is dried at a higher temperature, when the grain is partially charred. Stout has a higher sugar content than most beers. Lager contains less alcohol than beers or stout but it is absorbed more quickly into the blood stream. A different strain of yeast – which ferments at the bottom of the vat – increases the effervescence of lager. Barley wine is the most alcoholic – 6% by weight – and contains more energy (about 220 kilocalories per ½ pint), B vitamins, minerals and carbohydrate than all other beers. There is no truth in the idea that stout is particularly nutritious (see table).

Average nutrients in 100 grams (⅙ pint) Beer

	draught bitter	draught mild	keg bitter	bottled lager	bottled pale ale	bottled stout
Energy kilojoules	132	104	129	120	133	156
kilocalories	32	25	31	29	32	37
Protein grams	0.3	0.2	0.3	0.2	0.3	0.3
Total fat grams	0	0	0	0	0	0

	draught bitter	draught mild	key bitter	bottled lager	bottled pale ale	bottled stout
Saturated fat grams	0	0	0	0	0	0
Polyunsaturated fat grams	0	0	0	0	0	0
Alcohol grams	3.1	2.6	3.0	3.2	3.3	2.9
Sugars grams	2.3	1.6	2.3	1.5	2.0	4.2
Starch grams	0	0	0	0	0	0
Dietary fibre grams	0	0	0	0	0	0
Sodium milligrams	12	11	8	4	10	23
Potassium milligrams	38	33	35	34	49	45
Calcium milligrams	11	10	8	4	9	8
Magnesium milligrams	9	8	7	6	10	8
Iron milligrams	0.01	0.02	0.01	0	0.02	0.05
Copper milligrams	0.08	0.05	0.01	0	0.04	0.08
Zinc milligrams	–	–	0.02	–	–	–
Vitamin A micrograms	0	0	0	0	0	0
Vitamin D micrograms	0	0	0	0	0	0
Vitamin C milligrams	0	0	0	0	0	0
Vitamin E milligrams	–	–	–	–	–	–
B vitamins:						
Thiamin (B_1) milligrams	0	0	0	0	0	0
Riboflavin (B_2) milligrams	0.04	0.03	0.03	0.02	0.02	0.04
Nicotinic acid milligrams	0.60	0.40	0.45	0.54	0.52	0.43
Pyridoxine (B_6) milligrams	0.02	0.02	0.02	0.02	0.01	0.01
Vitamin B_{12} micrograms	0.17	0.15	0.15	0.14	0.14	0.11
Folic acid micrograms	8.8	4.5	4.6	4.3	4.1	4.4
Pantothenic acid milligrams	0.1	0.1	0.1	0.1	0.1	0.1
Biotin micrograms	0.5	0.5	0.5	0.5	0.5	0.5

(–) No information available   (0) Contains zero or trace amounts

Beetroot

Beetroot is related to the sugar beet and has as high a **sugar** content (10 grams per 100 grams) as apple. It also contains potassium and moderate amounts of **vitamin C** and **folic acid** (see table).

Average nutrients in 100 grams (3½ oz) Beetroot (boiled)

Energy kilojoules	189	Iron milligrams	0.4
kilocalories	44	Copper milligrams	0.08
Protein grams	1.8	Zinc milligrams	0.4
Total fat grams	0	Vitamin A micrograms	0
Saturated fat grams	0	Vitamin D micrograms	0
Polyunsaturated fat grams	0	Vitamin C milligrams	5
		Vitamin E milligrams	0
Cholesterol milligrams	0	B vitamins:	
Sugars grams	9.9	Thiamin (B_1) milligrams	0.02
Starch grams	0	Riboflavin (B_2) milligrams	0.04
Dietary fibre grams	4.1	Nicotinic acid milligrams	0.4
Sodium milligrams	64	Pyridoxine (B_6) milligrams	0.03
Potassium milligrams	350	Vitamin B_{12} micrograms	0
Calcium milligrams	30	Folic acid micrograms	50
Magnesium milligrams	17	Pantothenic acid milligrams	0.1
		Biotin micrograms	0

(–) No information available   (0) Contains zero or trace amounts

Beriberi

Beriberi is a nutritional disease, caused by a diet containing insufficient vitamin B₁ (**thiamin**). It is rare in Britain, except amongst alcoholics, but used to be endemic in communities where the diet was lacking in variety and based on highly milled unfortified **cereals**. It has not been completely eradicated from some **rice** eating countries because it is difficult in rural areas to enforce either parboiling of the rice before milling or subsequent replacement with synthetic vitamin B₁. The vitamin is replaced in all British white wheat **flours** and some refined **breakfast cereals**.

Beriberi is primarily a disease of the brain and nerves, which are more dependant on thiamin than other tissues. An initial general lassitude and loss of appetite is followed by impairment of skin senses and memory. Walking becomes difficult and work potential falls as the nerves degenerate and associated muscles atrophy. An infection or extra stress such as hard labour may precipitate death.

The thiamin content of breast milk reflects the dietary content, and infants may fall ill from beriberi even though the mother is seemingly in moderate health. The child may appear well fed, due to the accumulation of water in the tissues, but unless thiamin is supplied, is liable to die suddenly from heart failure.

Beverages

Beverages are essentially flavoured **water**, of which most people require at least 1½ pints to drink a day, and more in a hot climate.

The flavours in beverages are derived from essential **oils** in berries, fruits, herbs and grains. Some are valued chiefly for their **caffeine** and **alcohol** content. **Soft drinks** and alcoholic drinks contain **energy** and all except spirits may contain small quantities of minerals and vitamins. See individual entries: **beer, cocoa, coffee, mineral waters, soft drinks, spirits** and **tea**.

Bilberries

The bilberry is native to the British Isles, where it is also called whortleberry or blueberry, and to the USA, where it also called huckleberry. The juicy berries ripen from July to September and can be used as a side dish to meat or game, and for desserts and wine. Bilberries contain mainly sugar and are a good source of **vitamin C**.

Average nutrients in 100 grams (3½ oz) Bilberries (fresh)

Energy kilojoules	240	Iron milligrams	0.7
kilocalories	56	Copper milligrams	0.11
Protein grams	0.6	Zinc milligrams	0.1
Total fat grams	0	Vitamin A micrograms	20
Saturated fat grams	0	Vitamin D micrograms	0
Polyunsaturated fat grams	0	Vitamin C milligrams	22
		Vitamin E milligrams	–
Cholesterol milligrams	0	B vitamins:	
Sugars grams	14.3	Thiamin (B₁) milligrams	0.02

Average nutrients in 100 grams (3½ oz) Bilberries (fresh) *(continued)*

Starch grams	0	Riboflavin (B$_2$) milligrams	0.02
Dietary fibre grams	–	Nicotinic acid milligrams	0.5
Sodium milligrams	1	Pyridoxine (B$_6$) milligrams	0.06
Potassium milligrams	65	Vitamin B$_{12}$ micrograms	0
Calcium milligrams	10	Folic acid micrograms	6
Magnesium milligrams	2	Pantothenic acid milligrams	0.16
		Biotin micrograms	–

(–) No information available   (0) Contains zero or trace amounts

Bioflavonoids – including citrin and rutin

Bioflavonoids are derivatives of the flavones – widely distributed plant pigments (see **colour**). Rutin is found in cereals; citrin in citrus fruits, especially in pith.

One of the symptoms of **scurvy** is haemorrhage due to leakage of blood from the walls of small blood vessels (capillaries), noticed as bruises under the skin. In guinea pigs, natural sources of **vitamin C**, which contain bioflavonoids, heal the blood vessels more effectively than vitamin C alone, possibly by enhancing the absorption of vitamin C or inhibiting its breakdown.

The active substance was isolated from peppers in 1936 and named vitamin P, but diets deficient in vitamin P have not been found to adversely affect growth or health in animals or man. Bioflavonoids are not therefore classed as vitamins. They were once claimed as a cure for the common cold, but later experiments demonstrated that they have no effect.

Nevertheless, there are at least 2000 naturally occurring flavonoids in vegetables, cereals and fruits, and there is currently much speculation about their effect on human health. Some have a chemical structure similar to a class of carcinogens and as such are able to stimulate liver **enzymes** which metabolise this class of chemicals. However, the net effect in human diets is uncertain because either a harmless result is produced, or a more active carcinogen. Animal studies suggest that two flavonoids quercitin and rutin can act as carcinogens and mutagens – but on the other hand, they can also both stimulate the enzymes concerned and offset the effect of other carcinogens. Until more is known about the effect of these naturally occurring inhibitors and promoters, the safest route lies in eating plenty of vegetables and fruits, as part of a healthy **diet**. Several studies suggest that people who eat vegetables are at less risk of **cancer** than others.

Biotin

Biotin is part of the **vitamin B complex**. It is an important co**Enzyme**, necessary for many vital body processes, but, except under very unusual circumstances (see below), adult deficiency is unknown. The average daily diet contains 30 micrograms, but bacteria normally present in the intestines synthesise at least 2–5 times this amount, some of which is absorbed into the blood stream. The vitamin is widespread in food (liver, kidney, egg yolk and yeast are rich sources) and it is unaffected by cooking and processing. Breast milk contains very little: infants suffering from diarrhoea occasionally become deficient in biotin.

Egg white contains a **protein**, avidin, which combines with biotin making it unavailable for absorption into the blood stream. However, in cooked eggs, heat inactivates avidin and the availability of biotin is unimpaired. One or two raw eggs a day are harmless, but large quantities of raw egg white inactivate both the vitamin in food and that synthesised in the intestine. A diet taken for 3–4 weeks by volunteers, containing the equivalent of 80 raw egg whites a day, resulted in a variety of symptoms – including nervous disturbances and skin lesions (seborrhoeic dermatitis) – all of which were cured with injections of 100–300 micrograms of biotin. Some freak diets, for instance one dozen raw eggs each day, have also occasionally resulted in biotin deficiency.

Excess intakes of biotin are harmless and eliminated from the body in urine. In the treatment of skin disorders large doses are of dubious value, except when deficiency has been induced with egg white.

Animal experiments suggested that induced deficiency of biotin might promote regression of some cancers, but raw egg white diets were found to be of no value when used to treat human cancer.

Biscuits

Biscuits became popular in the 1860s when there was a radical change in food habits – from breakfast at 10 am and dinner at 4–5 pm, to current meal patterns which allowed time for lunch and tea. Before this time, biscuits (the word comes from the French *biscuit* meaning twice cooked) were consumed either for their supposed medicinal value (for example, Bath Olivers were invented by Dr William Oliver in the early eighteenth century) or as expensive sweet biscuits at formal parties. Ships biscuits were manufactured until the end of the nineteenth century, when it became possible to bake bread successfully at sea.

Recently consumption has declined – due again partly to changes in eating habits. Sweet biscuits contain about one fifth of their weight as **sugar**, and up to one third of their weight as **fat** (see table). Digestive biscuits are as high in fat as other biscuits and are not particularly 'healthy'. Rye crispbreads and matzo however contain very little fat.

Average nutrients in 100 grams (3½ oz) Biscuits

	cream crackers	rye crispbreads	water biscuits	digestive	rich tea	Lincoln
Energy kilojoules	1857	1367	1859	1981	1925	1966
kilocalories	440	321	440	471	457	469
Protein grams	9.5	9.4	10.8	9.8	6.7	6.2
Total fat grams	16.3	2.1	12.5	20.5	16.6	23.4
Saturated fat grams	–	0.3	–	–	7.9	11.6
Polyunsaturated fat grams	–	0.9	–	–	1.7	2.4
Cholesterol milligrams	–	–	–	–	–	–
Sugars grams	0	3.2	2.3	16.4[a]	22.3[a]	24.1[a]
Starch grams	68.3	67.4	73.5	49.6	52.5	38.1
Dietary fibre grams	3.0	11.7	3.2	5.5	2.3	1.7
Sodium milligrams	610	220	470	440	410	360
Potassium milligrams	120	500	140	160	140	110

	cream crackers	rye crispbreads	water biscuits	digestive	rich tea	Lincoln
Calcium milligrams	110	50	120	110	120	87
Magnesium milligrams	25	100	19	32	17	15
Iron milligrams	1.7	3.7	1.6	2.0	2.1	1.8
Copper milligrams	–	0.35	0.08	0.23	0.08	0.11
Zinc milligrams	0.6	3.1	0.6	0.6	0.6	0.6
Vitamin A micrograms	0	0	0	0	0	0
Vitamin D micrograms	0	0	0	0	0	0
Vitamin C milligrams	0	0	0	0	0	0
Vitamin E milligrams	–	0.5	–	–	1.4	1.3
B vitamins:						
Thiamin (B_1) milligrams	0.13	0.28	0.11	0.13	0.13	0.16
Riboflavin (B_2) milligrams	0.08	0.14	0.03	0.08	0.08	0.04
Nicotinic acid milligrams	3.4	1.8	3.1	3.5	2.9	2.2
Pyridoxine (B_6) milligrams	0.06	0.29	0.06	0.06	0.06	0.05
Vitamin B_{12} micrograms	0	0	0	0	0	0
Folic acid micrograms	13	40	8	8	8	8
Pantothenic acid milligrams	–	1.1	–	–	–	–
Biotin micrograms	–	7	–	–	–	–

(–) No information available   (0) Contains zero or trace amounts

[a]Mostly sucrose

Black pudding

A mixture of pigs' blood, pork fat and cereal stuffed into pig's intestine and boiled. It is remarkably rich in **iron** (see table).

Average nutrients in 100 grams (3½ oz) Black pudding

Energy kilojoules	1270	Iron milligrams	20.0
kilocalories	305	Copper milligrams	0.37
Protein grams	12.9	Zinc milligrams	1.3
Total fat grams	21.9	Vitamin A micrograms	0
Saturated fat grams	–	Vitamin D micrograms	0
Polyunsaturated fat grams	–	Vitamin C milligrams	0
		Vitamin E milligrams	0.24
Cholesterol milligrams	68	B vitamins:	
Sugars grams	–	Thiamin (B_1) milligrams	0.09
Starch grams	15.0	Riboflavin (B_2) milligrams	0.07
Dietary fibre grams	–	Nicotinic acid milligrams	3.8
Sodium milligrams	1210	Pyridoxine (B_6) milligrams	0.04
Potassium milligrams	140	Vitamin B_{12} micrograms	1
Calcium milligrams	35	Folic acid micrograms	5
Magnesium milligrams	16	Pantothenic acid milligrams	0.6
		Biotin micrograms	2

(–) No information available   (0) Contains zero or trace amounts

Blackberries

A native of Britain and Europe, blackberries are good sources of **vitamin C**, and rich in **vitamin E**. Cultivated blackberries contain less vitamin E (0.6 milligrams per 100 grams) than wild ones.

Average nutrients in 100 grams (3½ oz) Blackberries (fresh)

Energy kilojoules	125	Iron milligrams	0.9
kilocalories	29	Copper milligrams	0.12
Protein grams	1.3	Zinc milligrams	–
Total fat grams	0	Vitamin A micrograms	17
Saturated fat grams	0	Vitamin D micrograms	0
Polyunsaturated fat grams	0	Vitamin C milligrams	20
		Vitamin E milligrams	3.5
Cholesterol milligrams	0	B vitamins:	
Sugars grams	6.4	Thiamin (B$_1$) milligrams	0.03
Starch grams	0	Riboflavin (B$_2$) milligrams	0.04
Dietary fibre grams	7.3	Nicotinic acid milligrams	0.6
Sodium milligrams	4	Pyridoxine (B$_6$) milligrams	0.05
Potassium milligrams	210	Vitamin B$_{12}$ micrograms	0
Calcium milligrams	63	Folic acid micrograms	–
Magnesium milligrams	30	Pantothenic acid milligrams	0.25
		Biotin micrograms	0.4

(–) No information available   (0) Contains zero or trace amounts

Blackcurrants

Blackcurrants grow wild across Europe and northern Asia, and they are also cultivated. They are very rich in **vitamin C**, containing between 150–230 milligrams per 100 grams when raw. Canned blackcurrants contain an average 100 milligrams per 100 grams and blackcurrants stewed in sugar, 140 milligrams per 100 grams (see table).

Average nutrients in 100 grams (3½ oz) Blackcurrants (stewed with sugar)

Energy kilojoules	254	Iron milligrams	1.0
kilocalories	59	Copper milligrams	0.11
Protein grams	0.8	Zinc milligrams	–
Total fat grams	0	Vitamin A micrograms	27
Saturated fat grams	0	Vitamin D micrograms	0
Polyunsaturated fat grams	0	Vitamin C milligrams	140
		Vitamin E milligrams	0.8
Cholesterol milligrams	0	B vitamins:	
Sugars grams	15.0	Thiamin (B$_1$) milligrams	0.02
Starch grams	0	Riboflavin (B$_2$) milligrams	0.05
Dietary fibre grams	6.8	Nicotinic acid milligrams	0.3
Sodium milligrams	2	Pyridoxine (B$_6$) milligrams	0.05
Potassium milligrams	290	Vitamin B$_{12}$ micrograms	0
Calcium milligrams	47	Folic acid micrograms	–
Magnesium milligrams	13	Pantothenic acid milligrams	0.28
		Biotin micrograms	1.9

(–) No information available   (0) Contains zero or trace amounts

Bland diet see dyspepsia

Blood pressure

Blood pressure depends on the strength of the pumping action of the heart and the resistance produced as blood flows through smaller vessels like capillaries. It is measured by wrapping a cuff around the arm, increasing the pressure in the cuff, and then releasing the pressure slowly until the blood supply returns into the arteries below the cuff and can be heard with a stethoscope. The first sounds are the (systolic) pressure of the blood in the arteries when the heart contracts. It is usually about 100 to 120 millimetres of mercury but varies a great deal depending on, for example, nervousness and whether it is taken standing up or sitting down. The second measurement is the (diastolic) pressure when the heart relaxes and is usually 60 to 80 millimetres of mercury.

In many people, blood pressure rises with age. The medical name for this type of high blood pressure is essential hypertension. Diastolic pressures higher than 100 millimetres need treatment because they are associated with a higher risk of **stroke** and **heart disease**. The main cause of mildly raised blood pressure or essential hypertension is overweight (**obesity**) and treatment usually consists of a **slimming diet** if necessary and often a diet low in **salt**. Drugs may be necessary if these are ineffective and in more seriously raised blood pressures.

In some primitive societies blood pressure does not rise with age. There are a number of reasons why this could be so – including the fact that obesity is rare in primitive cultures – but the most generally accepted cause for higher blood pressures in affluent societies, in addition to overweight, is a high salt (**sodium**) intake. A low **calcium** diet has also recently been implicated as a cause of high blood pressure in studies carried out in the USA. The effect of calcium in these studies was very small however, and much less significant than the connection with overweight. The results also do not fit in with worldwide comparisons, because individuals living in societies where blood pressure is low generally do not have access to milk and cheese and can be expected to consume minimal amounts of calcium. So far, there have been one or two studies to determine whether or not very large doses of calcium can reduce blood pressure, but the results are contradictory. In general, the effect of overweight and salt are thought at present to be more important.

Body weight

Statistics from life insurance companies are used to work out 'desirable' body weights for adults which are associated with less risk of premature deaths or disabling disease. An example of one of these sets of standards is shown in the table below. See also **obseity**.

Desirable weights for adults

Height (no shoes)		Women[a]		Men[b]	
metres	ft/in	kilograms	st/lbs	kilograms	st/lb
1.45	4.9	42–53	6.8–8.5		
1.48	4.10	42–54	6.8–8.7		
1.50	4.11	43–55	6.11–8.9		
1.52	5.0	44–57	6.13–8.13		
1.54	5.1	44–58	6.13–9.1		
1.56	5.2	45–58	7.1–9.1		
1.58	5.2	46–59	7.3–9.4	51–64	8.1–10.1
1.60	5.3	48–61	7.6–9.8	52–65	8.2–10.3

metres	ft/in	kilograms	st/lbs	kilograms	st/lb
1.62	5.4	49–62	7.10–9.10	53–66	8.5–10.5
1.64	5.5	50–64	7.12–10.1	54–67	8.7–10.7
1.66	5.6	51–65	8.1–10.3	55–69	8.9–10.12
1.68	5.6	52–66	8.2–10.5	56–71	8.11–11.2
1.70	5.7	53–67	8.5–10.7	58–73	9.2–11.6
1.72	5.8	55–69	8.9–10.12	59–74	9.4–11.9
1.74	5.8	56–70	8.11–11.00	60–75	9.6–11.11
1.76	5.9	58–72	9.1–11.4	62–77	9.10–12.1
1.78	5.10	59–74	9.4–11.9	64–79	10.0–12.6
1.80	5.11			65–80	10.3–12.8
1.82	6.0			66–82	10.5–12.12
1.84	6.1			67–84	10.7–13.0
1.86	6.1			69–86	10.12–13.7
1.88	6.2			71–88	11.2–13.13
1.90	6.2			73–90	11.6–14.2
1.92	6.3			75–93	11.11–14.8

[a]Deduct 2kg (4 lb) if weighed with clothes   [b]Deduct 4kg (9lb) if weighed with clothes
Derived from WHO/FAO/UNO Tech. Rep. Ser. 724 1985

Bran

Bran is the outer husk of **wheat** weighing about 13% of the whole grain. It is a rich source of dietary **fibre** containing about 40 grams per 100 grams, and as such 20 grams bran (12 teaspoons) taken with milk, fruit, soup or yogurt each day are recommended by some doctors for the treatment of constipation. However, raw bran contains much **phytic acid** which interferes with the absorption of **minerals** such as calcium, iron, zinc and magnesium. Most nutritionists prefer to see fibre intakes boosted by wholemeal bread because phytic acid is reduced by **enzymes** present in yeast during proving and baking. Four slices (150 grams) of wholemeal bread supplies as much fibre as 12 teaspoons of bran.

Average nutrients in 100 grams (3½ oz) Bran

Energy kilojoules	872	Iron milligrams	12.9[a]
kilocalories	206	Copper milligrams	1.3
Protein grams	14.1	Zinc milligrams	16.2[a]
Total fat grams	5.5	Vitamin A micrograms	0
Saturated fat grams	0.9	Vitamin D micrograms	0
Polyunsaturated fat grams	2.9	Vitamin C milligrams	0
		Vitamin E milligrams	1.6
Cholesterol milligrams	0	B vitamins:	
Sugars grams	3.8	Thiamin (B_1) milligrams	0.9
Starch grams	23.0	Riboflavin (B_2) milligrams	0.4
Dietary fibre (NSP) grams	44.0	Nicotinic acid milligrams	3.0
Sodium milligrams	28	Pyridoxine (B_6) milligrams	1.4
Potassium milligrams	1160	Vitamin B_{12} micrograms	0
Calcium milligrams	110[a]	Folic acid micrograms	260
Magnesium milligrams	520[a]	Pantothenic acid milligrams	2.4
		Biotin micrograms	14

(–) No information available   (0) Contains zero or trace amounts

[a]Bran is rich in **phytic acid** and these minerals are not available to the body

Brazil nuts

Brazil nuts are richer in **thiamin** (vitamin B_1) than most nuts, and in **fat** (see table). They are also rich in **minerals**, but little of their iron, calcium, magnesium and zinc is likely to be absorbed, due to their high content of **phytic acid**. Commercial supplies of Brazil nuts are derived entirely from wild trees, chiefly in Brazil and Venezuela. The fruit weighs 2 to 4 lbs and contains 12–24 nuts.

Average nutrients in 100 grams (3½ oz) Brazil nuts

Energy kilojoules	2545	Iron milligrams	2.8
kilocalories	619	Copper milligrams	1.10
Protein grams	12.0	Zinc milligrams	4.2
Total fat grams	61.5	Vitamin A micrograms	0
Saturated fat grams	15.7	Vitamin D micrograms	0
Polyunsaturated fat grams	22.9	Vitamin C milligrams	0
		Vitamin E milligrams	6.5
Cholesterol milligrams	0	B vitamins:	
Sugars grams	1.7	Thiamin (B_1) milligrams	1.0
Starch grams	2.4	Riboflavin (B_2) milligrams	0.12
Dietary fibre grams	9.0	Nicotinic acid milligrams	4.2
Sodium milligrams	2	Pyridoxine (B_6) milligrams	0.17
Potassium milligrams	760	Vitamin B_{12} micrograms	0
Calcium milligrams	180	Folic acid micrograms	–
Magnesium milligrams	410	Pantothenic acid milligrams	0.23
		Biotin micrograms	–

(–) No information available   (0) Contains zero or trace amounts

Bread

Bread is an important source of **starch, protein, fibre** and B **vitamins**, but there are many differences in the nutrient and **additive** contents of different breads. The nutritional differences are discussed below, and the additives in bread, on page 36.

Nutritional differences of breads

Wholemeal contains five times more **fibre** than white, **vitamin E** (not found in white), and more potassium, magnesium, iron, copper, zinc, thiamin, riboflavin, pyridoxine, pantothenic acid, folic acid and biotin (see table). Wholemeal bread also contains over twice as much **chromium**, ten times as much **manganese**, and one and a half times as much **selenium**. Most of the calcium, magnesium and zinc in wholemeal bread however is not absorbed because it contains almost 100 times as much **phytic acid** as white. Iron is poorly absorbed from all bread. All bread is high in salt (sodium).

These differences are due to the different kinds of **flour** used to make bread. Wholemeal has to be made from the wholegrain, so that all the fibre, vitamins and minerals are retained. In white flour, about 30% of the grain, as the **bran** and wheat germ, is removed. **Iron, thiamin** and **nicotinic acid** are added by law to white flour to replace some of the losses. Since most of the nicotinic acid in wholemeal flour is not available for digestion, white flour ends up with more than wholemeal (see table). Brown bread is intermediate between wholemeal and white, about 15% of the bran and germ being removed during milling.

Wheat germ (Hovis) bread must contain at least 10% of added germ. Granary bread is brown bread with added malted flour (see **maltose**) and kernels of wheat or other cereals. It is not equivalent to wholemeal.

The addition of **calcium** and other nutrients to bread and flour is an anomaly. Calcium, as chalk (calcium carbonate) was originally added to the brown Second World War loaf to overcome the possible harmful effects of phytic acid on calcium absorption. Brown bread contains 50 times more phytic acid than white and at that time calcium rich foods such as milk and cheese were in short supply. Fortification continued with calcium and also iron, nicotinic acid and thiamin, in all flour after the war, except for wholemeal which it was felt should be left free of additives for people who did not want to consume them. The net result is that white, brown and Hovis breads contain about five times more calcium than wholemeal (see table). There have been many attempts to rationalise these regulations over the past 40 years; the last, in 1981, was met with a public outcry and the proposals to stop fortifying white and brown bread with these nutrients were consequently abandoned.

Apart from calcium and nicotinic acid, it is clear from the table that wholemeal and brown bread are superior foods to white. A crucial experiment carried out by the British Medical Research Council in 1947 however contradicted the opinion of most eminent nutritionists of the day that these differences are associated with better health. Five groups of undernourished children in Germany were each fed one of five types of bread; wholemeal, brown, white with no added vitamins and iron, white with vitamins and iron added to the level found in brown bread, and white with vitamins and iron added to the level found in wholemeal bread. All the breads were fortified with calcium, and supplied three quarters of the children's food intake. The rest was made up mainly of vegetables, with very little meat or milk. Unexpectedly, all the children grew equally well. For this reason, until recently, there have been no campaigns or subsidies to encourage wholemeal bread consumption.

In the early 1970s it was suggested that the higher fibre content of wholemeal bread might be protective against a number of large bowel disorders, including cancer. There is still only limited evidence to support this but nevertheless most nutritionists recommend that bread should be brown or wholemeal. There is also widespread agreement that everybody should eat more starch, including bread whether white or brown, and less fat – see **diet**, in order to reverse the trends in food habits seen over the past 30 years. In 1956 for example, the average person ate about five and a half large slices (200 grams) of bread each day, but this has fallen to present day levels of 3 slices (125 grams) per day. There is no truth in the belief that bread is particularly fattening; it contains only half the energy (Calories) found in, for instance, cream crackers. As can be seen from the table, starch reduced bread ('slimming bread') is much higher in energy (Calories) than other breads. Strictly such bread should be called high protein bread, and people eating it should not be led to believe that it can aid slimming.

Average nutrients in 100 grams (3½ oz) Bread

	wholemeal	brown	Hovis	white	starch reduced
Energy kilojoules	918	948	968	991	1631
kilocalories	216	223	228	233	384
Protein grams	8.8	8.9	9.7	7.8	44.0
Total fat grams	2.7	2.2	2.2	1.7	4.1
Saturated fat grams	0.5	0.4	0.4	0.4	0.6
Polyunsaturated fat grams	1.2	0.9	0.9	0.7	1.8
Cholesterol milligrams	0	0	0	0	0
Sugars grams	2.1	1.8	2.4	1.8	1.6
Starch grams	39.7	42.9	42.7	47.9	44.1
Dietary fibre (NSP) grams	5.7	4.2	4.2	2.0	–
Sodium milligrams	540	550	580	540	650
Potassium milligrams	220	210	210	100	130
Calcium milligrams	23	100[a]	150[a]	100[a]	47
Magnesium milligrams	93	75	60	26	63
Iron milligrams	2.5	2.5[a]	4.5[a]	1.7[a]	4.0
Copper milligrams	0.27	0.23	0.18	0.15	0.52
Zinc milligrams	2.0	1.6	–	0.8	–
Vitamin A micrograms	0	0	0	0	0
Vitamin D micrograms	0	0	0	0	0
Vitamin C milligrams	0	0	0	0	0
Vitamin E milligrams	0.2	0	–	0	–
B vitamins:					
Thiamin (B₁) milligrams	0.26	0.24[a]	0.52[a]	0.18[a]	–
Riboflavin (B₂) milligrams	0.06	0.06	0.10	0.03	–
Nicotinic acid milligrams	1.7	3.4[a]	3.4[a]	2.5[a]	–
Pyridoxine (B₆) milligrams	0.14	0.08	0.09	0.04	–
Vitamin B₁₂ micrograms	0	0	0	0	0
Folic acid micrograms	39	36	20	27	–
Pantothenic acid milligrams	0.6	0.3	0.3	0.3	–
Biotin micrograms	6	3	2	1	–

(–) No information available (0) Contains zero or trace amounts

[a]Added nutrients

Additives used in bread

Apart from caramel (E150) and some **enzymes**, wholemeal flour is not permitted by the 1984 Bread and Flour Regulations to contain any additives (see table). Bread however is allowed to contain a substantial number, particularly white bread. In white bread these include bleaches and improvers to strengthen **gluten** thus making a better quality loaf. They are undesirable additives (see notes to the table) and of these only **vitamin C** (E300) and ammonium sulphate and phosphate salts are allowed in wholemeal bread.

As can be seen from the table, bread is allowed to contain **preservatives, emulsifiers** and **raising agents**. Lactic and **acetic acids** are allowed in order to inhibit the growth of bacteria that cause 'rope'. 'Rope' causes yellow-brown spots in the middle of loaves and in severe cases the loaf turns brown and can be pulled into threads. Yeast stimulating preparations, such as ammonium chloride and calcium sulphate, promote vigorous yeast growth during bread making.

Purpose	Wholemeal flour	Wholemeal bread	other flour	other bread	Notes & example Name
Colour	E150	E150	E150	E150	Caramel, not permitted in white
Preservatives	–	E280–283	E280–283	E280–283	Propionic acid
	–	E290	–	E290	Carbon dioxide
Acids which prevent the growth of 'rope' bacteria	–	E260 E262 E270	–	E260 E262 E270	Acetic and lactic acids
Emulsifiers	–	E322	E322	E322	Lecithin
	–	E471–472	–	E471–472	Glycerides
	–	E481–483	–	E481–483	Stearyl tartrate
Yeast stimulators	–	510	–	510	Ammonium chloride
	–	516	516	516	Calcium sulphate
Raising agents	–	E336	E336	E336	Potassium tartrate
	E341[b]	E341[a]	E341[b]	E341[b]	
	E450	E450	E450	E450	
	–	–	541 575[a] 500	541 575[b] 500	Sodium aluminium phosphate & bicarbonate
	–	*	–	*	Nitrogen
Bleach	–	–	925	–	Chlorine in cake flour
	–	–	926	926	Chlorine dioxide[c]
	–	–	*	*	Benzoyl peroxide[d]
Improvers	–	–	924	924	Potassium bromate[e]
	–	–	927	927	Azodicarbamide[f]
	–	E300	E300	E300	Vitamin C
	–	*	–	*	Ammonium sulphate & phosphate
	–	–	920	920	Cysteine hydrochoride[g]
	–	–	E220 E223	–	Sulphur dioxide[h]
Enzymes	–	*	–	*	Proteinases[i]
	*	–	*	–	Amylases[i]
Acidifier	–	–	–	E330–333	Citric acid[j]
Cellulose	–	–	–	E460	Used in 'slimming' breads [k]
Vitamins calcium & iron	–	*,E170	*,E170	*,E170	

Key to symbols – see Appendix for full list of names of additives
– Not permitted
* E or serial number not yet assigned to this additive
a Permitted in soda bread
b Permitted in self raising flours
c Used for about 80% of white flour. Destroys vitamin E

^d Used for 60–70% of white flour. Destroys vitamin E and converted to benzoic acid on baking (see preservatives)
^e One of the most widely used of improvers. Leaves a residue of bromide
^f Converted to a harmless substance (biurea) in bread
^g An amino acid
^h Sulphur dioxide (see preservatives) destroys vitamin B_1 and is only permitted in flours intended for biscuit and pastry making
ⁱ Added to overcome the natural variation of enzymes in flours. Can be added as malt or soya, and more recently isolated from bacteria.
^j Permitted in rye bread
^k E170 is calcium carbonate (chalk). The other materials, vitamin B_1 (thiamin), nicotinic acid, and iron, do not have numbers

Bread baking and staling, and toast

Traditionally bread is raised (or proved) during a three to four hour period before baking. **Enzymes** in the flour and yeast cause the gas carbon dioxide to be formed, which is trapped in the dough. During proving and kneading the protein **gluten** is stretched and made more elastic so that more gas can be held in the dough and a lighter loaf produced. The flavour of baked bread is due to yeast and the crust. In the heat of the oven, caramel, and a reddish brown complex are formed, colouring the crust. The protein in the crust has a slightly lower nutritive value than the crumb: **amino acids** in the colour complex (see **colour**) are inactivated. Crusty loaves are cooked at a lower temperature and for a longer time than slicing ones. Although bread is not actually steamed or baked in steam, the higher temperature needed for slicing loaves is achieved in ovens heated with steam-containing pipes (steam baked).

The Chorleywood Bread Process (CBP) is a new bread process that eliminates the need for proving. It allows bakers to use more British (weak) flours in bread – previously only strong imported flours, containing more gluten, were used to make the standard British loaf – and produces more loaves from the same quantity of flour. In traditional methods up to 7% of the weight of the flour is lost during proving: alcohol is also formed by the yeast and is driven off from the dough during baking. The gluten fibres are stretched by a few minutes of intense mixing with high powered machinery. Improvers are necessary. About three quarters of all bread eaten is now made by this process but it is largely confined to large bread making plants that have the capital available for high powered equipment. CPB bread has a slightly lower protein content than normal bread – because of its higher proportion of British wheat – but otherwise it has the same nutrient composition.

Activated Dough Development (ADD) is another new bread making process which also eliminates the need for proving but does not require high powered machinery. The required changes in the structure of the gluten are produced by a combination of the improving agents ascorbic acid E300 (usually together with potassium bromate 924) and L cysteine hydrochloride 920.

Staling of bread is due to chemical changes similar to those which take place when starch, sauces and puddings set. Part of the molecules become linked closer together, squeezing water out of the middle of the loaf. The crumb becomes dry and the crust soft and tough. In the early stages, staling can be reversed by heating the bread in an oven.

Toasting of bread drives off some of the moisture and browns the surface by causing caramel and **dextrins** to be formed. Toast bread contains more sugar than normal bread so that browning is achieved in a shorter time. Toasting destroys up to 30% of the thiamin (vitamin B$_1$) in bread. More is lost from thin than thick toasted slices.

Breakfast

Children benefit from breakfast. They need more nutrients in proportion to their weight than adults to allow for growth and are more likely to fulfil their needs if they have three – rather than two – meals a day. About two-thirds of British children eat **breakfast cereals** – a large bowl plus a third of a pint of milk supplies about one sixth of a twelve year old's **energy** requirements for the day.

For adults, there is no evidence that breakfast promotes greater mental efficiency during the morning and in fact nearly one fifth of adults in the UK eat no breakfast. One study has suggested that a *change* in breakfast habits was more deleterious to mental performance than the habitual lack of it. However, people with demanding physical jobs should eat something – morning accident rates are lower in steel workers given a glucose drink at work than in those who are not.

In contrast to 50 years ago, when half of all Britons ate a cooked breakfast, only 20% do so now. Most people eat either breakfast cereal (30%) or toast (30%).

Breakfast cereals

Ready-to-eat breakfast cereals were invented in the second half of the nineteenth century, in the first instance to meet the needs of American vegetarian religious groups, such as the Seventh Day Adventists. Their development owed much to J.H. Kellogg, a food reformist, who invented 'Granola' in the 1860s, and, notably, the cornflake in 1899. Shredded wheat was invented in 1882 by H.D. Perky of Denver; Grape Nuts in 1898 by C.W. Post, and puffed wheat in 1902 by A. Anderson. U.K. based industries were set up in the 1920s–1930s; Weetabix (the only UK cereal invention) was founded in 1932. Since that time the consumption of ready to eat breakfast cereals by the average person in the UK has increased over six-fold, to 5.8 kilograms (13 lbs.) per year in 1983. They have largely replaced the traditional cooked breakfast on weekdays, and porridge. Cornflakes continue to dominate the market and the only major recent arrival has been the introduction of **muesli** in 1972.

Kellogg developed breakfast cereals as a health food, and many of the originals remain so, due to their low fat and sugar, high **starch, fibre** and **vitamin** content. This is especially true of those cereals eaten with fruit, no sugar, and with skimmed or semi-skimmed milk or yogurt. The low salt wholegrain cereals – shredded and puffed wheat – are particularly recommended. However, cereals such as cornflakes, puffed wheat and puffed rice coated in sugar may contain over 50% of their weight in sugar (**sucrose**) and are not recommended, particularly for children.

Most brand-name breakfast cereals are fortified with some of the **vitamins** and **iron**. Many breakfast cereals are unsuspected sources of **salt** (sodium), (see table).

Broccoli

Average nutrients in 100 grams (3½ oz) Breakfast cereals

	All-bran[a]	Cornflakes	Special K[a]	Puffed wheat	Rice Krispies[a]	Shredded wheat	Weetabix
Energy kilojoules	1055	1567	1510	1386	1500	1378	1440
kilocalories	249	368	355	325	351	324	340
Protein grams	15.1	8.6	15.3	14.2	5.9	10.6	11.4
Total fat grams	5.7	1.6	0.4	1.3	0.4	3.0	3.4
Saturated fat grams	–	0.3	–	0.2	–	0.4	0.5
Polyunsaturated fat grams	–	0.8	–	0.6	–	1.3	1.5
Cholesterol milligrams	0	0	0	0	0	0	0
Sugars grams	15.4	7.4	9.6	1.5	9.0	0.4	6.1
Starch grams	27.6	77.7	68.6	67.0	79.1	67.5	66.5
Dietary fibre (NSP) grams	23.6	0.7	0.7	10.7	0.9	10.7	10.4
Sodium milligrams	1470[b]	1160[b]	1150[b]	4	1270[b]	8	360[b]
Potassium milligrams	887	99	235	390	154	330	420
Calcium milligrams	70	3	70	26	20	38	33
Magnesium milligrams	370	14	52	140	50	130	120
Iron milligrams	12.0[b]	0.6	13.3[b]	4.6	6.7[b]	4.2	7.6
Copper milligrams	1.2	0.03	0.26	0.6	0.1	0.4	0.5
Zinc milligrams	8.4	0.3	1.9	2.8	1.1	2.3	2.1
Vitamin A micrograms	0	0	0	0	0	0	0
Vitamin D micrograms	2.8[b]	0	2.8[b]	0	2.8[b]	0	0
Vitamin C milligrams	0	0	0	0	0	0	0
Vitamin E milligrams	2.0	0.4	0.5	1.7	0.6	1.0	1.8
B vitamins:							
Thiamin (B$_1$) milligrams	1.0[b]	1.8[b]	1.2[b]	0	1.0[b]	0.27	1.0[b]
Riboflavin (B$_2$) milligrams	1.5[b]	1.6[b]	1.7[b]	0.06	1.5[b]	0.05	1.5[b]
Nicotinic acid milligrams	16.0[b]	21.9[b]	18.3[b]	2.9	16.0[b]	2.1	14.3[b]
Pyridoxine (B$_6$) milligrams	1.8[b]	0.03	2.2[b]	0.14	1.8[b]	0.24	0.24
Vitamin B$_{12}$ micrograms	0	0	2.2[b]	0	1.7[b]	0	0
Folic acid micrograms	100	7	37	19	14	29	50
Pantothenic acid milligrams	–	–	–	–	–	–	–
Biotin micrograms	–	–	–	–	–	–	–

(–) No information available   (0) Contains zero or trace amounts

[a]Includes data from manufacturer, 1986
[b]Added salt or vitamins or minerals

Broccoli

Broccoli is related to the **cabbage** and is rich in **vitamin A, vitamin C, folic acid, riboflavin** and **potassium**. These nutrients are highly variable, depending on the amount of flower, leaf or stalk eaten, and the freshness and green colouration. The nutrients and flavour are best kept by steaming, when it is unnecessary to add salt during cooking. The **iron** in broccoli is better absorbed than from most other vegetables, partly because of its high vitamin C content.

Average nutrients in 100 grams (3½ oz) Broccoli (boiled)

Energy kilojoules	78	Iron milligrams	1.0
kilocalories	18	Copper milligrams	0.08
Protein grams	3.1	Zinc milligrams	0.4
Total fat grams	0	Vitamin A micrograms	150–1167
Saturated fat grams	0	Vitamin D micrograms	0

40

Polyunsaturated fat grams	0	Vitamin C milligrams	20–70
		Vitamin E milligrams	1.1
Cholesterol milligrams	0	B vitamins:	
Sugars grams	1.5	Thiamin (B₁) milligrams	0.06
Starch grams	0.1	Riboflavin (B₂) milligrams	0.20
Dietary fibre grams	4.1	Nicotinic acid milligrams	1.2
Sodium milligrams	6	Pyridoxine (B₆) milligrams	0.13
Potassium milligrams	220	Vitamin B₁₂ micrograms	0
Calcium milligrams	76	Folic acid micrograms	110
Magnesium milligrams	12	Pantothenic acid milligrams	0.7
		Biotin micrograms	0.3

(–) No information available   (0) Contains zero or trace amounts

Brussels sprouts

Brussels sprouts are related to the **cabbage** (*Brassica*) family. They are good sources of **vitamin C** and **folic acid**, although some of these nutrients are lost in boiling. Steaming or microwaving are preferred methods, both from the nutritional and flavour point of view – when no salt needs to be added.

Average nutrients in 100 grams (3½ oz) Brussels sprouts

	raw	boiled		raw	boiled
Energy kilojoules	111	75	Iron milligrams	0.7	0.5
kilocalories	26	18	Copper milligrams	0.06	0.05
Protein grams	4.0	2.8	Zinc milligrams	0.5	0.4
Total fat grams	0	0	Vitamin A micrograms	20–92	20–92
Saturated fat grams	0	0	Vitamin D micrograms	0	0
Polyunsaturated fat grams	0	0	Vitamin C milligrams	70–140	30–90
			Vitamin E milligrams	1.0	0.9
Cholesterol milligrams	0	0	B vitamins:		
Sugars grams	2.6	1.6	Thiamin (B₁) milligrams	0.1	0.06
Starch grams	0.1	0.1	Riboflavin (B₂) milligrams	0.15	0.10
Dietary fibre grams	4.2	2.9	Nicotinic acid milligrams	1.5	0.9
Sodium milligrams	4	2	Pyridoxine (B₆) milligrams	0.28	0.17
Potassium milligrams	380	240	Vitamin B₁₂ micrograms	0	0
Calcium milligrams	32	25	Folic acid micrograms	110	87
Magnesium milligrams	19	13	Pantothenic acid milligrams	0.40	0.28
			Biotin micrograms	0.4	0.3

(–) No information available   (0) Contains zero or trace amounts

Bulimia nervosa

This is a psychological condition causing powerful urges to overeat, but overweight is avoided by vomiting, purgatives and periods of starvation. Bulimics are usually shy, hardworking women who keep their problem to themselves, awaiting binge-eating episodes with apprehension. When these occur, there are feelings of loss of control, self-disgust, anger and depression. The binge foods are usually sweet and starchy, and enormous amounts can be consumed. **Potassium** depletion, causing fits, tetany and fever can result from the repeated vomiting and use of laxatives.

Butter

Butter is virtually all **fat**, two thirds of it saturated **fatty acids**. It contains **vitamins A, D** and **E** – more in summer than in winter, see the range of values given in the table. The amount of added **salt** varies from 0 to 3 grams, leading to a wide range in the **sodium** content of butter. In contrast to other dairy products, butter contains little calcium and no B vitamins.

Butter is a high fat food and current recommendations for **diet** suggest that less of it and all other fats should be eaten. Replacing butter with hard **margarine** is of little benefit, and with polyunsaturated margarine of less benefit than cutting down on both.

The natural **colour** of butter is due to **carotene** (from grass), but annatto or turmeric may be added to pale butter, especially in winter. The flavour of butter is mainly due to diacetyl and short chain **fatty acids**. Sweet butter, made from fresh cream, contains less diacetyl than ripened butter – made from cream soured with cultures of **lactic acid** producing bacteria. **Antioxidants** may not legally be added to retail butter, but butter sold for manufacturing or catering purposes is permitted to contain them. Butter in – for example – biscuits and cakes, and butter served in individual packs in restaurants will contain antioxidant.

Average nutrients in 100 grams (3½ oz) Butter

Energy kilojoules	3041	Iron milligrams	0.16
kilocalories	740	Copper milligrams	0.03
Protein grams	0.4	Zinc milligrams	0.15
Total fat grams	82.0	Vitamin A micrograms	580–1078
Saturated fat grams	49.0	Vitamin D micrograms	0.63–1.0
Polyunsaturated fat grams	2.2	Vitamin C milligrams	0
		Vitamin E milligrams	2.0
Cholesterol milligrams	230	B vitamins:	
Sugars grams	0	Thiamin (B$_1$) milligrams	0
Starch grams	0	Riboflavin (B$_2$) milligrams	0
Dietary fibre (NSP) grams	0	Nicotinic acid milligrams	0
Sodium milligrams	0–1300	Pyridoxine (B$_6$) milligrams	0
Potassium milligrams	15	Vitamin B$_{12}$ micrograms	0
Calcium milligrams	15	Folic acid micrograms	0
Magnesium milligrams	2	Pantothenic acid milligrams	0
		Biotin micrograms	0

(–) No information available   (0) Contains zero or trace amounts

Cabbages, see also vegetables

Cabbages and other members of the *Brassica* species, such as **broccoli, Brussels sprouts** and **spring greens** have a deservedly healthy reputation. They contain no fat, and are good sources of dietary **fibre, minerals**, particularly potassium, and vitamins, especially **vitamin C** and **folic acid**. The outer dark green leaves are particularly noted for **vitamin A** and **vitamin E** (see table). Note, however, that the vitamin C, folate and other nutrient content of cooked cabbage is less than that of raw. See **vegetables** for a discussion of cooking losses.

Brassicas are part of the family of cruciferae which also includes radishes and mustards. The pungency of these foods when eaten raw is due to the formation of isothiocyanates and a number of other chemicals by the action of **enzymes** liberated during slicing and shredding. If, however, the vegetables are boiled the enzymes are destroyed and the precursers of the isothiocyanates are formed into other substances responsible for the unpleasant smell of overcooked cabbage.

A number of research studies have shown that people who eat plenty of green vegetables, including cabbages and other brassicas, are at less risk of **cancer**. Whether this is due to the high vitamin content of these vegetables or to some of the many other chemical compounds in brassicas is not certain.

Average nutrients in 100 grams (3½ oz) Cabbage

	red raw	white raw	Savoy raw	Savoy boiled[a]	Spring boiled[a]	January King raw	January King boiled[b]
Energy kilojoules	85	93	109	40	32	92	66
kilocalories	20	22	26	9	7	22	15
Protein grams	1.7	1.9	3.3	1.3	1.1	2.8	1.7
Total fat grams	0	0	0	0	0	0	0
Saturated fat grams	0	0	0	0	0	0	0
Polyunsaturated fat grams	0	0	0	0	0	0	0
Cholesterol milligrams	0	0	0	0	0	0	0
Sugars grams	3.5	3.7	3.3	1.1	0.8	2.7	2.2
Starch grams	0	0.1	0	0	0	0.1	0.1
Dietary fibre grams	3.4	2.7	3.1	2.5	2.2	3.4	2.8
Sodium milligrams	32	7	23	8	12	7	4
Potassium milligrams	300	280	260	120	110	390	160
Calcium milligrams	53	44	75	53	30	57	38
Magnesium milligrams	17	13	20	7	6	17	8
Iron milligrams	0.6	0.4	0.9	0.7	0.5	0.6	0.4
Copper milligrams	0.09	0.03	0.07	0.07	0.07	0.06	0.03
Zinc milligrams	0.3	0.3	0.3	0.2	0.2	0.4	0.2
Vitamin A micrograms	3	0	50[c]	50[c]	83	50[c]	50[c]
Vitamin D micrograms	0	0	0	0	0	0	0
Vitamin C milligrams	55	40	50–80	10–40	10–50	40–70	10–40
Vitamin E milligrams	0.2	0.2	0.2[d]	0.2[d]	0.2	0.2[d]	0.2[d]
B vitamins:							
Thiamin (B₁) milligrams	0.06	0.06	0.06	0.03	0.03	0.06	0.03
Riboflavin (B₂) milligrams	0.05	0.05	0.05	0.03	0.03	0.05	0.03
Nicotinic acid milligrams	0.6	0.6	0.8	0.4	0.4	0.8	0.5
Pyridoxine (B₆) milligrams	0.21	0.16	0.16	0.10	0.10	0.16	0.10
Vitamin B₁₂ micrograms	0	0	0	0	0	0	0

	red raw	white raw	Savoy raw	Savoy bolied[a]	Spring bolied[a]	January raw	King bolied[b]
Folic acid micrograms	90	26	90	35	50	90	35
Pantothenic acid milligrams	0.32	0.21	0.21	0.15	0.15	0.21	0.15
Biotin micrograms	0.1	0.1	0.1	0	0	0.1	0

(–) No information available   (0) Contains zero or trace amounts

[a]Boiled 30 minutes, no added salt
[c]Average value; outer leaves may contain 50 times the inner ones

[b]Boiled 15 minutes, no added salt
[d]Value for inner leaves; outer leaves contain 7.0 milligrams

Caffeine

Caffeine is the most active of three drugs found in **tea, coffee** and **cocoa**, to which most people in industrialised societies are habituated. One cup of tea contains 60–90 milligrams, one cup of coffee 40–150 milligrams and most cola drinks (see **soft drinks**) 40–70 milligrams per can. Decaffeinated coffee contains virtually none.

Only 4–5 cups of tea or coffee per day, containing about 250 milligrams, is sufficient to obtain a pharmacological effect. People who regularly drink caffeinated drinks report increased alertness and decreased irritability from it, but people who usually abstain find that an unaccustomed dose causes jitters, nervousness and an upset stomach.

The toxic dose of caffeine, about 600 milligrams, causes tremor, sweating, palpitations, rapid breathing, insomnia and depression. A study in Australia found a direct relationship between some of these symptoms and the amount of tea or coffee taken each day by normal people. Caffeine can also provoke **migraine**. In many patients, excess tea and coffee drinking has been found to be responsible for symptoms of tiredness and depression, rather than **allergy**.

Some expectant mothers who drank as much as 17–52 cups of coffee, cola and tea per day have given birth to babies with missing fingers and toes. The American Food and Drugs Administration suggest that caffeine consumption should be limited during pregnancy, to about 500 milligrams a day.

Cakes, see also pastries

There is a great variety of cakes; the nutrient contents of some typical ones are shown in the table below, ranged in order of their **energy** (Calorie) contents. Those containing a lot of **fat**, such as Victoria sponges and cream-filled chocolate eclairs are the most fattening. Swiss rolls are made without fat and are the least fattening. Most cakes also contain a high level of **sugar**, and when baking powder is used, **sodium**. Baking powder destroys vitamin B_1 (thiamin), consequently most cakes contain little or none. The vitamins A, D and E are derived from the margarine (or butter) and eggs used in the recipes. Swiss rolls are also high in cholesterol but contain little saturated fat.

Bought cakes and cake mixes are liable to contain a variety of food **additives**, ranging from **emulsifiers** (which enable less fat to be used than in conventional recipes), **antioxidants, colours** and **preservatives**.

Average nutrients in 100 grams (3½ oz) Cakes

	Swiss roll	fruit cake	doughnuts	scones	chocolate eclairs	Victoria sponge
Energy kilojoules	1280	1403.	1467	1562	1569	1941
kilocalories	302	332	349	371	376	464
Protein grams	4.2	3.7	6.0	7.5	4.1	6.4
Total fat grams	4.9	11.0	15.8	14.6	24.0	26.5
Saturated fat grams	1.9	3.9	–	5.6	12.4	9.7
Polyunsaturated fat grams	0.8	1.7	–	2.2	1.6	3.9
Cholesterol milligrams	260	50	–	5	90	130
Sugars grams	47.7	46.7	15.0	6.1	26.3	30.5
Starch grams	16.5	11.6	33.8	49.8	11.9	22.7
Dietary fibre grams	1.2	3.5	–	2.1	–	1.0
Sodium milligrams	420	170	60	800	160	350
Potassium milligrams	140	430	110	140	92	82
Calcium milligrams	44	75	70	620	48	140
Magnesium milligrams	14	26	16	19	16	10
Iron milligrams	1.6	1.8	1.9	1.5	1.0	1.4
Copper milligrams	0.2	0.3	0.11	0.12	0.15	0.10
Zinc milligrams	0.5	–	–	0.6	0.4	0.6
Vitamin A micrograms	–	121	0	151	210	300
Vitamin D micrograms	–	1.14	0	1.23	0.91	2.76
Vitamin C milligrams	0	0	0	0	0	0
Vitamin E milligrams	–	1.4	–	1.3	1.2	2.7
B vitamins:						
Thiamin (B_1) milligrams	0.04	0.08	–	0	0.05	0
Riboflavin (B_2) milligrams	0.07	0.08	–	0.08	0.09	0.12
Nicotinic acid milligrams	1.3	1.3	1.2	2.7	1.3	2.2
Pyridoxine (B_6) milligrams	–	0.13	–	0.08	0.04	0.06
Vitamin B_{12} micrograms	0	0	0	0	0	0
Folic acid micrograms	–	4	–	8	5	7
Pantothenic acid milligrams	–	0.2	–	0.2	0.3	0.5
Biotin micrograms	–	4	–	2	4	8

(–) No information available   (0) Contains zero or trace amounts

Calcium

Calcium is an important **mineral** in the diet. The bones – the supportive framework of the body – are hardened with calcium absorbed from food during growth. It is also necessary for tooth formation and for the normal activity of nerves and muscles.

Milk, most **cheeses** and **yogurt** are the richest sources of calcium. Three quarters of a pint of milk supplies the daily requirement for a child between the ages of two and nine years. White and brown (but not wholemeal) **bread**, biscuits and other foods made from white **flour** are also good sources. There is virtually no calcium in butter, double cream, cream cheese and artificial coffee whiteners. Some dark green **vegetables**, like watercress, are good sources, but spinach, and beet greens contain **oxalic acid** which renders most of the calcium unabsorbable. Wholegrain cereals, nuts and pulses contain **phytic acid** which also interferes with calcium absorption. Meat, fruit and fish (except **whitebait, sardines, sprats, herrings** and **shrimps**) are poor sources. Hard water may add significant quantities of calcium to the diet, but soft water contains little. There is evidence that calcium in hard water may be beneficial, but it is not known if calcium itself is the protective factor – see **water**.

The daily recommended intake for adults is 500 milligrams of calcium. 1200 milligrams of calcium is recommended during pregnancy and during breast feeding to meet the increased needs of the growing child and children require more in proportion to their weight than adults to allow for growth (see Appendix). The average British diet contains about 900 milligrams of calcium, excluding water, of which over half (56%) is supplied by milk and cheese, and a quarter (25%) is supplied by cereals.

During **digestion** under the influence of **vitamin D**, calcium is absorbed out of food into the blood stream and transported to the bones. The protein (gristle) element is hardened with calcium and **phosphorus** during growth, so that by adulthood, most people have accumulated about 1200 grams of calcium (one gram is equal to 1000 milligrams). A good intake of calcium is particularly important for children: not only may dietary insufficiency stunt growth, but a skeleton containing plenty of calcium may be protected against **osteoporosis** developing in middle age. Once growth has ceased, a diet high in calcium is less effective in protecting against osteoporosis.

The majority of calcium is in bone, although a small but vital amount – about 10 grams – is held in the blood stream and cells of the body. A portion of this calcium regulates the activity of nerves and muscles, stimulates the secretion of some hormones, and assists in the clotting of blood. Together with vitamin D, two hormones – parathormone and calcitonin – delicately maintain the level of calcium in the blood stream.

Although no more bone is formed in adulthood, calcium is constantly withdrawn from the skeleton and, in health, replaced at an equal rate. A small but uncertain quantity is required in the diet for daily replacement. Usually the diet contains far more than daily needs and less than one third of that in food is absorbed into the blood stream. An equivalent amount is eliminated from the body by the kidneys in urine. If the diet is rather low in calcium (for example if no milk is taken) there is an adaptive response – provided there is sufficient available vitamin D – and proportionately more calcium is eventually absorbed from food. The adaptive response is less efficient with increasing age.

When the adaptive response, together with a reduction of the calcium eliminated in the urine, is insufficient to maintain the blood calcium level, it is withdrawn from the fairly large reserves in the bone. Only when the bone reserves are depleted does the blood calcium level fall, causing tetany (muscular twitching) which can be fatal. A temporary alteration of blood calcium and tetany can be induced by overbreathing. It is alleviated by rebreathing into a paper bag. In normal health, that is when the skeleton has not been depleted, calcium in food is not a 'sedative'.

In practice, the skeleton is rarely depleted by a shortage of calcium alone in the diet – most diets supply at least 200 milligrams per day, which is usually sufficient to maintain the reserves. It can be depleted however by an insufficiency of vitamin D, as in old age; by increased needs, not compensated by an increase in calcium and vitamin D (for example in pregnancy); and if nutrients are not absorbed into the blood stream as a result of digestive disorders (see malabsorption). In rare cases disease of the parathormone-producing glands can cause too much hormone to be secreted, depleting the bones of calcium and causing kidney stones. It is cured by surgical removal of part of the overactive glands.

In pregnancy and breast feeding, calcium is supplied to the growing child, regardless of the adequacy of the mother's diet, by withdrawal from her skeleton. A low intake of vitamin D and calcium, coupled with successive pregnancies results in gradual weakening of the bones – **osteomalacia**.

For the majority, a high calcium diet is not harmful because intakes in excess of needs are not absorbed into the blood stream, but there are some people who absorb more calcium than normal from food (see below). Vitamin D is toxic when taken in excess: too much calcium is absorbed from food and deposited in blood vessels, with sometimes fatal results.

Low calcium diets

These may be prescribed for the treatment of idiopathic hypercalcuria, a condition in which the proportion of calcium absorbed from food is greater than normal. As a result, abnormally large quantities of calcium are eliminated from the body in urine. Unless the urine is kept dilute, deposits of calcium tend to form in the kidney (kidney stones) and may eventually obstruct the flow of urine, resulting in kidney failure. Small stones may be passed (and cause much pain). Larger stones may have to be surgically removed. Idiopathic hypercalcuria can be treated by a low calcium and high water diet but this treatment may not be suitable for the many other causes of kidney stones. At least four pints of water or other beverages should be drunk. More may be needed in hot climates or working conditions. Usually, not taking milk, cheese and yogurt is sufficient: other foods may have to be avoided in more serious cases.

Calcium supplements

The USA is at present experiencing a 'calcium craze' – sales of calcium supplements having reached $120 million in 1986 – seven times the level in 1980. This is because of the connection with osteoporosis, which causes 1.3 million fractures a year in the USA, with high **blood pressure**, and with **cancer** of the large bowel. Intakes of calcium in the USA are much lower than in Britain where white and brown flour is fortified with it. Calcium has been described as the 'wonder drug' of the mid–eighties akin to vitamin C and vitamin E, but people prone to kidney stones should not take calcium supplements.

Calorie – other name kilocalorie (kcal)

An expression of the **energy** contained in food and required for daily life and activity. It is a unit of heat – one of the many forms of energy. One calorie is the amount of heat required to raise the temperature of 1 gram of water by 1°C.

The calorie is a very small unit, consequently the Calorie, which is 1000 times greater than the calorie, has always been used for nutritional measurements. The kilocalorie is synonymous with Calorie and avoids confusion, and resultant printing errors, between calorie and Calorie.

Kilocalories have been replaced by the general unit for measuring energy, the kilo**joule**. However, since most people are unfamiliar with this unit, kilocalories have been retained in the text of all entries.

Cancer

Cancer occurs when the process of cell division during growth and renewal becomes out of control and leads to the development of malignant cells. These multiply in an uncontrolled way independent of the normal growth control mechanisms to form a tumour. Cells from the original cancer site travel via the blood stream or lymph vessels to form cancers elsewhere. Tumours that do not spread are called benign.

Cancer is second only to **heart disease** as a cause of death in westernised countries, in Britain accounting for 23% of all deaths. It can occur in a number of different parts of the body but 90% are in the 'lining' (epithelial) tissues, such as the digestive system, breast, skin and lungs. Table I shows the league table of incidence of different cancers; lung cancer is the most common in men, and breast cancer in women. Cancer of the large bowel is the second most common cancer in both men and women. Cancers with which diet is most strongly associated are marked with an asterisk.

Within any one population, risk of cancer is affected by genetic factors which are poorly understood. Two important observations however strongly suggest that diet can influence the risk of populations as a whole. First, there are widely differing rates for cancers of different organs in different parts of the world. In non-westernised countries, for example rural Africa, Japan and China, stomach, liver and oesophagus (food pipe) cancer are usually at the top of the league. These different rates could be due to racial factors, but studies of the cancer patterns of migrants suggest that they are not entirely. The Japanese for example have low rates of breast and large bowel cancer and high rates of stomach cancer. Japanese who migrate to the USA however take on the same pattern as their host country, that is high rates of large bowel and breast cancer, and low rates for stomach cancer. These rates change within one generation for the stomach and large bowel, and within two generations in cancer of the breast.

If racial factors are not the main reason for geographical variations in patterns of cancer, then differences in cancer risk must be due to factors in the environment of any particular locality, such as climate, air, water, food or lifestyle. Of these, diet has been shown to be most strongly associated and a variety of other circumstantial evidence supports this supposition.

The development of cancer is thought to be a two stage process of *initiation*, followed by *promotion*. The initiation step is bought about by substances, carcinogens, which are widespread in the environment and which cause changes in the genetic blueprint, DNA, of cells. Before malignancy develops, a second stage, promotion, is necessary. In general, diet is thought to be particularly important in the promotion of cancer and in protection against the effects of carcinogens, rather than as a carrier of carcinogens themselves.

Table I
Incidence rates per 100,000 for some cancers in Britain

Cancer	Men	Cancer	Women
Lung	113	Breast*	56
Large bowel*	43	Large bowel*	44

Skin	39	Skin	24
Stomach★	29	Uterus	22
Bladder★	29	Stomach★	19
Prostate★	29	Lung	15
Pancreas and liver	14	Ovary	13
Lymph glands etc	11	Pancreas★	7
Leukaemias	8	Lymph glands etc	9
Brain	8	Bladder★	7
Lip, mouth etc	8	Brain	8
Oesophagus★	8	Oesophagus★	5
Thyroid	2	Lip, mouth etc	5
		Leukaemias	5
		Thyroid	2

★Cancers with which diet is most strongly associated

All age rates, Birmingham area, taken from J. Waterhouse et al. *Cancer Incidence in Five Continents*, Volume IV, IARC, Lyon 1982

Initiators

Table II lists some of the known carcinogens in foods. Most of them are natural products of plants, or are produced by moulds or cooking and preserving practices. They are most commonly implicated in cancer of tissues which have direct contact with them, such as the oesophagus, stomach and liver which are the organs first involved in the digestion and metabolism of food constituents. High rates of stomach cancer in Iceland for example are thought to be due to smoked and pickled food, coupled with salt as a promoter, and lack of protective factors such as vitamin C, see below. It is possible that genetic differences affect the way in which carcinogens are handled; a carcinogen may for example be inactivated by the liver or by bacteria in the large bowel, or it may be turned into a more active product which may then affect organs elsewhere, such as the bladder or breast.

The agent responsible for bowel and breast cancer is not known, although in the case of the large bowel, worldwide rates are most strongly associated with meat consumption and it is possible that the heterocyclic amines in cooked meat may be important, together with other factors associated with a high meat diet, such as low levels of dietary fibre (see below). High levels of meat and other animal protein consumption are also associated with cancer of the pancreas and prostate although there are no good explanations for this. It must also be remembered that tobacco smoke increases the carcinogen load substantially, either by introducing polycyclic hydrocarbons or via nitrosamines – see nitrite and nitrate.

Table II
Carcinogens in foods[a]

Food or item	Type	Example
Plants	Pyrrolizidine alkaloids	Ragwort and comfrey
	Hydrazines	Edible mushroom *Agaricus bisporus*
	Benzene derivatives	Oil of sassafras, tarragon
	Cycasin	Cycad nuts
	Coumarin	Tonka beans

Food or item	Type	Example
	Quercitin[b]	Onion, tea, red wine
	Bracken fern	Related to 'fiddle heads'
Moulds	Afflatoxins[a]	Peanuts
	Other mycotoxins[a]	Mouldy food
Yeast products	Ethyl carbamate	Beer
Additives	Nitrites[c]	Cured foods, some vegetables
Contaminants	Polycyclic aromatic hydrocarbons[a]	Found in most foods, especially vegetables from smoky areas, but also smoked foods and barbecued or burnt meat
Cooked meat	Heterocyclic amines	Formed in meat cooked at relatively low temperatures.

[a] See poisons in food
[b] See Bioflavonoids
[c] See nitrite and nitrate in food

Promoters

The major promoters in diet are **fat** and **alcohol**. Drinkers who smoke for example are at much greater risk of cancer of the oesophagus, mouth and larynx than others. A high level of salt in the diet may also promote stomach cancer when coupled with the other factors discussed above.

Fat is particularly important in the two most common diet related cancers, breast and bowel, and possibly prostate cancer. Breast cancer is most common in populations where menstruation starts comparatively early and it is thought to be affected by changes in the patterns of some hormones which are induced by a high fat diet from childhood onwards. Breast cancer is also more common in **obesity** and a large number of studies have shown that breast cancer develops earlier in animals fed a high fat diet. The risk of prostate cancer may also be increased via fat and changes in hormonal levels. In large bowel cancer, studies have shown that a high fat diet increases the output of bile acids (see digestion) in humans, and in animals, fed carcinogens, high fat diets and increased bile acid output lead to the promotion of bowel tumours.

Protectors

The major protecting factors in diet are **vitamins A, C**, and possibly **riboflavin** and **vitamin E**, all of which are found in **vegetables**. Dietary **fibre** and some **starch** may also be important in large bowel cancer. Some **trace elements** have also been linked with different cancers. In addition, plants contain diverse numbers of other constituents such as phenols, sterols, flavones, indoles and isothiocyanates (see for example cabbage) which are able to inhibit the effect of carcinogens in animal studies.

In general, protectors act in three different ways. Vitamin C, vitamin E and phenols (such as caffeic acid and ferulic acid) are thought to block the formation of carcinogens from precursor substances, as is the case with vitamin C and nitrosamines, formed from nitrites in food. Dietary fibre may also allow bacteria inhabitating the large bowel to divert potential carcinogens or promoters, such as ammonia, into their own needs for protein and energy. Other inhibitors prevent carcinogens from reacting with tissues, in some cases by increasing the activity of **enzymes** responsible for their breakdown. The third mechanism suppresses the formation of malignant cells damaged by carcinogens, for example vitamin A. Some of these constituents act in all three ways.

Too little **calcium** has also been proposed as a risk factor in large bowel cancer, and it is suggested that higher calcium levels may be important in 'mopping up' excess levels of bile acids arising from high fat consumption, which damage the cells of the large bowel wall, in addition to their promoting effects. A reduction in the fat content of the diet is more likely to be beneficial to general health however than calcium pills.

Dietary recommendations

The American National Research Council recommends various measures likely to reduce the risk of cancer – recognising that most of the evidence with respect to humans is circumstantial. These include a reduction in the fat content of the diet, an increased consumption of fresh fruits and vegetables, less salty, smoked and pickled food, moderation in drinking habits, and avoidance of mouldy food. These, coupled with reduced cigarette smoking and avoidance of obesity are very similar to the general guidelines on a healthy diet outlined in **diet**, which also are thought to reduce the risk of heart disease and stroke in particular.

Capsicums – see **peppers**

Carbohydrate - chemical names, mono, di, and polysaccharides

In human nutrition, both **starch** and **sugars** have been traditionally classified together, as carbohydrate, but this is becoming increasingly difficult to justify, given present day recommendations on diet, see below. 'Complex carbohydrate' is another confusing term, meaning starch and dietary **fibre**.

Flour, bread, pulses, unsweetened breakfast cereals, and potatoes are the best sources of starch carbohydrate, and glucose powder, sugar, sweets, cakes, biscuits, honey, soft drinks and jams contain carbohydrates as sugars. Fruits, vegetables, nuts and milk contain smaller amounts of sugars. Fats, cheese, eggs, meat and fish contain none. The table on page 52 shows amounts of food containing 10 grams of total carbohydrate, but see individual entries for the amounts of sugars and starches in different foods.

Carbohydrates are used in the body for **energy**: starches and **dextrins** are split to their component units of glucose during **digestion**; sucrose to its component units of **glucose** and **fructose**: lactose (milk sugar) to its component units of glucose and **galactose**. These simple sugars are absorbed into the blood stream and used either immediately for energy or stored for later use in the form of **fat** or **glycogen**. All carbohydrates contain the same amount of energy – approximately 16 kilojoules (4 Calories) per gram. Glucose and sugar are not superior sources of energy, although they may be absorbed into the blood stream at a faster rate.

Carbohydrate ingested as starch has different effects to that eaten as sucrose (sugar) on **metabolism**, which is also affected by the amount and type of dietary **fibre** eaten. This is important in the treatment of **diabetes** and some disorders of **lipid** metabolism, and may be related to the onset of these diseases. Over the past century, starch consumption has halved and sucrose consumption doubled in Britain, so that starch now only provides 26% of total energy and sucrose 13%. Sucrose is a well known promoter of **tooth decay**. For this reason, modern recommendations for **diet** make a distinction between starches and sugar (sucrose) and stipulate that the amount of starch and dietary **fibre** should be increased primarily because the proportion of energy derived from **fat** in the diet is now, at 40% total energy, too high. However, the amount of sugar (sucrose) eaten should not be increased. Practically this means that more bread, potatoes and other cereals should be eaten, but less biscuits, cakes and sweets – see **diet**.

Quantities of foods containing approximately 10 grams carbohydrate

	Food	Portion containing 10 grams sugar or starch
Sugar	White or brown	10 grams (2 level teaspoons)
	Boiled sweets	10 grams (⅓ oz)
	Jam, marmalade or honey	15 grams (1 teaspoon)
	Toffees	15 grams (½ oz)
	Chocolate	20 grams (2/3 oz)
	Others	a
Cereals	Flour	15 grams (1 level tablespoon)
	Tapioca, sago, rice, cornflour, custard powder, other thickenings	10 grams (2 heaped teaspoons)
	Unsweetened breakfast cereals	15 grams (3 heaped tablespoons)
	Boiled rice	35 grams (1 tablespoon)
	Boiled spaghetti, macaroni	40 grams (2 tablespoons)
	Bread (all)	20 grams (½ large slice)
	Crispbread	15 grams (½ oz)
	Cream crackers	20 grams (2 biscuits)
	Sweet biscuits	15 grams (2 'Marie' type)
	Shortcrust pastry and scones	20 grams (2/3 oz)
	Other cakes and biscuits	a
Fruit	Currants, dates, sultanas, raisins	15 grams (½ oz)
	Bananas (without skin)	50 grams (½ large)
	Grapes and tinned fruit	60 grams (2 oz)
	Raspberries, strawberries	180 grams (6 oz)
	Most other fresh fruit	120 grams (1 medium apple)
Vegetables	Lentils and other dried pulses	20 grams (⅔ oz)
	Chips	30 grams (about 4 large)
	Boiled potatoes	50 grams (2 oz)
	Baked beans, sweetcorn	50 grams (2 oz)
	Parsnips (boiled)	75 grams (2½ oz)
	Beetroot (boiled)	100 grams (about 1 medium)
	Peas, broad beans, fresh or frozen	130 grams (4 tablespoons)

	Carrots (boiled)	230 grams (very large portion)

Most other vegetables are virtually carbohydrate free

Dairy foods	Milk, fresh	200 grams (1 glass)
	Milk, dried skimmed	20 grams (5 heaped teaspoons)
	Milk, evaporated	80 grams (2 tablespoons)
	Yogurt, low fat unsweetened	150 grams (1 carton)
	Single cream	300 grams (½ pint)
	Cottage cheese	220 grams (8 oz)

Other cheese, butter and double cream is virtually carbohydrate free

Meat, fish, eggs	Sausages, cooked	70 grams (2½ oz)
	Other made up meat and fish foods	a

Fresh meat, fish (except some shell fish) and eggs are carbohydrate free

Beverages	Port	90 mls (1 small glass)
	Wine, sweet (Sauternes)	170 mls (1 glass)
	Beer (bitter)	330 mls (just over ½ pint)
	Soft drinks	a

Miscellaneous	Ice cream	50 grams (1 small brick)
	Peanuts (shelled)	120 grams (4 oz)
	Chestnuts (shelled)	25 grams (1 oz)

Soups (clear are virtually carbohydrate free)[a]

Fats and oils are carbohydrate free

a – Made up and manufactured products are very variable. Booklets containing imformation about brand products are available from some supermarkets

Carnitine – obsolete name, vitamin B_T

Carnitine is a growth factor for some insects and bacteria, involved in the production of **energy** from **fats**. It is found in meat and dairy products and also synthesised from **lysine** and **methionine**.

Normally, carnitine is both synthesised and eaten in food in amounts of about 100 milligrams per day. However, some recent cases of deficiency in newborn infants and adults treated with intravenous feeding or dialysis for kidney failure have been reported. The symptoms of deficiency include muscle weakness and a fatty liver which are remedied by carnitine supplements. There is also a rare **Inborn error of metabolism** which results in carnitine deficiency.

Carotene – also called provitamin A

Carotene is a precursor of **vitamin A**. It is an orange pigment, found in yellow and orange fruits and vegetables. Green vegetables also contain carotene, masked by the green pigment, chlorophyll. White vegetables and fruits contain none.

Carotene contents are proportional to the orange or yellowness of fruits and vegetables: old **carrots** are particularly rich and contain more than young ones. **Apricots** and **pumpkins** are the best fruit sources. In some red and purple fruits and vegetables, the colour is due to anthocyanins, which do not have vitamin A activity. In green vegetables, the carotene content is proportional to greenness:

outer dark leaves of lettuce and cabbage contain much more carotene than the inner pale ones. **Spinach** and **watercress** are the best green vegetable sources.

About one third of the total vitamin A in the average diet is supplied by carotene. When butter and margarine were rationed during the war, carotene supplied half the vitamin A equivalents.

Several forms of carotene exist. The most common and potent form, β carotene, is referred to here. α carotene (in palm oil), and cryptoxanthene, in maize, have only half the potency of β carotene.

During **digestion**, some carotene is absorbed intact and some is converted to vitamin A in the cells lining the small intestine. This together with other vitamin A in food, is transported to the liver. In vegetables and fruits only one sixth is converted to vitamin A. This is partly because carotene is poorly absorbed from fat free foods. The average conversion rate of carotene is taken into account when assessing the vitamin A values of foods.

Animals and fish convert carotene in grass and feeds to vitamin A, which is colourless. In cows, intact absorbed carotene escaping conversion is passed into the milk, together with vitamin A. The creamy colour of milk fat (in milk, butter, cream etc.) is due to carotene, but in eggs, the yellow colour of the yolk is due to another pigment which does not have vitamin activity. Carotene is added to vegetable (kosher) margarine for both colouring and enrichment purposes. In fatty foods - margarine and dairy products – three times as much carotene is absorbed, and therefore half the carotene is converted to vitamin A.

There are little or no losses of carotene in cooking because it does not dissolve in water and is stable to boiling. Canned and frozen vegetables retain almost all of their carotene. However, carotene is destroyed (oxidised) in the presence of oxygen in air and ultra violet light in daylight. **Antioxidants** in fats, and vitamin C and the **preservative** sulphur dioxide in fruits and vegetables, protect against these losses. Sun-dried pulses and currants contain no carotene, but apricots and peaches that have retained their colour will contain some. There are smaller losses of carotene in modern methods of dehydration. Carrots lose about 40% when dried by hot air and about 20% when freeze dried.

Carotenaemia and cancer

In humans, most of the carotene that is absorbed during digestion is not converted to vitamin A, except when liver stores of vitamin A are low. The intact carotene circulates in the blood stream and is deposited in layers of fat under the skin. When a lot of carotene, from for example carrots, is eaten the skin turns yellow. In contrast to vitamin A intoxication this condition, carotenaemia is harmless and the stain wears off after stopping the high dietary intake.

Because it is not held under close storage in the liver, in contrast to vitamin A, carotene has been proposed as the active substance responsible for the apparent protective effect of fruits and vegetables in **cancer** (see also **vitamin A**). A comprehensive American trial is at present in progress to test this. Meanwhile helpings of fruit and vegetables are beneficial for many other reasons, see individual entries and **diet**.

Carragheenin

Carragheenin is a red seaweed, which dissolves when boiled and sets to a firm jelly. The jelly is usually called carragheen or Irish Moss and can be eaten as a sweet. It is a rich source of minerals, especially **iodine**. Laver, another red seaweed also rich in iodine, is used for laver bread.

Carragheen is sometimes used as a stabiliser and thickener (see **emulsifiers**) in foods, number E407.

Carrots

Carrots are noted for their **vitamin A** content, in the form of **carotene**. A 100 gram helping of carrots contains at least three times the **recommended intake** of vitamin A but the carotene content varies depending largely on maturity and variety. In general, the darker coloured varieties will be at the top end of the range; young carrots contain rather less carotene than old ones. Canned carrots may contain less carotene than fresh because they are usually canned when young. It is probable that the carotene is better absorbed from cooked carrots, rather than raw, especially if eaten with fat, which aids absorption.

Average nutrients in 100 grams (3½ oz) Carrots

	boiled	canned		boiled	canned
Energy kilojoules	79	82	Iron milligrams	0.4	1.3
kilocalories	19	19	Copper milligrams	0.08	0.04
Protein grams	0.6	0.7	Zinc milligrams	0.3	0.3
Total fat grams	0	0	Vitamin A micrograms	1667–2333	1167
Saturated fat grams	0	0	Vitamin D micrograms	0	0
Polyunsaturated fat grams	0	0	Vitamin C milligrams	4	3
			Vitamin E milligrams	0.5	0.5
Cholesterol milligrams	0	0	B vitamins:		
Sugars grams	4.2	4.4	Thiamin (B_1) milligrams	0.05	0.04
Starch grams	0.1	0	Riboflavin (B_2) milligrams	0.04	0.02
Dietary fibre grams	3.1	3.7	Nicotinic acid milligrams	0.5	0.4
Sodium milligrams	50	280[a]	Pyridoxine (B_6) milligrams	0.09	0.02
Potassium milligrams	87	84	Vitamin B_{12} micrograms	0	0
Calcium milligrams	37	27	Folic acid micrograms	8	7
Magnesium milligrams	6	5	Pantothenic acid milligrams	0.18	0.10
			Biotin micrograms	0.4	0.4

(–) No information available   (0) Contains zero or trace amounts

[a]Contains added salt

Cauliflower, see also **cabbage**

Cauliflowers are members of the *Brassica* (cabbage) family and the white part usually eaten is the immature flowering head and stalk. The white part contains little vitamin A (see table) when compared with darker green brassicas like broccoli, and also less of the vitamins such as riboflavin and folic acid. As with all vegetables, nutrients leach out during boiling and some of the vitamins are susceptible to heat - see **vegetables** for details of cooking losses. Steaming, or microwave cooking in little water, is the best way of conserving the nutrients and the flavour, and needs no added salt.

Average nutrients in 100 grams (3½ oz) Cauliflower

	raw	boiled		raw	boiled
Energy kilojoules	56	40	Iron milligrams	0.5	0.4
kilocalories	13	9	Copper milligrams	0.03	0.03
Protein grams	1.9	1.6	Zinc milligrams	0.3	0.2
Total fat grams	0	0	Vitamin A micrograms	1–8	1–8
Saturated fat grams	0	0	Vitamin D micrograms	0	0
Polyunsaturated fat grams	0	0	Vitamin C milligrams	50–90	15–40
			Vitamin E milligrams	0.2	0.1
Cholesterol milligrams	0	0	B vitamins:		
Sugars grams	1.5	0.8	Thiamin (B$_1$) milligrams	0.10	0.06
Starch grams	0	0	Riboflavin (B$_2$) milligrams	0.10	0.06
Dietary fibre grams	2.1	1.8	Nicotinic acid milligrams	1.1	0.8
Sodium milligrams	8	4	Pyridoxine (B$_6$) milligrams	0.20	0.12
Potassium milligrams	350	180	Vitamin B$_{12}$ micrograms	0	0
Calcium milligrams	21	18	Folic acid micrograms	39	49
Magnesium milligrams	14	8	Pantothenic acid milligrams	0.6	0.4
			Biotin micrograms	1.5	1.0

(–) No information available   (0) Contains zero or trace amounts

Celery and celeriac

Celery was originally grown as a medicinal herb, only being cultivated for salads and cooked vegetables by the French and Italians in the Middle Ages. It was introduced into the British Isles in the late 17th century, although wild celery is indigenous in Britain as well as Europe.

Celeriac is a different variety of celery and the swollen stem, rather than the stalk, is eaten. The flavour is less pronounced, especially when boiled, and celeriac has never become as popular in Britain.

The nutrient content of both is similar. Celery is often thought to be rich in iron, but it contains no more than other vegetables. White celery and celeriac contain no vitamin A, although green stems and leaves will supply some, as **carotene**.

Average nutrients in 100 grams (3½ oz) Celery and Celeriac

	raw celery	boiled celeriac		raw celery	boiled celeriac
Energy kilojoules	36	59	Iron milligrams	0.6	0.8
kilocalories	8	14	Copper milligrams	0.11	0.13
Protein grams	0.9	1.6	Zinc milligrams	0.1	–
Total fat grams	0	0	Vitamin A micrograms	0	0
Saturated fat grams	0	0	Vitamin D micrograms	0	0
Polyunsaturated fat grams	0	0	Vitamin C milligrams	7	4
			Vitamin E milligrams	0.2	–
Cholesterol milligrams	0	0	B vitamins:		
Sugars grams	1.2	1.5	Thiamin (B$_1$) milligrams	0.03	0.04
Starch grams	0.1	0.5	Riboflavin (B$_2$) milligrams	0.03	0.04
Dietary fibre grams	1.8	4.9	Nicotinic acid milligrams	0.5	0.8
Sodium milligrams	140	28	Pyridoxine (B$_6$) milligrams	0.10	0.10

Potassium milligrams	280	400	Vitamin B$_{12}$ micrograms	0	0
Calcium milligrams	52	47	Folic acid micrograms	12	–
Magnesium milligrams	10	12	Pantothenic acid milligrams	0.4	–
			Biotin micrograms	0.1	–

(–) No information available   (0) Contains zero or trace amounts

Cellulose (E460–466)

Cellulose is a component of dietary **fibre** found in all plants. It is a **polysaccharide** composed of glucose units but humans possess no digestive **enzymes** capable of breaking the linkages apart. The nutrients in tough raw vegetables are consequently not well digested. Cooking softens the cellulose cell walls and renders the nutrients inside more accessible for digestion.

Methyl cellulose is the basis for some slimming products. It swells in the stomach and is said to reduce appetite. It may also be used for proprietary constipation remedies: wholemeal bread is more effective and less expensive.

Cellulose is used as an **emulsifier** and thickener in foods, E460 to 466.

Cereals see also **Breakfast cereals**

Cereals are the seeds of cultivated plants in the grass family. The seven major cereals grown are barley, maize, millet, oats, rice, rye and wheat (see individual entries). The term 'corn' refers to the indigenous cereal – wheat in Europe and maize in some parts of America.

Cereals have a similar nutritional value, containing mostly **starch**. Although wholegrain cereals contain small quantities of all other **nutrients** they cannot support life when eaten alone because they are lacking in vitamin A (except yellow maize), B$_{12}$ and C. Wholegrain cereals also contain **phytic acid** which interferes with the absorption of iron, calcium and some trace elements. They are however a valuable base (staple), supplying **energy, protein** and **vitamin B**, in the diet which can be balanced with small quantities of vegetables and animal foods (see **diet**).

About 2% of the weight of cereals is the prospective plant (germ), about 13% the outer husk (bran) and about 85% the inner starchy food store (endosperm). Most of the B vitamins, fat, fibre, iron, trace elements and vitamin E are concentrated in the bran, germ and outer layers of the endosperm. Protein is distributed thoughout the wholegrain.

The bran and germ are easily removed from rice and wheat. Highly milled (refined) cereals are more palatable (because they are lacking in fibre) and easier to store (because they are lacking in fat) but of comparatively poor nutritional value. 80%, for instance, of vitamin B$_1$ is removed when rice is milled and polished. Some of the nutrients are partly replaced in white **flour** in Britain, but white flour is still a comparatively poor source of fibre, vitamin E and B$_6$ (pyridoxine) and some trace elements compared to wholemeal flour.

All cereals can be ground to flour but in Western countries wheat is the preferred cereal because it contains sufficient **gluten** to make acceptable leavened bread. The other cereals are chiefly used for animal feed, brewing and breakfast cereals. **Breakfast cereals** are toasted or puffed, which may destroy the B vitamins – in particular vitamin B_1. Some manufacturers replace these losses.

Other starchy dry foods eaten in this country – **sago, tapioca** and **arrowroot** – are sometimes called cereals. They are plant food stores but not seeds and consequently do not contain the germ and are low in protein. They are of very inferior nutritional value, but fortunately are not staple foods in this country and of little importance in the diet.

Starchy foods are the cheapest article of the diet and may supply at least 70% of the total energy in impoverished communities. Their nutritive value is therefore of crucial importance in determining the health of consumers. The lack of protein in cassava (tapioca) is the main cause of the disease **kwashiorkor** in communities subsisting on it. **Pellagra** used to be endemic in the southern states of America, where maize was the main food in the diets of the poor. **Beriberi** has not yet been completely eradicated from some communities where polished rice is the staple cereal. When circumstances – usually income – allows a variety of foods to be eaten the diet is more easily balanced and the nutritive value of the staple cereal is of less importance. However, other nutritional problems then arise, see **diet**.

Cheese

Most cheeses are rich in **protein, calcium** and **phosphorus**. They are good sources of **riboflavin**, and supply other B **vitamins**, but are lacking in vitamin C. All except those made with skimmed **milk** (like some cottage cheeses) are good sources of **vitamin A**, and contain vitamins D and E. All cheeses are poor in iron, but supply other **minerals**.

Nearly all cheeses however are high fat foods, mostly saturated **fatty acids** containing up to 40% by weight or over 75% of total energy. They should be eaten with care; many recipes can do with less cheese. Fat reduced, Feta, and Edam contain less and some cottage and curd cheese made only with skimmed milk are much lower in fat and can be eaten liberally. Cream cheese is one of the highest in fat (see table), and cheeses made with added cream, like Stilton are also high. 'Full fat' soft cheese can contain even more – up to 60%.

All cheeses contain added **salt** and processed cheese, Feta, Stilton and Camembert contain the most. Cheddar and Parmesan are the best sources of calcium: about 60 grams (2 oz) of Cheddar will supply the adult **recommended intake** for calcium. Soft cheeses, like cottage, tend to be lower in calcium than other cheeses – they are made in a similar way to **yogurt** and the calcium combines with the acid and is carried out in the whey.

Processed cheeses are pasteurised (see **milk**) to prevent over-ripening, treated with emulsifiers to prevent separation of the fat and packed into moisture proof coverings. Processed cheeses have a slightly lower protein and higher water content than ordinary cheese. Cheese spreads are treated in approximately the same way as processed cheese, but they are appreciably higher in water and lower in nutritional value than ordinary cheese – and more expensive.

Average nutrients in 100 grams (3½ oz) Cheeses

	blue	Camembert	Cheddar/ Cheshire	cottage	cream	curd
Energy kilojoules	1471	1246	1682	402	1807	567
kilocalories	355	300	406	96	439	135
Protein grams	23.0	22.8	26.0	13.6	3.1	11.0
Total fat grams	29.2	23.2	33.5	4.0	47.4	11.0
Saturated fat grams	17.4	13.9	20.0	2.4	28.3	–
Polyunsaturated fat grams	0.8	0.6	0.9	0.1	1.3	–
Cholesterol milligrams	88	72	70	13	94	–
Sugars grams	0	0	0	1.4	0	0
Starch grams	0	0	0	0	0	0
Dietary fibre grams	0	0	0 .	0	0	0
Sodium milligrams	1420	1410	610	450	300	–
Potassium milligrams	190	110	120	54	160	–
Calcium milligrams	580	380	800	60	98	–
Magnesium milligrams	20	17	25	6	10	–
Iron milligrams	0.17	0.76	0.40	0.10	0.12	–
Copper milligrams	0.09	0.08	0.03	0.02	0.04	–
Zinc milligrams	–	3.0	4.0	0.47	0.48	–
Vitamin A micrograms	300	237	344	35	422	–
Vitamin D micrograms	0.23	0.18	0.26	0.03	0.28	–
Vitamin C milligrams	0	0	0	0	0	–
Vitamin E milligrams	0.7	0.6	0.8	–	1.0	–
B vitamins:						
Thiamin (B₁) milligrams	0.03	0.05	0.04	0.02	0.02	–
Riboflavin (B₂) milligrams	0.4–0.8	0.3–0.9	0.3–0.8	0.19	0.14	–
Nicotinic acid milligrams	5.4–7.7	5.3–7.3	6.2–6.3	3.3	0.8	–
Pyridoxine (B₆) milligrams	0.1–0.2	0.2	0.1	0.01	0.01	–
Vitamin B₁₂ micrograms	0.6–2.7	1.2	1.5	0.5	0.3	–
Folic acid micrograms	20–80	35–95	10–40	9	5	–
Pantothenic acid milligrams	1.0–3.5	0.4–3.6	0.1–0.7	–	–	–
Biotin micrograms	1.0–3.6	1.2–17.8	0.4–2.3	–	–	–

(–) No information available   (0) Contains zero or trace amounts

Average nutrients in 100 grams (3½ oz) Cheeses

	Edam	Feta	low fat	Parmesan	processed	Stilton
Energy kilojoules	1262	1017	1062	1696	1291	1915
kilocalories	304	245	253	408	311	462
Protein grams	24.4	16.5	29.5	35.1	21.5	25.6
Total fat grams	22.9	19.9	15.0	29.7	25.0	40.0
Saturated fat grams	13.7	–	–	17.7	14.9	23.9
Polyunsaturated fat grams	0.6	–	–	0.8	0.7	1.1
Cholesterol milligrams	72	–	–	90	88	120
Sugars grams	0	0	0	0	0	0
Starch grams	0	0	0	0	0	0
Dietary fibre grams	0	0	0	0	0	0
Sodium milligrams	980	1260	–	760	1360	1150
Potassium milligrams	160	70	–	150	82	160
Calcium milligrams	740	384	–	1220	700	360
Magnesium milligrams	28	20	–	50	24	27
Iron milligrams	0.21	0.2	–	0.37	0.50	0.46
Copper milligrams	0.03	0.1	–	–	0.50	0.03
Zinc milligrams	4.0	1.1	–	4.0	3.2	–
Vitamin A micrograms	237	270	–	357	260	408
Vitamin D micrograms	0.18	0	–	0.27	0.14	0.31

	Edam	Feta	low fat	Parmesan	processed	Stilton
Vitamin C milligrams	0	–	–	0	0	0
Vitamin E milligrams	0.8	–	–	0.9	–	1.0
B vitamins:						
Thiamin (B_1) milligrams	0.04	0.03	–	0.02	0.02	0.07
Riboflavin (B_2) milligrams	0.4	0.11	–	0.50	0.29	0.30
Nicotinic acid milligrams	5.8	–	–	8.5	6.1	6.0
Pyridoxine (B_6) milligrams	0.1	–	–	0.1	–	–
Vitamin B_{12} micrograms	1.4	1.4	–	1.5	–	–
Folic acid micrograms	5–35	15	–	20	2	–
Pantothenic acid milligrams	0.1–1.3	–	–	0.3	–	–
Biotin micrograms	0.7–5.1	–	–	1.7	–	–

(–) No information available   (0) Contains zero or trace amounts

Hard cheese is permitted to contain the **preservatives** nisin and sorbic acid and specified permitted natural **colours** or their synthetic equivalents. Mineral hydrocarbons are permitted on the rind. Soft cheese, cheese spreads, and processed cheese may also contain **flavourings** and certain specified **emulsifiers** (like gums, alginates and lecithin). All except Cheddar, Cheshire and soft cheese may contain nitrite.

There are minimal losses of nutrients when cheese is cooked. It hardens when cooked but this can be prevented if it is combined with starch to prevent separation of the fat. When grilling cheese on toast, it is advisable to mix the grated cheese with a little milk, cornflour or mustard and cook under a hot grill for as short a time as possible.

Cheese and drugs

Tyramine (see **tyrosine**) occurs naturally in cheese, extracts, baked beans, alcohol and yoghurt. It is normally detoxicated by a group of enzymes called the monoamine oxidases (MAO), but certain antidepressant drugs, such as Nardil, inhibit their action. These foods must not be eaten in conjunction with MAO inhibiting drugs: an alarming rise in blood pressure – with sometimes fatal results – has been recorded. Old cheese may contain large amounts of **histamine**.

Cherries

Cherries were probably first cultivated in the near East, in the orchards of Mesopotamia, but their cultivation in Europe is relatively recent. Sour (Morello) cherries are used widely for making liqueurs, such as Kirsch. They differ little in their nutritional content from sweet cherries when cooked with sugar (see table).

Average nutrients in 100 grams (3½ oz) Cherries

	sweet raw	stewed with sugar		sweet raw	stewed with sugar
Energy kilojoules	201	328	Iron milligrams	0.4	0.2
kilocalories	47	77	Copper milligrams	0.07	0.07
Protein grams	0.6	0.4	Zinc milligrams	0.1	0.1
Total fat grams	0	0	Vitamin A micrograms	20	15
Saturated fat grams	0	0	Vitamin D micrograms	0	0
Polyunsaturated fat grams	0	0	Vitamin C milligrams	5	3
			Vitamin E milligrams	0.1	0.1
Cholesterol milligrams	0	0	B vitamins:		
Sugars grams	11.9	19.7	Thiamin (B_1) milligrams	0.05	0.03
Starch grams	0	0	Riboflavin (B_2) milligrams	0.07	0.06
Dietary fibre grams	1.7	1.2	Nicotinic acid milligrams	0.4	0.3
Sodium milligrams	3	2	Pyridoxine (B_6) milligrams	0.05	0.02
Potassium milligrams	280	230	Vitamin B_{12} micrograms	0	0
Calcium milligrams	16	15	Folic acid micrograms	8	3
Magnesium milligrams	10	9	Pantothenic acid milligrams	0.26	0.13
			Biotin micrograms	0.4	0.2

(–) No information available   (0) Contains zero or trace amounts

Chestnuts

Chestnuts were widely distributed in prehistoric times and were probably used as food by early hunter gatherers. There are many varieties of chestnut, and they have been used as a staple food, for example in southern Italy. They are much lower in fat than other nuts, and much higher in **starch**, so that it is possible to use them as flour. Chestnuts contain a little protein, and are good sources of B vitamins **thiamin, riboflavin** and **pyridoxine**.

Average nutrients in 100 grams (3½ oz) Chestnuts

Energy kilojoules	720	Iron milligrams	0.9
kilocalories	170	Copper milligrams	0.2
Protein grams	2.0	Zinc milligrams	–
Total fat grams	2.7	Vitamin A micrograms	0
Saturated fat grams	0.5	Vitamin D micrograms	0
Polyunsaturated fat grams	1.1	Vitamin C milligrams	0
		Vitamin E milligrams	0.5
Cholesterol milligrams	0	B vitamins:	
Sugars grams	7.0	Thiamin (B_1) milligrams	0.20
Starch grams	29.6	Riboflavin (B_2) milligrams	0.22
Dietary fibre grams	6.8	Nicotinic acid milligrams	0.6
Sodium milligrams	11	Pyridoxine (B_6) milligrams	0.33
Potassium milligrams	500	Vitamin B_{12} micrograms	0
Calcium milligrams	46	Folic acid micrograms	–
Magnesium milligrams	33	Pantothenic acid milligrams	0.47
		Biotin micrograms	1.3

(–) No information available   (0) Contains zero or trace amounts

Chicken

It is likely that the jungle fowl was the main ancestor of the domestic hen, which is indigenous to northern India. It had appeared in Egypt by the fourteenth century BC. The flesh is relatively low in **fat** when compared with red meats, although chicken eaten with the skin is surprisingly fatty (see table). Like all meats, chicken contains **iron** and **zinc** in well-absorbed forms; dark meat contains twice as much as the breast. The white breast meat contains twice as much **pyridoxine** as dark meat.

Average nutrients in 100 grams (3½ oz) Chicken (roast)

	meat and skin	light meat	dark meat		meat and skin	light meat	dark meat
Energy kilojoules	902	599	648	Iron milligrams	0.8	0.5	1.0
kilocalories	216	142	155	Copper milligrams	0.12	0.11	0.13
Protein grams	22.6	26.5	23.1	Zinc milligrams	1.4	1.0	2.1
Total fat grams	14.0	4.0	6.9	Vitamin A micrograms	0	0	0
Saturated fat grams	4.6	1.3	2.3	Vitamin D micrograms	0	0	0
Polyunsaturated fat grams	2.1	0.6	1.0	Vitamin C milligrams	0	0	0
				Vitamin E milligrams	–	0.08	0.15
Cholesterol milligrams	–	74	120	B vitamins:			
Sugars grams	0	0	0	Thiamin (B_1) milligrams	–	0.08	0.09
Starch grams	0	0	0	Riboflavin (B_2) milligrams	–	0.14	0.24
Dietary fibre grams	0	0	0	Nicotinic acid milligrams	–	15.3	10.4
Sodium milligrams	72	71	91	Pyridoxine (B_6) milligrams	–	0.35	0.16
Potassium milligrams	270	330	290	Vitamin B_{12} micrograms	0	0	1
Calcium milligrams	9	9	9	Folic acid micrograms	–	7	13
Magnesium milligrams	21	26	22	Pantothenic acid milligrams	–	1.1	1.3
				Biotin micrograms	–	2	3

(–) No information available   (0) Contains zero or trace amounts

Chicory

The compact blanched heart of 'witloof' chicory is a gourmet food for use in salads. It is sometimes also called Belgian endive. Its nutritional composition is shown in the table.

The chicory root is derived from the same variety as salad chicory although varieties grown for this purpose have larger roots. When roasted and ground it is used as a coffee substitute, particularly in liquid coffee extract.

There are several other types of chicory - more popular in France and Italy as salad vegetables. Red chicories are especially good.

Average nutrients in 100 grams (3½ oz) Chicory

Energy kilojoules	38	Iron milligrams	0.7
kilocalories	9	Copper milligrams	0.14
Protein grams	0.8	Zinc milligrams	0.2
Total fat grams	0	Vitamin A micrograms	0
Saturated fat grams	0	Vitamin D micrograms	0
Polyunsaturated fat grams	0	Vitamin C milligrams	4
		Vitamin E milligrams	–

Cholesterol milligrams	0	B vitamins:		
Sugars grams	–	Thiamin (B₁) milligrams	0.05	
Starch grams	0ᵃ	Riboflavin (B₂) milligrams	0.05	
Dietary fibre grams	–	Nicotinic acid milligrams	0.6	
Sodium milligrams	7	Pyridoxine (B₆) milligrams	0.05	
Potassium milligrams	180	Vitamin B₁₂ micrograms	0	
Calcium milligrams	18	Folic acid micrograms	52	
Magnesium milligrams	13	Pantothenic acid milligrams	–	
		Biotin micrograms	–	

(–) No information available   (0) Contains zero or trace amounts

ᵃ Contains 1.5 grams inulin

Chlorine

Chlorine is an **electrolyte**, closely associated with **sodium** in the body and food. Adults contain about 70 grams of chlorine, most of which is in the fluids surrounding cells.

The majority of chlorine in the diet is dervied from salt (sodium chloride). Salt free diets contain about ½ gram of chlorine; diets containing salt in cooking and added as a preservative contain 5-9 grams per day. Chlorinated water supplies a negligible amount – about 3 milligrams per day.

Chlorine is absorbed out of food and discarded from the body in urine and sweat with sodium. Though an essential nutrient, chlorine deficiency does not occur in otherwise normal health without a corresponding deficit of sodium.

Chocolate and confectionery

By weight, chocolate and confectionery is at least half sugar (**sucrose**), which contributes to **tooth decay**. Chocolate, made from **cocoa**, sugar, cocoa butter and flavourings, contains up to 30% **fat** – mostly saturated. A single Mars bar or 50 grams chocolate contains a whole Megajoule – one eighth of the day's energy needs for most women. Diabetic chocolate is not less fattening than ordinary chocolate.

Fruit gums, toffee and milk chocolate contain calcium and other minerals and small amounts of protein. Milk chocolate has more calcium and protein, from the milk, than plain, but boiled sweets and peppermints contain no nutrients apart from sugar. Toffee and fudge contain added salt and may have to be avoided in low **sodium** diets (see table).

Confectionery contains most types of food **additives** – including flavours, colours and mineral hydrocarbons. Antioxidants and preservatives are permitted ingredients and may be 'carried over' into the finished food.

Average nutrients in 100 grams (3½ oz) Sweets and Chocolate

	boiled sweets, peppermints	fruit gums	toffee	milk chocolate	plain chocolate	Mars
Energy kilojoules	1533	734	1810	2214	2197	1853
kilocalories	359	172	430	529	525	441
Protein grams	0	1.0	2.1	8.4	4.7	5.3
Total fat grams	0	0	17.2	30.3	29.2	18.9

	boiled sweets, **peppermints**	fruit gums	toffee	milk chocolate	plain chocolate	Mars
Saturated fat grams	0	0	–	17.7	17.4	–
Polyunsaturated fat grams	0	0	–	1.1	1.0	–
Cholesterol milligrams	0	0	–	–	–	–
Sugars grams	95.0	42.6	70.1	56.5	59.5	65.8
Starch grams	0	2.2	1.0	2.9	5.3	0.7
Dietary fibre (NSP) grams	0	0	0	0	0	0
Sodium milligrams	17	64	320	120	11	150
Potassium milligrams	4	360	210	420	300	250
Calcium milligrams	6	360	95	220	38	160
Magnesium milligrams	2	110	25	55	100	35
Iron milligrams	0.3	4.2	1.5	1.6	2.4	1.1
Copper milligrams	0.05	1.4	0.4	0.3	0.7	0.3
Zinc milligrams	–	–	–	0.2	0.2	–
Vitamin A micrograms	0	0	0	6	6	6
Vitamin D micrograms	0	0	0	0	0	0
Vitamin C milligrams	0	0	0	0	0	0
Vitamin E milligrams	0	0	0	0.5	0.5	–
B vitamins:						
Thiamin (B_1) milligrams	0	0	0	0.1	0.1	0
Riboflavin (B_2) milligrams	· 0	0	0	0.2	0.1	0.2
Nicotinic acid milligrams	0	0	0	1.6	1.2	1.2
Pyridoxine (B_6) milligrams	0	0	0	0.02	0.02	0.02
Vitamin B_{12} micrograms	0	0	0	0	0	0
Folic acid micrograms	0	0	0	10	10	–
Pantothenic acid milligrams	0	0	0	0.6	0.6	0.6
Biotin micrograms	0	0	0	3	3	3

(–) No information available   (0) Contains zero or trace amounts

Cholesterol

A raised *blood* cholesterol is an important risk factor in **heart disease**. Levels of blood cholesterol are relatively high in western countries such as Britain and most people would do well to reduce them. This is particularly true for people who have a close relative who suffers from heart disease.

The most effective way of doing this is to eat less **fat** especially saturated **fatty acids**. Some foods, notably **eggs, kidney, liver** and **roe** (including tar-amasalata) are rich in cholesterol and should be eaten occasionally. However the body normally synthesises at least twice as much as is eaten in food each day and blood cholesterol levels are not markedly affected in most people by intakes from food – but see **lipid**. The claim 'low in cholesterol' without information of the fat content on food **labels** is misleading.

Cholesterol is part of the body structure and a normal constituent of the blood stream. Most adults contain about 140 grams (5 oz). It is needed for cell membranes – particularly nerves – and also for the synthesis of some hormones and vitamin D, but it is not an essential nutrient. All animal foods (except egg white) contain cholesterol, and lean meat does not contain less than fatty meat. Plant foods do not contain cholesterol.

Normally cholesterol gains from diet and body synthesis are balanced by losses, mainly in bile. As already stated, the level of cholesterol circulating in the blood stream can be reduced by eating less saturated fat. Polyunsaturated **fatty acids**, found in some plant **oils** and **margarines** reduce the blood cholesterol, by hastening the loss of cholesterol in bile. However, they are *less effective* in reducing blood cholesterol than the saturated fats are in raising it. So except under medical advice (see **lipid**), it is better to reduce total fat than to eat more polyunsaturated fat, for a number of reasons – see **diet**.

Some forms of dietary fibre, notably oats and **pectin** found in vegetables and fruits are also able to reduce the blood cholesterol, possibly by hastening the loss in bile. This is an added reason for including plenty of them in a healthy diet.

For details of the way in which cholesterol is carried in the blood stream – the LDL and HDL – see **lipid**.

Choline

In diets containing sufficient **protein**, choline can be made in the human body, notably from **methionine**, an **amino acid**. Most people probably synthesise about 10 milligrams a day. Although it is rarely an essential **nutrient** for man (in contrast to some animals) choline is abundant in food. For example 1 egg and 100 grams (3½ oz) of meat and cereal contain 500, 600 and 100 milligrams respectively.

Choline has several important functions in the body, including the formation of lecithin and other **phospholipids**. When the diet is low in protein, for instance in alcoholism and **kwashiorkor**, insufficient choline may be formed. This may cause accumulation of fat in the liver.

Chromium

Chromium is a **trace element**, only recently recognised as an essential **nutrient** for humans. It enhances the action of insulin – the main hormone controlling the utilisation of **glucose** (see **diabetes**) – but this is probably not its only function in the body.

During **digestion**, only small amounts of chromium are absorbed from food into the blood stream. One of the several forms of chromium (called Glucose Tolerance Factor) is probably absorbed more efficiently and may be more potent than other forms. As yet, estimates of either total chromium or GTF contents of foods are uncertain. The best source of GTF found so far is brewers' yeast. Diets high in fats, refined starches and sugar contain less chromium than those including plenty of fresh vegetables and wholegrain cereals. Large amounts of chromium (which is labile to heat) may be lost during cooking and processing.

The daily needs for chromium are thought to be 5–10 micrograms (one microgram is one millionth of a gram). Depending on the source, 20 to 500 micrograms might be needed in food to replace daily losses. American diets reportedly contain 5 to 100 micrograms per day.

Needs for chromium are increased when the diet is excessively high in sugar or starch. These nutrients require more insulin for their utilisation and correspondingly induce more chromium to be released from tissues and lost in the urine after exerting its effect. Since refined starches and sugars are poor sources of chromium, even moderate intakes may cause a gradual depletion of body stores, resulting in mild deficiency in middle or old age. The body content of chromium is reported to fall with increasing age in Americans, but there have been no comparable studies in the UK.

Under certain circumstances, severe chromium deficiency in animals causes a syndrome similar to diabetes. Whilst chromium supplements cannot cure frank diabetes in humans, mild intolerance to **carbohydrates** (resulting in occasional glucose losses in urine – see **diabetes**) has been improved in middle aged and elderly people deficient in chromium. Chromium deficiency is also likely to occur in diabetics treated with insulin injections (which are thought to increase chromium losses in the urine), after successive pregnancies, and prolonged subsistence on formula diets deficient in chromium. It frequently occurs in children suffering from the protein deficiency disease **kwashiorkor**.

Other symptoms occurring in animals fed chromium deficient diets are raised blood **cholesterol**, increased incidence of **atherosclerosis** and decreased life span. The possible preventative effects of chromium in heart disease – in view of suspected large losses in food processing – is under investigation.

Citric acid (E330)

Citric acid is widely distributed in fruits, especially citrus fruits, vegetables and yogurt. It can be commercially manufactured and used as an acid flavouring agent in jams, soft drinks and sweets, and as a sequestrant, see **miscellaneous additives**. It is the most commonly used food additive and the average person eats about one gram every day.

Citric acid is continually made and broken down in the body. It takes part in a vital chain of reactions called the citric acid (or Kreb's) cycle whereby **energy** is liberated from food, see **glucose** and **metabolism**. Carbon dioxide and hydrogen (which is later combined with oxygen to form water) are the end products: they are removed from the blood stream by the lungs and kidneys.

Cobalt

Cobalt occurs in its free form in plants, but it is utilised by man only as part of the essential nutrient **vitamin B_{12}**, supplied by animal foods. Like other **trace elements**, cobalt is toxic in excess. Doses 1000 times greater than normally present in food have caused heart failure. It is more toxic when taken with alcohol: before this was realised, cobalt salts were used as foaming agents in beer.

Work with animals suggests that cobalt may be an antagonist to another trace element, **iodine**.

Cocoa

Cocoa contains **protein, minerals** and small quantities of B vitamins and vitamin A. It is a rich source of iron, but probably little is available for absorption into the blood stream. It also contains copper and zinc (see table). Because so little is used, cocoa is not an intrinsically importance source of **nutrients**, but it is a nourishing drink when made with milk.

Cocoa contains the stimulants **caffeine** (about 20 milligrams per cup) and theobromine (about 200 milligrams per cup). Theobromine is a weaker stimulant than caffeine.

Cocoa nibs (the separated beans) contain up to 60% of their weight in **fat** (cocoa butter) rich in saturated **fatty acids**. It is partially removed before the nibs are ground: otherwise it would separate out from the beverage. Although cocoa powder contains less saturated fat (20 to 25%) than nibs, it should be used in moderation in **cholesterol** lowering diets. Darker powders contain more fat and have a richer flavour.

Drinking chocolate contains cocoa (usually treated with alkali to prevent less sediment forming in the beverage) and sugar. Note that drinking chocolate contains much more sugar and less protein, iron and minerals than cocoa. Milk powder, salt and vanilla flavour may also be added.

Average nutrients in 100 grams (3½ oz) Cocoa and Drinking chocolate

	cocoa	drinking chocolate		cocoa	drinking chocolate
Energy kilojoules	1301	1554	Iron milligrams	10.5	2.4
kilocalories	312	366	Copper milligrams	3.9	1.1
Protein grams	18.5	5.5	Zinc milligrams	6.9	1.9
Total fat grams	21.7	6.0	Vitamin A micrograms	7	–
Saturated fat grams	12.8	3.5	Vitamin D micrograms	0	0
Polyunsaturated fat grams	0.6	0.2	Vitamin C milligrams	0	0
			Vitamin E milligrams	0.4	0.1
Cholesterol milligrams	0	–	B vitamins:		
Sugars grams	0	73.8	Thiamin (B_1) milligrams	0.16	0.06
Starch grams	11.5	3.6	Riboflavin (B_2) milligrams	0.06	0.04
Dietary fibre (NSP) grams	–	–	Nicotinic acid milligrams	7.3	2.1
Sodium milligrams	950	250	Pyridoxine (B_6) milligrams	0.07	0.02
Potassium milligrams	1500	410	Vitamin B_{12} micrograms	0	0
Calcium milligrams	130	33	Folic acid micrograms	38	10
Magnesium milligrams	520	150	Pantothenic acid milligrams	–	–
			Biotin micrograms	–	–

(–) No information available   (0) Contains zero or trace amounts

Cod

One of the virtues of cod, like all white fish, is its low content of **fat**. Consequently it is low in **energy** (Calories). Cod fried in batter is about twice as high in energy (see table). Cod contains reasonable amounts of well absorbed **iron** and **zinc**, but not as much as fatty fish such as **herrings**. It is also a good source of **iodine**.

Average nutrients in 100 grams (3½ oz) Cod

	steamed	fried		steamed	fried
Energy kilojoules	350	834	Iron milligrams	0.5	0.5
kilocalories	80	199	Copper milligrams	0.10	0.07
Protein grams	18.6	19.6	Zinc milligrams	0.5	–
Total fat grams	0.9	10.3	Vitamin A micrograms	0	0

	steamed	fried			steamed	fried
Saturated fat grams	0.2	–	Vitamin D micrograms		0	0
Polyunsaturated fat grams	0.3	–	Vitamin C milligrams		0	0
			Vitamin E milligrams		0.54	–
Cholesterol milligrams	60	60[a]	B vitamins:			
Sugars grams	0	–	Thiamin (B_1) milligrams		0.09	–
Starch grams	0	7.5	Riboflavin (B_2) milligrams		0.09	–
Dietary fibre grams	0	–	Nicotinic acid milligrams		5.6	–
Sodium milligrams	100	100	Pyridoxine (B_6) milligrams		0.37	–
Potassium milligrams	360	370	Vitamin B_{12} micrograms		3	–
Calcium milligrams	15	80	Folic acid micrograms		12	–
Magnesium milligrams	21	24	Pantothenic acid milligrams		0.20	–
			Biotin micrograms		3	–

(–) No information available   (0) Contains zero or trace amounts

[a]Will contain more if egg used in the batter

Coeliac disease

Coeliac disease is a common form of **malabsorption**, causing loss of weight and vitamin and mineral deficiencies. It is estimated to affect about one in every 2000 people in Britain.

Coeliacs are sensitive to gliadin, part of the protein **gluten** in wheat, rye, and to a lesser extent barley and oats. Most are affected in childhood after gluten containing cereals are first introduced into the diet. The cause of the disease is uncertain; it may be due to the absence of an **enzyme** necessary for the **digestion** of gliadin, a fraction of gluten, or to an abnormal reaction of one of the protective immunoglobulins A (see **allergy**) in the digestive system which causes an allergic type of reaction and damage to the intestine. Whatever the cause, gliadin irritates the cells lining the villi in the small bowel, which are responsible for absorbing nutrients and transferring them to the blood stream. When the villi become inflamed and eventually degenerate, nutrients are not absorbed, but are carried out of the body, usually as fatty diarrhoea. The child fails to thrive, is often irritable, has a characteristic pot belly, and may suffer from **anaemia** and **rickets**. Milder forms may pass unnoticed, but in adult life may result in general ill health, loss of weight, tiredness and **osteomalacia**.

Severe coeliac disease used to be fatal, but now is cured by complete removal of gluten from the diet. All untreated wheat flour must be excluded and barley and rye are usually prohibited. Treatment in hospital is usually necessary to allow regeneration of the villi and full recovery.

Maize (for instance in cornflakes, cornflour), rice and potatoes are gluten free. These starches, together with fresh meat, fish, cheese, eggs, fruits, vegetables and preserves are allowed freely. Special gluten-free biscuits, pasta, bread and flour (which can be made into bread, cakes and biscuits) made from treated wheat are available on prescription. Many convenience foods are unsuspected sources of gluten (for example pepper compound, vending machine coffee) and to enable successful adherence to the diet, instruction should be given by a qualified dietitian. The Coeliac Society, P.O. Box 181, London NW2 2QY, publishes an annual list of gluten-free convenience foods and is a valuable source of help and information.

Some children are apparently able to tolerate gluten eventually but, because anaemia, osteomalacia and more serious complications can develop insidiously and without discomfort, it is usually necessary for children to adhere to a lifelong gluten-free diet. Coeliacs diagnosed in adulthood are rarely able to return to a normal diet.

Coffee

Coffee contains at least 300 substances and some of them, notably **caffeine** are pharmacologically active. A strong cup of coffee, made from 50 grams (2 oz) coffee in 500 grams (1 pint) of water, contains approximately 150 milligrams of **caffeine**, 100 milligrams of **potassium** and 1 milligram of **nicotinic acid**. Black coffee contains hardly any **energy**.

Roasted chicory root (which has a bitter flavour but is lacking in caffeine), is added to French coffee. Legally French coffee must contain a minimum of 51% by weight of coffee, and Viennese coffee (coffee with figs) 85%. Instant coffees are spray – or freeze – dried coffee infusions. One teaspoon (2 grams) of instant coffee contains about 100 milligrams of caffeine. Coffee essences contain concentrated coffee infusions and sugar. Both instant and coffee essence may contain **preservative** and **emulsifier**.

Decaffeinated coffee must not contain more than 0.3% caffeine (approximately 6 milligrams per cup). The caffeine is removed by treatment with a solvent, dichloromethane, which is then mostly removed by steaming – a small residue (up to 10 parts per million) may be left.

Coley (saithe)

A white **fish** with similar nutritional virtues to **cod**. It is considerably less expensive and contains more **protein** and B **vitamins** (see table).

Average nutrients in 100 grams (3½ oz) Coley (steamed)

Energy kilojoules	418	Iron milligrams	0.6
kilocalories	99	Copper milligrams	–
Protein grams	23.3	Zinc milligrams	–
Total fat grams	0.6	Vitamin A micrograms	0
Saturated fat grams	0.1	Vitamin D micrograms	0
Polyunsaturated fat grams	0.2	Vitamin C milligrams	0
		Vitamin E milligrams	0.47
Cholesterol milligrams	75	B vitamins:	
Sugars grams	0	Thiamin (B_1) milligrams	0.12
Starch grams	0	Riboflavin (B_2) milligrams	0.26
Dietary fibre grams	0	Nicotinic acid milligrams	8.4
Sodium milligrams	97	Pyridoxine (B_6) milligrams	0.62
Potassium milligrams	350	Vitamin B_{12} micrograms	5
Calcium milligrams	19	Folic acid micrograms	–
Magnesium milligrams	31	Pantothenic acid milligrams	0.40
		Biotin micrograms	8

(–) No information available   (0) Contains zero or trace amounts

Colours in food

There are three main groups of the many naturally occurring colours in foods; chlorophyll (green) found particularly in leafy vegetables, **carotenes** (orange/ yellow) and anthocyanins (red/blue). Anthocyanins are flavonoids (see **bio-flavonoids**) and colour fruits such as strawberries, blackcurrants and other berries. All of these are complex chemical compounds which change readily with heat or acidity, see below.

A number of colours are added to food to replace losses in manufacture, standardise appearance, and to make foods containing little of the food they represent look fit to eat – orangeade for example, or strawberry flavoured desserts. There are several alternatives for each colour because some only dissolve in fat, others in water, and others may react with the food. Cakes, salad cream and squash may all contain different yellows.

Twelve of the natural colours or their synthetic equivalents are permitted in foods by the 1978 Regulations. A full list of colours and other food additives is shown in Appendix II. The natural colours are curcumin found in turmeric (E100), **riboflavin** (E101), cochineal (E120) extracted from the Coccus beetle, chlorophyll (E140-1), caramel (E150), carbon black (E153), carotene (E160), flavones (E161), beetroot red (E162) and anthocyanins (E163). Caramel accounts for 98% by weight of all colours permitted in food and is the only colour permitted in **bread**. Only specified natural colours like annatto (E160) are permitted in cheese and butter. Two inorganic colours, titanium dioxide (white, E171) and iron oxide (red/brown, E172) are also permitted.

Sixteen coal tar dyes are also permitted in food. They are preferred by the food industry because they are more stable in food, but their use is continually being questioned. Amaranth (E123) for example is a non-specific carcinogen in rats. As with the natural colours, they are permitted in any food except raw or processed meat, fish, fruit, vegetables, white bread, tea, coffee, and milk. A full list is shown in Appendix II. Yellows are E102 (**tartrazine**), E104, E110; reds are E122, E123, E127; blues are E131, E132; green is E142; and black E151. Five have no E numbers - yellow 2G (107), red 2G (128), brilliant blue (133) and brown FK (154) and HT (155).

A few colours are restricted. E180 is only allowed on cheese rind, methyl violet (no number) to mark cheese and fruit, and aluminium (E173), silver (E174) and gold (E175) are allowed on cake decorations.

Allergy to food colours

Colours, together with **preservatives** and **flavours** are the additives most commonly implicated in allergy – see, for example, **tartrazine**. This is partly because of their widespread use in cosmetics and drugs in addition to foods. Both the natural and the coal tar colours can be responsible for reactions – in one study annatto was responsible for 26% of positive reactions in a group of patients with **urticaria**, compared with 11% from tartrazine and from 9 to 17% from other coal tar dyes.

Changes of colour during cooking and processing of food

Natural plant colours are complex substances, easily altered by heat, light, acids and alkalis. Myoglobin changes from red to brown when meat is cooked: but the colour can be stabilised by **nitrite**. Chlorophyll in green leaves changes from bright to bronze green when cooked. Alkalis in cooking water (like bicarbonate of soda) preserve the green colour but destroy vitamin C. Carotene (in orange and yellow fruits and vegetables) is destroyed at high temperatures in air: apricots turn brown when they are dried unless the **preservative** sulphur dioxide is added. Anthocyanins in red, purple and blue fruits and vegetables, turn red in acids (for instance vinegar) and blue in alkaline cooking water. Flavones in white fruits and vegetables (like cauliflower) yellow on cooking in alkaline water: the colour change can be prevented by acids – lemon juice, vitamin C or vinegar.

Another important change which occurs when food is cooked or processed is browning, brought about by three different processes:

Heat – caramel is formed when sugars are heated. It is a permitted colour and added to many foods, including brown bread, marmalade and pickles.

Enzymes – cutting, peeling and chopping of vegetables and fruits releases enzymes from the damaged cells. Flavones in white vegetables and fruits are changed from white to brown in the presence of oxygen in air. Browning of potatoes, bananas, apples, can be prevented by excluding oxygen (by covering with water or adding vitamin C), or blanching (dipping in hot water) or by adding sulphur dioxide.

Maillard reaction–**Amino acids**–particularly lysine–and sugar combine to form a brown coloured complex when food is heated, and during storage of some processed foods. Although Maillard browning is desirable in cooked foods (for instance the skin of milk pudding, the crust of bread) in others – like milk powder – it is not: the nutritional value of the protein and flavour of the food are adversely affected.

Convenience foods

Manufactured foods requiring little additional preparation in the home have become known as convenience foods. For example, meat pies, dehydrated and frozen meals, instant puddings and soups, cake mixes and breakfast cereals.

Convenience foods save time for the consumer but, even allowing for lack of waste, they are generally a more expensive way of obtaining essential nutrients than fresh foods: labour and fuel used in preparation, packaging and transport have to be paid for. Losses of essential nutrients during processing are not much greater than in normal home cooking, but the nutrient content depends on the ingredients used: convenience foods are likely to contain less of the more expensive ingredients (such as meat) than a home prepared dish. In Australia, a study demonstrated that convenience foods (rice with curry or meat sauce) contained only 55% of the protein and 60% of vitamin B_1 on average compared with meals prepared in the home.

An additional reason for taking only moderate quantities of convenience foods is that they contain more food **additives** than fresh or lightly processed foods. As a safety factor many food additives are not permitted in foods eaten in large quantities. Convenience foods are assumed to be eaten infrequently and are thus subject to more lenient additive regulations.

Cooking fats - lard, dripping, suet, white fat

Cooking fats are remarkable for their complete absence of all nutrients, except **fat**, mostly saturated **fatty acids** (see table). Together with **oils** these foods are the most fattening (high in energy) of all human foods: a 250 gram block contains the average person's complete day's intake.

Lard is extracted from pig fat, dripping from sheep or beef bones or fat. Suet is extracted from beef or sheeps' kidney fat: block suet must contain 99% fat, but shredded suet contains up to 15% rice or wheat flours (to keep the pieces apart).

Lard substitutes (compound cooking fats, white fats or shortenings) are made from blends of oils – usually vegetable. They contain no cholesterol but are hardened (or hydrogenated – see **margarine**) and therefore are contraindicated in high polyunsaturated, low saturated fat diets.

All cooking fats are permitted to contain **antioxidant**.

Average nutrients in 100 grams (3½ oz) Cooking fats

	lard	dripping	suet	lard substitute (white fat)
Energy kilojoules	3663	3663	3402	3674
kilocalories	891	891	826	894
Protein grams	0	0 ·	0	0
Total fat grams	99.0	99.0	86.7	99.3
Saturated fat grams	41.8	42.0	49.2	40.0
Polyunsaturated fat grams	9.0	4.0	1.1	14.0
Cholesterol milligrams	70	60	74	–
Sugars grams	0	0	0	0
Starch grams	0	0	12.1	0
Dietary fibre grams	0	0	0	0
Sodium milligrams	2	5	0	0
Potassium milligrams	1	4	0	0
Calcium milligrams	1	1	0	0
Magnesium milligrams	1	0	0	0
Iron milligrams	0.1	0.2	0	0
Copper milligrams	0.02	–	0	0
Zinc milligrams	–	–	0	0
Vitamin A micrograms	0	0	64	0
Vitamin D micrograms	0	0	0	0
Vitamin C milligrams	0	0	0	0
Vitamin E milligrams	0	0.3	1.5	0
B vitamins:				
Thiamin (B_1) milligrams	0	0	0	0
Riboflavin (B_2) milligrams	0	0	0	0
Nicotinic acid milligrams	0	0	0	0
Pyridoxine (B_6) milligrams	0	0	0	0
Vitamin B_{12} micrograms	0	0	0	0

Folic acid micrograms	0	0	0	0
Pantothenic acid milligrams	0	0	0	0
Biotin micrograms	0	0	0	0

(–) No information available   (0) Contains zero or trace amounts

Copper

Copper is a **trace element**, necessary for growth of children and part of many **enzymes** including those needed for the formation of blood and bone. It is used as a growth promoter in animal feeds, and calves and lamb's **liver** are outstanding sources; 25 grams (1 oz) will supply the adult estimated daily needs. Unrefined cereals (wholemeal bread) supply more copper than refined (like white bread): milk, most dairy products and eggs are notably poor sources, see individual entries.

Adults probably require between 1.5 and 2 milligrams of copper per day – an amount which is supplied by a well balanced **diet**, containing a variety of foods. Children require more in proportion to their weight than adults to allow for growth, and more is required during pregnancy to ensure an adequate liver store of copper in the newborn child.

Adults contain between 100 and 150 milligrams of copper, distributed throughout all the tissues of the body but in highest concentration in the liver, brain and kidneys. Copper-containing enzymes are known to be necessary for the release from liver stores of **iron** used in new red blood cell formation (see **anaemia**); for the formation of **proteins** in bone, skin and blood vessels; and for the formation of melanin – the pigment in skin and hair. The most vital role of copper containing enzymes is probably the final stages of removal of energy from food and transferring it to 'energy rich' substances (like ATP – see **phosphorus**). These are a source of energy in – for example – the synthesis of many complex substances including **phospholipids**.

Adults are unlikely to suffer from a deficiency of copper except when suffering from diseases causing **malabsorption** of nutrients from food. Most foods contain small amounts and a mixed diet (see **diet**) is protective. However, infants, who are dependent on one food (milk) for the first few months of life, are more at risk. Normally, copper is transferred from the mother towards the end of pregnancy and held in store in the baby's liver. This store tides the infant over until weaning. Symptoms of copper deficiency – which have occurred in premature babies and those fed for a long time with fresh or evaporated cows' milk – include failure to thrive, diarrhoea, anaemia and bone fractures. (In some cases the bone fractures resembled those found in battered babies.) Cows' milk contains less copper than breast milk: it is added to some powdered baby milks.

Like other trace elements, copper is toxic when taken in excess. It causes diarrhoea, and over the long term accumulates in the body causing liver damage. Rarely food may be contaminated with copper-containing fungicides. Legal maxima for copper include a general limit of 2 milligrams per 100 grams for most foods: soft drinks may only contain 0.2 milligrams per 100 millilitres.

There are two rare **inborn errors of metabolism** caused by copper excess and deficiency. Wilson's disease results in accumulation of copper in the brain and liver. Although previously fatal, this disease can be treated with drugs which remove copper from the body. In Menkes syndrome, too little copper is absorbed from food, causing brain damage (possibly because too little phospholipid is formed) and other symptoms of copper deficiency.

Animal experiments suggest that other trace elements – cadmium, lead (see **poisons in food**) and **zinc** may interfere with the absorption of copper from food. The high ratio of zinc to copper, in cows' milk compared with breast milk, may be a contributory factor in copper deficiency in infancy. When given to animals in excess **molybdenum**, another trace element, causes a syndrome resembling copper deficiency. Knock knees and other skeletal abnormalities have been reported in adults and adolescents subsisting on very restricted diets in India where the soil is high in molybdenum and **fluorine**. Low intakes of copper, or high intakes of copper antagonists may be of relevance in **heart disease:** in animals a low copper diet results in a raised blood **cholesterol.**

Couscous

A North African speciality, made by steaming or boiling soaked grain, usually millet, eaten with a spiced meat sauce. The few analyses available (see table) are for couscous made with millet.

Average nutrients in 100 grams (3½ oz) Couscous

Energy kilojoules	950	Iron milligrams	5.0
kilocalories	227	Copper milligrams	–
Protein grams	5.7	Zinc milligrams	–
Total fat grams	1.0	Vitamin A micrograms	0
Saturated fat grams	–	Vitamin D micrograms	0
Polyunsaturated fat grams	–	Vitamin C milligrams	0
		Vitamin E milligrams	–
Cholesterol milligrams	0	B vitamins:	
Sugars grams		Thiamin (B$_1$) milligrams	0.20
Starch grams	} 51.3	Riboflavin (B$_2$) milligrams	0.06
Dietary fibre grams	–	Nicotinic acid milligrams	–
Sodium milligrams	–	Pyridoxine (B$_6$) milligrams	–
Potassium milligrams	–	Vitamin B$_{12}$ micrograms	0
Calcium milligrams	19	Folic acid micrograms	–
Magnesium milligrams	–	Pantothenic acid milligrams	–
		Biotin micrograms	–

(–) No information available   (0) Contains zero or trace amounts

Crab

Crab is comparatively higher in **sodium, iron** and **zinc** than white sea fish. Fresh crab also contains moderate amounts of **fat**. Canned crab according to the analyses shown below, contains noticeably less fat, copper and vitamin B, and more iron than fresh. The higher calcium and sodium levels are probably due to the addition of sequestrants, see **miscellaneous additives**. Tinned crab meat may also contain the **preservative** sulphur dioxide, hence vitamin B$_1$ is absent.

Average nutrients in 100 grams (3½ oz) Crab

	fresh	canned		fresh	canned
Energy kilojoules	534	341	Iron milligrams	1.3	2.8
kilocalories	127	81	Copper milligrams	4.8	0.4
Protein grams	20.1	18.1	Zinc milligrams	5.5	5.0
Total fat grams	5.2	0.9	Vitamin A micrograms	0	0
Saturated fat grams	0.6	0.1	Vitamin D micrograms	0	0
Polyunsaturated fat grams	1.9	0.3	Vitamin C milligrams	0	0
			Vitamin E milligrams	–	–
Cholesterol milligrams	100	100	B vitamins:		
Sugars grams	0	0	Thiamin (B$_1$) milligrams	0.10	0
Starch grams	0	0	Riboflavin (B$_2$) milligrams	0.15	0.05
Dietary fibre grams	0	0	Nicotinic acid milligrams	6.3	4.5
Sodium milligrams	370	550	Pyridoxine (B$_6$) milligrams	0.35	–
Potassium milligrams	270	100	Vitamin B$_{12}$ micrograms	0	0
Calcium milligrams	29	120	Folic acid micrograms	20	–
Magnesium milligrams	48	32	Pantothenic acid milligrams	0.6	–
			Biotin micrograms	0	0

(–) No information available   (0) Contains zero or trace amounts

Cranberries

An acid fruit, native to Europe and the British Isles. The American variety is larger. Cranberries are mainly used as a tart sauce for turkey and venison; they contain small amounts of **vitamin C, B vitamins** and **minerals** (see table). Cranberries contain relatively large amounts of fruit acids up to 2 grams per 100 grams, mainly as malic acid and **citric acid**.

Average nutrients in 100 grams (3½ oz) Cranberries

Energy kilojoules	63	Iron milligrams	1.1
kilocalories	15	Copper milligrams	0.14
Protein grams	0.4	Zinc milligrams	–
Total fat grams	0	Vitamin A micrograms	3
Saturated fat grams	0	Vitamin D micrograms	0
Polyunsaturated fat grams	0	Vitamin C milligrams	12
		Vitamin E milligrams	–
Cholesterol milligrams	0	B vitamins:	
Sugars grams	3.5	Thiamin (B$_1$) milligrams	0.03
Starch grams	0	Riboflavin (B$_2$) milligrams	0.02
Dietary fibre grams	4.2	Nicotinic acid milligrams	0.2
Sodium milligrams	2	Pyridoxine (B$_6$) milligrams	0.04
Potassium milligrams	120	Vitamin B$_{12}$ micrograms	0
Calcium milligrams	15	Folic acid micrograms	2
Magnesium milligrams	8	Pantothenic acid milligrams	0.22
		Biotin micrograms	–

(–) No information available   (0) Contains zero or trace amounts

Cream

Cream has a similar nutritional value to **butter** in that it contains **fat, vitamins A, D, E,** and is a poor source of protein, calcium and B vitamins. Summer cream contains more vitamin A, D and E than winter (see table).

Double cream contains about one third of its weight as saturated **fatty acids** and 48% of its weight as total fat. In many recipes calling for double cream, the amount can be reduced, or single cream or **yogurt** substituted. Single cream contains about half the fat of double, and whipping cream is intermediate between the two.

Regulations concerning the nutritional content of cream are based on minimum fat contents – specifications which are becoming difficult to justify given current recommendations for **diet**. By law, clotted cream must contain 55% of fat; double cream 48%; whipped and whipping cream 35%; sterilised cream 23%; single cream 18%; half cream and sterilised cream (including longlife UHT creams) 12%. Milk contains 3–4% fat. Whipped and sterilised cream may contain **emulsifiers** and stabilisers which must be declared on the label. Whipped cream may also contain sugar; clotted and canned cream, the **preservative** nisin. No other additives are allowed. The table below compares the nutrient content of single and double cream.

Sour cream is made from single cream, inoculated with lactic acid producing bacteria, see **yogurt**. Acid soured cream is made by adding acid directly and has the same nutritional value as single cream. Imitation cream is made from vegetable oils, emulsifiers and water and contains no nutrients, apart from fat.

Average nutrients in 100 grams (3½ oz) Cream

	single	double		single	double
Energy kilojoules	876	1841	Iron milligrams	0.31	0.21
kilocalories	212	447	Copper milligrams	0.20	0.13
Protein grams	2.4	1.5	Zinc milligrams	0.26	0.17
Total fat grams	21.2	48.2	Vitamin A micrograms	157–220	356–500
Saturated fat grams	12.6	28.8	Vitamin D micrograms	0.08–0.16	0.18–0.38
Polyunsaturated fat grams	0.6	1.3	Vitamin C milligrams	1.2	0.8
			Vitamin E milligrams	0.5	0.9–1.2
Cholesterol milligrams	66	140	B vitamins:		
Sugars grams	3.2	2.0	Thiamin (B$_1$) milligrams	0.03	0.02
Starch grams	0	0	Riboflavin (B$_2$) milligrams	0.12	0.08
Dietary fibre (NSP) grams	0	0	Nicotinic acid milligrams	0.64	0.40
Sodium milligrams	42	27	Pyridoxine (B$_6$) milligrams	0.03	0.02
Potassium milligrams	120	79	Vitamin B$_{12}$ micrograms	0.2	0.1
Calcium milligrams	79	50	Folic acid micrograms	4	2
Magnesium milligrams	6	4	Pantothenic acid milligrams	0.30	0.19
			Biotin micrograms	1.4	0.8

(–) No information available   (0) Contains zero or trace amounts

Croissant

A pastry, first made in 1686, as a privilege to the bakers of Budapest who had raised the alarm during an attempted attack by the Turks, who had tunnelled underground the beseiged city. The special pastry had to take the form of a crescent – after the emblem of the Ottoman flag.

Croissants can be made from puff pastry (see **pastries**) or, preferably, from a dough leavened with yeast, which is lower in **fat**.

Cucumber

Cucumbers are believed to have originated in southern Asia, and have been grown in India for at least 3000 years. They were well known in ancient Egypt, Greece and Rome. Although unremarkable nutritionally (see table), they are a particularly refreshing salad ingredient, containing a very high proportion (96%) of **water**.

Average nutrients in 100 grams (3½ oz) Cucumber

Energy kilojoules	43	Iron milligrams	0.3
kilocalories	10	Copper milligrams	0.09
Protein grams	0.6	Zinc milligrams	0.1
Total fat grams	0	Vitamin A micrograms	0[a]
Saturated fat grams	0	Vitamin D micrograms	0
Polyunsaturated fat grams	0	Vitamin C milligrams	8
		Vitamin E milligrams	0
Cholesterol milligrams	0	B vitamins:	
Sugars grams	1.8	Thiamin (B_1) milligrams	0.04
Starch grams	0	Riboflavin (B_2) milligrams	0.04
Dietary fibre grams	0.4	Nicotinic acid milligrams	0.3
Sodium milligrams	13	Pyridoxine (B_6) milligrams	0.04
Potassium milligrams	140	Vitamin B_{12} micrograms	0
Calcium milligrams	23	Folic acid micrograms	16
Magnesium milligrams	9	Pantothenic acid milligrams	0.3
		Biotin micrograms	0.4

(–) No information available (0) Contains zero or trace amounts

[a] Value for the flesh. The skin will contain carotene

Currants

Dried currants are produced from a small-fruited black grape variety which has been grown in Greece for more than 2000 years. Some are also produced in Australia. They are rich in the sugars **glucose** and **fructose**, with a little **sucrose**, and also contain small amounts of some vitamins and minerals. They contain no vitamin C, which is lost during drying.

Average nutrients in 100 grams (3½ oz) Currants

Energy kilojoules	1039	Iron milligrams	1.8
kilocalories	243	Copper milligrams	0.48
Protein grams	1.7	Zinc milligrams	0.1
Total fat grams	0	Vitamin A micrograms	5
Saturated fat grams	0	Vitamin D micrograms	0
Polyunsaturated fat grams	0	Vitamin C milligrams	0
		Vitamin E milligrams	–
Cholesterol milligrams	0	B vitamins:	
Sugars grams	63.1	Thiamin (B_1) milligrams	0.03
Starch grams	0	Riboflavin (B_2) milligrams	0.09
Dietary fibre grams	6.5	Nicotinic acid milligrams	0.6
Sodium milligrams	20	Pyridoxine (B_6) milligrams	0.30
Potassium milligrams	710	Vitamin B_{12} micrograms	0
Calcium milligrams	95	Folic acid micrograms	11
Magnesium milligrams	36	Pantothenic acid milligrams	0.10
		Biotin micrograms	–

(–) No information available (0) Contains zero or trace amounts

Cysteine and cystine

Cysteine and cystine are two non-essential **amino acids**. They are inter-changeable in the body: cystine is composed of two molecules of cysteine.

Cysteine and cystine are made in the body from the essential amino acid **methionine** but are also present in food **proteins**. They are required, like other amino acids, for synthesis of new protein needed for growth and repair, and are especially abundant in keratin, the protein in hair. Despite claims for pollen (which contains cystine) taking extra will not arrest hair loss.

Cystine and cysteine in the diet reduces the needs for methionine, and, since almost all the **sulphur** in the diet is derived from these three amino acids the sulphur content is sometimes used as an approximate assessment of the ade-quacy of a protein. Cysteine is an additive used in new **bread** making processes.

Dahl

The Indian name for a variety of **pulse**. The nutrient content of three cooked dahls, containing mung **beans** (green gram), **lentils** and chick **peas** are shown in the table. These recipes all contain butter, onion and spices; the use of oil rather than butter and the addition of milk to lentil dahl will alter the nutritional composition.

Average nutrients in 100 grams (3½ oz) Dahl (cooked)

	mung bean	masur (lentil)	channa (chickpea)		mung bean	masur (lentil)	channa (chickpea)
Energy kilojoules	447	380	407	Iron milligrams	2.6	1.7	1.8
kilocalories	106	90	97	Copper milligrams	0.29	0.12	0.20
Protein grams	6.4	4.9	5.3	Zinc milligrams	–	0.6	0.8
Total fat grams	4.2	3.1	4.5	Vitamin A micrograms	67	32	–
Saturated fat grams	–	–	–	Vitamin D micrograms	0.04	0.03	–
Polyunsaturated fat grams	–	–	–	Vitamin C milligrams	0	0	0
				Vitamin E milligrams	–	–	–
Cholesterol milligrams	–	–	–	B vitamins:			
Sugars grams	0.8	0.7	1.5	Thiamin (B$_1$) milligrams	0.09	0.07	0.08
Starch grams	10.4	10.7	8.9	Riboflavin (B$_2$) milligrams	0.04	0.03	0.03
Dietary fibre grams	6.4	2.4	5.2	Nicotinic acid milligrams	1.4	1.1	1.1
Sodium milligrams	820	320	480	Pyridoxine (B$_6$) milligrams	0.09	0.07	–
Potassium milligrams	270	150	260	Vitamin B$_{12}$ micrograms	0	0	0
Calcium milligrams	34	11	30	Folic acid micrograms	20	4	30
Magnesium milligrams	51	17	31	Pantothenic acid milligrams	–	0.20	–
				Biotin micrograms	–	–	–

(–) No information available   (0) Contains zero or trace amounts

Damsons

Damsons contain sugars, mostly **glucose** and **fructose** and small amounts of minerals, particularly potassium, and vitamins. They are not a particularly good source of vitamin C (see table). When stewed with sugar, the energy (Calorie) content of damsons approximately doubles.

Average nutrients in 100 grams (3½ oz) Damsons

	raw	stewed with sugar		raw	stewed with sugar
Energy kilojoules	162	293	Iron milligrams	0.4	0.3
kilocalories	38	69	Copper milligrams	0.08	0.05
Protein grams	0.5	0.3	Zinc milligrams	0.1	0.1
Total fat grams	0	0	Vitamin A micrograms	37	28
Saturated fat grams	0	0	Vitamin D micrograms	0	0
Polyunsaturated fat grams	0	0	Vitamin C milligrams	3	2
			Vitamin E milligrams	0.7	0.5
Cholesterol milligrams	0	0	B vitamins:		
Sugars grams	9.6	17.8	Thiamin (B₁) milligrams	0.10	0.06
Starch grams	0	0	Riboflavin (B₂) milligrams	0.03	0.02
Dietary fibre grams	4.1	3.1	Nicotinic acid milligrams	0.4	0.3
Sodium milligrams	2	2	Pyridoxine (B₆) milligrams	0.05	0.03
Potassium milligrams	290	220	Vitamin B₁₂ micrograms	0	0
Calcium milligrams	24	17	Folic acid micrograms	3	1
Magnesium milligrams	11	9	Pantothenic acid milligrams	0.27	0.18
			Biotin micrograms	0.1	0.1

(−) No information available (0) Contains zero or trace amounts

Dates

Dates are an important food crop, and they have been cultivated in the Middle East for at least 5000 years. They have been used as sugar substitutes, for wine, and for food; dry dates are quite hard, and can be ground into flour. Dates eaten in Europe and America are the semi-dry type. They are rich in **sugars** and contain good amounts of **minerals**. Their vitamin content however is quite low (see table).

Average nutrients in 100 grams (3½ oz) Dates

Energy kilojoules	1056	Iron milligrams	1.6
kilocalories	248	Copper milligrams	0.21
Protein grams	2.0	Zinc milligrams	0.3
Total fat grams	0	Vitamin A micrograms	8
Saturated fat grams	0	Vitamin D micrograms	0
Polyunsaturated fat grams	0	Vitamin C milligrams	0
		Vitamin E milligrams	−
Cholesterol milligrams	0	B vitamins:	
Sugars grams	63.9	Thiamin (B₁) milligrams	0.07
Starch grams	0	Riboflavin (B₂) milligrams	0.04
Dietary fibre grams	8.7	Nicotinic acid milligrams	2.9
Sodium milligrams	5	Pyridoxine (B₆) milligrams	0.15
Potassium milligrams	750	Vitamin B₁₂ micrograms	0
Calcium milligrams	68	Folic acid micrograms	21
Magnesium milligrams	59	Pantothenic acid milligrams	0.80
		Biotin micrograms	−

(−) No information available (0) Contains zero or trace amounts

Dextrins

Dextrins are formed when **starch** is subjected to dry heat, for instance when bread is toasted, in biscuits, bread crumbs and breakfast cereals; or when starch is subjected to strong acids; or to the action of **enzymes**, for instance in **digestion**, malting of cereals (see **maltose**), and bread making. Dextrins are brown, taste slightly sweet, dissolve in water and have the same **energy** value as starch.

Diabetes – full name Diabetes mellitus

A disease resulting from an insufficient or ineffective supply of the hormone insulin. It is quite common, affecting at least 1% of the British population. There is a familial tendency to diabetes.

The energy in **carbohydrate** (**sugar** and **starches**) reaches the blood stream in the form of **glucose**. Blood glucose (blood 'sugar') rises after a meal and, in response, insulin is secreted into the blood stream from cells of the pancreas – a gland (sweet-breads) situated below the stomach (see also **digestion**). Insulin enables body cells to take glucose out of the blood stream and use it either immediately for energy, or to store it for later use in the form of **fat** or **glycogen**. About four hours after eating, the blood glucose returns to normal.

In diabetes, although the glucose passes into the blood stream as before, insulin is not secreted in sufficient amounts, or is made but is ineffective. As a result, the blood glucose remains unacceptably high. The kidneys are unable to conserve the excessive quantities of glucose circulating in the blood stream, and allow it to escape into the urine. Usually, glucose (sugar) in the urine confirms the presence of diabetes.

There are two main types of diabetes, but it may also be caused by other hormone disturbances, some drugs, and liver disease.

Diabetes treated without insulin – or maturity onset diabetes

About 80% of diabetics develop the disease in middle or old age. The majority are obese, and women are more affected than men. See also **obesity** and **chromium**.

In this type of diabetes, there are often no intense symptoms of thirst or loss of weight (see below), and the disease may only be found as a result of a routine urine test. In other cases, the side effects of the disease, such as intense itching around the genital area (caused by the growth of yeasts on the sugary urine), impotence, eye changes, tingling in fingers, loss of feeling in the legs or boils and other infections on the skin initiate a visit to the doctor. First symptoms may also be experienced as a result of stress, for instance a car accident or operation, but shock cannot cause diabetes – it merely unmasks a latent form of the disease.

Obese people with large stores of fat (as **adipose tissue**) are resistant to the action of insulin, probably because high fat diets chronically increase the amount of circulating insulin in the body, causing in turn a reduction in the number of receptors in cells capable of using it. Blood glucose rises but often all that is needed to restore the blood glucose to normal is a determined effort to lose weight. Drugs that lower the blood glucose, either by stimulating the production of more insulin from the pancreas, or by enabling body cells to use it more efficiently, are sometimes needed, particularly for those who are not overweight.

Insulin dependant diabetes

Usually this type of diabetes occurs in childhood or early adulthood, causing serious symptoms which, unless treated, are rapidly fatal.

Before treatment, there may be a complete lack of effective insulin, and large quantities of glucose spill over into the urine. Water is drawn out of the body and a thirst develops to keep pace with the excessive volumes of urine passed. Fats are also withdrawn from the body stores (adipose tissue), but the large quantities released cannot be used completely for energy purposes and accumulate as acids in the blood stream, causing a dangerous disturbance of the delicate acid/alkali balance in the body. The loss of incompletely used fat and glucose in urine causes a marked loss of weight. Other symptoms are pain in the abdomen, vomiting and weakness. Unless treated, coma results.

Insulin (extracted from animal pancreases) restores the condition to normal. Unfortunately it cannot be taken by mouth (it is a protein and would be digested) and has to be injected daily. There are several different types. Some are short acting, effective only for a few hours and necessitating more than one daily injection : others are effective for 24 hours. The diet (see below) is adjusted to match the type of insulin needed – more carbohydrate is given when the insulin is at its highest peak of activity. The total daily amount of carbohydrate needed depends on age and activity: a very active adolescent would require more than an older office worker.

Once established on a regime, diabetics are able to live fairly normal lives, balancing their diet with injections of insulin. However, it is a difficult situation and imbalances can occur. Increases in activity, too little to eat, and too much insulin can all result in a low blood glucose. The brain and nervous tissues are particularly dependent on a supply of glucose and if the blood level falls, their activity is depressed, resulting in drowsiness and eventual coma. A rapidly absorbed form of glucose – usually sugar (sucrose) – is carried by all diabetics treated with insulin and taken when the first symptoms occur. These precautions are not necessary for diabetics treated by diet alone.

Diets for diabetics

After the discovery of insulin in 1922, a 'free' diet with daily adjustments of insulin was the treatment of choice for all diabetics. Later it was realised that late onset diabetics are often resistant to the action of insulin, and that the regime could result in overweight and wide fluctuations of the blood glucose level. For these reasons, free diets have been largely abandoned in favour of treatment with diet alone, or diet with insulin or drugs. Overweight and blood sugar are easier to control if a dietary regime is followed, and there is probably less risk of complications (eye changes, nervous degeneration, kidney disease, **atherosclerosis** affecting the limbs and heart) in both types.

Before 1922, the only treatment for diabetes was to virtually exclude all carbohydrate and the practice of cutting down has continued until very recently. Once weight has been stabilised the diet could be varied with an exchange system for carbohydrate foods. Most clinics use a system of 10 grams carbohydrate exchanges and some foods containing this amount are shown under **carbohydrate**. Full lists are available from the British Diabetic Association, 3 Alfred Place, London WC1.

However, low carbohydrate diets are also high in **fat**. Diabetics are at greater risk of **heart disease** and many recent studies have shown that as good or better control of the blood glucose can be achieved if the diet is high in **fibre** and starch. This is partly because sugars are absorbed less quickly from some fibre containing foods. In 1982 the British Diabetic Association endorsed the use of diets containing less fat, less **salt**, more fibre, and up to 50% of the total energy as starch - about double the national average. High sucrose (sugar) foods are still discouraged because they contain little dietary fibre.

Practically, this means that diabetics are being advised to eat more of the same foods currently being encouraged for everyone else - wholegrain cereals, bread, pasta, potatoes, peas, beans and lentils - and to cut down on fatty meats, cheese, butter, margarine and all other sources of fat. Nevertheless, the precise amounts and pattern need to be tailored to individual needs with the help of a qualified dietitian.

Other reasons for sugar (glucose) in urine

A chance finding of glucose in the urine is not always indicative of diabetes. In young people, and sometimes during pregnancy, the kidneys may fail to conserve glucose completely, even though the blood glucose is normal. Other people may absorb glucose very quickly from food (particularly if part of the stomach has been surgically removed) and it is lost in the urine whilst the blood level is temporarily high. It is normal for these reasons to perform a confirmatory test - the glucose tolerance test - which measures the body's response to a test done of carbohydrate (usually a glucose drink). Blood is withdrawn every half hour for two hours after taking the dose and its content of glucose measured. Diabetics have a characteristic response. Prolonged fasting and very low carbohydrate **slimming diets** (for example the 'quick weight loss diet' and Atkins diet) can also cause a diabetic curve; normal food should therefore be taken for several days before undergoing a glucose tolerance test.

Diet

Man has been preoccupied from the earliest times with diet. There are numerous references to the dietetic treatment of common diseases in the writings of Hippocrates, and complex classifications of foods according to their 'elemental qualities' survived in orthodox teaching for almost 2000 years. However only over the past 200 years with the development of the science of, **nutrition** has it become possible to ascribe quantitative requirements and hence make recommendations about the amount and type of food (the diet) that should be eaten to maintain health. The treatment of the symptoms of disease by

therapeutic diets continues to play an important part in the management of many clinical conditions.

The first principle of healthy eating is that the requirements for the essential nutrients – **amino acids, vitamins, minerals,** essential **fatty acids**, and **energy** – must be met. Most foods contain a variety of nutrients but, as nearly all are deficient in one or more, requirements for essential nutrients are most likely to be met if a wide variety of foods is eaten in moderation. In general the essential nutrients are found in greater amount and in more bio-available forms in animal products such as meat, fish, cheese, eggs and milk. Hence these food groups, together with vegetables and fruit, have traditionally been emphasised in guidelines for healthy eating particularly for those at most risk of classic deficiency disease – the young, pregnant or breast-feeding women and the elderly (see below). However, in westernised countries the occurrence of malnutrition, as judged by poor growth rates, or frank clinical symptoms, is now rare, and confined to well-defined circumstances – for example vitamin D deficiency in Asian immigrants. This is in contrast to the situation in, for example, Britain at the opening of the twentieth century, when overt signs of malnutrition such as **rickets**, stunting, deformities and **anaemia** were wide-spread, and the infant mortality rate was as high as 25% in some areas. During the course of the two World Wars (and partly as a consequence of being unable to recruit sufficient men of satisfactory physical fitness for army service in the Boer and First World War) the Government came eventually to assume responsibility for the provision of adequate nutrition for the nation as a whole. The institution of welfare food policies, fortification, legislation and education culminated in the Second World War food policy under the direction of Sir Jack Drummond, Minister of Food.

With the control also of infectious diseases, partly as a consequence of improved nutrition, interest in other diseases that may be caused by inappropriate dietary habits has increased. Now, the commonest causes of death (excluding lung cancer) in westernised countries are **cancer** of the breast and bowel, and **strokes** and **heart disease**. Studies of migrants show clearly that a major cause of these diseases is environmental, since the migrants acquire the incidence rate of the host country within one or two generations. Worldwide comparisons of the diet eaten in different populations show that animal protein intake, particularly from **meat**, is strongly associated with cancer of the colon, **fat** with cancer of the breast, and **salt** and animal (saturated) fat in particular with stroke and heart disease. These associations do not prove causation but those who consider all individuals in western populations to be at risk, recommend that salt, fat and sugar in the diet should be reduced, and starch and dietary **fibre** be increased, towards levels found in populations where the occurrence of these diseases is rare.

What then constitutes current concepts of a 'balanced' diet containing an optimum supply of nutrients, both essential and non essential? If fat in the diet is to be reduced, less of it in all foods needs to be eaten. This includes full cream milk, butter, margarine, cheese, fatty meat, cakes, biscuits and all fried food (see **fat** for more information). Sugar has always been recognised as an undesirable source of energy and less of it needs to be eaten in sweets, pastry and other cooked foods and drinks. Greater emphasis needs to be placed on wholegrain cereals, such a wholemeal bread, wholemeal pasta and rice, and on potatoes, vegetables and fruit which contain very little fat, much starch, and notable amounts of protein, vitamins, fibres, and minerals. The table below sets out foods grouped according to the nutrients they supply.

Cereals, particularly whole grain, together with potatoes (Group 1) should be eaten in generous amounts at each main meal to satisfy appetite. Three or more portions of fresh vegetables or fruit, preferably green or yellow, (Group 2) should be eaten per day and two or more portions of low fat foods containing the most protein (Group 3). Low fat dairy foods (Group 4) should be chosen in preference to high fat ones and all sugar, refined starches, and foods made from them, such as biscuits, cakes, sweets, etc. (Groups 5 and 6) should be used sparingly. They can be excluded without any risk of unbalancing the diet. An excessive intake of alcohol (more than 80 g per day for men and 50 g per day for women) should be avoided, together with foods cooked or preserved in excessive quantities of salt. Table salt should be avoided.

Groups with special needs are:

Women of child-bearing age who require more iron and may benefit from at least one portion of well absorbed iron, as red lean meat or sardines, pilchards etc. or **soya**, in the daily diet.

In pregnancy and breast-feeding more of all nutrients are required to ensure adequate supplies for the growing child. The inclusion of extra low fat milk, yogurt or cheese (Group 4), and vegetables (Group 2), most easily meets these extra needs.

Foods grouped according to the nutrients they supply

Group	Food	Best sources of	Notes
1	Bread, pasta, rice, flour, low salt breakfast cereals, potatoes	Energy, protein, B vitamins, fibre, minerals, essential fatty acids	Wholegrain cereals are preferable to refined. Vitamin C in fresh potatoes.
2	Fresh vegetables and fruit	Vitamin C, folic acid, vitamin A, minerals, vitamin E, essential fatty acids	Vitamin A only in green and yellow vegetables
3	Lean meat, poultry, shell-fish, fish, peas, beans, lentils, eggs	Protein, B vitamins, minerals, essential fatty acids	Red meat and soya are good sources of iron. Liver, eggs and fatty fish contain vitamin A.
4	Yogurt, semi-skimmed or skimmed milk, low fat cheese	Calcium	Full cream milk contains vitamin A.

5	Butter, margarine, oils, cooking fat	Vitamin A in butter and margarine, vitamin E and essential fatty acids in oils	All fats are high in energy.
6	Sugar, sweets, alcoholic and soft drinks, cornflour	Energy	Poor source of all other nutrients

Children and adolescents require more nutrients in proportion to their weight than adults to allow for growth. Milk is a good source of these nutrients but, to avoid excessive fat intake, semi-skimmed or skimmed milk or yogurt is preferable to full cream milk for children over the age of five years. If there is little exposure of the skin to sunlight (for example, Asian children) extra vitamin D as vitamin drops is required.

The elderly are generally advised to keep as active, and therefore as fit, as possible. If physical activity is allowed to decline less energy is required and foods high in energy and poor sources of essential nutrients like fried food, sugar, cakes, pastries and biscuits are best avoided. At least one half pint of milk (preferably skimmed or semi-skimmed) should be taken each day, together with extra vitamin D if there is little exposure of the skin to sunlight.

Digestion

Digestion is the dismantling of **protein**, **fats** and **carbohydrate** in food into particles small enough to be transferred into the blood stream.

One of the smallest animals, the amoeba, forms a sac of cell tissue around its food and secretes digestive juices into the sac. Complex digestive systems have evolved in man and higher animals, but the basic process is the same. **Enzymes** are used to dismantle proteins mostly to **amino acids**, carbohydrates to **glucose** and other simple sugars, and fats partly to **fatty acids**. To a minute extent, similar changes can be brought about by heat and acids used in cooking.

The digestive system consists of a series of passages (beginning at the mouth and ending at the anus) whose contents are kept moving from one section to the next by sequential contractions of circular muscles in the walls. Digestive juices, containing enzymes, manufactured by glands whose outlets open on to the digestive system, are mixed with the food as it is forced along. The whole system is controlled by hormones and the nervous system.

Digestion begins as soon as food is put into the mouth. The primary role of the mouth in digestion is the mastication of food, but saliva, secreted by the salivary glands, also contains an enzyme which begins the digestion of **starch**. Bread, for instance, if chewed for a long time, begins to taste sweet.

After swallowing, food is pushed down the oesophagus into the stomach, where hydrochloric acid and an enzyme, pepsin, are secreted by glands lining the stomach wall. Muscular contractions mix the food and secretions to a porridge consistency, and pepsin begins to dismantle proteins. Small quantities of the mixture are forced out of the stomach at intervals, and six hours after eating a meal it has all passed into the first section of the small intestine, the duodenum. A valve normally prevents food from passing back into the stomach. The stomach also secretes the 'intrinsic factor' for the absorption of **vitamin B$_{12}$**.

Bile, made by the liver and held in the gall bladder, and pancreatic juice, from the pancreas, pass down the bile duct to the duodenum as food enters. The salts in bile emulsify (finely divide) fat into microscopic globules and pancreatic enzymes initiate the digestion of lipids, continuing the digestion of proteins and carbohydrates.

The next stage is the entry into the rest of the small intestine – the ileum and jejunum. This tube is about nine metres long, and its surface area is made eight times greater by millions of finger-like villi which project into the centre of the tube. The villi themselves have microvilli, microscopic hair-like borders, projecting from them which increases the absorptive area twenty fold. Here the nearly digested food is absorbed by the surface cells of the villi, and enzymes in the cells complete the breakdown of proteins and carbohydrate and reform fatty acids to triglycerides.

The main products of digestion are glucose, fructose, galactose, amino acids and an emulsion of microscopic **lipid** particles coated with a layer of protein (chylomicrons). Some particles of protein are absorbed intact, which is of importance in the development of **allergy**. All except the chylomicrons are passed directly to the blood stream and are transported to the liver, whereas most fats travel, as chylomicrons, in lymph vessels which run parallel to the intestine and are later released into the blood stream. Glucose and fructose already present in food (for example in fruits) do not have to be digested and pass directly into the villi. Alcohol, most minerals and vitamins are also small enough to be absorbed intact. Fat soluble vitamins A, D, E and K, are transported with fat and therefore cannot be absorbed in the absence of bile.

Usually at least 95% of carbohydrate, fat and protein is absorbed out of food in the small intestine, and eight to nine hours after eating a meal, the fluid residue has passed into the large intestine. Here most of the water is absorbed. The residues, **fibre**, insoluble salts, undigested nutrients, residues of bile and digestive juices, mucus and dead cells from the lining of the digestive system are fermented by bacteria, which multiply, increasing faecal weight. Large amounts of fibre therefore increase faecal weight, and shorten the time residues spend in the large bowel. By-products of this fermentation process may also be beneficial to the health of the large bowel wall.

The digestive system is complex and subject to many disorders. Some require hospital treatment and/or modification of diet. (See also **dyspepsia**, peptic **ulcers**, **malabsorption**, **coeliac disease**, **lactose**, **allergy**, and **therapeutic diets**).

Disaccharides

These are two combined simple sugars or monosaccharides. The most important are sucrose – table sugar, lactose – milk sugar and maltose – malt (see individual entries).

During **digestion**, disaccharides are split to their component monosaccharides which are absorbed into the blood stream. Sucrose is divided to **glucose** and **fructose**, lactose to glucose and **galactose**, and maltose to glucose. Dilute acids can also divide disaccharides – for example **invert sugar**, in honey and used in the food industry, is formed from sucrose in this way. Most of the added sugar (sucrose) in canned fruits is divided whilst in the can and ends up being eaten as glucose and fructose.

Duck

The meat of duck is a good source of **protein**, **iron**, **zinc** and most B **vitamins**. However, roast duck eaten with the **fat** and skin has twice the **energy** (Calorie) content of the meat alone. To remove as much fat as possible the skin should be pricked and the duck roasted on a rack above the pan.

Average nutrients in 100 grams (3½ oz) Duck (roast)

	meat and skin	meat only		meat and skin	meat only
Energy kilojoules	1406	789	Iron milligrams	2.7	2.7
kilocalories	339	189	Copper milligrams	0.3	0.3
Protein grams	19.6	25.3	Zinc milligrams	1.8	2.6
Total fat grams	29.0	9.7	Vitamin A micrograms	–	–
Saturated fat grams	7.9	2.6	Vitamin D micrograms	–	–
Polyunsaturated fat grams	3.5	1.2	Vitamin C milligrams	–	0
			Vitamin E milligrams	–	0.02
Cholesterol milligrams	–	160	B vitamins:		
Sugars grams	0	0	Thiamin (B_1) milligrams	–	0.26
Starch grams	0	0	Riboflavin (B_2) milligrams	–	0.47
Dietary fibre grams	0	0	Nicotinic acid milligrams	–	10.5
Sodium milligrams	76	96	Pyridoxine (B_6) milligrams	–	0.25
Potassium milligrams	210	270	Vitamin B_{12} micrograms	–	3
Calcium milligrams	12	13	Folic acid micrograms	–	10
Magnesium milligrams	16	20	Pantothenic acid milligrams	–	1.5
			Biotin micrograms	–	4

(–) No information available   (0) Contains zero or trace amounts

Dyspepsia

Dyspepsia can be felt as nausea, heartburn, discomfort or distension felt after taking meals. It is usually described as severe 'indigestion', but in the majority of cases, **nutrients** in food are completely digested in the normal way (see **digestion**).

Dyspepsia can be a symptom of any disease of the digestive system but it is often brought about by worry, overwork, hurried meals, and over-indulgence in cigarettes and alcohol. It is usually alleviated by the simple measures shown below, but medical advice should be sought, especially if these fail and when it occurs in previously unaffected middle aged people.

Advice for sufferers from dyspepsia

1. All food must be chewed slowly and thoroughly. Water or other beverages should not be taken with food because it encourages swallowing before food has been properly chewed.

2. Beverages should be taken between or after meals, and strong coffee, tea and alcohol should not be taken on an empty stomach.

3. Cigarettes should be avoided.

4. Large fatty meals should not be taken. Small, frequent meals should be taken at regular times during the day. It is advisable to rest if possible before and after meals.

5. A bland diet (see below) may help in acute attacks for a few days, but apart from avoiding fried food, pickles and highly spiced meals the diet should be normal over the long term. For most cases of dyspepsia the advice above, and avoidance of worry and overwork, together with adequate sleep, are more effective than elaborate dietary regimes. Some authorities recommend that the diet should be low in sugar (**sucrose**): others recommend a high **fibre** diet.

Bland diet - typical menu

Small helpings of all food should be taken

Breakfast	Cornflakes or Rice Krispies, with a little sugar and milk
	Toast, with a little butter and jelly, jam, marmalade or honey
	Weak tea or coffee
Lunch (or evening meal)	Lean, tender meat (no sausages, fatty or twice cooked meat) or white baked fish in milk
	Mashed, jacket or boiled potatoes
	A small helping of tender vegetables or salad
	Milk pudding
Tea	Plain biscuit (Marie type)
	Weak tea
Supper (or lunch)	Cream soup
	Grated cheese, boiled, poached, scrambled egg or lean, tender ham
	Toast or mashed, jacket or boiled potatoes
	A small helping of tender vegetables or salad (if wanted)
	Junket or jelly or mousse or yogurt (if wanted)
Before bed	Warm milk or plain biscuits

Rose hip or blackcurrant syrup or orange or grapefruit juice (diluted with water) should be taken if the diet is continued for more than 2 to 3 days

E numbers

Additives in foods which are approved for sale throughout the EEC have had E numbers assigned to them. With the introduction of recent legislation on **labelling** of food, either the E number or the additive's specific name must be declared. Foods on sale in Britain contain a number of other additives which have no E numbers and are declared by their specific name.

There is a full list of E numbers, and the other additives permitted in Britain in Appendix II.

Eczema

Eczema is an inflammation of the skin, causing an itchy, red soreness and sometimes blisters which weep and form scabs. It occurs most commonly in infancy and often disappears during adolescence. Stress, such as teething, is a common precipitating factor but food **allergy** is often involved. The foods commonly implicated are cows' milk, hens' eggs, wheat, fish, shellfish and nuts.

Babies with parents prone to allergy are twice as likely to develop eczema. Breast feeding cannot always prevent allergies, since breast milk itself often contains allergens passed on by the mother. Allergic eczema is 50% more likely in children given solid food before the age of four months when the protective immune system has fully developed. Guidelines from St George's Hospital, London for weaning babies of allergic parents suggest that breast feeding should continue for six months, provided vitamin and iron supplements are given. Milk-free baby rice, mixed with water, should be introduced first, followed by puréed vegetables. Wheat, fish, milk and eggs are not recommended until eight, ten and 12 months respectively.

Edible gums

Edible gums are extracts from seeds and exudates (saps) of trees, used as thickeners and stabilisers (see **emulsifiers**) in the food industry and for confectionery. Examples are carob gum (E410), gum guar (E412) (from seeds), and gum arabic (E414), gum tragacanth (E413) and gum ghatti (E415) (exudates). They are not split to their component parts by human digestive **enzymes** and contribute to the dietary **fibre**.

Eels

Eels are classified nutritionally with the fatty **fish**. They are rich sources of **vitamin A** (see table), and the oil is a rich source of **vitamin D**. The flesh also contains good amounts of B vitamins, and well absorbed **zinc** and **iron**.

Average nutrients in 100 grams (3½ oz) Eel

Energy kilojoules	700	Iron milligrams	0.7
kilocalories	168	Copper milligrams	0.05
Protein grams	16.6	Zinc milligrams	0.5
Total fat grams	2.2-27.8[a]	Vitamin A micrograms	260-2500[a]

Average nutrients in 100 grams (3½ oz) Eel *(continued)*

Saturated fat grams	–	Vitamin D micrograms	b
Polyunsaturated fat grams	–	Vitamin C milligrams	0
		Vitamin E milligrams	–
Cholesterol milligrams	–	B vitamins:	
Sugars grams	0	Thiamin (B_1) milligrams	0.20
Starch grams	0	Riboflavin (B_2) milligrams	0.05–0.50
Dietary fibre grams	0	Nicotinic acid milligrams	6.6
Sodium milligrams	89	Pyridoxine (B_6) milligrams	0.30
Potassium milligrams	270	Vitamin B_{12} micrograms	1
Calcium milligrams	19	Folic acid micrograms	–
Magnesium milligrams	19	Pantothenic acid milligrams	0.15
		Biotin micrograms	–

(–) No information available   (0) Contains zero or trace amounts

[a] Higher values for mature eels
[b] The oil contains 120 micrograms

Eggs

Eggs are a useful and convenient food. They are a source of high value **protein, zinc, vitamins A, D**, and **E** and **B vitamins**. A dark coloured yolk does not imply that the egg has a higher vitamin A (**carotene**) content – other pigments in grass and feeds colour the yolk. The only detectable nutritional difference between free range and battery eggs is in the vitamin B_{12} content (see table). The iron in eggs is poorly absorbed due to a protein, conalbumin, in the white. Another protein, avidin, prevents the absorption of **biotin** but it is inactivated on cooking and all the biotin in cooked eggs is absorbed. Eggs are not a notable source of calcium – it is concentrated in the shell.

Eggs are well known for their high content of **cholesterol**, which, like the fat (mostly saturated **fatty acids**) and vitamins A, D, and most B vitamins, is concentrated in the yolk. Egg white contains no fat or cholesterol and is a useful food in low fat or fat free diets. It also contains minerals and vitamin B_2.

There is no significant nutritional difference between white and brown eggs – in general white hens lay white eggs and brown hens lay brown eggs. Other kinds of eggs have approximately the same composition as hens' eggs – duck eggs have a marginally higher fat content.

Freshness of eggs

Class A eggs are the only ones usually available in shops and they must not have been preserved or refrigerated. Boxes stamped 'extra' must not be more than seven days old. Class B eggs may have been preserved in carbon dioxide or refrigerated, and Class C eggs are for food manufacturers only.

A fresh egg has very little thin white, and the round yolk is supported on a thick circle of white. As the egg becomes older, water moves from the white to the yolk and a stale egg has a flat yolk surrounded by a thin, runny white. The white and yolk become more alkaline as the gas carbon dioxide diffuses out through the shell, the white proteins and muscular supporting strands (chalazae) are thinned, and the yolk moves away from its central position. If eggs are stored blunt end uppermost the yolk sustains less damage because it is cushioned against the air space. In time the air space increases in size and very stale eggs float in water. Eventually the yolk breaks and the proteins are broken down, causing the bad egg smell of hydrogen sulphide.

Eggs keep relatively well because the shell, membranes and white are designed to protect the developing chick and its food store (the yolk) from infection by bacteria and other micro-organisms. Should micro-organisms penetrate the layer of mucin on the shell (which hardens when the egg is laid); the shell; or the membranes their growth is retarded by the alkalinity of the white. Iron and biotin (necessary for the growth of bacteria) are also inactivated by conalbumin and avidin. Other proteins prevent the growth of some viruses and are able to liquify bacteria.

Washing or extensive handling remove the mucin coat, exposing shell pores and hastening the loss of water from the inside. If eggs do have to be washed it should be done in warm rather than cold water, otherwise shrinkage and drawing in of micro-organisms occurs. It is best to store eggs in covered containers which retard water evaporation and flavour penetration through the shell.

Cooked eggs

On cooking, the egg proteins are coagulated (see **protein**) and are made firm and easier to eat. Lightly boiled eggs leave the stomach more quickly than raw or hard boiled eggs but all egg is equally well digested. The almost complete absence of residue left after digestion, may be the basis for the belief that eggs are 'binding'. Provided that the egg is not overcooked, the protein suffers no damage. Vitamins A, D and nicotinic acid are completely retained but up to 16% of vitamins B_1 and B_2 may be lost, depending on the length of time the egg is cooked.

A green ring around the yolk in a hard boiled egg is due to a reaction between sulphide (released from the white proteins) and iron in the yolk. It can be prevented by boiling for the shortest possible time and quick cooling in cold water. This reduces the amount of sulphide formed and draws it out of the egg away from the yolk. Stale eggs are more likely to develop green rings than fresh because the protein has already partially decomposed.

Eggs are used extensively in cooking, to thicken and bind foods. Overcooking causes the white to shrink and squeeze water out (for example in an overcooked baked egg custard or scrambled egg). Eggs are also useful **emulsifiers**, used in mayonnaise and meringues.

Average nutrients in 100 grams (2 eggs) Eggs (boiled, poached or raw)

Energy kilojoules	612	Iron milligrams	2.0
kilocalories	147	Copper milligrams	0.10
Protein grams	12.3	Zinc milligrams	1.5
Total fat grams	10.9	Vitamin A micrograms	140
Saturated fat grams	3.4	Vitamin D micrograms	1.75
Polyunsaturated fat grams	1.2	Vitamin C milligrams	0
		Vitamin E milligrams	1.6

Average nutrients in 100 grams (2 eggs) Eggs
(boiled, poached or raw)*(continued)*

Cholesterol milligrams	450	B vitamins:	
Sugars grams	0	Thiamin (B$_1$) milligrams	0.09
Starch grams	0	Riboflavin (B$_2$) milligrams	0.47
Dietary fibre grams	0	Nicotinic acid milligrams	3.68
Sodium milligrams	140	Pyridoxine (B$_6$) milligrams	0.11
Potassium milligrams	140	Vitamin B$_{12}$ micrograms	1.7[a]-2.9[b]
Calcium milligrams	52	Folic acid micrograms	25
Magnesium milligrams	12	Pantothenic acid milligrams	1.8
		Biotin micrograms	25

(–) No information available   (0) Contains zero or trace amounts

[a]Value for battery eggs
[b]Value for deep litter and free range eggs

Electrolytes – see also **water**

Electrolytes are salts and other substances dissolved in the body fluids.

The body is composed of millions of cells (sacs of protoplasm enclosed in a membrane) bathed in fluid. This extracellular fluid resembles sea water in having as its chief electrolytes sodium and chlorine (common salt). The extra-cellular fluid is made up of one part blood plasma and four parts of interstitial fluid. However, cells also contain water – the intracellular fluid, which occupies twice the volume of extracellular fluid. The chief electrolytes in intracellular fluid are potassium, magnesium, phosphates and proteins: it contains very little sodium and chlorine.

Most of the **energy** expended by the resting body is used in maintaining the differential between the two fluids: **enzymes** cannot function efficiently if the electrolyte composition varies outside normal limits. Maintenance at a constant level of the total concentration of electrolytes is the job of the kidneys in particular. The balance can be upset if electrolytes are not absorbed from food (for example in diarrhoea) and in certain diseases, particularly of the kidneys.

Emulsifiers and stabilisers, including thickeners – see also **additives**

Emulsifiers and stabilisers are used extensively in the food industry in foods like bread, cakes, biscuits, meringues, cooking fats, sweets, soft drinks, jams, sauces and instant puddings. Emulsifiers aid the incorporation of air into a liquid – as in ice cream; fat into water – as in synthetic cream and salad dressings; and water into fat – as in margarine. Stabilisers prevent the mixture from separating, but some emulsifiers also act as stabilisers.

Substances like oil and vinegar (mainly water) can be made to mix by beating with a whisk or shaking in a bottle, when the oil is divided into globules and disperses evenly throughout the vinegar. However, the globules of oil soon coalesce and rise to the top of the vinegar if the dressing is allowed to stand. But if the oil is beaten into an emulsifier, such as egg yolk, it is divided into much smaller globules, and the emulsifiers and stabilisers in the egg yolk surround the globules, preventing them from joining together. At the same time, because of the chemical structure of the emulsifiers, the globules of oil are repelled by each other and attracted to the water in the vinegar. The resulting emulsion (mayonnaise) is thick and does not separate.

Emulsifiers and stabilisers are used in most processed foods and the manufacture of new convenience foods has been facilitated by the development of new emulsifiers. Instant puddings and soups, whips, coffee whiteners and powdered drinks contain emulsifiers to prevent caking and allow the powder to dissolve completely and quickly without lumpiness. They are also used to thicken puddings and other foods without the necessity for heat. Emulsifiers added to aerated soft drinks prevent particles of fruit clumping together and forming sediment, and trap air in the foam at the top of the drink. In bread and rolls they retard staling, in cakes and cake mixes they can substitute for egg, and they are added to processed cheese and peanut butter to prevent separation of the fat. In ice cream and mousses, stabilisers hold globules of fat around pockets of air, allowing them to keep their foamy structure after thawing – in contrast to home made ice cream. In chocolate, emulsifiers prevent stiffening during manufacture and bloom on storage – caused by sugar (**sucrose**) crystallising out of the fat, sugar and cocoa emulsion. In cooking fats, emulsifiers prevent droplets of water coalescing and spluttering out of the fat when it is heated for frying food. In easy cook rice, starch can be prevented from leaching out of the grain and causing stickiness if emulsifier is added. Instant potato also contains emulsifier.

There are many emulsifiers, each with a different chemical structure which determines the combination of foods it will emulsify. The use of the majority is controlled by the Emulsifiers and Stabilisers in Food Regulations 1980, which permit 56 specified substances. The permitted list includes 21 miscellaneous substances, like **edible gums**, **lecithin**, **agar** and **alginates**: 30 chemically modified fats (see **triglyceride**) E470–483, and six chemically modified forms of **cellulose** (E460–466). A full list of all food additives is shown in Appendix II. There are few restrictions on their use except for **bread**, soft drinks, cheese and cocoa. Milk and cream may contain none (except for whipped or sterilised cream). **Modified starches** are also used as emulsifiers but at present their use is not controlled by law. Emulsifiers such as eggs yolk, dextrin, proteins, glucose syrup and malt extract are not controlled because they are classified as foods.

Endive

Endive is a salad plant, which is probably a native of southern Asia and northern China. It is of the same species as chicory which is known as endive in Europe. It is relatively resistant to cold and therefore can often be found in winter and early spring. Endive is a rich source of the B vitamin **folic acid**, and iron (see table). If blanched it contains no vitamin A, but the fresh green leaves contain useful amounts, as **carotene**.

Average nutrients in 100 grams (3½ oz) Endive

Energy kilojoules	47	Iron milligrams	2.8
kilocalories	11	Copper milligrams	0.09
Protein grams	1.8	Zinc milligrams	–
Total fat grams	0	Vitamin A micrograms	380–1000

Average nutrients in 100 grams (3½ oz) Endive *(continued)*

Saturated fat grams	0	Vitamin D micrograms	0
Polyunsaturated fat grams	0	Vitamin C milligrams	12
		Vitamin E milligrams	–
Cholesterol milligrams	0	B vitamins:	
Sugars grams	1.0	Thiamin (B$_1$) milligrams	0.06
Starch grams	0	Riboflavin (B$_2$) milligrams	0.10
Dietary fibre grams	2.2	Nicotinic acid milligrams	0.7
Sodium milligrams	10	Pyridoxine (B$_6$) milligrams	–
Potassium milligrams	380	Vitamin B$_{12}$ micrograms	0
Calcium milligrams	44	Folic acid micrograms	330
Magnesium milligrams	10	Pantothenic acid milligrams	–
		Biotin micrograms	–

(–) No information available   (0) Contains zero or trace amounts

Energy

Many people think of energy as good, and Calories as bad (fattening), but they are one and the same thing. Calories are just one way of measuring energy, and have been replaced by the more general energy units, kilo**joules**. In health eating extra energy does not ensure an 'energetic' or zestful life – despite the impression created by advertisements for glucose drinks and sweets. The need for energy in food is dictated by the amount the body uses up – not the other way round. In fact, 'energetic' people are usually those who have managed to achieve the fine tuning necessary to keep in energy balance and are neither too fat nor too thin, (see **body weight**), despite the 20 tonnes of food eaten in an average life time.

In the human body, energy is constantly required for **metabolism** and is dissipated as heat. It is replaced ultimately from food; each day an average of 1.3 kg food is eaten and about 100 watts of heat (9 megajoules per day) produced, incidental to metabolism. Energy requirements are increased during growth, but in both adults and children excess energy from food is stored as **adipose tissue** or **glycogen**. The energy reserves of fat in adipose tissue are however much greater than those of glycogen. The 13 kg of fat stored in an average man for example would supply sufficient energy for 45 days without food, whereas glycogen reserves are only sufficient to last for 2 days.

Carbohydrates, **proteins**, **fats** and **alcohol** in food can all be converted into fat for storage as adipose tissue, although the energy cost of converting carbohydrates and proteins into fats is greater than that of direct storage of fat from the diet. As energy is thus converted from one form to another in the body, it is an inescapable fact that weight (adipose tissue) is gained if input has exceeded output, and lost if output exceeds input. However, many factors affect the two sides of the energy equation, and the question of whether or not the maintenance of energy balance in man is primarily under natural control, or subject to conscious effort, is the subject of much controversy.

Small mammals, such as the rat, when fed their normal diet are able to balance daily input with output with remarkable precision. The majority of food is eaten at night, and during the day energy is withdrawn from stores laid down the previous night. If the amount of food available is restricted at night, the rat compensates by eating more in the day. Feeding behaviour is under the control of a variety of transmitters in the brain, and much interest centres on new work providing some insight into this complex system of appetite suppressors and stimulants. However, energy balance is easily over ridden by offering some strains of adult rat a selection of popular, human foods, such as Mars bars, cornflakes and cheese in place of the normal monotonous stock diet, and then **obesity** results. Given the enormous variety of foods offered for sale in western societies, this has obvious implications for the development of obesity in man.

Nevertheless, it is well known that individuals vary widely in the amount of food they are able to eat without gaining or losing weight, and that both volunteers and rats have failed to gain the expected amount of weight when overfed. Consequently a 'natural' mechanism for maintaining energy balance has been proposed, whereby the body compensates for increased supply by 'burning off' unwanted food, or for scarcity by 'adapting' to low energy intakes. Brown adipose tissue is a possible site for such an adaptive mechanism, see **adipose tissue**, but its importance in adult man is still controversial.

Arguments for 'natural' control of body weight apart, the various factors that are known to affect the two sides of the energy balance equation are discussed in the following two sections. Two of them, the type of food eaten, and the amount of exercise taken, are important ways in which energy balance can be controlled, by conscious effort if necessary.

Energy in the diet

The energy in food is held in the form of fat, sugar, starch, protein and alcohol. Fats contain the most energy 37 kilojoules (9 kilocalories) per gram, and proteins, starches and sugars the least – about 16 kilojoules (4 kilocalories) per gram. Alcohol supplies 29 kilojoules or 7 kilocalories per gram.

People who eat foods high in fat and sugar regularly are far more likely to eat more energy than they need. This is mainly because such foods have a low bulk (are 'energy dense') and, for the unsuspecting, attractive to eat. A small cake or chocolate bar containing 1300 kilojoules (300 kilocalories) only weighs 60 grams, yet a helping of boiled new potatoes, dressed with fresh herbs and no butter, would have to weigh as much as 400 grams to give the same amount of energy. In general, vegetables, fruits, bread, lean meat, fish and cereals are safe to eat with no fear of gaining weight because they are low in fat and sugar and contain a lot of **water**. Immediately fat or sugar is added, the energy content is boosted – as happens with chips, crisps, biscuits, cakes, cheese, cream desserts, gold top milk, fatty meat and over-buttered bread. Also, the fact that it costs more energy to convert protein and carbohydrates into fats (for storage as adipose tissue) means that expenditure is slightly greater if the diet contains little of the energy as fats. For these and other reasons, modern recommendations for a balanced **diet** specify a reduction from the present levels of 40% total energy as fat in the diet to 30 to 35%. For most people this is equivalent to eating about 25 grams less fat each day (see **fat**).

The table on page 96 shows foods grouped according to their approximate energy content – but see individual entries.

Approximate energy values in 100 grams (3½ oz) of foods

		Megajoules	kilocalories
Energy rich foods	Cooking fats, oils, butter, margarine,	3.0 – 3.7	750 – 900
	biscuits, cakes, dry cereals, nuts, sugar, cheese, fatty meat, double cream, chocolate.	1.4 – 2.7	350 – 650
Moderate sources	Lean meat, fatty fish, eggs, bread, single cream.	0.6 – 1.4	140 – 340
Low in energy	White fish, most fresh fruit and vegetables, skimmed and semi-skimmed milk, yoghurt	below 0.5	below 140

Energy needs, or expenditure

Energy is needed throughout the day to maintain metabolism and other processes which are measured as the basal **metabolic rate**. As with any other human characteristic, such as colour of hair, this varies naturally between individuals and may account for some of the problems that some people at the extremes may have in putting on weight or losing it, see below and metabolic rate.

The other major determinant of energy expenditure, and which can be altered if necessary, is activity. This varies according to the intensity of exercise. During sleep, when no muscles are being used, the basal metabolic rate (BMR) is about 4 kilojoules or 1 kilocalorie per minute. Immediately on rising, energy expenditure increases to 1.4 times the BMR to maintain posture, and to 2.5 times when walking around. Jogging can raise energy expenditure to at least six times the BMR. The table on page 97 shows how much various activities cost in energy expenditure compared with the BMR. Some of the values differ between men and women because of the nature of the work, for example in the electrical industry, but also because of differences in body weight between the sexes. Greater weights take more energy to move against the forces of gravity. For example, walking at a normal pace uses up to 3.2 times the BMR but with a 10 kilogram (22 lb) load it uses up to 3.5 times the BMR.

Most people spend very little of their time on strenuous activity, and most of the 24 hours is spent asleep, sitting, or standing and walking around. Careful studies at the Dunn Clinical Nutrition Centre, Cambridge, of a few individuals have shown that most use up about 1.4 times their BMR energy on average each day and some only 1.2 times the BMR. Recent World Health Organisation recommended levels for people in sedentary jobs are however 1.5 times the BMR which includes an average of 20 minutes strenuous activity each day, such as jogging, football or tennis. This improves fitness and reduces the risk of **heart disease**.

The fact that individuals living sedentary lives manage to raise their energy expenditure to only such a small extent above the BMR accounts for much of the problem so many people face in trying to maintain an acceptable body weight. Recommended levels for people with moderately active jobs, such as postmen, are 1.8 times the BMR, and for those with very heavy jobs, such as labourers, 2.1 times the BMR.

The values given in the tables for BMR (see metabolic rate) are averages. They are a useful guide for anyone who wants to estimate how much energy they might be using each day but no more than this. This is because any one individual can be expected to differ naturally by more or less than 20% away from the average. A 55 kilogram (8 ½ stone) women aged 35 years may need as little as 4.3 megajoules just for the BMR, and if she is inactive, expending only 1.4 times her BMR her total energy needs would be only 6 Megajoules, or 1500 kilocalories. Another of the same weight and age but at the top of the distribution using up 1.8 times her BMR would use up twice as much, 11.6 Megajoules or 2800 kilocalories. This second lady would be able to eat twice as much food as the first, and have no difficulty in keeping her weight within acceptable limits. People also perform the same tasks with greater or less efficiency and this introduces another factor of uncertainty when estimating how much individuals need. Over the long term, a constant body weight, with no gains or losses of adipose tissue, remains the only way of ensuring that energy needs are being met with the right amount of energy in food.

Energy used up in various activities as a proportion of basal metabolic rate

	Men	Women
Sleeping	1.0	1.0
Sitting quietly (for instance watching TV)	1.2	1.2
Standing quietly	1.4	1.5
Cooking	1.8	1.8
Light cleaning	2.7	2.7
Moderate cleaning (for instance polishing)	3.7	3.7
Walking, normal pace	3.2	3.4
Walking uphill, normal pace	5.7	4.6
Walking, normal pace with a 10 kilogram load	3.5	4.0
Sedentary work – office	1.3	1.7
driving	1.4	1.4
Light industry – garage repairs, laundry work	3.6	3.4
electrical work	3.1	2.0
Labouring, shovelling, digging	5.7	4.6
Recreations		
Seated; playing cards, knitting	2.2	1.4
Light; golf, bowls, billiards	2.2-4.4	2.1-4.2
Moderate; dancing, swimming, tennis	4.4-6.6	4.2-6.3
Heavy; jogging, football, athletics	6.6+	6.3+

Derived from FAO/WHO/UNO Tech. Rep. Ser. 724, 1985

Enzymes

Enzymes are **proteins** that act as biological catalysts, accelerating the speed of chemical reactions in living tissues. Reactions that would normally require great heat, strong acids or many years can take place almost immediately with the aid of enzymes. They are essential for the existence of life.

Enzymes are formed inside each cell, according to genetic instructions inherent in cells and specific to each species. Some enzymes work outside cells (for instance those required for **digestion** of food) but most are held inside.

Only minute amounts of enzymes are needed to bring about reactions – in some cases an enzyme can transform a million times its own weight of one compound (substrate) into another. They need a strictly defined acidity or alkalinity in their surroundings and work best at normal body temperature.

Enzymes are specific (each enzyme reacts with one specific substrate or a group of substrates closely resembling each other) and used to be named after the substrate they caused to react. Thus the digestive enzyme that splits lactose (milk sugar) to form **glucose** and **fructose** is called lactase. In modern classification, enzymes are numbered according to the type of reaction they control and are also given a chemical name if their structure is known. Most of the millions of enzymes thought to exist in nature remain to be purified, named and classified.

The activity of an enzyme can be inhibited – thus slowing or stopping a reaction. Many drugs work on this principle, although often the enzyme involved is not known. See also **inborn errors of metabolism**.

Some enzymes are unable to function unless another, non-protein substance is associated with them. These are called coEnzymes and about 20 are known – many contain **B vitamins**. In addition, enzymes may need small amounts of **minerals** (cofactors) to function; molybdenum, iron, copper, manganese, selenium and zinc are known cofactors.

Enzymes are present in foods or added to foods as micro-organisms (yeasts, bacteria and fungi). They are responsible for many of the changes in texture, flavour and colour when foods are stored and prepared. Some of the changes are undesirable, for instance the browning (see **colour**) of potatoes and the destruction of vitamin C. In other cases, enzymes take part in the preserving of food, and in making it palatable. For instance, when meat is hung enzymes partially degrade the protein fibres so tenderising it. Enzymes in yeast and flour are necessary for bread making; enzymes in bacteria are necessary to convert lactose to lactic acid in yogurt making; and enzymes in fungi are necessary for the flavour of some cheeses.

Many enzymes can now be extracted from micro-organisms (as yet, they cannot be synthesised) and a wide range is used in the food industry. Starch splitting enzymes are used to make glucose syrup from starch, and sugar (sucrose) splitting enzymes are used in soft centre chocolates (see **invert sugar**). **Pectin** splitting enzymes can be used to make vegetable purées. As yet, the use of enzymes is not controlled by law.

Essential fatty acids – obsolete name, vitamin F

Essential **fatty acids** are two classes of polyunsaturated fatty acids with a particular chemical structure that cannot be imitated by the human body. They are involved in the formation of **phospholipids** in cell membranes and the structure and functioning of cells, particularly nervous tissue. About 10 grams of essential fatty acids are needed per day.

The characteristic pattern of essential fatty acids depends on the position of the first double bond (see **fatty acids**) counting from the end not attached to glycerol. In the group with the initiator *linoleic acid* the first double bond is at the *sixth* carbon atom and in the second group, with the initiator α *linolenic acid*, the first double bond is at the *third* carbon atom. In theory these fatty acids can be elongated in the body to make long chain fatty acids particularly required, as phospholipids, in nervous tissue and, in milligram amounts, to form potent muscle stimulators and substances involved in blood clotting – the prostaglandins.

At least 13 prostaglandins have been identified in different parts of the body, including the eye, kidney, lungs, brain and nervous tissue, intestines and reproductive organs. Some are able to make the heart beat with greater force; others lower blood pressure, stimulate the intestinal muscles to contract, and inhibit the release of fat from **adipose tissue** (fat stores). Others are involved in the allergic response, for instance in asthma.

Safflower, sunflower, soya, cotton seed and corn oils are rich sources of linoleic acid – over half their fatty acids are linoleic. Peanut oil and chicken fat are good sources; olive oil and pig fat (bacon, lard, pork) are moderate (about 10% of their fatty acids are linoleic). Beef fat, milk fat (butter, cheese and cream), coconut and cocoa butter are poor (less than 5% of their fatty acids are linoleic). However, few foods contain the next in that class, γ linolenic acid. There are probably individual differences in the ability to form γ linolenic acid which may be important for a variety of disorders in man. Evening primrose oil contains large amounts, and liver and lean meat contain acids higher up in that class.

Sufferers from multiple sclerosis, a condition in which the myelin sheath of nerves is lost, often causing disablement, have abnormal levels of linoleic acid in their blood stream. In the initial stages (when the myelin sheath is being broken down) the levels are raised; afterwards they fall. It has been suggested that supplements of linoleic acid (from sunflower seed oil) might increase the chances of myelin regeneration. It is, however, very uncertain if supplements are able to ameliorate the disease: attempts to establish their value are in progress.

Green leafy vegetables contain α linolenic acid, and vegetable oils also contain it but to a lesser extent than linoleic acid. Soya bean and rapeseed **oil** (used most extensively in oils labelled 'vegetable oil') and wheat germ found in wholemeal bread contain the most. Small amounts are found in meats. Most interest however centres around the fatty acids higher up in the class, such as eicosapentaenoic acid (EPA) which are found particularly in fish oils. They are known to inhibit the tendency of blood to clot and Eskimos, who eat large amounts of fish containing these oils such as seal, herring and mackerel, have a low risk of **heart**

disease and **stroke**. For this reason, including some fatty fish in the diet is probably beneficial, but most experts caution against taking supplements except under medical advice, because they may alter the action of the linoleic class of essential fatty acids and prostaglandins.

Extracts – from meat and yeast

Most meat extract is a by-product of the corned beef industry. Successive batches of meat are heated in a tank of water when flavours and B vitamins are leached out of the meat. Fat is skimmed off and the extract is concentrated or dried by boiling. Brand products, such as Bovril and Oxo, have added flavours (like **hydrolysed protein** and yeast extract), salt, starch and caramel. They are low in fat and high in **salt** – Oxo contains about one fifth of its weight as salt – and contain **vitamin B**, **minerals** (including iron), and protein.

Yeast extract is made by autolysis (a process of self digestion); **enzymes** produced by dead cells destroy cell walls liberating the contents. In brand products, such as Marmite (which contains no meat), salt, spices and vegetable extract are added to the concentrated yeast extract. Yeast extract is a source of B vitamins, including B_{12}, and protein. Its high salt content makes it unsuitable for babies.

The table shows the nutrient content of 100 grams of Marmite, Bovril and Oxo. About 10 grams (1 teaspoonful) is used to make a cup of extract, and about 3 grams is used to spread on a slice of toast.

Average nutrients in 100 grams (3½ oz) Extracts

	Marmite	Bovril	Oxo		Marmite	Bovril	Oxo
Energy kilojoules	759	737	969	Iron milligrams	3.7	14.0	24.9
kilocalories	179	174	229	Copper milligrams	0.3	0.4	0.7
Protein grams	41.4	39.1	38.3	Zinc milligrams	2.1	1.8	–
Total fat grams	0.7	0.7	3.4	Vitamin A micrograms	0	0	0
Saturated fat grams	–	–	–	Vitamin D micrograms	0	0	0
Polyunsaturated fat grams	–	–	–	Vitamin C milligrams	0	0	0
				Vitamin E milligrams	–	–	–
Cholesterol milligrams	–	–	–	B vitamins:			
Sugars grams	0	0	–	Thiamin (B_1) milligrams	3.1	9.1	–
Starch grams	1.8	2.9	12.0	Riboflavin (B_2) milligrams	11	7.4	–
Dietary fibre grams	–	0	0	Nicotinic acid milligrams	58	85	–
Sodium milligrams	4500	4800	10300	Pyridoxine (B_6) milligrams	1.3	0.5	–
Potassium milligrams	2600	1200	730	Vitamin B_{12} micrograms	0.5	8.3	–
Calcium milligrams	95	40	180	Folic acid micrograms	1010	1040	–
Magnesium milligrams	180	61	59	Pantothenic acid milligrams	–	–	–
				Biotin micrograms	–	–	–

(–) No information available (0) Contains zero or trace amounts

Fat – see also **lipid, butter, margarine, cooking fat, oils, cream**

Fat is the highest **energy** yielding **nutrient**. Foods which are nearly all fat, like vegetable oils, provide more **energy** (Calories) weight for weight than any other food.

Although generally used to describe concentrated fatty foods like fat on meat and separated fat like butter, the term 'fat' applies equally to the non-visible fat contained in nearly all foods. Lean roast beef and eggs, for instance, contain 4–11% of their weight as fat; peanuts about half. The exceptions (fat-free foods) are fruits, most vegetables, sugar, egg white, and the majority of beverages. Foods containing very little fat include flour and bread, skimmed milk, cottage cheese, very lean poultry, veal and rabbit, and some shell fish and white fish.

The table on pp.104–5 shows portions of foods containing approximately 10 grams of fat, but there are variations in the non-visible fat content of some fresh foods at different times of the year and between different species. See individual entries.

Apart from the **essential fatty acids**, the liver is able to make all the fat the body requires from **carbohydrates** and **protein**, provided these are eaten in sufficient quantities. Weight for weight, fat supplies over twice as much energy to the body as carbohydrates (sugar and starches): each gram of fat supplies about 37 kilojoules (9 kilocalories) and each gram of carbohydrate or protein about 16 kilojoules (4 kilocalories). Fat also takes less energy to store as adipose tissue than starches or proteins, so there is an added 'fattening' effect with a high fat diet.

About 10 grams of essential fatty acids are needed in the human diet, but the average person in Britain eats ten times this amount, or 100 grams total fat a day, which provides 40% of the energy in the diet. About half the average intake is obtained from meat, fatty fish, eggs, milk, cream and cheese. A further third is eaten as butter, margarine and other separated fats; and pastries, cakes and biscuits contribute about 8 grams. The rest is supplied by small amounts of fat in cereals.

The incidence of ischaemic **heart disease** and breast **cancer** in a community can be correlated with the average individual fat content in the diet. In general, people living in industrialised countries (one exception is Japan) eat more fat and have a higher rate of death from heart disease. People from less affluent countries eat less fat on average and have lower death rates from heart disease and breast cancer. The 'cut off' point where these diseases become less common is about 75 grams of fat in the diet or 30 to 35% of total energy as fat. For this reason, modern recommendations for **diet** suggest that food intakes should be reduced to these levels. Changing from silver or gold top milk to semi-skimmed, eating low fat spread rather than butter or margarine, and eating only lean meat (no sausages or other fatty meat) goes a long way to achieving this. Children below the age of five however should still be given silver top milk.

An easy way of getting down to a lower fat diet is to use the table on pp. 104–5, and choose six to eight portions from it each day. Men on average will need the higher level, woman the lower, and some very tall people may need more. The diet will be bulkier and more satisfying if choices are made primarily from the right hand columns of the table – Swiss roll for example rather than full fat Victoria sponge. It is also essential to include plenty of fresh green vegetables in the diet, and to eat wholemeal or brown bread, to make sure that the needs for essential nutrients are met, see **diet**. Choose at least two foods from the meat, fish, cheese, eggs, or milk categories – or include peas, beans and lentils and nuts. A sample day's meal for a woman could be:

		Fat score
Breakfast	Shredded wheat, large helping	0
	Fresh or dried fruit, like sultanas	0
	Semi-skimmed milk (1 pint for the day)	1
Lunch	Wholemeal bread, large helping	0
	Tomatoes, large helping	0
	Edam or cheese spread, 45 grams	1
	Low fat spread or salad cream, 25 grams	1
	Large helping fresh fruit	0
Supper	Grilled steaklets, 90 grams	1½
	Large helping any vegetables, like peas	0
	Boiled potatoes (no butter), large helping	0
	Herbs or pickle	0
	Apple crumble, 150 grams	1
	Low fat yogurt or custard made with skimmed milk	0
Snack	Rich tea biscuits, 30 grams	½
Total		6

Many convenience foods are not on the list, but all packaged foods will be required to be labelled with their fat content in the near future, when they can be added into a counting system like this. It is advisable to weigh out foods to begin with – 12 grams mayonnaise, butter or margarine is surprisingly little.

Low fat diets, containing about 40 grams a day, may be prescribed as part of the treatment of some diseases of the liver and digestive system (see **malabsorption**) and occasionally prior to the removal of gall stones. For modified fat diets see **lipid**.

In low fat diets separated fats are severely restricted and fatty fish and meat, ordinary milk, most cheese, cream, pastry, cakes and biscuits made with fat, chocolate and confectionery, and ice cream are usually forbidden. Fat free foods, especially sugar and starch, should be taken liberally: low fat diets are invariably low in energy and can result in severe weight loss. Fruit juice with extra glucose is often readily accepted. Special purified oils – medium chain triglycerides (MCT) (see **fatty acids**) – can be used for frying and to make margarine, for spreading and baking. MCT oil is expensive, though available in some circumstances on prescription, but a valuable source of extra energy in a low fat diet.

Fatty acids

Structurally, a fatty acid is a chain of carbon atoms, each with hydrogen atoms attached. At the end of the chain is an acidic group of atoms, able to combine with **glycerol**. Three fatty acids attached to one molecule of glycerol is called a simple fat (chemical name **triglyceride**). Nearly all **fat** in the diet is composed of triglycerides – see also **lipid**.

Short chain fatty acids contain 2 to 6 carbon atoms, medium chain 8 to 10 and long chain 12 to 30. Most fatty acids are long chain, but some short chain – like butyric acid – are found in milk fat, butter and cream. Medium chain fatty acids are extracted from oils to make medium chain triglycerides (MCT) – water miscible fats used as a source of extra energy in some low fat diets.

Fatty acids containing their full quota of hydrogen atoms are called *saturated fatty acids*. Animal fats and hardened fats (see **margarine**) tend to contain more saturated fat than plant and fish oils and be solid at room temperature. Three saturated fatty acids – lauric, myristic and palmitic acids – have been found to raise the blood **cholesterol** level of humans, but other saturated fatty acids have little effect. The three cholesterol raising fatty acids are the most commonly occurring saturated fatty acids. Palmitic acid is very common: in animal fats and palm oil it makes up to 35% of all fatty acids, and up to 17% in other plant oils and fish oils.

Fatty acids with less than their full quota of hydrogen atoms are called *unsaturated fatty acids*. The hydrogen is replaced by a double bond between the carbon atoms. Most plant and fish oils contain a greater proportion of unsaturated fatty acids than animal fats and are liquid at room temperature. Fatty acids with only 2 hydrogen atoms missing (and therefore only one double bond) are called *monounsaturated fatty acids*. Monounsaturated fatty acids have no effect on the blood cholesterol. In nature, oleic acid – a monounsaturated fatty acid with 18 carbon atoms – is the most common fatty acid, most fats and oils contain 30 to 65% of their total fatty acids as oleic.

Fatty acids with four or more hydrogen atoms missing (and therefore two or more double bonds) are called *polyunsaturated fatty acids* (or PUFA or polyunsaturates). Polyunsaturates have been found to lower the blood cholesterol, but they are less effective in lowering the blood cholesterol than are saturated fats in raising it.

The positioning of the double bonds is important in determining biological activity. Generally, naturally occurring PUFA are in the 'cis' form, when they are 'doubled back' on themselves. This is important for the formation of prostaglandins and for the positioning of fatty acids in cell membranes, see **essential fatty acids** and **lipids**. The cis formation is lost to some extent when oils are hydrogenated, for example to make hard margarine, and the resulting straight chains of fatty acids are called 'trans' fatty acids. These have no biological activity in, for example, lowering blood cholesterol or forming prostaglandins and are either stored in **adipose tissue** or used for **energy**. Animal studies suggest that they are no more harmful than saturated or monounsaturated fats in influencing either **heart disease** or **cancer**.

Linoleic acid is one of the most abundant polyunsaturated fatty acids (18 carbon atoms and 2 double bonds) and is found especially in plant oils, although animal fats contain small amounts. It is the initiator of one of the classes of **essential fatty acids**. Fish oils, in fatty fish, contain large amounts of fatty acids higher up in one of those classes, which are important in reducing the tendency of the blood to clot; thus being a possible factor influencing the risk of heart disease.

Apart from the need for essential fatty acids, about 10 grams per day, the human body is able to make all the fat it requires from simple precursors. Most of the 100 grams of fatty acids eaten each day by the average person are superfluous to actual needs – see **fat**.

Weights of foods containing 10 grams fat

Category	High fat (20g + in 100g food)	Medium fat (10-20 grams in 100 grams food)	Low fat (5-10 grams in 100 grams food)	Very low fat or fat-free alternative
Biscuits	Chocolate (orange creams, Penguin etc), 35g Filled wafers, 35g Custard creams, 40g Chocolate digestive, 40g Shortbread, 40g Homemade Easter, 45g Lincoln, crunch biscuits, 45g	Cream crackers, 60g Rich Tea, 60g Oatcakes 55g Ginger nuts, 65g Water biscuits, 80g	Starch reduced, 130g	Matzo, rye crispbread Fresh fruit
Cakes	Flaky Pastry, 25g Short pastry, 30g Victoria sponge, 40g Chocolate eclairs, 40g Mince pies, 50g	Madeira, rock cakes, 60g Doughnuts, jam tarts, 65g Scones, 70g Plain iced cakes, 70g Fruit cake, 85g	Currant bun, 130g Sponge with no fat, like Swiss roll, 150g	Meringues Fresh fruit
Puddings	Cheese cake, 30g	Custard tart, 60g Pancakes, 60g Sponge pudding, 60g Fruit pie (two crust) 65g Lemon Meringue pie, treacle tart, 70g	Trifle, 165g Fruit tart, 130g Bread and butter pudding, 130g Ice cream, 140g Apple crumble, 150g Egg custard, 170g	Jelly, low fat yogurt, fresh, canned or frozen fruit, custard or other milk pudding made with skim milk (fresh or powdered)
Milk, cream	Gold top milk [a], 1/3 pint Butter, 12g Double cream, 20g Whipping cream, 30g Milk powder, 40g Single or soured cream, 50g	Silver top milk [a], 1/2 pint Full fat yogurt, 300g	Semi-skimmed milk [a], 1 pint Evaporated, condensed milk, 100g	Skimmed milk, fresh or dried, low fat yogurt
Oils, fats, spreads	Vegetable oils, lard, dripping, 10g Margarine, butter, 12g Mayonnaise, 12g	Low fat spread, 25g Salad cream, 35g		Bottled sauces and pickles, marmite, jams honey, bovril, tomatoes etc, onions, herbs, spices
Eggs	Scrambled eggs, 45g Fried eggs, 50g Scotch egg, 50g	Boiled eggs, 100g (2)		Egg white
Cheese	Stilton, 25g Cream cheese, 20g Cheddar, Cheshire, 30g Danish blue, Parmesan, 35g Edam, cheese spread, like Dairylea, 45g	Feta, 50g Tendale, 70g Curd cheese, 90g		Cottage cheese. Use mustard to boost the flavour and use less cheese in recipes.

104

Weights of foods containing 10 grams fat

Cheese dishes	Quiche, 35g Welsh rarebit, 40g	Cheese soufflé, 55g Pizza, 90g Cheese pudding, 95g	Macaroni cheese, 110g Cauliflower cheese, 125g	
Meats	Fried streaky bacon, 20g Boiled brisket, 40g Lamb chop, with fat 30g Port chop, with fat 40g Roast duck, with fat, 25g Liver pâté, 40g Luncheon meat, 40g Pork sausages, 40g Sausage roll, 25g Pork pie, 35g Pastie, meat pie, 50g	Grilled lean back bacon, 50g Fried rump steak, with fat 70g Stewed mince, 70g Lean lamb chop, 85g Lean pork chop 85g Roast chicken, with skin, 70g Fried lamb's liver, 70g Corned beef, 80g Steaklets, beefburgers, hamburgers, 60g Moussaka, 75g Bolognese sauce, 100g	Home cooked lean ham, 100g Lean grilled rump steak, 170g Lean roast beef, 110g Lean roast leg lamb, 120g Lean roast leg pork 150g Roast chicken, no skin, 185g Grilled lamb's kidney, 100g Canned lean ham, 195g Lean meat in stew, hot pot, shepherd's pie, curry, 150-200g	Turkey breast White fish Peas, beans, lentils
Fish	Taramasalata, 20g Fried whitebait, 20g Fried scampi, 55g	Fried cod in batter, 100g Canned salmon, 120g Sardines, 85g Fish fingers, 100g	Pilchards in tomato sauce, 185g	All poached or steamed white fish and shellfish
Vegetables Nuts and soups	Crisps, 30g Low fat crisps 50g Frozen fried chips, 50g Soya beans, 45g Avocado pears, 45g Nuts and nut butters, 20g	Thick chips, 100g Olives, 90g Cream and thick soups, like tomato, lentil, oxtail, 250g	Roast potatoes, 200g Oven ready chips 140g	All potatoes cooked without fat. All vegetables, salad, peas, beans, lentils (except soya) with no added fat.
Sweets and chocolates	Milk chocolate, 35g	Mars bar, 50g Toffees, 60g		All plain sweets
Breads, Breakfast cereals	Fried bread, 25g	Chapatis, 80g	Muesli, 133g Ready Brek, 115g Soft rolls, 150g	All other bread, pasta, rice, cereals, breakfast cereals

[a] Milk contains the following fat per 100g; gold top (Jersey) 4.8g; silver and red (homogenised) tops, 3.8g; silver (Fresian) and red (semi-skimmed) 2.0g; blue (skimmed) 0.1g

Fennel

Fennel is a familiar **herb** but the fleshy stem base of cultivated Florence fennel can be eaten as an interesting vegetable, raw in salads or cooked. Its distinctive flavour of aniseed is best preserved in cooking by steaming or braising in a little water. No nutritional analyses are available but its vitamin content is probably similar to **celery**.

Fibre

Dietary fibre is found in leaves, stems, roots, seeds and fruits of plants. It is not broken down by enzymes produced by the human digestive system (see **digestion**) and passes through to the large bowel, where some of it absorbs water. Most however is fermented by bacteria inhabiting the large bowel and the by-products of this fermentation, such as **acetic** and butyric acids, may be important in preserving the health of the large bowel. Some types of fibre, notably **edible gums** and **pectin**, found in fruits and vegetables, lower the blood **cholesterol** and reduce the blood glucose (see **diabetes**), probably by interfering with their absorption from the small intestine. Other sources of dietary fibre, notably wholewheat cereals are important, partly because of their water holding effect, and because of the increased bacterial mass from fermentation, in increasing the bulk of the daily bowel motion, thus relieving constipation.

Nearly all vegetable foods contain some fibre. Foods made from wholewheat, containing the **bran**, supply more than milled. Thus wholemeal **bread** contains three and a half times that in white bread, and wholewheat **breakfast cereals** (like shredded wheat and weetabix) contain more than sixteen times that in cornflakes or rice krispies. Of the vegetables, **cabbage**, and **peas, beans** and **lentils** are especially good sources, although salad vegetables contain only half that found in cabbage. Fleshy fruits, such as apple and banana contain less than berries, such as blackberries, and the fibre is concentrated when foods are dried. Potatoes, and rice, even brown rice, contain relatively little, and meats, fish, fats, vegetable oils, sugar, eggs and cheese and dairy products contain none.

Chemically, dietary fibre is a **polysaccharide**, like starch, but it is a complex system of different sugars which are difficult to analyse. Modern methods of analysis measure dietary fibre as *non-starch polysaccharides (NSP)* and wherever possible values for NSP have been used in the tables for individual foods. Other (outdated) names for dietary fibre are roughage, bulk, unavailable carbohydrate, and hemicellulose. The average British diet contains 12 grams of dietary fibre, of which 3 grams is **cellulose**, 2 grams is **pectin** and the remainder is polysaccharides of four different sugars, including **glucose**. The total amount of NSP is much less than the 150 grams of the other polysaccharide in food, starch.

In the late 1960s, a group of surgeons and physicians proposed that lack of dietary fibre in Britain and other westernised populations, including Europe and the USA, was the cause of a wide variety of large bowel problems, including **cancer**, diverticular disease and appendicitis; and of gall stones, **tooth decay, obesity, diabetes, heart disease**, varicose veins, haemorrhoids and hiatus hernia. All of these are very common and important causes of ill health and premature death, and the possibility that they might be prevented by simple dietary measures has stimulated a massive amount of research into both dietary fibre and other aspects of the western diet.

The fibre hypothesis was based partly on the fact that it increases and softens the contents of the large bowel causing a faster rate of passage, and in the case of diverticular disease, reducing pressure. In the absence of dietary fibre it was suggested that herniations in the bowel wall form, rather like a blown tyre, which may become infected. It was suggested that the increased pressure forces residue into the appendix, causing appendicitis, forces the stomach up through the diaphragm, causing hiatus hernia, and transfers pressure to the veins which collect blood from the anal area, causing eventual haemorrhoids and varicose veins. In large bowel cancer, the faster rate of passage and the less concentrated bowel contents would mean that putative carcinogens would be in contact with the large bowel walls for a shorter time.

Most doctors now recommend **bran** for the treatment of diverticular disease and constipation, although it is preferable to eat the bran as bread and wholegrain cereals, see bran. The importance of dietary fibre in *preventing* all these diseases, apart from constipation, is however still open for debate.

A cornerstone of the fibre hypothesis was that these diseases are rare in rural Africa, where more dietary fibre mainly from unrefined maize and millet was thought to be eaten. Whilst this was true some time ago, most maize eaten in Africa has the bran removed and actual intakes are uncertain. More definitely, the Japanese and Chinese do not suffer (as yet) from high rates of diverticular disease and large bowel cancer, but recent studies have shown that they have traditionally eaten no more dietary fibre than in Britain – 12 to 13 grams per day – because of the low fibre content of rice. Both the Japanese and Africans eat more starch than the British. This may be important because recent research has consistently shown that some starch escapes digestion in the small bowel and enters the large bowel where bacteria use it for fermentation, as with dietary fibre.

Another factor is that in all areas where diverticular disease and large bowel cancer are uncommon, little meat and fat is eaten, together with much starch. The Japanese for example still only eat an average of 70 grams meat, compared with 150 grams a day in Britain. If fibre is protective against these large bowel disorders, it probably is so only in populations at high risk eating large amounts of meat and fat. Limited studies in Britain and Scandinavia suggest that this might be true.

The role of fibre in other diseases is even more uncertain, although it has been found to have definite physiological effects which are now used in the treatment of diabetes. Nevertheless, there is a common theme in many of them, namely that eating more starchy foods and vegetables and fruits, containing dietary fibre, and less animal foods, containing fat, form the basis of modern recommendations for a balanced **diet**.

Figs

Fresh figs contain vitamin A, as carotene, and a little vitamin C. Dried figs are a concentrated source of **sugar**, and together with dates were used as sweeteners by the Assyrians. Other nutrients are also concentrated in dried figs, so that they are good sources of minerals including iron, although this is not well-absorbed from plant foods. Dried figs contain little vitamin A and no vitamin C because it is not preserved. Figs contain ficin, a protein tenderising enzyme.

Average nutrients in 100 grams (3½ oz) Figs

	fresh	dried		fresh	dried
Energy kilojoules	174	908	Iron milligrams	0.4	4.2
kilocalories	41	213	Copper milligrams	0.06	0.24
Protein grams	1.3	3.6	Zinc milligrams	0.3	0.9
Total fat grams	0	0	Vitamin A micrograms	83	8
Saturated fat grams	0	0	Vitamin D micrograms	0	0
Polyunsaturated fat grams	0	0	Vitamin C milligrams	2	0
			Vitamin E milligrams	–	–
Cholesterol milligrams	0	0	B vitamins:		
Sugars grams	9.5	52.9	Thiamin (B₁) milligrams	0.06	0.10
Starch grams	0	0	Riboflavin (B₂) milligrams	0.05	0.08
Dietary fibre grams	2.5	18.5	Nicotinic acid milligrams	0.6	2.2
Sodium milligrams	2	87	Pyridoxine (B₆) milligrams	0.11	0.18
Potassium milligrams	270	1010	Vitamin B₁₂ micrograms	0	0
Calcium milligrams	34	280	Folic acid micrograms	–	9
Magnesium milligrams	20	92	Pantothenic acid milligrams	0.30	0.44
			Biotin micrograms	–	–

(–) No information available   (0) Contains zero or trace amounts

Fish

Fish are a valuable source of good quality **protein** and **minerals**. All fish contain **phosphorus**, sea fish are important for their **iodine** content, and fish with small bones that cannot be separated from the flesh are a source of **calcium**. All fish contain B **vitamins**, and fatty fish are a source of fat soluble vitamins A, D and E, and **essential fatty acids**.

White fish and some fresh water fish like bream, perch and pike, contain minimal fat and a high proportion of water. With their low **energy** and high protein content they are ideal foods for slimmers. Compared with meat, white fish are as good a source of B vitamins, but a poorer source of iron. The slightly fattier white fish (like halibut) sometimes contain small amounts of vitamin A, but usually the flesh of white fish contains no fat soluble vitamins. The livers of white fish are however rich sources of vitamins A, D and E. **Roes**, including caviar, are rich in protein and B vitamins – particularly **thiamin**, and contain about as much **iron**, weight for weight, as lamb or pork. Roes, including taramasalata, are rich in **cholesterol** and may have to be avoided in some diets.

Fatty fish and some fresh water fish like salmon, eel and trout are between 5 and 30% fat, depending on season and species. Their fat is high in polyunsaturated essential fatty acids. They are generally fattest in late summer and early autumn, and leanest after spawning in early spring. In nutritive value fatty fish are superior to white, containing more energy, fat soluble vitamins A, D and E and iron. Sardines contain as much iron weight for weight as lamb, sprats as much as beef. Their bones, which are often eaten, are rich sources of calcium. In view of their cheapness, herrings and mackerel are particularly valuable foods. Some contain at least 25 micrograms of vitamin D in a 100 grams (3⅓ oz) portion - enough to fulfill the adult **recommended intake** for ten days.

Shell fish including crustaceans (like crabs, shrimps) and molluscs (like mussels, whelks) contain twice as much salt as other fish, and about the same protein, fat and energy as white fish. Only the flesh of crustacea is eaten and their vitamin and other mineral contents are similar to white fish. Molluscs are eaten whole (including their organs) and are better sources of iron and vitamin A. Without shell, cockles, whelks and oysters contain as much iron, weight for weight as beef, winkles as much as liver. Some oysters contain vitamin C.

Despite their nutritional virtues, only 5 ounces of fish were eaten in the average British diet (excluding meals taken outside the home) in 1985, compared with 38 ounces of meat. Their greatest contribution to the average intake of nutrients in the diet was about 15% of vitamin D - mostly from fatty fish.

Bought fish should have bright eyes, red gills and plenty of firmly attached scales. They should smell fresh (slightly seaweedy) and have firm creamy (not yellow) white flesh. Their markings, for instance spots on plaice, should be clear. Shell fish should be heavy in proportion to their size.

Unlike meat, fish contains no connective tissue and consequently is never tough - unless overcooked when the flesh becomes rubbery and dry. Only sufficient heat to coagulate the protein, turning the flesh white, is required. On boiling, nearly half the minerals - including **iodine** of which fish is one of the few reliable sources - leach into cooking water. All can be recovered if the liquor is used for sauce. Baking, steaming, grilling and frying cause little loss of nutrients.

Fish can be frozen, canned or cured. Freezing causes no loss in nutritive value, though some B vitamins and flavour are lost in the drip on thawing. To avoid these losses, small pieces of fish should be cooked without thawing beforehand. The proteins of fish are less stable to freezing than meat, so that water and flavour are lost unless frozen fish is glazed with ice. A current Code of Practice recommends that this should not exceed 15% of the total weight. **Polyphosphates** (E450) may also be used, and these should be declared on the label.

Of the many fish products, only the composition of fish cakes and spreads are controlled by specific regulations. Legal minimum weights of fish in these products are shown in the table on page 110. Fish fingers (not subject to control) usually contain 50 to 70% of fish. Fish products may contain **additives: colours** (brown in kippers, yellow in smoked fillet); **flavours; emulsifiers;** and **miscellaneous additives**, like sequestrants added to prevent struvite formation in tins of shell fish. Struvite crystals are harmless but may be mistaken for glass. Other additives, not yet subject to permitted lists, like smoke solutions, may also be used. Smoke solutions and polyphosphates avoid the loss of water which usually occurs with traditional curing processes. **Antioxidants** and **preservatives** may be present in ingredients, and although not directly added, will be 'carried over' to the finished food. Frozen fried fish for instance will contain antioxidant.

Fish is rarely a cause of food poisoning – fresh fish becomes unpalatable when subjected to conditions favouring the multiplication of food poisoning bacteria. It is also usually cooked immediately before eating (unlike some meat foods). Smoked fish, which is not cooked before eating is a possible danger if it is not kept in a refrigerator – particularly smoked trout which, in contrast to sea fish, can be contaminated with the botulism toxin – see **poisons in food**.

Most episodes of poisoning by shell fish are due to **allergy** but 'wild' molluscs can be contaminated with sewage and should be gathered with care. They also accumulate a potent nerve toxin formed by plankton which sometimes multiplies in the sea in summer time (colouring it red), causing poisoning of wild life and humans. Although outbreaks of mussel poisoning are quite common elsewhere, the first recorded outbreak in England occurred in 1968 when about 80 people were affected. It is probably wise to avoid gathering shell fish in summer months.

Fish is the main source of methyl mercury, the most toxic form of mercury – see **poisons in food**. The average mercury content of fish landed in Britain is quite low and about 1 lb a day would have to be eaten to exceed the adult provisional tolerable intake. Tuna and shell fish contain more than other fish. However, fish caught in some British estuaries (particularly the Thames and Mersey) has a much higher mercury content – 1 lb a week would exceed the tolerable limit.

Composition of fish products

Food	Legal minimum fish content
Fish cakes	35%
Fish pastes and spreads	70%
Fish pastes and spreads labelled 'requires grilling'	None
Potted fish	95%
Potted fish and butter	96% (fish and butter)
Fish paste with one other main ingredient	80%

Flavour

Flavour is a mixture of many chemicals in minute quantities, recognised by taste and aroma. It is important in stimulating appetite and identifying foods, but the way in which flavour is perceived in only partly known. **Zinc** and perhaps **vitamin A** are necessary for flavour perception.

The taste buds on the surface of the tongue are sensitive to sweet, sour (acid), bitter and salt. However, aroma (which stimulates the sense of smell) is much more important in distinguishing foods and promoting appetite. An apple tastes the same as an onion when the nose and sinuses are blocked. Heat intensifies aroma – the chemicals are volatile – but overcooking can drive most of the flavour out of food. In cooked foods, flavour depends partly on that of the raw ingredients (which may be affected by breed, maturity, and environment); changes brought about by cooking; and substances rich in flavouring chemicals – flavouring agents – added to impart their own flavour.

An enormous number of flavourings, at least 1500, are currently used by the food industry. They account for much of food **additives** used, 20% of the total or about 2 grams average consumption per day. They may be used to enhance the flavour of the food, replace losses in processing, or flavour manufactured foods (for instance jellies, instant puddings, margarine, soft drinks, **novel proteins**). There are four main groups of flavouring agents: foods (about 30); **herbs** and **spices** (about 150); essential oils, extractives and distillates (about 250); and synthetics (about 1000 specified chemicals). **Salt, sweeteners** and **monosodium glutamate** are also used.

Examples of foods with flavouring properties are **hydrolysed protein**, yeast **extract**, anchovies, vegetables and soy sauce.

The essential oils, extractives and distillates are essences or concentrations of the flavouring chemicals in fruits, herbs, spices and vegetables obtained by pressing, distillation, or treatment with a solvent. Ginger oil, oil of lemon, gum benzoin and vanilla extract are some examples. This group of flavours and the foods from which they are derived are common causes of contact **allergy** (from cosmetics and drugs as well as food). Examples are oil of lemon, vanilla, limonene (from oranges and lemons), anise oil, cinnamon, and clove oil. Many cross-react with balsam of Peru which is a notorious cause of this type of allergy. Cross-reaction can also occur between for example celery and oranges, and with benzoates (see **preservatives**) and **salicylates**.

Mixtures of synthetic chemicals can simulate a natural flavour. Synthetic flavours can be made for apple, apricot, banana, blackberry, brandy, rum, butter, cherry, chocolate, almond, raspberry, strawberry, cranberry, date, garlic, grape, honey, lemon, peach, pineapple, vanilla, even cheese (Cheddar or Roquefort) and bacon. However, synthetic flavours cannot exactly mimic a natural flavour and are usually inferior. Although some synthetics are identical to their natural counterparts, comparatively few of the thousands of flavour components that exist naturally are known and can be synthesised. Examples of synthetics also occurring in a natural flavour are acetaldehyde (apple), benzaldehyde (almond), diacetyl (butter), diallyl disulphide (garlic), vanillin (vanilla), citral (lemon), and probably undecalactone (peach).

Flour

Flour is usually prepared from **wheat**, though other **cereals**, pulses and nuts may also be ground into flour. Wheat flour has a high **gluten** content and can be made into leavened **bread**. Cornflour (see **maize**) is virtually pure **starch**.

Flour can be milled to different extraction rates. In 100% extraction flour (wholemeal), all the grain is used and 100 lb of flour is obtained from 100 lb of wheat. The flour is dark because it contains the outer layers of the grain – **bran** and germ, rich in **minerals, fibre** and **vitamins**. In 70% extraction flour, 70 lb of white flour is obtained from 100 lb of grain. All the outer layers are removed, leaving only the inner part (endosperm). Brown flours can be between 85 and

95% extraction (containing most of the germ and some or most of the bran) or they may be a blend of white flour with sufficient bran to make the fibre up to that of brown.

All flour used to be made by grinding wheat between stones. Some of the bran could be separated off by forcing (bolting) through cloth but the 'white' flour produced was probably equivalent to an 80% extraction flour. It was cream coloured due to the presence of most of the germ and some of the bran. It was very expensive: most people ate wheaten (made with coarser cloths and containing more bran) or household (wholemeal, or wholemeal with rye) breads. In the 1880s roller mills were introduced. These separated the bran and germ, enabling millers to produce cheap white flour of 70% extraction or lower. This white flour was inferior nutritionally, but more popular and replaced brown and wholemeal in the average diet. The health of working people (who were still dependent on bread for most of their essential **nutrients**) probably declined as a result.

Since 1953, three 'token' nutrients (**iron**, and two B vitamins – **thiamin** and **nicotinic acid**) must legally be partially replaced (up to the level of 80% extraction flour) in white flour. Although white flour remains nutritionally inferior to wholemeal, the significance of the difference in a normal balanced **diet** remains uncertain. See **bread** and **fibre**. These nutrients are also usually added to all brown flours – though this is not strictly necessary if the flour is of a high extraction rate (above 80%). No added nutrients are permitted in wholemeal flour. **Calcium** (see **phytic acid**) is also added by law to all flours except wholemeal. Two **additives** are permitted in wholemeal flour, and 20 in other flours. These include bleaches and improvers, which hasten changes which occur naturally when flour is stored – the colour of white flour changes from cream to white and in most the gluten is 'strengthened' enabling a taller, lighter loaf to be made. Two additives – chlorine (926) and sulphur dioxide (E220) – are only permitted in cake and biscuit flours respectively. See **bread** for a full list of additives in flours.

Technological advances (including the use of additives and modern mills) enable millers to produce standardised blends of flours for specific purposes, despite natural variations in gluten (protein) content and baking properties. In general, flours intended for bread, pasta and puff pastry contain more gluten and are said to be 'stronger' than cake and biscuit flours. Self raising flour, which is intended for cake baking, usually contains less protein than plain. Bread flours are usually made from imported wheat, though new baking techniques have enabled more British wheat flour to be used, see **bread**.

Self raising flour, which accounts for about 80% of retail sales, is usually white, containing permitted additives and **raising agents**. It may be an unsuspected source of sodium (salt) - see table. Government regulations specify a minimum amount of gas (carbon dioxide) which must be produced when self raising flour is cooked. It should be kept dry and used as soon as possible after buying because its potency declines during storage, particularly in damp conditions.

Average nutrients in 100 grams (3½ oz) Wheat flour

	whole-meal	white self raising		whole-meal	white self raising
Energy kilojoules	1351	1443	Iron milligrams	4.0	2.6
kilocalories	318	339	Copper milligrams	0.4	0.1
Protein grams	13.2	9.3	Zinc milligrams	3.0	0.6
Total fat grams	2.0	1.2	Vitamin A micrograms	0	0
Saturated fat grams	0.3	0.2	Vitamin D micrograms	0	0
Polyunsaturated fat grams	0.9	0.5	Vitamin C milligrams	0	0
			Vitamin E milligrams	1.0	0
Cholesterol milligrams	0	0	B vitamins:		
Sugars grams	2.3	1.7	Thiamin (B$_1$) milligrams	0.46	0.28
Starch grams	63.5	76.1	Riboflavin (B$_2$) milligrams	0.08	0.02
Dietary fibre (NSP) grams	8.9	2.3	Nicotinic acid milligrams	2.5	3.6
Sodium milligrams	3	350	Pyridoxine (B$_6$) milligrams	0.50	0.15
Potassium milligrams	360	170	Vitamin B$_{12}$ micrograms	0	0
Calcium milligrams	35	350	Folic acid micrograms	57	19
Magnesium milligrams	140	42	Pantothenic acid milligrams	0.8	0.3
			Biotin micrograms	7	1

(–) No information available   (0) Contains zero or trace amounts

Fluorine – see also **tooth decay**

Fluorine is a **trace element**. Like other trace elements, it may be an essential **nutrient** in very minute quantities, but is toxic in excess. In small quantities, fluorine appears to increase the resistance of **teeth** to decay – other trace elements, for instance **molybdenum** and **vanadium**, may also have an effect. Free fluorine is a toxic gas (like **chlorine**) but in nature fluorine is in the form of salts, or fluorides. Fluorine in food and drink is usually called fluoride.

All diets contain some fluoride. Most foods contain traces – about 0.02 milligrams in each 100 grams (3½ oz) of food, or 0.2 parts per million (ppm). Sea fish contain more – between 5 and 15 ppm – but tea is the only significant source in the British diet. It contains up to 100 ppm dry weight, and a cup of tea supplies between 0.2 and 0.5 milligrams. The daily intake from food (including tea) is estimated to be between 0.6 and 1.8 milligrams, though heavy tea drinkers will consume more. Children consume the least because they drink little tea and eat a smaller total quantity of food.

Water contains variable amounts of fluoride. In Britain, waters contain between nil and 6 parts per million of fluoride, adding between nil and 6 milligrams to the daily average intake. Most people drink about 1 litre (1¾ pints) of water each day (ppm = milligrams per litre). People who work in hot environments and others who drink more than a litre a day will consume more.

Fluoride is absorbed out of food and water into the blood stream: calcium decreases the amount that can be absorbed. Once in the blood stream fluoride is transported around the body and some is retained in the bones and – during the growth period before eruption – tooth enamel. The rest is eliminated from the body in urine and sweat. More is retained whilst bones and teeth are being hardened with calcium during growth, but little is otherwise certain of the fate of fluoride. It has recently been reported as an essential nutrient for animals, but not yet been shown to be essential for humans.

Fluoride is toxic in excess. A lethal acute dose for an adult is likely to be 2 grams, or about 1000 times the normal intake. Over the long term, chronic poisoning – fluorosis – has been reported in areas where the water supply contains over 10 ppm, and in workers in contact with fluoride-containing substances – for instance aluminium smelters. The pelvis, backbone and limb bones become increasingly dense, and the ligaments of the spine are hardened with calcium, resulting in an immobile back (poker back). In Britain, the only food which was likely to be contaminated with toxic quantities of fluoride was baking powder, because the acid part (see **raising agents**) used to be obtained from rock phosphates which also contain fluoride. These are no longer used, but present day regulations still specify maximum permissible quantities of fluoride in baking powder and self raising flour – 15 and 3 ppm respectively, or 1.5 and 3 milligrams per 100 grams.

In areas where the fluoride content of water is low, children usually have more decayed (or missing or filled) teeth than in areas where the fluoride content of water is between 1 and 2 ppm (adding between 1 and 2 milligrams to the average diet). Fluoride probably becomes part of the chemical structure of tooth enamel and when bacteria multiply on the enamel and produce acids, the fluoridated enamel is thought to dissolve less readily. Fluoride may also inhibit the growth of bacteria.

When the fluoride concentration of water is greater than 1.5 ppm, teeth become increasingly mottled. The enamel becomes opaque and there can be white specks (mild mottling) or yellow, brown or black markings (moderate to severe mottling). Mild mottling can also occur when there is virtually no fluoride in the water and is assumed to be idiopathic (having an unexplained cause). When water contains 1 ppm of fluoride, mottling occurs but is hardly detectable and similar to idiopathic mottling. At 2 ppm, about 10% of teeth are moderately mottled, and when the fluoride content of water is high (over 3 to 5 ppm) mottling of the teeth is common.

Water containing 1 ppm (adding 1 milligram to the average diet) of fluoride is considered to be ideal. At this level, there is least mottling and the incidence of decay is low.

Dental decay in children is a serious problem in most industrialised countries, and there have been many experiments to see if it can be reduced by adding fluoride at the optimum level to mains water supplies naturally low in fluoride. The reduction in decay claimed varies from 60 to 30%, depending on whether the results are compared with those of a 'control' – see below. Fluoride is usually added as sodium fluoride, or sodium silicofluoride or hydrofluosilicic acid – these separate out into fluoride, **sodium** and **silicon** particles once in the water. Hence, there is no difference between added and natural fluoride.

Since 1955, a Government study has been assessing the effects of fluoridation: in three towns where the water content of fluoride was low, fluoride was added to the level of 1 ppm. The children in these towns were compared with those in three similar 'control' towns where the water content of fluoride – also low – was left unchanged.

The children in study and control towns were divided into groups, according to age. The amount of dental decay was assessed by counting the number of decayed, missing and filled teeth in individual mouths and calculating the average total for each group of children. This measurement cannot be used to assess decay in adults, where more teeth are lost as a result of gum disease. Consequently, the effects of fluoridation after adolescence are not certain.

Between 1956 and 1967 the amount of dental decay in one fluoridated town (Watford) decreased by an average of between 50 and 60% for children aged three to ten years. This supports the common statement 'Fluoride cuts dental decay by half. However, the amount of decay in its control town – unfluoridated Sutton – also decreased by an average of 20 to 30% over that period. A decrease of 30% – or one third – would be more accurate.

The average numbers of decayed, missing or filled teeth counted in these towns are shown in the table on page 117. In terms of average numbers of teeth, children who received fluoridated water for eight to ten years had an average of one tooth less decayed, missing or filled compared with those who did not. Those children in the fluoridated area aged three to seven years had an average of 1.7 less decayed, missing, or filled teeth compared with those in the control town. In the older age group (eleven to fourteen years) there was less improvement (or reduction in decay) probably because these children had not been given fluoridated water all their lives. Fluoride is more effective if it is taken whilst the dental enamel is being formed before teeth erupt. Once the teeth erupt, the enamel is not in contact with the blood stream.

Taking control towns into account, there have been 28 and 58% reductions in fluoridated towns in Michigan and East Germany respectively for children aged ten years. In one study in New York there was a reduction of 45% – which included an increase in the control area of 15%.

In 1963, following five years of fluoride trials in Britain, the Minister of Health advised local authorities that they were free to add fluoride up to 1 ppm in waters that were naturally low in fluoride in order that the amount of dental decay could be reduced. However, in 1969, only two million people were drinking fluoridated water in Britain. Fluoridation has not been universally introduced because it has been vigorously opposed at parliamentary and local authority level. Unfortunately, personal convictions have led to unsupportable claims being made about the safety of fluoride. As stated in a recent *Current Contents* review '. . . decisions about fluoridation have too often been affected by emotional appeals and charges that are not related to the available scientific evidence'.

Many studies have shown no changes in the health of people drinking water fluoridated to a level of 1 ppm, except that the amount of dental decay in children is reduced. The members of the Government Research Committee on Fluoridation, and the American Institute of Nutrition in 1985, have categorically stated that at a level of 1 ppm fluoridation is completely safe. On the available evidence, fluoridation does not increase the incidence of rheumatism, bone disease (see also **osteoporosis**), cancer, gout, goitre, Down's syndrome, and heart disease. However, it is uncertain (though unlikely in view of the absence of complaint from millions of tea drinkers) that fluoride is a cause of allergy. People treated with artificial kidney machines (which require large volumes of water for each treatment) could accumulate sufficient fluoride to cause fluorosis. Other people who need to drink large volumes of water (for instance steel workers and those suffering from some kidney stones, see **calcium**) may also be at risk, especially if they also consume a lot of strong tea.

Postulated health risks to adults apart, fluoridation opponents challenge the statistical methods used in fluoridation studies and maintain that the actual benefits for the individual are small. Even if fluoride is beneficial for children's teeth, opponents feel that adding fluoride to water supplies is wasteful because only about 1% is actually drunk. It is feared that large quantities of fluoride which would be released will eventually result in unacceptably high levels in the diet as a whole – especially where food is processed in fluoridated water.

The most important opposition argument is a moral one: fluoridation is a form of mass medication. In other nutritional improvement programmes, alternatives are available – for instance ordinary salt is available for those who do not wish to take extra iodine, and wholemeal flour is available for those who do not wish to take extra calcium and nicotinic acid in their bread. Although water fluoridation may reduce dental decay in childhood, its benefits in adult life are not certain. In adult life most teeth are lost as a result of gum disease, caused principally by poor eating habits and inadequate tooth brushing. Water fluoridation does not encourage children to take care of their teeth over the long term and has been called a 'technological fix'.

There are other methods of increasing the fluoride content of tooth enamel which are almost or as effective, see below, but require positive action on the part of parents and children. Many people are taking this action and, coupled with greater awareness of the harmful effect of sugar containing foods on teeth, the extent of dental decay has fallen markedly in recent years.

Flouride tablets, toothpaste and fluoride preparations painted onto teeth by dentists are the most effective alternatives to water fluoridation. Fluoride tablets are as effective, provided they are taken daily. Each contains 1 milligram of fluoride (as 2.2 milligrams of sodium fluoride). The recommended dose from birth to two years is a quarter tablet daily which may be dissolved in water or sucked before swallowing. From the age of two to four years half a tablet should be taken daily, and one a day until about sixteen years of age when all the teeth have erupted. Like other medicines, large quantities of tablets should be kept out of reach of children. After the teeth have erupted, fluoride tablets are probably of little benefit, though externally applied fluoride – as toothpaste or other preparations – is probably worthwhile even in adulthood.

Most toothpastes contain monofluophosphate (MFP) which when compared with a control reduces dental decay by about 20%. MFP contains approximately 13% of fluoride, and 10 grams (1 inch) of a toothpaste containing 0.8% of MFP supplies approximately 1 milligram of fluoride. Concentrations are stated on toothpaste containers (0.8% = 800 milligrams per 100 grams of toothpaste). If toothpaste is swallowed, fluoride tablets should not be given in addition.

Fluoride preparations applied topically to the teeth by dentists probably reduce dental decay in children by about 30%, provided they are carried out regularly (once to twice yearly). Unfortunately, this treatment is not available under the National Health Service.

Average numbers of decayed, missing or filled teeth per child★

		Average per child		Percentage reduction	Difference
		1956	latest year	%	%
Age 3–7	Watford	4.8	1.8	63	33
	Sutton	4.1	2.8	30	
Age 8–10	Watford	3.0	1.5	50	31
	Sutton	3.0	2.5	19	
Age 11–14	Watford	6.4	4.3	33	19
	Sutton	6.3	5.5	14	

★Ref. *Rep. Pub. Health and Med. Subj.* no 122 HMSO

Folic acid

– Group names – folic acid, folate, folacin
- Obsolete names – vitamin B_c, vitamin M, Wills factor, leucovorin factor
- Chemical name for synthetic form – pteroylglutamic acid (PGA)

Folic acid is part of the **vitamin B complex**, and is required for the synthesis of many fundamental substances, including DNA, the genetic blueprint in cells. In its absence, cell division and therefore replication and renewal is affected. This is clearly important during growth, and the possibility that some birth defects arise at conception due to folic acid deficiency is currently under investigation. **Anaemia** is one of the first consequences of a diet lacking in folic acid.

The best sources of folic acid are dark green **vegetables**, like **broccoli, endive** and **spinach, liver, kidney, nuts**, and wholemeal **bread** and wholegrain **breakfast cereals**. This is one of the many reasons why plenty of vegetables and wholegrain cereals should be included in a healthy **diet**. However, up to 90% of folic acid can be lost in overcooked vegetables because it is sensitive to heat, light, oxygen and readily diffuses into the cooking water. See **vegetables** for the best ways of cooking them. White bread, most meats, fish, fruit, milk and cheese are only poor sources.

There are many different forms of the vitamin: folate and folic acid are used to describe the group as a whole. Folacin – another group name – is used particularly in the USA. Folates in food are usually complex and it is uncertain how much of the very complex forms are available to the body. The synthetic form of folic acid – PGA – is one of the most simple and potent forms but only small amounts of PGA occur naturally in food. Because of its complexity it is difficult to measure in food and even the values given in the official British food tables, used thoughout this book, are probable underestimates. It is also very uncertain how much is actually needed, and for this reason, **recommended allowances** for it were withdrawn in Britain. The USA recommendation of 400 micrograms minimum and 800 micrograms during pregnancy are controversial and probably too high.

During **digestion** the vitamin is converted to its active form by cells lining the small intestine. It is transferred to the blood stream and carried to the liver, where it may be stored. Well nourished people have sufficient liver stores for three to four months. When needed the vitamin is withdrawn from the liver and carried in the blood stream to cells where it fulfills a fundamental role: it is a co**Enzyme** required for the replication and renewal of cells. When there is insufficient, growth and replacement slow down and eventually cease. Cells in the blood, skin and digestive system – among the most rapidly renewed – are first affected by lack of folic acid, resulting in anaemia, and skin and digestive disorders. It is also important in the nervous system, particularly in the brain, leading to mental symptoms in severe deficiency.

Deficiency of folic acid is common during pregnancy: it is difficult to meet the growing child's needs for the vitamin from food alone – particularly when multiple births are expected. Initially folic acid is withdrawn from the mother's liver stores to make good the inadequacy, but this may be insufficient. The ensuing anaemia checks the baby's growth and puts the mother's life at risk. Extra **iron** is also required during pregnancy, and the two nutrients are usually routinely prescribed as a combined tablet. During breast feeding a nutritious diet (containing plenty of green vegetables) will enable the mother to supply her child with sufficient folic acid.

Other groups of people at risk from folic acid deficiency are the very young and the elderly. Babies have become anaemic when fed artificially with goats' milk, which is a very poor source and the elderly may not eat a diet containing enough fresh vegetables; this may be important in causing premature mental deterioration. Epileptics taking some anticonvulsant drugs also seem to be more prone to folic acid anaemia.

Because of its importance in cell division, folic acid taken before conception is presently under investigation to see if it prevents various congenital diseases of the nervous system, including spina bifida. In the initial studies, mothers who had already given birth to a baby with one of these defects were asked to take the vitamin as tablets for one month before conceiving again, and for two months after conception. The numbers of children born with defects were substantially reduced, as compared with a similar group of women who did not take the vitamins. However, the folic acid was given as multivitamin tablets, also containing iron, calcium, and vitamins A, D, C and other B vitamins. Consequently it is not certain which was the active ingredient. All are therefore having to be tested in several large scale preconceptual trials. The need to wait for the outcome of these has been criticised, but in the past treatments which seemed to be 'safe' have been used before proper testing with tragic results. 100% oxygen was given to premature babies for example before proper testing, assuming that it was safe, and only when it was too late was it found to cause blindness.

Large doses of folic acid may apparently cure pernicious anaemia (see vitamin B_{12}) but not the degeneration of the nervous system. For this reason the British Code of Advertising Practice forbids the advertisement of over the counter vitamin preparations that contain sufficient folic acid to mask pernicious anaemia.

Fructose - other name, fruit sugar - chemical name, laevulose

Fructose is a simple sugar (**monosaccharide**). For the same sweetness, just over half as much fructose as sucrose (ordinary sugar) needs to be used.

The only foods which contain more than traces of free fructose are **honey** and a few fruits, for instance apples and pears. Nearly all fructose is eaten in a combined form as sucrose, which is split during **digestion** to fructose and glucose. **Invert sugar** is also used in the food industry.

Pure fructose used to be very expensive because it was in such short supply. It used to be made from **inulin**. Now, however, it can be made from starch using **enzymes** and a series of chemical manipulations. It is often sold as 'natural fruit sugar'.

Fructose supplies the same amount of **energy**, weight for weight, as other sugars and is not suitable for slimming diets. However, small amounts can be used in the liver without the need for insulin (see **diabetes**) and it is sometimes recommended for diabetics treated with insulin and diet. Fructose also increases the rate at which the body uses **alcohol**, though the effect varies with the individual.

Fructose should be used with care. Unlike glucose it is absorbed out of the body into the blood stream by simple diffusion and excess quantities can result in diarrhoea. More importantly, it tends to raise the level of some fats in the blood stream and may also precipitate attacks of **gout** in susceptible people.

Fructose may have to be excluded from the diet of some infants suffering from rare **inborn errors of metabolism**. In infancy ordinary milk – provided it is not sweetened with sucrose – can be given. After weaning, a low blood **glucose** and resulting fits and brain damage, can be avoided if no sucrose, fructose, fruit or invert sugar is taken.

Fruit

Refreshing, delicately flavoured foods, fruits are generally thought of as the sweet tasting parts of plants, though botanically many vegetables, nuts, and cereals are fruits.

Some fruits are good sources of **vitamin C, vitamin A** (as **carotene**) and **fibre**. In Britain, blackcurrants and rosehips are the richest fruit sources of vitamin C. One 100 gram (3½ oz) portion of stewed blackcurrants contains an average of five times the adult daily **recommended intake** of vitamin C. Strawberries and citrus fruits are also good sources – an average 100 gram portion has between two and three times the adult daily recommended intake. Mandarins contain slightly less than oranges, lemons and grapefruit. Apples, pears, bananas and grapes contain comparatively little – weight for weight, less than a properly cooked portion of cabbage or cauliflower.

Yellow (not white) melons, peaches and apricots are the best fruit source of vitamin A, though they contain much less than carrots. There is little or no carotene in white fruits (for instance pears). Fruits with tough skins and pips have more fibre than tender fleshy fruits.

Fresh fruits are 80–90% water and consequently they are low in **energy** and **fat**. Most of the energy in fruits is in the form of sugars (carbohydrates) – chiefly **glucose** and **fructose** but also (especially in pineapple) **sucrose**. Fruits also contain small amounts of B vitamins, **minerals** and vitamin E, but other foods are better sources of these nutrients. They also contain **bioflavonoids**.

The refreshing quality of fruits is due partly to their high water content and also to weak, sharp tasting acids. Vitamin C is an acid (**ascorbic acid**) and **citric acid** is in all citrus fruits, pineapple and soft summer fruits. Malic acid is in apples and plums, benzoic acid (also used as a **preservative**) in cranberries, and **oxalic acid** in strawberries and rhubarb. Although the acid taste of some fruits may be uncomfortable for those with digestive disorders (see dyspepsia), fruits do not increase the acidity of the body – see ash. As fruits ripen, their acid content falls. Unripe fruits also contain **starch** and **cellulose** which is converted to sugar as they ripen. See also pectin.

In the average British diet, about 27 oz of fruit and fruit products are eaten per person per week (excluding meals taken outside the home) which supplied about half (44%) of the total vitamin C intake in 1983. Apples are the most popular fruit in Britain, but they supply little vitamin C, and most in the average diet comes from **fruit juices**. The popularity of fruit juices has meant that vitamin C intakes have noticeably increased in recent years in Britain.

Freshly picked fruits contain more vitamin C than stored because the vitamin declines slowly during storage. Its destruction is hastened by warmth, bruising and drying out. In apples, pears and bananas (which are poor sources of vitamin C) these losses are not important, provided some vegetables or citrus fruits are taken each day. Citrus fruits however should be kept as cool as possible, preferably in a refrigerator.

During cooking, the acidity of fruits protects against severe loss of vitamin C, and compared with vegetables, little is lost. Up to 90% is normally retained, but prolonged soaking, cooking and keeping hot (especially if fruit is puréed) can destroy all vitamin C in apples.

Some **additives** are permitted on the skin of some fresh fruit, which should be washed or peeled before eating. Apples and pears may contain **antioxidant** to prevent browning of the flesh during storage, and bananas and grapes, and citrus fruits may have added **preservative** to prevent mould growth during storage. Citrus fruit is also allowed to be coated with **mineral hydrocarbons** to prevent drying out during storage. Dried and crystallised fruit is permitted to contain the preservative sulphur dioxide (which helps to protect vitamin A) and glacé fruit usually contains added **colour**. Crystallised fruit is made by dipping in hot sugar solutions, which destroys most of the vitamin C, but candied peel retains a little.

During bottling and canning heat destroys up to 60% of vitamin C: stored bottled fruit will lose more if exposed to sunlight. Blanching before freezing results in some loss of vitamin C, but the losses are smaller than those which would be caused by **enzyme** action during storage.

Canned or bottled citrus fruit juices (but not squashes – see soft drinks) are very reliable sources of vitamin C. They are acid and 80 to 90% of vitamin C is retained. Little is lost during storage but vitamin C in contact with oxygen rapidly declines: up to 50% can be lost from an open can in a week. Only small quantities should be opened and kept under refrigeration. Blackcurrant syrup is also a reliable source of vitamin C, but apple juice contains much less than citrus fruits. Fruit juices are permitted to contain the preservative sulphur dioxide (which aids retention of vitamin C) or benzoic acid.

Small amounts of fruit juices are used to make fruit squashes and cordials. The comminuted pulp may also be used – the drinks are called 'whole fruit'. Unless vitamin C is added, squashes contain little or no vitamin C – see soft drinks.

Fruit juices and drinks

Citrus fruit juices are reliable sources of **vitamin C** and tomato juice contains **vitamin A**. Pineapple juice contains less vitamin C than grapefruit, orange or tomato (see table). Legally, apple and citrus fruit juices must be made from a minimum of 50% fruit juice or purée. Pineapple juice may contain dimethyl polysiloxane (900), an anti-foaming agent (see **miscellaneous additives**), and all fruit juices may contain acids, added vitamin C, **flavourings** and **preservatives**. Additives are particularly likely in fruit drinks and squashes which also compare badly with fruit juices nutritionally. Compare for example orange juice with lemonade in the table below.

Average nutrients in 100 grams (3½ oz) Fruit juices and drinks

	grapefruit juice	orange juice	pineapple juice	tomato juice	orange drink	lemonade
Energy kilojoules	132	143	225	66	456	90
kilocalories	31	33	53	16	107	21
Protein grams	0.3	0.4	0.4	0.7	0	0
Total fat grams	0	0	0	0	0	0
Saturated fat grams	0	0	0	0	0	0
Polyunsaturated fat grams	0	0	0	0	0	0
Cholesterol milligrams	0	0	0	0	0	0
Sugars grams	7.9[a]	8.5[b]	13.4	3.2	28.5	5.6
Starch grams	0	0	0	0.2	0	0
Dietary fibre grams	0	0	0	–	0	0
Sodium milligrams	3	4	1	230	21	7
Potassium milligrams	110	130	140	260	17	1
Calcium milligrams	9	9	12	10	8	5
Magnesium milligrams	8	9	12	10	3	0
Iron milligrams	0.3	0.5	0.7	0.5	0.1	0
Copper milligrams	0.03	0.03	0.09	0.05	0.01	0.01
Zinc milligrams	0.4	0.3	–	0.4	–	–
Vitamin A micrograms	0	8	7	83	0	0
Vitamin D micrograms	0	0	0	0	0	0
Vitamin C milligrams	28	35	8	20	0	0
Vitamin E milligrams	0	0	–	0.2	0[c]	0
B vitamins:						
Thiamin (B$_1$) milligrams	0.04	0.07	0.05	0.06	0	0
Riboflavin (B$_2$) milligrams	0.01	0.02	0.02	0.03	0	0
Nicotinic acid milligrams	0.3	0.3	0.3	0.8	0	0
Pyridoxine (B$_6$) milligrams	0.01	0.04	0.10	0.11	0	0
Vitamin B$_{12}$ micrograms	0	0	0	0	0	0

Fruit juices and drinks

	grapefruit juice	orange juice	pineapple juice	tomato juice	orange drink	lemonade
Folic acid micrograms	6	7	–	13	0	0
Pantothenic acid milligrams	0.12	0.15	0.10	0.20	0	0
Biotin micrograms	1	1	–	1	0	0

(–) No information available   (0) Contains zero or trace amounts

[a]Sweetened contains 10 grams
[b]Sweetened contains 13 grams
[c]20 to 60 milligrams added to some brands

Galactose

Galactose is a simple sugar (or **monosaccharide**).

The majority of galactose in the diet is derived from **lactose** (milk sugar) which is split during **digestion** to its component sugars – **glucose** and galactose. These sugars are absorbed into the blood stream, and galactose is normally converted to glucose in the liver.

Galactosaemia is an **inborn error of metabolism** where the normal conversion of galactose to glucose does not take place. The accumulation of a toxic intermediate compound causes damage to many tissues, including the brain, liver and lens of the eye. Blindness and mental retardation can be avoided if galactose is excluded from the diet in time.

Special lactose-free milks are available on prescription for galactosaemic babies. After weaning, normal foods can be eaten, provided all galactose containing foods are avoided. These include milk and all milk products (for instance cheese and cheese spreads, yogurt) and offals like liver, brains and sweetbreads. Lactose and milk are also used in many processed foods (some breads, cakes, biscuits, soups, tinned meats) and **labels** must be read carefully. Lactose is sometimes added as a 'filler' in tablets.

Garlic

A member of the onion (*Allium*) family. Garlic was eaten in ancient Greece. The flavour of garlic is liberated on crushing or cutting by the action of an **enzyme** on a chemical compound, allyl cysteine sulphoxide, contained in the flesh. The nutrient content of garlic is shown in the table but it is more important for its flavour than nutritional value.

The equivalent of 30 grams (1 oz.) of raw garlic clove per day has been found to reduce the level of blood **cholesterol** in an experimental study, although the means by which it does so is not known.

Average nutrients in 100 grams (3½ oz) Garlic

Energy kilojoules	490	Iron milligrams	1.5
kilocalories	117	Copper milligrams	–
Protein grams	3.5	Zinc milligrams	0.9
Total fat grams	0.3	Vitamin A micrograms	0
Saturated fat grams	–	Vitamin D micrograms	0
Polyunsaturated fat grams	–	Vitamin C milligrams	10
		Vitamin E milligrams	–
Cholesterol milligrams	–	B vitamins:	
Sugars grams	} 26.7	Thiamin (B_1) milligrams	0.24
Starch grams		Riboflavin (B_2) milligrams	0.05
Dietary fibre grams	–	Nicotinic acid milligrams	0.4
Sodium milligrams	18	Pyridoxine (B_6) milligrams	–
Potassium milligrams	373	Vitamin B_{12} micrograms	0
Calcium milligrams	18	Folic acid micrograms	6
Magnesium milligrams	8	Pantothenic acid milligrams	–
		Biotin micrograms	–

(–) No information available   (0) Contains zero or trace amounts

Gelatine

A **protein** of limited nutritive value: it is lacking in the essential **amino acid** tryptophan and contains little phenylalanine. Commercially, gelatine is produced by simmering hide, skin and bones in water. It is added to many meat products and is the basis of sweet jellies and aspic.

When **meat** is cooked in water, collagen – the main protein in connective tissue responsible for toughness of meat – is converted to gelatine. Bones and gristle, which contain more connective tissue than meat, yield more gelatine. On cooling, gelatine causes the cooking liquor to set; 'richer' liquors contain more gelatine and form firmer jellies. Calves foot is a good source.

Meat jellies are easily contaminated with food poisoning organisms and care should be taken in keeping them (see **poisons in food**).

Glucose – other names, dextrose, grape sugar, blood sugar

Glucose is a simple sugar (or **monosaccharide**) which can be made in the body from many food constituents, including **protein**. Only a few natural foods – for instance **honey** and grapes – contain more than traces of free glucose, but it is found in abundance as combined forms – mostly as **starch** (a polymer of glucose) and as **sucrose** or sugar – a **disaccharide**. Commercially, glucose and glucose syrups are made from starch using acids or **enzymes**.

Despite claims for certain glucose drinks and sweets, glucose has no particular **energy** giving properties. Although it may be absorbed into the blood stream at a faster rate than starch, weight for weight it contains the same amount of energy as other **carbohydrates** (approximately 16 kilojoules or 4 kilo**calories** per gram). However, glucose has only half the sweetness of sugar (sucrose) and is sometimes useful for special high energy diets: for the same sweetness, twice as much glucose can be taken.

After **digestion** glucose, from sugars and starches, is absorbed into the blood stream and transported to the liver. Some is immediately circulated round the rest of the body, and some is converted into **glycogen**. The blood glucose level never falls to zero – the brain and nerves need a constant supply for continued activity – and between meals it is maintained by glucose released from liver glycogen. The liver is able to replenish its own glycogen reserves with glucose manufactured from protein, **galactose**, some **fructose**, and other substances released from cells.

This complex system is under the control of hormones and enzymes. The malfunctioning of one link can cause a variety of symptoms – see **diabetes**.

In cells, glucose is degraded in about twenty stages and its energy is harnessed for energy requiring reactions (see **metabolism**). The last series of reactions is called the **citric acid** cycle. Finally, oxygen is combined with hydrogen: waste products – carbon dioxide and **water** – diffuse into the blood stream and are eliminated from the body. Carbon dioxide is breathed out through the lungs, and the kidneys, skin and lungs remove excess water.

Glutamic acid (620)

An **amino acid**, glutamic acid is a component of food **proteins**, the vitamin folic acid, and **monosodium glutamate**, but is not an essential **nutrient**. It is readily synthesised by the body and incorporated into new proteins, required for replacement and growth, and plays an important part in the formation of other non essential amino acids. Excess intakes are converted to **glucose** and used for energy purposes. The nitrogen part is used to make other amino acids or converted to urea, later filtered out of the blood stream by the kidneys.

Monosodium glutamate is made from glutamic acid extracted from sugar beet and wheat gluten.

Gluten

Gluten is a **protein** capable of stretching when mixed with water and kneaded. Present in wheat, rye and, to a lesser extent, barley and oats. It is essential for leavened bread and cake making, when it expands and traps gas (see raising agent) to form a spongy cooked product.

When flour is stored, gluten becomes tougher and more elastic, resulting in a larger loaf. Flour improvers (see flour) accelerate this process which would otherwise take several weeks. Gluten is added to starch reduced and high protein breads. They are lighter (contain more air) but their **energy** value is greater than ordinary **bread**.

Strong flours – for instance Canadian – contain more gluten and are imported to make the British loaf. However, weak flours are best for cake and biscuit making. New methods of bread making now allow more British flour to be used – see bread.

A gluten-free diet is used in the treatment of **coeliac disease**. Special gluten-free flours and bread are available on prescription for those who need them: the difficulties encountered in baking with gluten-free flour can partially be overcome by adding protein in the form of milk or eggs.

Allergy to gluten has been suggested as a cause of multiple sclerosis, but is probably an unlikely one. See also **essential fatty acids**.

Glycerol – other name glycerine (E422)

A sweet substance, part of the structure of fats (see **fatty acids**), and made in the body. Excess intakes are used for energy by the same series of reactions which degrade **glucose**.

Glycerol is manufactured from fats and used as a humectant (moistening agent) – particularly in cakes – see **Miscellaneous additives** and as a **solvent**.

Glycine

Glycine is the simplest **amino acid**. Because of its sweet taste, it is sometimes used in conjunction with saccharin. Glycine is contained in all food proteins, but is not an essential **nutrient**. Excess intakes are converted to **glucose** and used for energy purposes. The **nitrogen** part is used to make other amino acids or converted to urea, which is later filtered out of the blood stream by the kidneys.

Glycine is used to make new body proteins needed for growth and repair and for other important substances, including bile. Potentially toxic substances, for instance benzoic acid (see **preservatives**) combine with glycine in the liver and are later eliminated in the urine.

Glycogen – other name, animal starch

Glycogen is a polymer of **glucose** (**polysaccharide**), used as an **energy** reserve in muscle and liver cells. Normally the energy stores of glycogen are small – most people contain less than 1 kilogram of glycogen, compared with up to 16 kilograms of fat in a 70 kilogram (11 stone) man.

Glucose released from liver glycogen stores maintains the blood glucose level, ensuring a continual supply of energy to the brain and nerves between meals. In muscles, glycogen is an emergency store of energy, independent of nutrients supplied in the blood. For sudden activities, like running, glycogen is broken down and a small amount of energy obtained by the conversion of glucose to **lactic acid**, without the need for oxygen. Modern athletic training regimes usually incorporate a high **carbohydrate** diet which increases muscle glycogen stores and probably enhances endurance during long distance events. The reserves are further increased if they are first depleted by several days' hard exercise and a carbohydrate-free diet.

Goose

Goose domestication probably began as early as Neolithic times. The goose was regarded as a sacred animal by the Romans and its meat and liver were highly prized by gourmets of this period. *Foie gras*, according to *Larousse Gastronomique*, is regarded as one of the greatest delicacies available – at least by those who do not mind the method of its production.

Only scanty data of the nutritional composition of goose is available (see table). *Foie gras* will be similar to other **liver**.

Average nutrients in 100 grams (3½ oz) Goose (roast)

Energy kilojoules	1327	Iron milligrams	4.6
kilocalories	319	Copper milligrams	0.49
Protein grams	29.3	Zinc milligrams	–
Total fat grams	22.4	Vitamin A micrograms	–
Saturated fat grams	–	Vitamin D micrograms	–
Polyunsaturated fat grams	–	Vitamin C milligrams	–
		Vitamin E milligrams	–
Cholesterol milligrams	–	B vitamins:	
Sugars grams	0	Thiamin (B$_1$) milligrams	–
Starch grams	0	Riboflavin (B$_2$) milligrams	–
Dietary fibre grams	0	Nicotinic acid milligrams	–
Sodium milligrams	150	Pyridoxine (B$_6$) milligrams	0.43
Potassium milligrams	410	Vitamin B$_{12}$ micrograms	–
Calcium milligrams	10	Folic acid micrograms	–
Magnesium milligrams	31	Pantothenic acid milligrams	–
		Biotin micrograms	–

(–) No information available   (0) Contains zero or trace amounts

Gooseberries

A member of the currant (*Ribes*) family, it is native to Europe and particularly popular in France and Britain. As mackerel is traditionally served with a gooseberry sauce in France; its French name is '*groseille à maquereau*'. Cooking gooseberries contain less sugar than the dessert variety, about 3 grams per 100 grams. Gooseberries are a good source of **vitamin C**, which is not lost on cooking and canning due to their high acidity.

Average nutrients in 100 grams (3½ oz) Gooseberries

	dessert	stewed with sugar		dessert	stewed with sugar
Energy kilojoules	157	215	Iron milligrams	0.6	0.2
kilocalories	37	50	Copper milligrams	0.15	0.10
Protein grams	0.6	0.9	Zinc milligrams	0.1	0.1
Total fat grams	0	0	Vitamin A micrograms	30	23
Saturated fat grams	0	0	Vitamin D micrograms	0	0
Polyunsaturated fat grams	0	0	Vitamin C milligrams	25-50	28
			Vitamin E milligrams	0.4	0.3
Cholesterol milligrams	0	0	B vitamins:		
Sugars grams	9.2	12.5	Thiamin (B$_1$) milligrams	0.04	0.03
Starch grams	0	0	Riboflavin (B$_2$) milligrams	0.03	0.02
Dietary fibre grams	3.5	2.5	Nicotinic acid milligrams	0.4	0.3
Sodium milligrams	1	2	Pyridoxine (B$_6$) milligrams	0.02	0.02
Potassium milligrams	170	160	Vitamin B$_{12}$ micrograms	0	–
Calcium milligrams	19	22	Folic acid micrograms	–	–
Magnesium milligrams	9	5	Pantothenic acid milligrams	0.30	0.11
			Biotin micrograms	0.1	0.4

(–) No information available   (0) Contains zero or trace amounts

Gout

Gout is a form of arthritis, caused by deposition of uric acid crystals in joints. There is a marked familial tendency to gout, and it is most common in middle aged men.

Uric acid is a waste product, continually made in the body and filtered out of the blood stream by the kidneys. Its precursors – purines – are components of the nucleic acids (DNA and RNA) which form the genetic code in cells. Nearly all foods contain some purine, but the body also manufactures it from **amino acids** using **folic acid** (which is a co**Enzyme**).

In many people (about 3 in every 100 in Britain), uric acid tends to accumulate resulting in a raised level in the blood stream. Few of those with a raised level of uric acid in the blood stream – only about 3 in every 1000 in Britain – actually develop gout. The disorder is exacerbated by a diet rich in meat and fats, and excessive alcohol. Occasionally gout is a side effect of other medical conditions.

A typical first attack manifests itself as an excruciating pain in the big toe. This is the joint most subjected to stress (from shoes), but other joints – though not the spine – can be affected. The joint is swollen and tender for a few days, but eventually the pain passes off. There is usually a long remission, but if not treated the attacks – accompanied by fever, misery, irritability, and disinclination to eat – become more frequent. In severe gout, lumps of uric acid crystals (tophi) appear in the skin.

Gout is treated by drugs, but diet is important in reducing the frequency of attacks. The majority of gout sufferers are overweight. A well balanced **slimming diet** can reduce the blood level of uric acid, and, with a reduction in weight, the stress on foot and leg joints is minimised.

Once weight has been reduced, the diet can be normal, but heavy meals, excessive **fat** and – when medically advised – foods rich in purines (see table) and large helpings of meat should be avoided. All alcoholic drinks raise the blood uric acid level: in severe gout alcohol may have to be omitted entirely. Fasting and excessive **fructose** are two other factors which can precipitate an attack and high fat, **carbohydrate** free diets are particularly harmful. Tea and coffee consumption can be normal: **caffeine** (although it is a purine) is not converted to uric acid.

Uric acid crystals tend to precipitate in the urine of gout sufferers and people with a high blood uric acid level, increasing the risk of kidney stones and possible kidney failure. The urine should be kept dilute: at least 4 pints of non alcoholic beverages – and more in hot working conditions – should be taken. See slimming diets for low energy drinks list.

Gout is to some extent inherited. Three quarters of sufferers have a family history and one quarter of near male relatives have a raised blood uric acid. It is probably an advantage for male relatives of gout sufferers to seek medical advice because a high blood uric acid is probably a risk factor in **heart disease**. Women, whose hormones exert a protective effect, are rarely affected by gout before the menopause.

Foods rich in purines

Offals	sweetbreads, liver, kidney, heart
Yeast	and yeast extracts
Roes	cod roe, caviar, herring roe, taramasalata
Fish	anchovies, whitebait, sprats, herrings, mackerel, salmon, sardines, mussels, scallops
Meat	partridge, guinea fowl, meat extracts (for instance Bovril), (other meats contain moderate quantities)

Grapefruit, see also **fruit juices**

Grapefruit is one of the most important citrus fruits thought to have originated outside Asia. It may have arisen as a 'sport' in the West Indies and only attained worldwide popularity within the past 100 years. Like all citrus fruits it contains **citric acid**, and is a reliable source of **vitamin C** (see table).

Average nutrients in 100 grams (3½ oz) Grapefruit

	fresh	canned with sugar		fresh	canned with sugar
Energy kilojoules	95	257	Iron milligrams	0.3	0.7
kilocalories	22	60	Copper milligrams	0.06	0.03

Protein grams	0.6	0.5 -	Zinc milligrams	0.1	0.4
Total fat grams	0	0	Vitamin A micrograms	0	0
Saturated fat grams	0	0	Vitamin D micrograms	0	0
Polyunsaturated fat grams	0	0	Vitamin C milligrams	35–45	30
			Vitamin E milligrams	0.3	0
Cholesterol milligrams	0	0	B vitamins:		
Sugars grams	5.3	15.5	Thiamin (B$_1$) milligrams	0.05	0.04
Starch grams	0	0	Riboflavin (B$_2$) milligrams	0.02	0.01
Dietary fibre grams	0.6	0.4	Nicotinic acid milligrams	0.3	0.3
Sodium milligrams	1	10	Pyridoxine (B$_6$) milligrams	0.03	0.02
Potassium milligrams	230	79	Vitamin B$_{12}$ micrograms	0	0
Calcium milligrams	17	17	Folic acid micrograms	12	4
Magnesium milligrams	10	7	Pantothenic acid milligrams	0.28	0.12
			Biotin micrograms	1.0	1.0

(–) No information available   (0) Contains zero or trace amounts

Grapes

Grapes have one of the highest sugar contents of the fruits, chiefly **glucose** and **fructose**; although differences in the amount and type of sugars will affect their taste. The grapevine is one of the oldest cultivated plants, having been known to the Egyptians about 6000 years ago. It probably originated in western Asia. There is little difference in the average nutritional composition of black and white dessert grapes (see table). The colour is due to the presence of anthocyanins. There are slight differences in the chemical composition of these in European grapes compared with those grown elsewhere and this can be used to prove whether wine is of European origin or not.

Average nutrients in 100 grams (3½ oz) Dessert Grapes

	black	white		black	white
Energy kilojoules	258	268	Iron milligrams	0.3	0.3
kilocalories	61	63	Copper milligrams	0.08	0.10
Protein grams	0.6	0.6	Zinc milligrams	0.1	0.1
Total fat grams	0	0	Vitamin A micrograms	0	0
Saturated fat grams	0	0	Vitamin D micrograms	0	0
Polyunsaturated fat grams	0	0	Vitamin C milligrams	4	4
			Vitamin E milligrams	–	–
Cholesterol milligrams	0	0	B vitamins:		
Sugars grams	15.5	16.1	Thiamin (B$_1$) milligrams	0.04	0.04
Starch grams	0	0	Riboflavin (B$_2$) milligrams	0.02	0.02
Dietary fibre grams	0.4	0.9	Nicotinic acid milligrams	0.3	0.3
Sodium milligrams	2	2	Pyridoxine (B$_6$) milligrams	0.10	0.10
Potassium milligrams	320	250	Vitamin B$_{12}$ micrograms	0	0
Calcium milligrams	4	19	Folic acid micrograms	6	6
Magnesium milligrams	4	7	Pantothenic acid milligrams	0.05	0.05
			Biotin micrograms	0.3	0.3

(–) No information available   (0) Contains zero or trace amounts

Gravy – and sauces

Gravy and sauces can be an opportunity to recover **minerals** and some water soluble **vitamins** leached out of food cooked in **water** or stock.

Heat sensitive water soluble vitamins (like vitamin C and B_1 (thiamin) are largely destroyed in the cooking liquor, especially if cooking is prolonged. Heat stable B vitamins and minerals are recoverable: in boiled or simmered meat and fish up to half the **riboflavin** (vitamin B_2) and nearly all the **nicotinic acid** leached out remains in the liquor.

Greengages

Greengages are a member of the *Prunus* genus, which includes plums, cherries, peaches etc. They were reintroduced into England in 1725 by Sir Thomas Gage, although they may have been cultivated in earlier times. The plums contain very little vitamin C (see table).

Average nutrients in 100 grams (3½ oz) Greengages (stewed with sugar)

Energy kilojoules	321	Iron milligrams	0.3
kilocalories	75	Copper milligrams	0.06
Protein grams	0.6	Zinc milligrams	0.1
Total fat grams	0	Vitamin A micrograms	–
Saturated fat grams	0	Vitamin D micrograms	0
Polyunsaturated fat grams	0	Vitamin C milligrams	2
		Vitamin E milligrams	0.5
Cholesterol milligrams	0	B vitamins:	
Sugars grams	19.2	Thiamin (B_1) milligrams	0.04
Starch grams	0	Riboflavin (B_2) milligrams	0.02
Dietary fibre (NSP) grams	2.1	Nicotinic acid milligrams	0.4
Sodium milligrams	1	Pyridoxine (B_6) milligrams	0.03
Potassium milligrams	240	Vitamin B_{12} micrograms	0
Calcium milligrams	13	Folic acid micrograms	1
Magnesium milligrams	5	Pantothenic acid milligrams	0.14
		Biotin micrograms	0

(–) No information available   (0) Contains zero or trace amounts

Grouse

A high protein, low **fat** game bird with a good ratio of polyunsaturated to saturated **fatty acids** (see table). It is rich in well-absorbed **iron**, but few other nutritional analyses are available.

Average nutrients in 100 grams (3½ oz) Grouse (roast)

Energy kilojoules	728	Iron milligrams	7.6
kilocalories	173	Copper milligrams	–
Protein grams	31.3	Zinc milligrams	–
Total fat grams	5.3	Vitamin A micrograms	–
Saturated fat grams	1.2	Vitamin D micrograms	–
Polyunsaturated fat grams	3.1	Vitamin C milligrams	–
		Vitamin E milligrams	–
Cholesterol milligrams	–	B vitamins:	

Sugars grams	0	Thiamin (B$_1$) milligrams	–
Starch grams	0	Riboflavin (B$_2$) milligrams	–
Dietary fibre grams	0	Nicotinic acid milligrams	–
Sodium milligrams	96	Pyridoxine (B$_6$) milligrams	–
Potassium milligrams	470	Vitamin B$_{12}$ micrograms	–
Calcium milligrams	30	Folic acid micrograms	–
Magnesium milligrams	41	Pantothenic acid milligrams	–
		Biotin micrograms	–

(–) No information available   (0) Contains zero or trace amounts

Guava

A tropical American fruit, with a remarkably high content of **vitamin C**. Canned guavas contain 180 milligrams per 100 grams. Raw guavas contain about 200 milligrams, but the value may range from 20 to 600 milligrams per 100 grams.

Average nutrients in 100 grams (3½ oz) Guava (canned)

Energy kilojoules	258	Iron milligrams	0.5
kilocalories	60	Copper milligrams	0.10
Protein grams	0	Zinc milligrams	0.4
Total fat grams	0	Vitamin A micrograms	17
Saturated fat grams	0	Vitamin D micrograms	0
Polyunsaturated fat grams	0	Vitamin C milligrams	180
		Vitamin E milligrams	–
Cholesterol milligrams	0	B vitamins:	
Sugars grams	15.7	Thiamin (B$_1$) milligrams	0.04
Starch grams	0	Riboflavin (B$_2$) milligrams	0.03
Dietary fibre grams	3.6	Nicotinic acid milligrams	1.0
Sodium milligrams	7	Pyridoxine (B$_6$) milligrams	–
Potassium milligrams	120	Vitamin B$_{12}$ micrograms	0
Calcium milligrams	8	Folic acid micrograms	–
Magnesium milligrams	6	Pantothenic acid milligrams	–
		Biotin micrograms	–

(–) No information available   (0) Contains zero or trace amounts

Haddock and halibut

Haddock and halibut are classified as white fish, although halibut contains some fat – about as much as chicken meat. Smoked haddock is very similar to fresh, apart from the added **salt**. Smoked haddock also contains added **colour** usually as **tartrazine** (E102) or quinoline yellow (E104). Traditional wood-smoking leads to the formation of known carcinogens (see **cancer**, **poisons in food**), and the colour can now be painted on in a 'liquid smoke' to give the appearance of the traditional process.

Average nutrients in 100 grams (3½ oz) Haddock and Halibut (steamed)

	haddock fresh	haddock smoked	halibut		haddock fresh	haddock smoked	halibut
Energy kilojoules	417	429	553	Iron milligrams	0.7	1.0	0.6
kilocalories	98	101	131	Copper milligrams	0.13	–	0.07
Protein grams	22.8	23.3	23.8	Zinc milligrams	0.4	–	–
Total fat grams	0.8	0.9	4.0	Vitamin A micrograms	0	0	0[a]
Saturated fat grams	0.1	0.2	0.4	Vitamin D micrograms	0	0	0[a]
Polyunsaturated fat grams	0.3	0.3	1.4	Vitamin C milligrams	0	0	0
				Vitamin E milligrams	–	–	1.0
Cholesterol milligrams	75	75	60	B vitamins:			
Sugars grams	0	0	0	Thiamin (B_1) milligrams	0.08	0.10	0.08
Starch grams	0	0	0	Riboflavin (B_2) milligrams	0.13	0.11	0.11
Dietary fibre grams	0	0	0	Nicotinic acid milligrams	9.4	6.1	9.6
Sodium milligrams	120	1220	110	Pyridoxine (B_6) milligrams	0.25	0.35	0.23
Potassium milligrams	320	290	340	Vitamin B_{12} micrograms	1	3	1
Calcium milligrams	55	58	13	Folic acid micrograms	16	5	14
Magnesium milligrams	28	25	23	Pantothenic acid milligrams	0.20	0.20	0.28
				Biotin micrograms	6	3	5

(–) No information available   (0) Contains zero or trace amounts

[a] Depends on type – Atlantic contains none but Pacific may contain 120 micrograms vitamin A, and 1 microgram vitamin D.

Ham, see also meat

The **energy** (Calorie) content of ham depends on whether it is eaten canned, or cooked from a gammon joint, and on the amount of **fat** eaten with it. A fatty cut (20% fat) contains 1119 kilojoules (269 kilocalories) per 100 grams, whereas lean ham contains about half this amount. Canned ham contains 10–20% more water than home-cooked ham, hence it is lower in energy and some nutrients (see table). Ham contains a lot of salt, but it is a good source of **vitamin B_1**. To reduce the risk of nitrosamine formation from the added **nitrite**, vitamin C (E300–304) is used in the curing of some brands of canned ham, hence ham may be an unsuspected source of this vitamin.

Average nutrients in 100 grams (3½ oz) Ham (boiled and canned)

	gammon lean	gammon with fat	ham canned		gammon lean	gammon with fat	ham canned
Energy kilojoules	703	119	502	Iron milligrams	1.5	1.3	1.2
kilocalories	167	269	120	Copper milligrams	0.2	0.1	0.2
Protein grams	29.4	24.7	18.4	Zinc milligrams	3.3	2.7	2.3
Total fat grams	5.5	18.9	5.1	Vitamin A micrograms	0	0	0
Saturated fat grams	2.2	7.6	1.9	Vitamin D micrograms	0	0	0
Polyunsaturated fat grams	0.4	1.4	0.5	Vitamin C milligrams	0	0	0[a]
				Vitamin E milligrams	0.05	0.11	0.08
Cholesterol milligrams	–	–	33	B vitamins:			
Sugars grams	0	0	0	Thiamin (B$_1$) milligrams	0.55	0.44	0.52
Starch grams	0	0	0	Riboflavin (B$_2$) milligrams	0.19	0.15	0.25
Dietary fibre grams	0	0	0	Nicotinic acid milligrams	9.7	8.0	6.9
Sodium milligrams	1110	960	1250	Pyridoxine (B$_6$) milligrams	0.33	0.26	0.22
Potassium milligrams	250	210	280	Vitamin B$_{12}$ micrograms	0	0	0
Calcium milligrams	10	9	9	Folic acid micrograms	1	0	0
Magnesium milligrams	21	18	18	Pantothenic acid			
				milligrams	0.5	0.4	0.6
				Biotin micrograms	3	2	1

(–) No information available   (0) Contains zero or trace amounts

[a]May contain 12 – 60 milligrams

Hare

Hares were domesticated for food by the Romans. The ancient Egyptians also probably used hare as food; they are depicted for example in the tombs of Harembob, Thebes, about 1420 BC. Wild hare has dark flesh and it is consequently a rich source of well-absorbed **iron**. Although not as commonly eaten today as other game, needing long, slow cooking t tenderise the meat, hare used to be very popular. *Larousse* lists over 20 recipes.

Average nutrients in 100 grams (3½ oz) Hare (stewed)

Energy kilojoules	804	Iron milligrams	10.8
kilocalories	192	Copper milligrams	–
Protein grams	29.9	Zinc milligrams	–
Total fat grams	8.0	Vitamin A micrograms	–
Saturated fat grams	3.3	Vitamin D micrograms	–
Polyunsaturated fat grams	2.6	Vitamin C milligrams	–
		Vitamin E milligrams	–
Cholesterol milligrams	–	B vitamins:	
Sugars grams	0	Thiamin (B$_1$) milligrams	–
Starch grams	0	Riboflavin (B$_2$) milligrams	–
Dietary fibre grams	0	Nicotinic acid milligrams	–
Sodium milligrams	40	Pyridoxine (B$_6$) milligrams	–
Potassium milligrams	210	Vitamin B$_{12}$ micrograms	–
Calcium milligrams	21	Folic acid micrograms	–
Magnesium milligrams	22	Pantothenic acid milligrams	–
		Biotin micrograms	–

(–) No information available   (0) Contains zero or trace amounts

Hazel (cob) nuts

Over a third of the weight of hazel nuts is **fat** (see table) so that if ground or well-chewed, hazel nuts are high in **energy** (Calories). They are also a rich source of **vitamin E**, and a good source of most B vitamins, except B_{12}.

Average nutrients in 100 grams (3½ oz) Hazel nuts

Energy kilojoules	1570	Iron milligrams	1.1
kilocalories	380	Copper milligrams	0.2
Protein grams	7.6	Zinc milligrams	2.4
Total fat grams	36.0	Vitamin A micrograms	0
Saturated fat grams	2.6	Vitamin D micrograms	0
Polyunsaturated fat grams	3.8	Vitamin C milligrams	0
		Vitamin E milligrams	21.0
Cholesterol milligrams	0	B vitamins:	
Sugars grams	4.7	Thiamin (B_1) milligrams	0.40
Starch grams	2.1	Riboflavin (B_2) milligrams	–
Dietary fibre grams	6.1	Nicotinic acid milligrams	3.1
Sodium milligrams	1	Pyridoxine (B_6) milligrams	0.55
Potassium milligrams	350	Vitamin B_{12} micrograms	0
Calcium milligrams	44	Folic acid micrograms	72
Magnesium milligrams	56	Pantothenic acid milligrams	1.15
		Biotin micrograms	–

(–) No information available   (0) Contains zero or trace amounts

Health foods

Strictly, any wholesome food containing a balanced proportion of essential **nutrients** and little fat and sugar is a health food, but it is generally accepted that health foods mean those sold in health food shops. They include **organic foods** and wholefoods. Wholefoods are sometimes described as being 'natural' and in general they are unprocessed and contain no food **additives**. Wholefoods include a wide variety of unusual nuts, cereals and grains, and by providing outlets for these, some health food shops have influenced diet for the better. Nuts, wholegrain cereals, peas and beans are tasty, nutritious and comparatively inexpensive foods. Cooperative wholefood stores are generally excellent value for money.

On the other hand, some health food shops are very expensive and mislead consumers over what is 'natural' as much as the large food processor. The 'natural' function of food is not that it should be eaten by man but that it should grow, reproduce, die and decay. Natural foods are not therefore necessarily safer or purer and contain many toxic factors – see **poisons in food**.

Some health food shops are also outlets for various pills, tonics, and 'miracle' foods claimed to prolong life and improve vitality. Miracle foods include **yeast** and wheat germ which are rich in vitamins and minerals, and **honey**. Products with misleading claims for cures and systems with no basis in fact may also be sold. These include cider vinegar for slimming, vitamins A and B_2 for cataracts, vitamin E for impotence, magnesium for epileptic fits, calcium for bad temper and vitamins A and D for asthma and acne. Health food shops lay themselves open to well founded criticism by allowing consumers to be misled in this way.

Heart

Like most offal, heart is rich in **iron, protein** and B **vitamins**. It is a particularly good source of **vitamin B₁₂**, and also contains some vitamin C – unusual for a meat product. It contains rather more **cholesterol** than other meats.

Average nutrients in 100 grams (3½ oz) Heart

	roast sheep's	stewed ox		roast sheep's	stewed ox
Energy kilojoules	988	752	Iron milligrams	8.1	7.7
kilocalories	237	179	Copper milligrams	–	0.7
Protein grams	26.1	31.4	Zinc milligrams	–	3.5
Total fat grams	14.7	5.9	Vitamin A micrograms	0	0
Saturated fat grams	5.7	2.9	Vitamin D micrograms	0	0
Polyunsaturated fat grams	1.4	0.2	Vitamin C milligrams	11	6
			Vitamin E milligrams	0.7	0.7
Cholesterol milligrams	260	230	B vitamins:		
Sugars grams	0	0	Thiamin (B₁) milligrams	0.45	0.21
Starch grams	0	0	Riboflavin (B₂) milligrams	1.5	1.1
Dietary fibre grams	0	0	Nicotinic acid milligrams	14.7	11.4
Sodium milligrams	150	180	Pyridoxine (B₆) milligrams	0.38	0.11
Potassium milligrams	370	210	Vitamin B₁₂ micrograms	14	15
Calcium milligrams	10	7	Folic acid micrograms	4	2
Magnesium milligrams	35	29	Pantothenic acid milligrams	3.8	1.6
			Biotin micrograms	8	4

(–) No information available   (0) Contains zero or trace amounts

Heart disease

Ischaemic heart disease (IHD) is the commonest cause of death in the United Kingdom. In recent years, countries such as the USA, Canada, Australia, New Zealand and Belgium have had a dramatic fall in the death rates for IHD, leaving the UK almost at the top of the league, second only to Finland. It is almost invariably caused by coronary artery disease, brought about by **atherosclerosis**, a contributor to **stroke**. These two diseases account for 40 out of every 100 deaths in the UK. Other names that mean or imply IHD are coronary heart disease (CHD), coronary thrombosis, heart attack or myocardial infarction.

The heart is a hollow muscle, nourished by **nutrients** and oxygen carried in the blood stream which circulates through a network of coronary arteries and veins. The coronary arteries are very susceptible to atherosclerosis: they become partially obstructed by fatty and fibrous material, and the muscle below the obstruction becomes deprived of oxygen (ischaemia). The resulting pain (angina) occurs especially during exercise and passes off after a rest. Eventually the obstruction – or, more frequently a blood clot (thrombus) – may occlude the artery completely. Unless blood from another artery is diverted to the ischaemic area, the cells below the obstruction die (myocardial infarction). Large areas of dead muscle can stop the heart altogether, but smaller areas are eventually healed by scar tissue. Minor heart attacks may pass unnoticed. Scar tissue cannot contract, consequently the extensively scarred heart is unable to cope with undue exertion.

There are widely differing rates of death from IHD in different parts of the world. Evidence that these are due to factors associated with lifestyle comes from the fact that when people born in a low risk area migrate to a high risk area, they eventually become as prone to IHD as the host population. Of the many lifestyle factors that could be important, diet seems to be the most strongly associated with death rates. Worldwide comparisons between one population and another show that death rates from IHD are most strongly associated with the average **fat** content of the diet and with the average blood **cholesterol**. Rates for IHD, fat intake, and blood cholesterol levels are all low in Japan for example, and vice versa in Britain. Other evidence has shown that blood cholesterol may be reduced by a diet low in saturated **fatty acids**, or by increasing the level of polyunsaturated fats, and that diseased arteries with atherosclerosis contain 5 – 10 times more cholesterol than healthy ones.

The missing link is that *within* any one population it has not been possible to show that individuals with a high fat diet either have a consistently higher blood cholesterol, or that these people are noticeably more likely to develop heart disease, despite numerous attempts to do so. This is why some authorities, particularly in Britain, have been slow to emphasise the importance of reducing fat in the diet.

The reason for this is that there are a number of other risk factors involved, in addition to a high blood cholesterol, which affect an *individual's* likelihood of succumbing to IHD. Another is that it is exceedingly difficult to measure the fat contents of diets eaten by individuals over the necessary long periods of time.

The two other main risk factors are a high blood pressure and smoking habit. Somebody who smokes, has a high blood pressure and a high blood cholesterol has a much greater risk of heart disease than others. Also, the level of blood cholesterol is to a large extent under genetic control (see **lipids**) and within any one high risk population, some individuals are able to cope with a high fat diet better than others. The long chain **essential fatty acids** which arise from the α linolenic acid class also seem to confer some protection by virtue of the fact that they are precursors of the factors which delay the tendency of the blood to clot.

Nevertheless, removal of the causative factors – smoking, high fat diets and high blood pressure – reduces the risk of everyone in that population to a greater or lesser extent. Some people will still be susceptible to even lower levels of fat, but the *numbers* of people at risk in that population will be reduced. The individual who decides to limit fat intake, stop smoking and reduce blood pressure if necessary is therefore to some extent troubleshooting. This is particularly worthwhile if a close relative suffers from IHD because of the fact that the way in which cholesterol is handled in the body is to some extent inherited. People who have a family history of heart trouble are well advised to ask for a blood cholesterol check up from their doctor. Reducing the fat content of the whole family's diet is particularly important because atherosclerosis is a progressive disease which begins in childhood.

Ways in which fat may be reduced are set out in the section on fat. Children under the age of five should not be given skimmed milk except under medical advice. High blood pressure is also amenable to diet. It is particularly common in people who are overweight (obese) and heart disease mortality for example is 30% greater in younger men who are only 10% above their ideal **body weight**. Cutting down on **salt** may also be important.

In women, IHD is six times less common than in men up to the menopause; but there are other good reasons, for instance breast **cancer** and obesity, why women should also cut down on fat.

Several other dietary factors may have an influence on IHD, though none are as generally important as fat, smoking, and high blood pressure. These are dietary **fibre, trace elements** and some **vitamins**. The levels of these can be improved by cutting down on high fat diets and eating more wholegrain cereals and fresh vegetables. The risks also increase with increasing age, particularly in people with a tendency to **gout** or **diabetes**, which are also related to being overweight.

Too little exercise (see **energy**) is also very important, partly because obesity is more likely and because a successful recovery from a heart attack is less likely in unfit individuals. Endomorphs who have a short broad shape are also at greater risk than tall thin individuals (ectomorphs), as are highly competitive people who subject themselves to greater stress. Some of this aggressiveness is best diverted into a planned schedule of regular strenuous exercise, leading to an average of for example 20 minutes swimming, jogging or running each day. Sudden strenuous exercise in unfit people must however be avoided, by both the middle aged and elderly, otherwise a heart attack might be precipitated.

Heat in foods

All other things being equal, hot foods contain slightly more **energy** than cold ones. When hot foods (approximate temperature 60°C) are eaten, they cool to normal body temperature (37°C), transferring their heat to the body. Heat is measured in kilo**calories**.

For instance, a hot mug of tea cools down 23°C (from 60°C to 37°C), and has a volume of about ½ pint (300 ml). Since 1 litre of water releases 1 kilocalorie when it cools by 1°C (see calories), the energy given off by the tea is $\frac{23 \times 300}{1,000}$ which is equal to 7 kilocalories.

Herbs

Herbs are usually leaves of plants containing aromatic oils. Small quantities added during cooking enhance and impart **flavour** to savoury foods, stimulating appetite.

Herbs have a similar nutritive value to other green **vegetables**, but as such small amounts are needed their contribution to the average intake of **nutrients** is usually negligible. Parsley however, can be used more generously: 2 teaspoons (2 grams), freshly chopped, sprinkled onto a portion of food contains an average of 3 milligrams of vitamin C and 70 microgram equivalents of vitamin A – about one tenth of the adult daily **recommended intake** for these nutrients.

Vitamin C rapidly declines after chopping and pounding. Dried herbs that have lost their colour will also have lost their vitamin A and C.

Herring

Herrings have long been recommended as a nutritious food. They are rich in **vitamins D**, and **B₁₂** and **protein**. The fat content varies according to season, as does the **vitamin A** and **D** content; highest values being found in late summer, lowest in the spring. Herrings also contain well absorbed **iron** and **zinc**.

Herrings and other fatty fish have attracted more recent attention because of their relatively high content of long-chain **essential fatty acids**, such as eicosa-pentanenoic acid (EPA). These reduce the tendency of the blood to clot and may be important in lessening the risk of **stroke** or **heart disease**.

Average nutrients in 100 grams (3½ oz) Herring (grilled)

Energy kilojoules	828	Iron milligrams	1.0
kilocalories	199	Copper milligrams	0.1
Protein grams	20.4	Zinc milligrams	0.5
Total fat grams	5–20	Vitamin A micrograms	6–120
Saturated fat grams	2.6	Vitamin D micrograms	7–42
Polyunsaturated fat grams	2.3	Vitamin C milligrams	0
		Vitamin E milligrams	0.3
Cholesterol milligrams	80	B vitamins:	
Sugars grams	0	Thiamin (B₁) milligrams	0
Starch grams	0	Riboflavin (B₂) milligrams	0.18
Dietary fibre grams	0	Nicotinic acid milligrams	7.8
Sodium milligrams	170	Pyridoxine (B₆) milligrams	0.57
Potassium milligrams	370	Vitamin B₁₂ micrograms	11
Calcium milligrams	33	Folic acid micrograms	10
Magnesium milligrams	32	Pantothenic acid milligrams	0.88
		Biotin micrograms	10

(–) No information available   (0) Contains zero or trace amounts

Histamine

Histamine is formed from **histidine** and is released from tissues of the body following injury. It increases the permeability of small blood vessels, allowing white blood cells to penetrate the damaged area and limit the infection or intrusion. It is responsible for some of the inflammatory reaction in **allergy** for example in **urticaria**.

Some foods, such as shellfish and strawberries can provoke histamine release in susceptible people and it is also formed by bacteria when some foods are fermented or stored badly; old cheese for example contains large amounts of histamine and it is also found in sauerkraut, pepperoni and salami. Canned or badly smoked unrefrigerated fish, particularly mackerel which contains a lot of histidine, have sometimes caused poisoning from their high content of his-tamine. Some cheaper red wines contain substantial amounts of histamine which may contribute to the after effects of **alcohol**.

Histidine

Histidine is a semi-essential **amino acid**. Children do not grow if it is absent from their diet, but adults can probably synthesise enough for their daily needs. It is found in all food proteins, and amounts eaten in excess of needs are converted to **glucose** and used for **energy** purposes. The **nitrogen** part is converted to urea, later filtered out of the blood stream by the kidneys.

Like all other amino acids, histidine is needed to make new body proteins for growth and repair. It is also the precursor of **histamine**.

Honey

Almost all primitive and ancient civilised societies the world over have relied on honey as a food, preservative and sweetener. The fact that milk and honey were frequently mentioned as offerings to gods, and that they often occur in myth and religious rites, indicates their importance to ancient civilisations. Some of this mystery surrounding honey has survived into modern times.

On average, 10 grams (1 teaspoon) of honey contains about 4 grams of **fructose**, 3 grams of **glucose**, 1½ grams of water, and 1 gram of **sucrose**. It also has small quantities of **dextrins, maltose,** wax, and **protein**. There is pollen in comb honey, but it is usually strained off from blended varieties. **Colour** and **flavour** in different honeys are due to pigments and flavours from the nectar of flowers visited by bees.

Honey is sweeter than sugar (sucrose), because it contains fructose, and lower in energy, because of its water content. For the same sweetness, honey supplies less energy and it is therefore preferable to sugar for people living sedentary lives.

Sweetness apart, honey contains only minimal quantities of **minerals** and **vitamins** and compared with other foods has no special nutritional benefits. Honeycomb and honey in jars differ little in their content (see table).

Average nutrients in 100 grams (3½ oz) Honey

	comb	in jars		comb	in jars
Energy kilojoules	1201	1229	Iron milligrams	0.2	0.4
kilocalories	281	288	Copper milligrams	0.04	0.05
Protein grams	0.6	0.4	Zinc milligrams	–	–
Total fat grams	0	0	Vitamin A micrograms	0	0
Saturated fat grams	0	0	Vitamin D micrograms	0	0
Polyunsaturated fat grams	0	0	Vitamin C milligrams	0	0
			Vitamin E milligrams	–	
Cholesterol milligrams	0	0	B vitamins:		
Sugars grams	74.4	76.4	Thiamin (B₁) milligrams	0	0
Starch grams	0	0	Riboflavin (B₂) milligrams	0.05	0.05
Dietary fibre grams	0	0	Nicotinic acid milligrams	0.2	0.2
Sodium milligrams	7	11	Pyridoxine (B₆) milligrams	–	–
Potassium milligrams	35	51	Vitamin B₁₂ micrograms	0	0
Calcium milligrams	8	5	Folic acid micrograms	–	–
Magnesium milligrams	2	2	Pantothenic acid milligrams	–	–
			Biotin micrograms	–	–

(–) No information available   (0) Contains zero or trace amounts

Hummus

A spread, made from chick peas (see **peas**), onion and oil. The available information is shown in the table.

Average nutrients in 100 grams (3½ oz) Hummus

Energy kilojoules	773	Iron milligrams	1.9
kilocalories	185	Copper milligrams	0.3
Protein grams	7.6	Zinc milligrams	1.4
Total fat grams	12.6	Vitamin A micrograms	–
Saturated fat grams	–	Vitamin D micrograms	0
Polyunsaturated fat grams	–	Vitamin C milligrams	1
		Vitamin E milligrams	–
Cholesterol milligrams	–	B vitamins:	
Sugars grams	} 11.1	Thiamin (B$_1$) milligrams	0.16
Starch grams		Riboflavin (B$_2$) milligrams	0.05
Dietary fibre grams	–	Nicotinic acid milligrams	–
Sodium milligrams	665	Pyridoxine (B$_6$) milligrams	–
Potassium milligrams	195	Vitamin B$_{12}$ micrograms	0
Calcium milligrams	41	Folic acid micrograms	–
Magnesium milligrams	62	Pantothenic acid milligrams	–
		Biotin micrograms	–

(–) No information available   (0) Contains zero or trace amounts

Hydrolysed protein

Hydrolysed protein is animal or vegetable protein partially split to its constituent **amino acids**. It is used to give a meaty **flavour** to food, or as a flavour enhancer, often with **monosodium glutamate**.

Hyperactivity

An excessive level of restlessness and inattentiveness in children, resulting in underachievement at school and disruptive behaviour. Some studies suggest that hyperactive children become a troubled group, more vulnerable to alcohol or drug abuse in early adult life. Estimates of hyperactivity are 3–10% in schools in the USA but much lower in Britain.

In 1973, Feingold suggested that artificial colourings and flavours in food were a cause of hyperactivity in the USA and that treatment with the 'Feingold diet' would restore the child to normal behaviour. The diet involves elimination of all foods containing artificial colours, preservatives and other **additives** and, initially, those containing natural **salicylates**. Because of the potential importance of this suggestion, many controlled trials have been held in an attempt to verify it – but so far with little success. Two recent American reports from the National Institutes of Health and the American Council on Science and Health, concluded that there was no evidence that the behaviour of hyperactive children improved with the Feingold diet in particular. However, both the mental and physical health of children will benefit from food that is prepared for them with tender loving care – as has to be the case with the Feingold diet.

Hypoglycaemia

Hypoglycaemia is a very low blood sugar associated with hunger, sweating, headache, vague feelings of ill–health and occasionally bizarre and aggressive behaviour. It is important in **diabetes**. In healthy adults it is possible to provoke hypoglycaemia by giving a large dose of **glucose** after a fast of several hours and it sometimes occurs after excessive drinking with little food, see **alcohol**. However the suggestion that it causes **hyperactivity** in children and aggressive behaviour in adults and is a result of eating 'junk' foods high in sugar is controversial. Nevertheless, there are good reasons for avoiding large amounts of sugar rich foods; see **sugar**.

Ice cream

Ice cream is a mixture of milk, **fat, sugar, emulsifiers, flavours** and **colour**. Except for dairy ice cream, commercial varieties do not contain cream. Legally, ice cream must have a minimum of 5% fat, which is usually hardened vegetable **oil** (see **margarine**), containing **antioxidants**. About half the volume of ice cream is air, and half its weight water. It contains less fat than cream, but **yogurt** is a better topping for desserts.

Average nutrients in 100 grams (3½ oz) Ice cream

	dairy	non-dairy		dairy	non-dairy
Energy kilojoules	704	691	Iron milligrams	0.2	0.3
kilocalories	167	165	Copper milligrams	0.03	0.03
Protein grams	3.7	3.3	Zinc milligrams	0.4	0.4
Total fat grams	6.6	8.2	Vitamin A micrograms	14	–
Saturated fat grams	4.3	4.2	Vitamin D micrograms	0	0
Polyunsaturated fat grams	0.2	0.6	Vitamin C milligrams	0	0
			Vitamin E milligrams	0.4	1.2
Cholesterol milligrams	21	11	B vitamins:		
Sugars grams	22.6	19.7	Thiamin (B_1) milligrams	0.04	0.04
Starch grams	2.2	1.0	Riboflavin (B_2) milligrams	0.18	0.15
Dietary fibre grams	–	–	Nicotinic acid milligrams	1.0	0.9
Sodium milligrams	80	70	Pyridoxine (B_6) milligrams	0.02	0.02
Potassium milligrams	180	150	Vitamin B_{12} micrograms	0	0
Calcium milligrams	140	120	Folic acid micrograms	2	2
Magnesium milligrams	13	11	Pantothenic acid milligrams	–	–
			Biotin micrograms	–	–

(–) No information available   (0) Contains zero or trace amounts

Inborn errors of metabolism

This term applies to very rare inherited defects affecting the synthesis of a specific **protein** – usually an **enzyme** – in the body. Over two hundred different defects are known, and most result in disease early in life. Some involving an enzyme are treated with special diets – which may need to be synthetic. See also **malabsorption**.

In **metabolism**, complex body constituents are built up and broken down by specific sequences of chemical reactions (metabolic pathways). Each chemical reaction is controlled by an enzyme. If an enzyme is lacking (or ineffective) in a metabolic pathway, substances produced before it in the chain accumulate in the body; later products are missing. Depending on the enzyme, the defect may pass unnoticed or lead to damage of the brain, liver and other vital organs. Damage can either be caused by toxic intermediates or by deficiency of nutrients at the end of the pathway.

Some defects respond to massive doses of **vitamins** – particularly those in the B complex, which are co**Enzymes**. In others, damage can be avoided by giving a diet low in substances at the beginning of the metabolic pathway. Phenylketonuria and galactosaemia – occurring in about one in every 15,000 and 70,000 infants respectively in Britain – are the two commonest inborn errors of metabolism successfully treated by diet. See phenylalanine and galactose. With prompt detection and treatment, mental retardation can be avoided. All infants are screened for phenylketonuria in the first few days of life, and although national screening is expensive, the cost is amply justified by the numbers of children who would otherwise be confined to mental institutions.

Gout, diabetes, and some blood fat (**lipid**) disorders have a familial tendency.

Inositol – obsolete names, Bios I, inosite, meat sugar

Like **para amino benzoic acid**, and **choline**, inositol is sometimes classed as a B complex vitamin. However, although it is required for the multiplication of yeasts and growth of some animals, inositol is not thought to be an essential **nutrient** (and is therefore not a vitamin) for humans. No human deficiency has ever been discovered, and sufficient quantities for daily needs are presumed to be made in the body.

All diets contain some inositol. It is part of **phytic acid** and good sources are wholegrain cereals and wholemeal bread. It is also part of **phospholipids** found in vegetables and animal protein foods – particularly meat. Most people eat about 1 gram a day – more than the daily needs for most of the known vitamins.

Mice fed on inositol free diet lose their fur, but supplements of inositol do not prevent hair loss in humans.

Inulin

Inulin is a polysaccharide (polymer) of **fructose**, found in many plants – for instance artichokes, endive and salsify. It used to be the commercial source of fructose. Inulin is not broken down during **digestion** and, like **fibre**, is fermented by bacteria in the large bowel.

Invert sugar

This is a type of syrup, extensively used in the food industry. It contains equal quantities of **glucose** and **fructose** and is made when **sucrose** (sugar) is heated or treated with acid or **enzymes**. It also occurs naturally, for instance in **honey**.

Iodine

Iodine is an essential **trace element** needed by the thyroid gland for synthesis of thyroid hormones which regulate many diverse and important body processes. Dietary insufficiency results in goitre and, in children, cretinism.

The daily needs of iodine are uncertain, but adults may require an average of 100 micrograms per day. During pregnancy, breast feeding, infancy, childhood and adolescence, needs may be increased to 150 micrograms to ensure adequate supplies of thyroid hormones during growth.

Seafish and seaweed are the only reliable natural sources of iodine. Sea salt contains a little, but it is lost during storage. Other foods vary depending on the soil content of the area in which they were grown. The level of iodine in water is an indication of the iodine content of local diets, but drinking water itself contributes little.

Iodised salt contains added iodine, but a more important source is milk. In winter iodine is added to cattle feed to prevent goitre and stillbirth and about half of this is excreted in milk. As a result, winter milk contains substantial amounts, about 40 micrograms per 100 grams. In summer, when cattle are grazing, levels fall to about 5 micrograms.

Foods such as canned strawberries, red sweets and pink biscuits also may contain the food **colour** erythrosine (E127) which is over half iodine by weight. The average intake in Britain is therefore quite high, 250 micrograms per day.

During **digestion**, iodine is absorbed out of food and carried in the blood stream to the thyroid gland, where it is extracted. The gland stores about half the body content of iodine, and incorporates it into thyroid hormone. Throughout the day, thyroid hormone is secreted into the blood stream, taken up by cells, and inactivated after it has exerted its effect. Iodine is then released and most is filtered out of the blood stream by the kidneys and eliminated in the urine. If iodine losses are not replaced by iodine in food, the thyroid gland increases in size in an attempt to trap more iodine from the blood stream and maintain an adequate supply of thyroid hormone. The enlarged gland causes the neck to swell, a condition known as goitre. Small goitres may be a natural adaptation. If treated early by increasing the iodine content of the diet, the gland returns to its normal size of about 30 grams (1oz). In severe untreated cases it becomes very large, interferes with breathing and has to be surgically removed. Goitre may also occur in two serious diseases only rarely caused by diet – thyrotoxicosis and myxoedema (respectively over and under activity of the thyroid gland).

Despite the formation of a goitre, if the mother's diet is lacking in iodine during pregnancy and breast feeding, she may be unable to maintain adequate supplies for the growing child. Most brain growth takes place during the last three months of pregnancy (but is not complete until the second year of life) and if there is insufficient thyroid hormone, the brain fails to develop adequately, resulting in deaf mutism and cretinism. Welfare vitamin tablets available in pregnancy and breast feeding also contain 100 micrograms of iodine and these complications are rare in Britain.

Worldwide however, the picture is very different. At least 300 million people suffer from goitre but this is the least harmful aspect of iodine deficiency. Children raised in iodine deficient areas suffer a wide range of development disorders, ranging from hearing disabilities, retarded mental development, speech disorders, and poor growth which are the results of cretinism. These could be prevented by efficient administration of iodised salt.

In some areas, goitre is found despite a moderate iodine water content, and genetic and other factors are thought to be involved. Plants of the *Brassica* family (for instance **cabbage**, mustard) contain goitrogens which can interfere with extraction of iodine out of the blood stream, or inhibit the synthesis of the hormone in the thyroid gland, causing goitre in animals. In Britain, humans consume too little of these foods to be affected, but goitrogens are thought to contribute to goitre formation in other parts of the world. Other trace elements, for instance cobalt and manganese, are antagonistic to iodine. In excess they provoke goitre in animals, but their effect in humans is not known.

Ionising radiations or irradiation of food

This has recently been recommended as an alternative to **preservatives** in food. Lower levels can also be used as a sprout inhibitor (for example in potatoes), for insect disinfestation of stored foods, and to delay fruit ripening.

Food is irradiated usually by passing it over **cobalt** made radioactive in a nuclear reactor. The level of treatment of food could, in theory, result in the food becoming more radioactive, but to an unmeasurable amount when compared with the natural background radioactivity of food, see page 229 (section on radiation in **poisons in food**) for more details of radioactivity. Radiation hastens rancidity of fats (see **antioxidants**) but in general is felt to result in the production of less carcinogens than are produced by present day methods of cooking and especially smoking of food. See pp. 229-33 (sections on other pollutants and on cooking and processing of food in **poisons in food**).

Iron

Iron is a vital **mineral** needed for red blood cell formation. **Anaemia** due to lack of iron in the diet is one of the commonest nutritional disorders, particularly likely to affect women.

Only a small proportion of iron in food is absorbed into the blood stream during **digestion**. The iron in some foods is better retained than in others. The richest sources of well absorbed iron are **black sausage, liver**, (including pâté and liver sausage), **kidney, heart**, game, (including **pigeon, hare, venison, pheasant**), **whitebait, mussels**, cockles and **winkles**. Other fatty fish such as **sardines, sprats, herrings**, and **pilchards**, corned **beef**, and other red meat such as beef and **lamb**, and possibly **soya** beans are good sources. White fish and white meat contain comparatively little, but the iron in these is well absorbed.

Some vegetable foods such as wholegrain cereals, peas, and other beans, cocoa, curry and nuts are apparently good sources of iron, but the iron in them is not well absorbed, partly because of the chemical form of the iron, and also because of the presence of **phytic acid** and other substances. Thus although spinach contains nearly half as much iron as beef, at least ten times the weight of spinach would have to be eaten for the same amount of iron to be absorbed. White flour and some breakfast cereals are fortified with iron, but the iron in them is poorly absorbed. **Vitamin C** in for instance a glass of orange juice helps absorption. Virtually none of the iron in eggs is absorbed.

Poor sources of iron are sugar, fats, milk, cheese, yogurt and fresh fruit. In other iron rich foods – like fruit gums, liquorice, glace cherries, dried fruits, molasses (black treacle) and some wines – the iron is taken up from tools and containers used in manufacture and storage. Cooking utensils such as steel knives, can also contribute to the iron in the diet. It is uncertain how much iron from these sources is normally absorbed.

Like other minerals, iron leaches out of food into cooking water, but it can be recovered if the liquor is used for sauce or gravy. The iron content of foods is otherwise little affected by cooking, storage and processing.

Adults contain 3 to 4 grams of iron (a gram is one thousand times a milligram) which is carefully conserved. About one third is stored – mostly in the liver – and nearly all the rest is held in haemoglobin, the red pigment in blood cells which transports oxygen from the lungs to all parts of the body. Although individual red cells are dismantled every four months, their iron is recycled in replacement red blood cells. A small but important quantity of iron is contained in **enzymes** – present in body cells – concerned with the release of energy from food. Provided there is no bleeding, the only iron lost is from iron in these enzymes as cells die and are sloughed off from the outside of the body (for instance from skin). A healthy man only has to absorb sufficient iron from his food to replace these losses, less than one milligram per day. **Recommended intakes** are however ten times greater than this to allow for the fact that most iron is poorly available from food.

Because their needs are so small, men rarely suffer from iron deficiency due to a poor diet. However, when new blood has to be made, the iron requirement is greatly increased. Ten millilitres (2 teaspoons) of blood contains about 5 milligrams of iron. These increased needs are partly compensated for by less wastage of iron in food: about 20% (three times that normally absorbed by healthy men) can be transferred into the blood stream when there is a shortage. If the diet is poor in meat and other well absorbed iron containing foods this adaptation may not supply sufficient.

If the diet is lacking in iron, it is initially withdrawn from liver stores to match the needs for new blood formation. When these are exhausted, anaemia develops – the newly formed red blood cells are small and contain less haemoglobin. Minor degrees of anaemia may not be noticed (especially if little exercise is taken) but eventually the anaemic person suffers from the lack of oxygen and becomes tired and breathless. In severe cases there may be difficulty in swallowing, and angina (see **heart disease**). Severe anaemias are life threatening.

Women are particularly at risk: even in affluent countries, about 10% are estimated to suffer from iron deficiency. During the child bearing years they must absorb at least twice as much iron from their food as men to compensate for the loss during periods. The recommended intakes are therefore greater for women than men. Women with a tendency to anaemia should choose iron rich foods, but iron tablets are necessary once anaemia has developed, and for women whose monthly losses are too great for sufficient iron to be absorbed, even from a good diet.

During pregnancy extra iron is required to reinforce iron stores in preparation for blood losses at childbirth and to ensure adequate supplies for the growing child. The needs are unlikely to be met from food alone and iron tablets are routinely supplied at antenatal clinics in the last three months of pregnancy: anaemia is associated with a greater risk of complications for both mother and child.

When available, iron is transferred from the mother in the last stages of pregnancy. This store tides the infant over the first few months of life of milk feeding (milk is a poor source of iron). The child may become anaemic if the stores are inadequate or if milk feeding is prolonged – but infants should not be weaned before four months. The iron in breast milk is better absorbed than in fresh cows' milk, but iron and vitamin C is added to some powdered baby milks.

Children and adolescents with inadequate iron stores may not be able to meet the needs for new blood during growth spurts without becoming anaemic. The recommended allowances for iron during adolescence are as great as those for pregnant women. Needs for iron are not increased in the elderly, but their diet is often poor. Corned beef and sardines are particularly valuable sources of iron – they are easy to chew and require no cooking.

Anaemia due to blood loss is likely after surgery, and accidents. An iron rich diet should be given during convalescence. It can also occur following regular unnoticed blood loss from the digestive system – for instance as a result of ulcers, haemorrhoids and large intakes of aspirin – particularly in the elderly. See also **malabsorption**.

For most people, iron supplements are not harmful: if there is no storage, the iron is not absorbed. However, like other medicine, iron tablets should be kept out of the reach of children. Rarely, an inherited defect may allow abnormally large quantities of iron to be absorbed and an accumulation in the body may cause liver failure if not treated (by removal of blood). Alcoholics are likely to accumulate too much: some cheap wines are very rich sources, and alcohol and a low protein diet may interfere with regulatory processes, allowing too much iron to be absorbed.

Isoleucine

Isoleucine is an essential **amino acid** needed in the daily diet for the formation of new body **proteins** for growth and repair. Children fail to grow and adults lose weight if it is lacking in the diet.

Isoleucine is not a limiting amino acid – it is well supplied in all animal protein containing foods (except **gelatine**) and is also contained in vegetable proteins. Excess intakes are converted to **fat** or **glucose** and used for **energy**. The **nitrogen** part is converted to urea, a relatively harmless substance later filtered out of the blood stream by the kidneys.

Maple syrup urine disease is an **inborn error of metabolism** in which brain damage and early death can be avoided by a diet low in isoleucine and two other essential amino acids, leucine and valine.

Jelly

Home made jellies may contain vitamin C if they are made from **fruit** juices, but proprietary products – mixtures of sugars (sucrose, invert sugar, glucose), **gelatine**, flavouring and colour – do not contain fruit. Apart from **energy** and a small amount of poorly used protein, they are an insignificant source of **nutrients**. Milk jelly does however contain some nutrients (see table).

Average nutrients in 100 grams (3½ oz) Jelly

	made with water	made with milk		made with water	made with milk
Energy kilojoules	251	363	Iron milligrams	0.4	0.4
kilocalories	59	86	Copper milligrams	0.04	0.04
Protein grams	1.4	2.8	Zinc milligrams	–	–
Total fat grams	0	1.6	Vitamin A micrograms	0	14
Saturated fat grams	0	1.0	Vitamin D micrograms	0	0.01
Polyunsaturated fat grams	0	0	Vitamin C milligrams	0	0
			Vitamin E milligrams	0	0
Cholesterol milligrams	0	–	B vitamins:		
Sugars grams	14.2	16.0	Thiamin (B$_1$) milligrams	0	0.02
Starch grams	0	0	Riboflavin (B$_2$) milligrams	0	0.07
Dietary fibre grams	0	0	Nicotinic acid milligrams	0	0.3
Sodium milligrams	6	27	Pyridoxine (B$_6$) milligrams	0	0.02
Potassium milligrams	6	66	Vitamin B$_{12}$ micrograms	0	0
Calcium milligrams	7	59	Folic acid micrograms	0	2
Magnesium milligrams	1	6	Pantothenic acid milligrams	0	0.2
			Biotin micrograms	0	1

(–) No information available   (0) Contains zero or trace amounts

Joule

A joule is a basic unit for measuring **energy**. Unlike the **calorie**, which is only a unit for energy in the form of heat, the joule can apply to all forms of energy – for instance, work, heat, electricity, chemical energy, nuclear power. 4.184 joules equal one calorie.

Like the calorie, the joule is too small for practical dietary use and kilojoules (1000 joules) are used. 4.184 kilojoules (kJ) is equal to one kilocalorie (kcal). In some circumstances, when the total energy of a day's diet is measured. Mega-joules (MJ) are used. One Megajoule is one million joules (or one thousand kilojoules).

Scientific journals and food tables now contain energy values expressed in joules. In other books, calories will be gradually replaced by joules. This changeover, like metrication is a result of the acceptance by Britain of the International System of Units (SI units) in 1960.

Some conversion factors are shown in the table below.

One kilocalorie is equal to 4.184 kJ
One Btu is equal to 1.055 kJ
One hph is equal to 2.685 MJ
One kWhour is equal to 3.6 MJ

One gram of fat contains approximately 37 kJ
One gram of carbohydrate contains approximately 16 kJ
One gram of protein contains approximately 17 kJ
One gram of alcohol contains approximately 29 kJ

Kidney

Kidneys are a very rich source of **vitamin B$_{12}$**. 100 grams of lamb's kidney supplies about 40 times the daily requirement of vitamin B$_{12}$. Ox and pig's liver contain rather less (see table). Kidney is also very rich in the B vitamin, **biotin**, and contains **vitamin C**. Kidney requires gentle cooking for tenderness; over-cooked kidneys are tough and lacking in flavour.

Average nutrients in 100 grams (3½ oz) Kidney

	fried lamb's	stewed ox	stewed pig's		fried lamb's	stewed ox	stewed pig's
Energy kilojoules	651	720	641	Iron milligrams	12.0	8.0	6.4
kilocalories	155	172	153	Copper milligrams	0.65	0.66	0.84
Protein grams	24.6	25.6	24.4	Zinc milligrams	4.1	3.0	4.7
Total fat grams	6.3	7.7	6.1	Vitamin A micrograms	160	250	140
Saturated fat grams	–	3.2	2.0	Vitamin D micrograms	–	–	–
Polyunsaturated fat grams	–	0.5	0.9	Vitamin C milligrams	9	10	11
				Vitamin E milligrams	0.41	0.42	0.36
Cholesterol milligrams	610	690	700	B vitamins:			
Sugars grams	0	0	0	Thiamin (B$_1$) milligrams	0.56	0.25	0.19
Starch grams	0	0	0	Riboflavin (B$_2$) milligrams	2.3	2.1	2.1
Dietary fibre grams	0	0	0	Nicotinic acid milligrams	14.9	10.3	11.3
Sodium milligrams	270	400	370	Pyridoxine (B$_6$) milligrams	0.30	0.30	0.28
Potassium milligrams	340	180	190	Vitamin B$_{12}$ micrograms	79	31	15
Calcium milligrams	13	16	13	Folic acid micrograms	79	75	43
Magnesium milligrams	29	19	21	Pantothenic acid milligrams	5.1	3.0	2.4
				Biotin micrograms	42	49	53

(–) No information available   (0) Contains zero or trace amounts

Kippers and bloaters

Smoked and salted **herrings**. Bloaters are more lightly preserved than kippers and require immediate eating. Both are particularly good sources of **vitamin D** and **vitamin B$_{12}$**, and **biotin**. Kippers and bloaters are also sources of well absorbed **iron**.

Average nutrients in 100 grams (3½ oz) Kippers and Bloaters

	grilled bloater	baked kipper		grilled bloater	baked kipper
Energy kilojoules	1043	855	Iron milligrams	2.2	1.4
kilocalories	251	205	Copper milligrams	–	–
Protein grams	23.5	25.4	Zinc milligrams	–	–
Total fat grams	17.4	11.4	Vitamin A micrograms	49	49
Saturated fat grams	3.5	2.3	Vitamin D micrograms	25	25
Polyunsaturated fat grams	3.1	2.0	Vitamin C milligrams	0	0
			Vitamin E milligrams	0.3	0.3
Cholesterol milligrams	80	80	B vitamins:		
Sugars grams	0	0	Thiamin (B$_1$) milligrams	0	0
Starch grams	0	0	Riboflavin (B$_2$) milligrams	0.18	0.18
Dietary fibre grams	0	0	Nicotinic acid milligrams	8.4	8.8
Sodium milligrams	700	990	Pyridoxine (B$_6$) milligrams	0.57	0.57

Potassium milligrams	450	520	Vitamin B$_{12}$ micrograms	11	11
Calcium milligrams	120	65	Folic acid micrograms	10	10
Magnesium milligrams	45	48	Pantothenic acid milligrams	0.88	0.88
			Biotin micrograms	10	10

(–) No information available   (0) Contains zero or trace amounts

Kiwi fruit

The original name for Kiwi fruit was Chinese Gooseberry but these fruits have been 'adopted' by New Zealand which is now the major exporting country. They are good sources of **vitamin C**, containing twice as much as oranges.

Average nutrients in 100 grams (3½ oz) Kiwi fruit[a]

Energy kilojoules	230	Iron milligrams	0.34
kilocalories	54	Copper milligrams	0.20
Protein grams	1.2	Zinc milligrams	–
Total fat grams	0.6	Vitamin A micrograms	20
Saturated fat grams	–	Vitamin D micrograms	0
Polyunsaturated fat grams	–	Vitamin C milligrams	100
		Vitamin E milligrams	–
Cholesterol milligrams	0	B vitamins:	
Sugars grams	11.7	Thiamin (B$_1$) milligrams	0.62
Starch grams	0	Riboflavin (B$_2$) milligrams	0.62
Dietary fibre grams	–	Nicotinic acid milligrams	0.25
Sodium milligrams	2	Pyridoxine (B$_6$) milligrams	–
Potassium milligrams	360	Vitamin B$_{12}$ micrograms	0
Calcium milligrams	25	Folic acid micrograms	–
Magnesium milligrams	20	Pantothenic acid milligrams	–
		Biotin micrograms	–

(–) No information available   (0) Contains zero or trace amounts

[a]Ministry of Agriculture, Fisheries and Food, (unpublished data).

Kumquats

A close relative of citrus fruits, usually eaten raw and, in French cuisine, used for salads, marmalade and as a garnish. It looks like a small orange, and contains nearly as much **vitamin C** (see table).

Average nutrients in 100 grams (3½ oz) Kumquats (canned)

Energy kilojoules	577	Iron milligrams	0.8
kilocalories	138	Copper milligrams	–
Protein grams	0.4	Zinc milligrams	–
Total fat grams	0.5	Vitamin A micrograms	4·
Saturated fat grams	–	Vitamin D micrograms	0
Polyunsaturated fat grams	–	Vitamin C milligrams	40
		Vitamin E milligrams	–
Cholesterol milligrams	0	B vitamins:	
Sugars grams	35.4	Thiamin (B$_1$) milligrams	0.09
Starch grams	0	Riboflavin (B$_2$) milligrams	0.06
Dietary fibre grams	–	Nicotinic acid milligrams	–
Sodium milligrams	111	Pyridoxine (B$_6$) milligrams	–

Average nutrients in 100 grams (3½ oz) Kumquats (canned)*(continued)*

Potassium milligrams	156	Vitamin B$_{12}$ micrograms	0
Calcium milligrams	16	Folic acid micrograms	–
Magnesium milligrams	–	Pantothenic acid milligrams	–
		Biotin micrograms	–

(–) No information available   (0) Contains zero or trace amounts

Kwashiorkor

Kwashiorkor is one extreme of protein energy **malnutrition** (P.E.M.) in children. The other extreme is **marasmus.**

Although the name originated in Ghana, kwashiorkor (literally: the illness the older child gets when another child is born) is widespread in most developing countries. It usually occurs in the second year of life when the child is weaned onto a diet containing too little **protein**. The shortage of protein retards growth and affects all parts of the body but energy needs are often met (in contrast to marasmus). The skin flakes and may ulcerate; the hair is sparse and sometimes loses its dark colour (turning red); and the muscles may be so wasted that the child cannot crawl. The blood stream contains insufficient protein, and water accumulates: the child has a puffy appearance, and is less resistant to infections (which may themselves partly cause the disease). The liver may become infiltrated with fat (which sometimes leads to liver failure) and the digestive system degenerates. The resulting diarrhoea exacerbates the shortage of nutrients.

Any child is at risk but kwashiorkor occurs typically in areas where the staple food is low in protein (for instance tapioca – cassava). Severe cases may recover with hospital treatment. In less serious cases supplements of skimmed milk or other protein restore the child. Unless the mother takes milk supplements for the child or is taught how to feed the child with local protein containing foods (if available) recurrence is likely.

Labels on food

The labelling of food is controlled by the Food Labelling Regulations 1984. With a few exceptions, these cover nearly all retail prepacked foods. These are required to be labelled with the name of the food, a list of ingredients, the 'best before' or 'sell by' date, and the name of the manufacturer or packer.

Ingredients, including water, must generally be listed in decreasing order of weight. All **additives** must be listed by their category, for example, colours, antioxidants, and, except for **flavours** this must be followed by the specific name, or the **E number**. For additives which do not yet have an E number, a serial number is specified in the regulations, but usually the specific name is used. Foods exempted from a list of ingredients are fresh fruit and vegetables that have not been peeled or cut into small pieces, very small packages, and foods containing only one ingredient or covered by other food regulations such as flour, cheese, butter and plain yogurt.

Perishable foods which are intended to be eaten within six weeks of packing must have storage instructions, a 'sell by' date, and/or a 'best eaten before' date. Foods exempted from this are those which can be kept for longer than 18 months, frozen foods, ice cream, fresh fruit and vegetables (not peeled or cut into pieces) sugar, salt, wine, and cakes, buns and bread etc. which are normally eaten within a day of purchase.

The 1984 regulations also specify claims for foods that may legally be made. No food for example is allowed to be described as having 'tonic' properties. No food can be claimed to have specific slimming properties, but a food can be claimed to aid weight reduction as *part* of a diet low in **energy** (Calories) provided the energy content is less than three-quarters of a similar food, or if it contains less than 167 kilojoules (40 kilocalories) per 100 grams or 100 millilitres of food.

Foods may claim to contain **protein** if the food contains at least 3 grams of protein for every 420 kilojoules (100 kilocalories) the food supplies – but this is less than, for example, eggs. Foods may also be said to contain vitamins A, D, C and the B vitamins thiamin, riboflavin, nicotinic acid, folic acid and vitamin B_{12}, and calcium, iron, and iodine, if the quantity of food that would be consumed in a day would supply one sixth of the **recommended intake**. No claims for other vitamins and minerals are permitted. Claims relating to **cholesterol** and polyunsaturated **fatty acids** are also restricted to avoid misleading consumers. "Low in cholesterol" for example cannot be claimed unless those words are preceded by statements about the polyunsaturated fat content of the food, in larger or equal sized lettering. If a manufacturer wants to make claims about the high polyunsaturated content of foods, at least 45% of the fat must be polyunsaturated. The amounts of *cis* polyunsaturated fatty acids have also to be declared.

Lactic acid (E325 – 327)

Lactic acid is a natural **preservative** in food. Its acidity discourages the multiplication of putrefactive microorganisms.

Lactic acid is formed from **glycogen** in meat and game. It is also made by some bacteria as they multiply on sugars (for instance lactose, milk sugar). Cultures of these bacteria are deliberately added to milk in the making of cheese, yogurt, other cultured milks and sour cream. Apart from its preservative action, the lactic acid produced clots some of the milk protein, thickening yogurt and sour cream. Olives, and cabbage (sauerkraut) are also preserved by fermentation with lactic acid producing bacteria.

Lactose – milk sugar

Lactose is a sugar with about one fifth the sweetness of **sucrose** (sugar). It is a **disaccharide** made by the milk glands of mammals and only found naturally in milk and milk products. Human and cows' milk contain 7 and 4 grams of lactose respectively per 100 millilitres (½ glass). Sucrose or other sugars are added to cows' milk intended for baby feeding in an attempt to make it similar in **carbohydrate** content to human milk.

In infants and young children, lactose is split during **digestion** to its constituent sugars, **glucose** and **galactose**, by the **enzyme** lactase which is made by the cells lining the surface of the small bowel. These simple sugars are absorbed into the blood stream and ultimately used for **energy**. Caucasians are unusual in retaining the capacity to produce lactase after weaning – most races lose this ability and cannot tolerate large quantities of milk in adulthood. Only a small quantity of lactose can be digested and the remainder is fermented in the large bowel, causing diarrhoea. Cheese and some fermented milks (which contain less lactose) are better tolerated.

The capacity to produce lactase may also be lost as a result of **coeliac disease**, an **inborn error of metabolism**, and surgery of the small bowel. The resultant diarrhoea and failure to thrive in infants is cured by special lactose-free baby milks. A lactose free diet is also needed in the treatment of galactosaemia (see **galactose**).

Ladies' Fingers see Okra

Lamb

The nutrient contents of lean cuts of lamb are very similar, shoulder and chops having slightly more **fat** than roast leg (see table). Like all red **meats**, lamb is a good source of well absorbed **iron** and **zinc**.

Lamb eaten with fat, however, is much higher in fat, saturated **fatty acids** and **energy** (Calories). Roast shoulder eaten with fat, for example, contains 26 grams of fat per 100 grams. Grilled chops with fat contain more (29 grams), and roast leg with fat less (18 grams).

Average nutrients in 100 grams (3½ oz) Lamb (lean)

	grilled chops	roast leg	roast shoulder		grilled chops	roast leg	roast shoulder
Energy kilojoules	928	800	819	Iron milligrams	2.1	2.7	1.8
kilocalories	222	191	196	Copper milligrams	0.19	0.31	0.16
Protein grams	27.8	29.4	23.8	Zinc milligrams	4.1	5.3	5.3
Total fat grams	12.3	8.1	11.2	Vitamin A micrograms	0	0	0

Saturated fat grams	6.0	4.0	5.5	Vitamin D micrograms	0	0	0
Polyunsaturated fat grams	0.6	0.4	0.5	Vitamin C milligrams	0	0	0
				Vitamin E milligrams	0.10	0.10	0.10
Cholesterol milligrams	110	110	110	B vitamins:			
Sugars grams	0	0	0	Thiamin (B₁) milligrams	0.15	0.14	0.10
Starch grams	0	0	0	Riboflavin (B₂) milligrams	0.30	0.38	0.27
Dietary fibre grams	0	0	0	Nicotinic acid milligrams	13.1	12.9	9.4
Sodium milligrams	75	67	65	Pyridoxine (B₆) milligrams	0.22	0.22	0.22
Potassium milligrams	380	340	300	Vitamin B₁₂ micrograms	2	2	2
Calcium milligrams	9	8	9	Folic acid micrograms	4	4	4
Magnesium milligrams	28	28	22	Pantothenic acid milligrams	0.7	0.7	0.7
				Biotin micrograms	2	2	2

(–) No information available   (0) Contains zero or trace amounts

Lard see Cooking fats

Laverbread

Laverbread is a purée of seaweed, coated in oatmeal. It is a good source of **iodine** and contains most of the vitamins found in **vegetables**.

Average nutrients in 100 grams (3½ oz) Laverbread

Energy kilojoules	217	Iron milligrams	3.5
kilocalories	52	Copper milligrams	0.12
Protein grams	3.2	Zinc milligrams	0.8
Total fat grams	3.7	Vitamin A micrograms	–
Saturated fat grams	–	Vitamin D micrograms	0
Polyunsaturated fat grams	–	Vitamin C milligrams	5
		Vitamin E milligrams	1.1
Cholesterol milligrams	0	B vitamins:	
Sugars grams	0	Thiamin (B₁) milligrams	0.03
Starch grams	1.6	Riboflavin (B₂) milligrams	0.10
Dietary fibre grams	3.1	Nicotinic acid milligrams	1.1
Sodium milligrams	560	Pyridoxine (B₆) milligrams	–
Potassium milligrams	220	Vitamin B₁₂ micrograms	0
Calcium milligrams	20	Folic acid micrograms	47
Magnesium milligrams	31	Pantothenic acid milligrams	–
		Biotin micrograms	–

(–) No information available   (0) Contains zero or trace amounts

Lecithin – other name, phosphotidyl choline

Lecithin is a **phospholipid**, composed of glycerol, two fatty acids, phosphorous and choline (see individual entries). It can be made in the body and is not an essential **nutrient**, but it is found in most foods. Egg yolks are the richest food source (up to 10% by weight).

Commercially, crude lecithin is a mixture of several phospholipids obtained from soya beans and other oil seeds (like peanuts). Pure lecithin can be extracted out: both pure lecithin and the remaining phospholipids are important **emulsifiers** in the food industry.

Whilst all lecithins have the same basic structure, lecithins from different sources contain different types of fatty acids. Lecithins are the main phospholipids (emulsifiers) in the blood stream and are present in the myelin sheath of nerves, yet, despite claims by some enthusiasts extra lecithin is unlikely to promote healthy nerves and offset the risk of **heart disease**. The body makes enough lecithin to satisfy its requirements from the raw materials methionine (an amino acid converted into choline), sugars or fats (to make fatty acids and glycerol) and phosphorus. Small amounts of **essential fatty acids** are also required.

Leeks

Leeks have a long history as food and ancient Egypt was said to be a country where 'onions are adored and leeks are gods'. They are worn on St David's Day to commemorate the victory of King Cadwaller over the Saxons in 690 AD; during the battle the Welsh wore leeks to distinguish their own men from the enemy.

Leeks contain small amounts of **vitamins** and **minerals** and **fibre** (see table). The blanched, elongated bulb is generally eaten, consequently leeks usually contain little vitamin A; the green leafy parts contain much more (see table).

Average nutrients in 100 grams (3½ oz) Leeks

	raw	boiled		raw	boiled
Energy kilojoules	128	104	Iron milligrams	1.1	2.0
kilocalories	31	24	Copper milligrams	0.1	0.1
Protein grams	1.9	1.8	Zinc milligrams	0.1	0.1
Total fat grams	0	0	Vitamin A micrograms	7[a]	7[a]
Saturated fat grams	0	0	Vitamin D micrograms	0	0
Polyunsaturated fat grams	0	0	Vitamin C milligrams	15—30	10—25
			Vitamin E milligrams	0.8	0.8
Cholesterol milligrams	0	0	B vitamins:		
Sugars grams	6.0	4.6	Thiamin (B$_1$) milligrams	0.10	0.07
Starch grams	0	0	Riboflavin (B$_2$) milligrams	0.05	0.03
Dietary fibre grams	3.1	3.9	Nicotinic acid milligrams	0.9	0.7
Sodium milligrams	9	6	Pyridoxine (B$_6$) milligrams	0.25	0.15
Potassium milligrams	310	280	Vitamin B$_{12}$ micrograms	0	0
Calcium milligrams	63	61	Folic acid micrograms	–	–
Magnesium milligrams	10	13	Pantothenic acid milligrams	0.12	0.10
			Biotin micrograms	1.4	1.0

(–) No information available   (0) Contains zero or trace amounts

[a] White part; the green parts contain 300 micrograms

Lemons and limes

Lemons and limes are both citrus fruits, but the lime contains half as much **vitamin C** as the lemon (see table). The ability of lemon juice to protect against **scurvy** was demonstrated by James Lind in 1753, and in 1795 the Admiralty adopted lemon juice as the principal antiscorbutic ration. This was over 100 years before the active substance, vitamin C, was known. Consequently the possibility that there may have been differences in the ability of the juices to protect against scurvy was not appreciated and by the middle of the 19th century, lime juice, rather than lemon, was commonly issued – hence the name 'limey' for British seamen. Because of the lower vitamin C content of lime juice, and insufficient measures to preserve the juices on long campaigns and voyages, outbreaks of scurvy reappeared – leading to confusion and distrust of both lemon and lime juice. The situation was not properly investigated until during the First World War, when it was finally realised that lemon juice is a far more powerful preventative measure against vitamin C deficiency than lime juice.

Average nutrients in 100 grams (3½ oz) Lemons and Limes

	lemons	limes		lemons	limes
Energy kilojoules	65	151	Iron milligrams	0.4	–
kilocalories	15	36	Copper milligrams	0.26	–
Protein grams	0.8	0.5	Zinc milligrams	0.1	–
Total fat grams	0	2.4	Vitamin A micrograms	0	2
Saturated fat grams	–	–	Vitamin D micrograms	0	0
Polyunsaturated fat grams	–	–	Vitamin C milligrams	80[a]	46[a]
			Vitamin E milligrams	–	–
Cholesterol milligrams	0	0	B vitamins:		
Sugars grams	3.2	5.6	Thiamin (B₁) milligrams	0.05	0.03
Starch grams	0	0	Riboflavin (B₂) milligrams	0.04	0.02
Dietary fibre grams	5.2	–	Nicotinic acid milligrams	0.3	–
Sodium milligrams	6	2	Pyridoxine (B₆) milligrams	0.11	–
Potassium milligrams	160	82	Vitamin B₁₂ micrograms	0	0
Calcium milligrams	110	13	Folic acid micrograms	–	–
Magnesium milligrams	12	–	Pantothenic acid milligrams	0.23	–
			Biotin micrograms	0.5	–

(–) No information available   (0) Contains zero or trace amounts

[a] Lemon juice contains 40–60 milligrams, lime juice 25 milligrams

Lentils, see also pulses and dhal

Lentils are one of the oldest leguminous (pulse) crops; remains of lentils have been found at Swiss prehistoric sites. Like all **pulses** they are rich in **protein** and **starch**, and good sources of B **vitamins**. They contain **phytic acid** which interferes with the absorption of **iron**, **zinc**, **calcium** and **magnesium**. More iron is absorbed if lentils are eaten with foods containing vitamin C, such as tomatoes.

Average nutrients in 100 grams (3½ oz) Lentils

Energy kilojoules	1293	Iron milligrams	7.6
kilocalories	304	Copper milligrams	0.58
Protein grams	23.8	Zinc milligrams	3.1
Total fat grams	1.0	Vitamin A micrograms	10
Saturated fat grams	–	Vitamin D micrograms	0
Polyunsaturated fat grams	–	Vitamin C milligrams	0
		Vitamin E milligrams	–
Cholesterol milligrams	0	B vitamins:	
Sugars grams	2.4	Thiamin (B₁) milligrams	0.50
Starch grams	50.8	Riboflavin (B₂) milligrams	0.20
Dietary fibre grams	11.7	Nicotinic acid milligrams	5.8
Sodium milligrams	36	Pyridoxine (B₆) milligrams	0.60

Average nutrients in 100 grams (3½ oz) Lentils *(continued)*

Potassium milligrams	670	Vitamin B$_{12}$ micrograms	0
Calcium milligrams	39	Folic acid micrograms	35
Magnesium milligrams	77	Pantothenic acid milligrams	1.36
		Biotin micrograms	–

(–) No information available   (0) Contains zero or trace amounts

Lettuce

A member of the *Compositae* (daisy) family of uncertain origin, possibly Siberia or the Mediterranean region. Lettuce seeds have been found in plant remains in some of the ancient Egyptian tombs. It has a similar composition to other **vegetables**, being valuable for its **vitamin C**, **folic acid** and **vitamin A** content. The greenest leaves contain the most vitamin A.

Average nutrients in 100 grams (3½ oz) Lettuce

Energy kilojoules	51	Iron milligrams	0.9
kilocalories	12	Copper milligrams	0.03
Protein grams	1.0	Zinc milligrams	0.2
Total fat grams	0.4	Vitamin A micrograms	167[a]
Saturated fat grams	–	Vitamin D micrograms	0
Polyunsaturated fat grams	–	Vitamin C milligrams	10—30
		Vitamin E milligrams	0.5
Cholesterol milligrams	0	B vitamins:	
Sugars grams	1.2	Thiamin (B$_1$) milligrams	0.07
Starch grams	0	Riboflavin (B$_2$) milligrams	0.08
Dietary fibre grams	1.5	Nicotinic acid milligrams	0.4
Sodium milligrams	9	Pyridoxine (B$_6$) milligrams	0.07
Potassium milligrams	240	Vitamin B$_{12}$ micrograms	0
Calcium milligrams	23	Folic acid micrograms	34
Magnesium milligrams	8	Pantothenic acid milligrams	0.20
		Biotin micrograms	0.7

(–) No information available   (0) Contains zero or trace amounts

[a] Outer leaves may contain 50 times as much as inner ones

Leucine

Leucine is an essential **amino acid** needed in the daily diet for the formation of new body **proteins** for growth and repair. Children fail to grow and adults lose weight if it is lacking in the diet.

Leucine is not a limiting amino acid – it is well supplied in all animal protein containing foods (except gelatine) and is also contained in vegetable proteins. Excess intakes are converted to fat and used for **energy**. The **nitrogen** part is converted to urea, a relatively harmless substance later filtered out of the blood stream by the kidneys.

Maple syrup urine disease is an **inborn error of metabolism**, treated with a diet low in isoleucine, leucine and valine.

Limes see Lemons and Limes

Lipid

Lipid is a biochemical term, sometimes used to distinguish fatty substances in the body from fat in the diet. When referring to food, **fat** is used: nearly all (98%) of fat in the diet is in the form of simple fat (**triglycerides**).

In the body, lipid has two main functions: it is used for **energy** and it is part of the structure of all cells. The fat in food can either be used immediately for energy, or deposited in energy stores (**adipose tissue**). Between meals, most cells rely on **fatty acids** released from adipose tissue and carried in the blood stream for their supplies of energy.

Whereas the amount of lipid in adipose tissue can vary from day to day, the quantity of lipid in the structural part is normally not altered. The structural body lipids are of great variety and complexity. Nearly all contain fatty acids and most contain phosphorus (**phospholipids**). Some contain **carbohydrate** (for instance galactose). In brain and nervous tissue, large complexes form the myelin sheath, which acts as an electrical insulator. The steroids – for instance **cholesterol**, sex hormones and cortisone – are also classed as lipids. All these materials can be made in the body and, with the exception of small amounts of **essential fatty acids** fat is not an essential **nutrient**.

Triglycerides (simple fats) are not soluble in water and have to be emulsified (divided finely, see emulsifiers) before they can be transported in the blood stream. The emulsified particles are called lipoproteins, and consist of a core of cholesterol and fats, surrounded by phospholipid and detergent proteins (apoproteins) which are formed initially in the liver and small intestine. At least five of the lipoproteins and 12 apoproteins can be identified in the blood stream at any one time. Some of the apoproteins are cofactors for **enzymes** involved in the transfer of cholesterol and fatty acids from the lipoproteins into the cell, and others bind to receptor sites on cell membranes. On entry into the cell, and release of cholesterol, synthesis and receptor formation are suppressed.

The regulators of lipid transport – the apoproteins, cell receptors and enzymes – are proteins and hence under genetic control. The inherited type IIA disorder (see below) for example is due to a defect of apoprotein B receptors for lipoproteins that carry the majority of cholesterol, the LDL (low density lipoproteins). Consequently LDL levels are high in these patients, who have a ten fold increased risk of **heart disease**. LDL receptors in the liver can be induced by the drug cholestyramine, used for the treatment of this disorder, and by oestrogens. Since the liver is the main route by which cholesterol leaves the body, LDL (and therefore blood cholesterol) levels fall on treatment with cholestyramine. The effect of oestrogens may explain why women are relatively immune to heart disease until the menopause. However the extent to which cholesterol leaves the plasma by the LDL receptor pathway remains to be established – it may well account for only 30% of the total. Another problem is that the risk of heart disease may be more strongly predicted by low levels of another class of lipoproteins, the HDL fraction. Whereas LDL can be substantially altered by diet (by increasing the ratio of PUFA to saturated fatty acids and increasing the amount of dietary **fibre** eaten) in studies so far, HDL levels have not been amenable to dietary change.

Hyperlipoproteinaemias

A raised level of lipoprotein in the blood stream between meals is called hyperlipoproteinaemia: depending on the lipoprotein involved, blood cholesterol or triglycerides or both may be raised.

Hyperlipoproteinaemia is a risk factor in heart disease, and, like **gout** and **diabetes**, is partly inherited, partly caused by a faulty diet. The three disorders are likely to affect the same people and all are associated with **obesity**.

Alteration of the amount of fat in the diet, in an attempt to lower the level of lipid in the blood stream and offset the risk of heart disease, is particularly worthwhile for those suffering from hyperlipoproteinaemia. The diet may have to be augmented with drugs.

There are six types of hyperlipoproteinaemia, of which three are quite common. The exact disorder and individual treatment need to be medically decided. An outline of three of the diets used is given here, but specialised advice should be sought.

Type IV is the most common, affecting middle aged men in particular. It also occurs in alcoholism, some types of kidney disease, obesity, diabetes, and sometimes during pregnancy and use of contraceptive pills. The blood cholesterol is normal, but the blood triglycerides are raised. A reduction in weight where necessary and curtailment of drinking are most important. Thereafter the diet is low in carbohydrate (less than 200 grams a day) and restricted in fats, sugar and cholesterol.

Type IIA is mostly inherited: there is a very high level of cholesterol in the blood stream, and it is treated with a diet very low in cholesterol and saturated fats. Polyunsaturated fats are taken in place of saturated fats (see oils and margarine) and **alcohol** may be taken in moderation.

Type IIB may be inherited or result from a rich diet. Both cholesterol and triglycerides are raised. Reduction in weight is the most important treatment, followed by a diet high in protein and restricted in cholesterol, carbohydrate, fat, sugar and alcohol.

Lipoic acid

Lipoic acid is a growth factor for many micro-organisms. It takes part in the production of **energy** from **glucose**. It is found in most foods, but humans probably synthesise all they require so that it is not included in the vitamins.

Liquorice

A herb belonging to the pulse (legume) family, grown for the flavouring properties of its roots. Pontefract in Yorkshire used to be the centre of liquorice growing; 'Pontefract cakes' are now made using imports of liquorice from Russia and the Mediterranean. Powdered liquorice is very rich in iron, hence liquorice allsorts contain more than other sweets, 8.1 milligrams per 100 grams compared with 0.3 milligrams in boiled sweets.

The drug carbenoloxone derived from liquorice is now less commonly used for the treatment of peptic **ulcers**, having been largely replaced by inhibitors of gastric acid secretion, such as cimetidine.

Liver

Liver is often recommended by nutritionists because it is a rich source of nutrients such as well absorbed **iron, zinc, copper, vitamin A, riboflavin, pyridoxine, vitamin B₁₂, folic acid** and **pantothenic acid**. There are differences in nutrient content depending on the species – pigs' liver for example is particularly rich in iron, calves' in copper. Ox liver contains remarkably high levels of vitamin B₁₂ and used to be used to treat pernicious **anaemia**. All are rich in vitamin A, but there is a great range, highest levels being found in older animals. Liver pâté and sausages contain rather more **fat** than the liver alone, and added salt. However, they are good sources of iron and vitamin A. Liver sausage is legally allowed to contain 10% less lean meat than liver pâté.

These high levels of nutrients arise because the liver is a storage organ – hence the greater amount of nutrients with increasing age. Polar bear liver is toxic due to its very high content of vitamin A. Liver also contains a carbohydrate, **glycogen**, and useful amounts of vitamin C.

Average nutrients in 100 grams (3½ oz) Liver

	calf, fried	chicken, fried	lamb, fried	ox, stewed	pig, stewed	liver, pâté and sausage
Energy kilojoules	1063	810	970	831	793	1283
kilocalories	254	194	232	198	189	310
Protein grams	26.9	20.7	22.9	24.8	25.6	12.9
Total fat grams	13.2	10.9	14.0	9.5	8.1	26.9
Saturated fat grams	–	–	–	3.2	2.6	8.5
Polyunsaturated fat grams	–	–	–	2.0	2.2	2.1
Cholesterol milligrams	330	350	400	240	290	120
Sugars grams	0	0	0	0	0	0
Starch grams	(7.3)[a]	(3.4)[a]	(3.9)[a]	(3.6)[a]	(3.6)[a]	4.3
Dietary fibre grams	0	0	0	0	0	0
Sodium milligrams	170	240	190	110	130	860
Potassium milligrams	410	290	300	250	250	170
Calcium milligrams	15	15	12	11	11	26
Magnesium milligrams	26	23	22	19	22	12
Iron milligrams	7.5	9.1	10.0	7.8	17.0	6.4
Copper milligrams	12.0	0.5	9.9	2.3	2.5	0.63
Zinc milligrams	6.2	3.4	4.4	4.3	8.2	2.3
Vitamin A micrograms	8300-31700	5700-12800	3000-55000	11600-24000	5600-14200	8300
Vitamin D micrograms	0.25	–	0.50	1.13	1.13	0.6
Vitamin C milligrams	13	13	12	15	9	0
Vitamin E milligrams	0.50	0.34	0.32	0.44	0.16	0.10
B vitamins:						
Thiamin (B₁) milligrams	0.27	0.37	0.27	0.18	0.21	0.17
Riboflavin (B₂) milligrams	4.2	1.7	4.4	3.6	3.1	1.58
Nicotinic acid milligrams	21.4	14.9	20.1	15.6	17.0	6.7
Pyridoxine (B₆) milligrams	0.73	0.45	0.49	0.52	0.64	0.14
Vitamin B₁₂ micrograms	87	49	81	110	26	8

	calf, fried	chicken, fried	lamb, fried	ox, stewed	pig, stewed	liver, pâté and sausage
Folic acid micrograms	320	500	240	290	110	19
Pantothenic acid milligrams	8.8	5.5	7.6	5.7	4.6	1.5
Biotin micrograms	53	170	41	50	34	7

(–) No information available   (0) Contains zero or trace amounts

[a] Liver contains **glycogen** and some starch from flour added in cooking

Lobster

Lobsters are *Crustacea* weighing between 2 – 4 lbs. Catches in the UK from March to August are supplemented with lobsters from America for the summer season. Crawfish or *langouste* are the smaller spiny or rock lobster and usually only the tail meat is eaten. Plain boiled lobster is quite low in **fat**, and therefore energy (see table). Most recipes for lobster, however, call for the addition of large amounts of high fat foods, such as butter, cream and mayonnaise.

Average nutrients in 100 grams (3½ oz) Lobster (boiled)

Energy kilojoules	502	Iron milligrams	0.8
kilocalories	119	Copper milligrams	1.7
Protein grams	22.1	Zinc milligrams	1.8
Total fat grams	3.4	Vitamin A micrograms	0
Saturated fat grams	0.7	Vitamin D micrograms	0
Polyunsaturated fat grams	1.3	Vitamin C milligrams	0
		Vitamin E milligrams	1.5
Cholesterol milligrams	150	B vitamins:	
Sugars grams	0	Thiamin (B_1) milligrams	0.08
Starch grams	0	Riboflavin (B_2) milligrams	0.05
Dietary fibre grams	0	Nicotinic acid milligrams	5.6
Sodium milligrams	330	Pyridoxine (B_6) milligrams	–
Potassium milligrams	260	Vitamin B_{12} micrograms	1
Calcium milligrams	62	Folic acid micrograms	17
Magnesium milligrams	34	Pantothenic acid milligrams	1.6
		Biotin micrograms	5

(–) No information available   (0) Contains zero or trace amounts

Loganberries

Loganberries are a relative of raspberries and blackberries, containing slightly more **vitamin C**. The fresh loganberry is low in sugars (mostly glucose and fructose) and hence energy (Calories). Canned loganberries contain added sugar (see table).

Average nutrients in 100 grams (3½ oz) Loganberries

	fresh	canned		fresh	canned
Energy kilojoules	73	429	Iron milligrams	1.4	1.4
kilocalories	17	101	Copper milligrams	0.14	0.04
Protein grams	1.1	0.6	Zinc milligrams	–	–
Total fat grams	0	0	Vitamin A micrograms	13	12
Saturated fat grams	0	0	Vitamin D micrograms	0	0

Polyunsaturated fat grams	0	0	Vitamin C milligrams	35	25
			Vitamin E milligrams	0.3	–
Cholesterol milligrams	0	0	B vitamins:		
Sugars grams	3.4	26.2	Thiamin (B$_1$) milligrams	0.02	0.01
Starch grams	0	0	Riboflavin (B$_2$) milligrams	0.03	0.02
Dietary fibre grams	6.2	3.2	Nicotinic acid milligrams	0.6	0.4
Sodium milligrams	3	1	Pyridoxine (B$_6$) milligrams	0.06	0.04
Potassium milligrams	260	97	Vitamin B$_{12}$ micrograms	0	0
Calcium milligrams	35	18	Folic acid micrograms	–	–
Magnesium milligrams	25	11	Pantothenic acid milligrams	0.24	0.17
			Biotin micrograms	–	–

(–) No information available   (0) Contains zero or trace amounts

Lychee (Litchi)

The edible part of fresh lychees is white, with a sweet acid flavour, and good amounts of **vitamin C**. It is the fruit of the evergreen tree *Litchi chinensis* and is indigenous to China. Canned lychees are more familiar. They contain slightly more **sugar** (as glucose and fructose) and less vitamin C than the fresh fruit (see table).

Average nutrients in 100 grams (3½ oz) Lychees

	fresh	canned		fresh	canned
Energy kilojoules	271	290	Iron milligrams	0.5	0.7
kilocalories	64	68	Copper milligrams	–	0.1
Protein grams	0.9	0.4	Zinc milligrams	–	0.2
Total fat grams	0	0	Vitamin A micrograms	0	0
Saturated fat grams	0	0	Vitamin D micrograms	0	0
Polyunsaturated fat grams	0	0	Vitamin C milligrams	40	8
			Vitamin E milligrams	–	–
Cholesterol milligrams	0	0	B vitamins:		
Sugars grams	16.0	17.7	Thiamin (B$_1$) milligrams	0.04	0.03
Starch grams	0	0	Riboflavin (B$_2$) milligrams	0.04	0.03
Dietary fibre grams	0.5	0.4	Nicotinic acid milligrams	0.4	0.2
Sodium milligrams	3	2	Pyridoxine (B$_6$) milligrams	–	–
Potassium milligrams	170	75	Vitamin B$_{12}$ micrograms	0	0
Calcium milligrams	8	4	Folic acid micrograms	–	–
Magnesium milligrams	10	6	Pantothenic acid milligrams	–	–
			Biotin micrograms	–	–

(–) No information available   (0) Contains zero or trace amounts

Lysine

Lysine is an essential **amino acid** needed in the daily diet for the formation of new body **proteins** for growth and repair. Children fail to grow, and adults lose weight, becoming nauseated, dizzy, and intolerant of noise, when it is lacking.

Lysine is the limiting amino acid in **cereals**. Animal foods (meat, fish, cheese, eggs, milk) and pulses are, however, good sources – for instance the 9 grams of protein in 50 grams (under 2 oz) of cod supplies the estimated daily adult needs for lysine.

When eaten together, proteins supplement each other: good sources of lysine overcome the deficiencies of cereals. Bread and cheese, rice and lentils, cornflakes and milk are good combinations of proteins – the mixed protein is efficiently converted to new body protein and, provided the daily needs for protein are not exceeded, little is wasted.

In the USA, lysine is added to bread in an attempt to increase the amount of wheat protein used by the body. Similar proposals have not been accepted in Britain because lysine is not the limiting amino acid in mixed diets – see **methionine**.

Excess intakes of lysine are converted to fat and used for **energy**. The **nitrogen** part is converted to urea, a relatively harmless substance later filtered out of the blood stream by the kidneys.

Mackerel

A fatty **fish**, rich in **vitamin D** and containing well absorbed **iron**, and **vitamins A** and **B₁₂**, mackerel contains long chain **essential fatty acids** which may be important in reducing the tendency of blood to clot; see also **stroke** and **heart disease**.

Average nutrients in 100 grams (3½ oz) Mackerel (fried)

Energy kilojoules	784	Iron milligrams	1.2
kilocalories	188	Copper milligrams	0.2
Protein grams	21.5	Zinc milligrams	–
Total fat grams	11.3	Vitamin A micrograms	52
Saturated fat grams	4.0	Vitamin D micrograms	21
Polyunsaturated fat grams	4.0	Vitamin C milligrams	0
		Vitamin E milligrams	–
Cholesterol milligrams	80	B vitamins:	
Sugars grams	0	Thiamin (B₁) milligrams	0.09
Starch grams	0	Riboflavin (B₂) milligrams	0.38
Dietary fibre grams	0	Nicotinic acid milligrams	12.7
Sodium milligrams	150	Pyridoxine (B₆) milligrams	0.84
Potassium milligrams	420	Vitamin B₁₂ micrograms	12
Calcium milligrams	28	Folic acid micrograms	–
Magnesium milligrams	35	Pantothenic acid milligrams	0.96
		Biotin micrograms	8

(–) No information available   (0) Contains zero or trace amounts

Macrobiotic diets

Macrobiotic diets are part of a philosophy taken from a number of Eastern religions, particularly Zen Buddhism. The originator is thought to be a Japanese, George Ohsawa, who has written over 300 books on the subject but who, according to the first Zen Institute of America, is not a member of their religion.

The principles and philosophy behind macrobiotic diets are somewhat difficult to comprehend, based as they are on a combination of foods classified according to their 'yin' and 'yang' properties. This classification includes such factors as the colour, direction of growth (up or down), taste, season, and weight of foods. According to one macrobiotic food writer, only those foods grown within a 500 mile radius should be included in the diet, in order to achieve harmony with the environment. Literally translated, macrobiotic means 'large life', and it is claimed that the macrobiotic diet will lead its followers to a joyous, happy and wonderful life. This is in contrast to a statement by the American Medical Association in 1971 which condemned the diet as 'one of the most dangerous dietary regimes, posing not only serious hazards to the health of the individual but even to life itself'.

In practice, the diet is based largely on wholegrain (brown) **rice**, other wholegrain **cereals**, and **beans**, supplemented with locally grown **vegetables** in season, seaweeds and **soy** products. Some fish, poultry, shellfish, eggs and fruit can be eaten occasionally. As such, the diet could be as healthy and nutritious as a well planned **vegetarian** diet. However, as acknowledged by

Ohsawa, the philosophy can be taken up with a fanatical rigidity and problems occur when the seventh and highest stage, consisting of small quantities of rice and water, are followed. This cannot support health for long and there have been a number of medical reports of severe **malnutrition** occurring, most seriously in children maintained by their parents on macrobiotic diets.

Magnesium

Magnesium is a **mineral** which has many fundamental roles in the body. It is widespread in foods and frank deficiency is known to occur only as a result of underlying disease, or in conjunction with other essential **nutrients**.

Magnesium is evenly distributed in foods and beverages, except white sugar, fats, spirits, some **convenience foods**, and most **soft drinks** which contain virtually none. Wholegrain cereals, nuts and spinach are apparently good sources (particularly bran and wheat germ products) but **phytic acid** (and **oxalic acid** in spinach) is known to interfere with the absorption of magnesium. It is uncertain how much of the magnesium in these foods actually reaches the blood stream: wholemeal bread contains less phytic acid than other wholegrain cereals.

Magnesium is little affected by processing and cooking of foods – apart from losses in milling (wholemeal flour contains at least four times more than white), and leaching into cooking water. Up to two thirds can be lost when vegetables are boiled but it is recovered if the liquor is used for sauce or gravy. Fried, baked and grilled foods retain all their magnesium.

There are no British recommended intakes for magnesium, due to lack of information, but adults probably require about 300 milligrams a day – an amount contained in the average British diet. In pregnancy and breast feeding, needs for magnesium may be greater: American recommended allowances are set at 450 milligrams daily. The additional 150 milligrams is supplied by, for example, 200 grams (5 large slices) of wholemeal bread in place of white.

During **digestion**, about one third of the magnesium in a mixed diet is absorbed into the blood stream. Normally an equivalent amount is eliminated from the body by the kidneys, but in childhood and adolescence, more is retained (less is eliminated in the urine) to allow for growth. By adulthood, most people have accumulated about 25 grams (less than one ounce) of magnesium, of which two thirds is held as salts in the skeleton. The majority of the remainder is a vital component of cells: it is an **electrolyte**, helps to maintain the structure of cells, and is a cofactor for many important **enzymes**. It also influences the utilisation of two other important minerals, calcium and potassium.

Prolonged diarrhoea, and **malabsorption** syndromes (for instance, coeliac disease) can deplete the body of magnesium. None may be absorbed from food, and in severe cases up to four times more magnesium than is eaten in food may be carried out of the body in the stools. Abnormal losses in urine – due to some kidney diseases, excessive **alcohol** consumption and some drugs used to increase the flow of urine (diuretics) – can also induce magnesium deficiency.

Initially some of the magnesium stored in the bones can be withdrawn to overcome a temporary lack of magnesium in the diet, increased losses or inadequate absorption. Eventually, when the stores are exhausted, personality changes, irritation, lethargy, depression and fits ensue, and if not treated death may be precipitated by a heart attack.

It has been suggested that diets supplying marginal intakes of magnesium (less than 300 milligrams per day) may be a cause of **heart disease**. Diets of people living in unindustrialised countries (where the disease is comparatively rare) usually contain more magnesium. The magnesium content of the heart muscle of Americans who died from heart attacks has been found to be lower than in those who died from other causes. However, the suggestion is not generally accepted: too little is known of the factors governing magnesium utilisation, and the finding may be an effect rather than a cause of the disease.

Excess magnesium is not harmful in itself because it is not absorbed into the blood stream, but magnesium salts (for instance Epsom salts) have a laxative effect, drawing water and other minerals out of the body. Excessive use, particularly in the elderly, can result in **potassium** depletion.

Maize – Indian corn

Maize is a **cereal** associated in some countries with the deficiency disease **pellagra**. Its nutritional properties differ slightly from other cereals: it is deficient in **tryptophan** the precursor of the vitamin **nicotinic acid**. Yellow (but not white) maize contains **carotene** (provitamin A).

Maize originated in South America but became established as a staple food in many poverty stricken areas. It is resistant to drought, gives a good yield and has a short growing season. Where the traditional method of steeping maize in lime before cooking was not followed, pellagra became endemic. Its nutritional short-comings are not important in a mixed diet containing plenty of nicotinic acid or tryptophan (found in most other sources of protein).

Maize can be eaten whole, as popcorn. Like other cereals it is ground into flour: maize meal and popcorn retain all the nutritive value of the whole grain, but corn hominy or grits – where the nutrients in the germ and outer husk have been removed – are equivalent to white wheat flour. The germ is a valued source of **oil**. Maize flour cannot be made into leavened bread (it contains no **gluten**) but is usually eaten as a kind of porridge, for example polenta in Italy, or flat bread, for instance Mexican tortillas.

Cornflour is extracted after steeping the grain in water. It is a useful thickening agent, and is the basis of custard powder and blancmange, but is a source of 'empty calories'. It is virtually pure starch.

Sweetcorn is a different variety of maize, containing more water and sugar. It is eaten as a vegetable: its nicotinic acid is made available by ordinary cooking methods. See also **breakfast cereals**.

Average nutrients in 100 grams (3½ oz) Maize flour, Grits and Cornflour

	maize flour	grits	cornflour		maize flour	grits	cornflour
Energy kilojoules	1477	1515	1508	Iron milligrams	4.2	1.0	1.4
kilocalories	353	362	354	Copper milligrams	–	–	0.13
Protein grams	9.3	8.7	0.6	Zinc milligrams	–	–	0
Total fat grams	3.8	0.8	0.7	Vitamin A micrograms	4	44	0
Saturated fat grams	0.6	–	0.1	Vitamin D micrograms	0	0	0
Polyunsaturated fat grams	1.9	–	0.3	Vitamin C milligrams	3	0	0
				Vitamin E milligrams	–	–	0
Cholesterol milligrams	0	0	0	B vitamins:			
Sugars grams	0	0	0	Thiamin (B$_1$) milligrams	0.30	0.13	0
Starch grams	71.5	77.7	92.0	Riboflavin (B$_2$)			
				milligrams	0.08	0.04	0
Dietary fibre (NSP) grams	–	–	0.1	Nicotinic acid milligrams	–	–	0
Sodium milligrams	1	1	52	Pyridoxine (B$_6$)			
				milligrams	–	–	0
Potassium milligrams	284	80	61	Vitamin B$_{12}$ micrograms	0	0	0
Calcium milligrams	17	4	15	Folic acid micrograms	–	–	0
Magnesium milligrams	–	–	7	Pantothenic acid			
				milligrams	–	–	0
				Biotin micrograms	–	–	0

(–) No information available   (0) Contains zero or trace amounts

Malabsorption

Malabsorption is a disorder of **digestion** resulting in the failure to absorb one or more **nutrients** into the blood stream. It may be caused by lack of digestive **enzymes** (sometimes as a result of an **inborn error of metabolism** or disease of the pancreas) or bile; parasites or other infections; **coeliac disease**; or following surgery of the digestive tract.

Failure to absorb fat interferes with the absorption of any vitamin or mineral – commonly iron, calcium and folic acid – which is carried out of the body in the fatty diarrhoea. Loss of weight, flatulence and general ill health may be accompanied by **anaemia, osteomalacia** and skin disorders. The underlying condition may have to be treated with a special diet, for instance a **gluten** free diet. A low **fat** diet is sometimes necessary but aggravates weight loss (low fat diets are low in energy). Low fat diets are sometimes supplemented with special oils (MCT) which can be absorbed in the absence of bile or fat splitting enzymes.

Intolerance to **carbohydrate** commonly takes the form of **lactose** intolerance; inability to digest starch and other sugars occurs rarely. The undigested carbohydrate is fermented by bacteria in the large bowel, causing irritation. Food is hurried through the digestive system with resulting malabsorption of other nutrients. There is usually an acid diarrhoea. The disorders are treated by a diet without the relevant carbohydrate.

Malnutrition

Malnutrition is ill health brought about by a failure to eat a balanced **diet**. One, or more often, several, **nutrients** may be lacking or in excess. It may also be caused by underlying disease – for instance **malabsorption**.

In affluent countries, most malnutrition is associated with too much food – see **obesity, diabetes, heart disease** and **tooth decay**. Deficiency diseases due to lack of essential nutrients alone are comparatively rare, but see **anaemia** and **osteomalacia**.

Deficiency diseases are more likely in both adults and children when poverty restricts both the amount and type of food available. They are common in most developing countries, where protein energy malnutrition (PEM) is the most serious public health problem, estimated to affect up to 20% of children under the age of five. It is caused by too little food or lack of protein or both – most cases are intermediate between the two extremes of **kwashiorkor** and **marasmus**. Any other essential nutrient may be lacking, see for instance vitamin A.

A child may recover from PEM, provided he is given food in sufficient time, and in mild cases growth and development are not affected over the long term. In severe cases, modern treatment has reduced the risk of death, but although the child may later catch up with his peers in terms of growth, the effect of PEM on subsequent mental ability is uncertain.

Maltose

Maltose is a sugar (disaccharide) composed of two molecules of **glucose**. It is about 30% as sweet as sugar (sucrose), and is found naturally in small quantities in some plants and honey. Maltose is formed during the **digestion** of **starch** and is itself digested to glucose, which is absorbed into the blood stream.

Maltose is formed in sprouted wheat or barley. Malt extract is used in malted drinks, malt loaves, barley sugar and as a vehicle for cod liver oil, but has no special nutritive virtues. Malted barley gives **flavour** and **colour** to **beer**.

Manganese

Manganese is a **trace element**, which is thought to be an essential **nutrient** for humans, though no disorder resulting from a lack of manganese has ever been established. It is required as a cofactor for several **enzymes**; in animals, synthetic diets deficient in manganese cause infertility and defects in the bones and nervous system.

Wholegrain cereals, nuts and tea are rich sources of manganese: one cup of tea supplies over half the assumed minimum daily needs. Some green vegetables (like spinach) are good sources. Refined cereals, meat, fish, eggs, fruit, white sugar, milk, and cheese are comparatively poor.

The manganese content of diets varies between 2 and 9 milligrams per day, which is presumed to be sufficient. In excess (100 times greater than normally eaten), manganese may interfere with the absorption of iron in the diet, but it would be extremely unusual to eat this amount in food. Toxic manganese gases, inhaled by miners of manganese ores, cause a disease called manganic madness.

Mango

The mango is a very popular fruit in tropical countries, particularly India, which is becoming increasingly available worldwide. Fresh mangoes contain plenty of **vitamin C**, although the amount varies considerably from one fruit to another. Ripe, orange coloured mangoes also contain **vitamin A** but unripe, green ones contain only about a tenth of the amount shown in the table.

Average nutrients in 100 grams (3½ oz) Mango

	fresh	canned		fresh	canned
Energy kilojoules	253	330	Iron milligrams	0.5	0.4
kilocalories	59	77	Copper milligrams	0.12	0.09
Protein grams	0.5	0.3	Zinc milligrams	–	0.3
Total fat grams	0	0	Vitamin A micrograms	200	200
Saturated fat grams	0	0	Vitamin D micrograms	0	0
Polyunsaturated fat grams	0	0	Vitamin C milligrams	10–180	10
			Vitamin E milligrams	–	–
Cholesterol milligrams	0	0	B vitamins:		
Sugars grams	15.3	20.2	Thiamin (B$_1$) milligrams	0.03	0.02
Starch grams	0	0.1	Riboflavin (B$_2$) milligrams	0.04	0.03
Dietary fibre grams	1.5	1.0	Nicotinic acid milligrams	0.4	0.2
Sodium milligrams	7	3	Pyridoxine (B$_6$) milligrams	–	–
Potassium milligrams	190	100	Vitamin B$_{12}$ micrograms	0	0
Calcium milligrams	10	10	Folic acid micrograms	–	–
Magnesium milligrams	18	7	Pantothenic acid milligrams	0.16	–
			Biotin micrograms	–	–

(–) No information available   (0) Contains zero or trace amounts

Marasmus

Marasmus is one extreme of protein energy **malnutrition**, widespread in developing countries. It is the child equivalent of **starvation**.

Initially, lack of food checks growth. If given sufficient food in time, the child is likely to catch up with his peers. Otherwise the child wastes away: fat stores are lost and used for energy; later, muscles are broken down. The child has a wizened appearance, the stomach may be swollen and diarrhoea develops because proteins are not available to renew the digestive system and its **enzymes**. The child is lethargic and less resistant to infections which may themselves be a partial cause of the disease.

Any child is at risk from marasmus but it typically occurs in the early months of life, often following early weaning from the breast. It is more likely in impoverished urban areas: the mother may stop breast feeding because she needs to work, or in response to advertising campaigns for artificial baby milks. The child may be given too little (the milks are expensive) and in insanitary conditions the feeds are likely to become contaminated. The child's illness will be worsened if, in an attempt to cure the resultant diarrhoea, the mother feeds the child on a water only diet.

Margarine

Most margarines are virtually all **fat**, like **butter**. Margarine was first patented as a less expensive substitute for butter by Mège Mouries in Paris in 1869, it contained suet, skim milk, and minced cow's udder. Modern margarines are sophisticated products of food technology, often eaten for health and convenience rather than economic reasons. The most expensive brands now cost as much as butter.

Virtually any source of **fat**, whether artificial, animal or vegetable, can be used to make margarine: refining enables the production of oils and fats free of taste, smell and colour. Most margarines are blends of vegetable or fish oils – the type used depending on world supplies. Different margarines for specific purposes (for example ice cream, baking, table margarines) are made after modifying – particularly hydrogenating – and blending refined fats.

Oils are liquid at room temperature, due to their higher content of unsaturated **fatty acids**. They can be made more saturated, and harder (solid at room temperature), by treatment with hydrogen and a nickel catalyst. Oils are never completely hydrogenated and some of the double bonds remain. Some of the biological activity may be lost however when the fatty acids lose their 'cis' formation, see **fatty acids**. Hard and soft margarines contain about the same proportions of polyunsaturated fatty acids, and only polyunsaturated margarines contain a substantial proportion, see table below. Margarine supplies about one quarter of the total polyunsaturated fat intake in the average British diet.

Low fat spreads such as Gold or Outline contain only half the fat and energy (Calories) of other margarines and are recommended for cutting down on **fat** in the diet. Polyunsaturated and low fat margarines do not contain **cholesterol** and the cholesterol content of other margarines is variable, depending on whether plant or animal or fish oils have been used in their manufacture. The fact that a margarine is stated to be cholesterol free does not mean that it will lower the blood cholesterol – only less fat overall or polyunsaturated margarines can do this.

All margarines are required by law to contain added vitamins A and D, which are worked into the fat together with **flavours, colours, emulsifiers** and **antioxidants** in the final stages of manufacture by a complicated system of beating and cooling. Margarine supplied nearly half the vitamin D in the average British diet in 1983, and is a useful supplement for people likely to be at risk from low amounts (see **vitamin D**).

Average nutrients in 100 grams (3½ oz) Margarines

	low fat spread	hard	soft	polyun- saturated
Energy kilojoules	1506	3000	3000	3000
kilocalories	366	730	730	730
Protein grams	0	0.1	0.1	0.1
Total fat grams	40	81	81	81
Saturated fat grams	11	30	25	19
Polyunsaturated fat grams	12	10–14	16–18	42
Cholesterol milligrams	0	a	a	0
Sugars grams	0	0.1	0.1	0.1
Starch grams	0	0	0	0
Dietary fibre (NSP) grams	0	0	0	0
Sodium milligrams	690	800	800	800
Potassium milligrams	0	5	5	5
Calcium milligrams	0	4	4	4
Magnesium milligrams	0	1	1	1

	low fat spread	hard	soft	polyun-saturated
Iron milligrams	0	0.3	0.3	0.3
Copper milligrams	0	0.04	0.04	0.04
Zinc milligrams	0	–	–	–
Vitamin A micrograms	800–1000	800–1000	800–1000	800–1000
Vitamin D micrograms	7.0–8.8	7.0–8.8	7.0–8.8	7.0–8.8
Vitamin C milligrams	0	0	0	0
Vitamin E milligrams	4.0	8.0	8.0	25.0
B vitamins:				
Thiamin (B₁) milligrams	0	0	0	0
Riboflavin (B₂) milligrams	0	0	0	0
Nicotinic acid milligrams	0	0	0	0
Pyridoxine (B₆) milligrams	0	0	0	0
Vitamin B₁₂ micrograms	0	0	0	0
Folic acid micrograms	0	0	0	0
Pantothenic acid milligrams	0	0	0	0
Biotin micrograms	0	0	0	0

(–) No information available   (0) Contains zero or trace amounts

ᵃContains cholesterol if animal fats used

Marrow and courgettes (zucchini)

Courgettes or zucchini are the same species as the marrow, developed for eating when young. When mature they are no different from the marrow. Courgettes are eaten with the skin on, hence they contain more vitamin A, as **carotene**, which is found largely in the green skin. The values given for marrow in the table are for peeled, boiled marrow, cooked for 30 minutes. Steamed or lightly cooked marrow will be more similar to courgettes in its nutrient composition, apart from the vitamin A.

Average nutrients in 100 grams (3½ oz) Courgettes and Marrow

	raw courgettes	boiled marrow		raw courgettes	boiled marrow
Energy kilojoules	105	29	Iron milligrams	2.4	0.2
kilocalories	25	7	Copper milligrams	–	0.03
Protein grams	1.6	0.4	Zinc milligrams	–	0.2
Total fat grams	0.4	0	Vitamin A micrograms	58	5
Saturated fat grams	–	0	Vitamin D micrograms	0	0
Polyunsaturated fat grams	–	0	Vitamin C milligrams	16	2
			Vitamin E milligrams	–	0
Cholesterol milligrams	0	0	B vitamins:		
Sugars grams	4.5	1.3	Thiamin (B₁) milligrams	0.05	0
Starch grams	–	0.1	Riboflavin (B₂) milligrams	0.09	0
Dietary fibre grams	–	0.6	Nicotinic acid milligrams	0.4	0.3
Sodium milligrams	1	1	Pyridoxine (B₆) milligrams	–	0.03
Potassium milligrams	202	84	Vitamin B₁₂ micrograms	0	0
Calcium milligrams	30	14	Folic acid micrograms	48	6
Magnesium milligrams	6	7	Pantothenic acid milligrams	–	0.07
			Biotin micrograms	–	–

(–) No information available   (0) Contains zero or trace amounts

Meat

Meat is the best source of well absorbed **iron** and **zinc**, but on the other hand it can be high in **fat**, especially saturated **fatty acids**. It contains well utilised **protein** and most B **vitamins** but it is not an essential item of diet.

The fat in meat influences the nutritional value of different cuts considerably. Most of the vitamins, minerals and proteins are concentrated in the lean, which contains about a fifth of its weight as protein. The cost of a particular cut of meat is not a reflection of its nutritional value; lean stewing steak has a similar nutrient content to lean fillet steak. Lean meat contains a maximum of 10% fat, supplying **essential fatty acids, cholesterol**, and **phospholipids**, but the fat content in some cuts, like streaky bacon and breast of lamb, can reach 40%. This fat contains more saturated fatty acids than the structural fat (see **lipid**) found in lean cuts.

In 1983, meat supplied a quarter of all the fat eaten in the average British diet, and most nutritionists recommend that this should be reduced by transferring to lean cuts. Despite its high biological value, much of the protein in large helpings is wasted and used for **energy** (Calories) so that a better balanced **diet** is achieved by limiting portions to about 60 grams (2 oz) cooked weight. Excess meat has also been linked with large bowel **cancer** and **osteoporosis**. The main focus of meals should be **starch** foods, such as potatoes, pasta and rice, with plenty of **vegetables**, rather than meat. In many recipes, the amount of meat can be cut down.

Meat is however the best source of iron and zinc and for this reason it is a valuable food for women and the elderly who are most likely to be prone to **anaemia**. Generally, red meats, game, liver (including pâté) and kidney are the richest sources – but see **iron** and **zinc**. **Liver** and **kidney** are also rich sources of **vitamin A**, the B vitamins, particularly B_{12} and **folic acid**, and they contain **vitamin D**. By the time it is eaten, meat usually contains only traces of vitamin C, apart from liver, kidney, and ham with added vitamin C (E300–304). Lean, fresh pork is a rich source of **thiamin** (vitamin B_1) but is deficient in **vitamin E**.

Fresh and frozen meat is not permitted to contain **colours, antioxidants** or **preservatives**, though mince may have added sulphur dioxide (a preservative) in Scotland throughout the summer months. Sulphur dioxide destroys thiamin. Tenderisers are permitted, but must be declared on an adjacent notice or, if the meat is prepacked, on the label. Tenderisers may be directly added to meat, or injected into the animal just prior to slaughter. Other additives are not specifically banned (except for vitamin C and nicotinic acid which preserve the colour of fresh meat and may mislead the customer) but their misuse could lead to prosecution under the 1984 Food Act (see **additives**). Oven ready poultry is usually injected with **polyphosphates** and sometimes with butter or extracts of fat from older animals to improve the flavour. Meat may also contain traces of **antibiotics**. In sheep and cattle synthetic hormones increase the lean in the carcase. They are either implanted as pellets in the ear or given in the feed, but are discontinued before slaughter and there is hardly any detectable residue left in the meat. Hormone pellets are also implanted in the neck of capons and turkeys: they have the same effect as castration and produce a fatter bird with an improved flavour, but a small residue is left in the meat. Most (about 85%) chickens are consumed as broilers, which are not caponised (given hormones or castrated).

Cooking tenderises meat and also has a preservative action, killing growing forms of putrefactive micro-organisms. However, cooked meat can easily be recontaminated and cause food poisoning – see **poisons in food**.

At least a quarter of the weight of meat is lost during cooking: the protein shrinks, squeezing water out. Consequently, weight for weight, cooked meat contains more protein than raw. Fat is also released, but cooked meat may contain more than raw if it is fried or basted.

Vitamin and mineral losses during cooking are very variable and depend on the type of cooking and cut of meat. Generally minerals and two B vitamins (riboflavin and nicotinic acid) are all recovered in the cooking liquor. Thiamin (vitamin B_1) is sensitive to heat: up to 70% can be lost when meat is boiled, stewed or braised and up to 50% when roasted or grilled. Up to 50% of other B vitamins are also lost.

When meat is cooked in the can, nutrient losses are of the same order as those incurred during cooking. Corned beef however, which is cooked in water before canning, contains no thiamin and less of other B vitamins. The liquor is used for beef **extracts**.

Thiamin is well retained when meat is cured, and bacon and ham are good sources. However, modern bacon and ham contain less nutrients weight for weight than traditional products. Traditionally, pork was cured by rubbing salt in to the carcase and smoking over wood fires, which resulted in a loss of about 20% of water. Now, brine solutions are injected (or the meat is soaked in tanks of brine) and smoke solutions are painted onto the surface. Polyphosphates and waterproof wrappers also aid water retention. The change is most marked in wrapped, sliced or tinned hams, which are very moist. All added water must be declared in cooked ham, and amounts greater than 10% (to the nearest 5%) in uncooked.

When meat is frozen, all the nutrients are retained but thiamin decreases during storage. When held in a deep freeze for six months, losses of between 20 and 40% of the vitamin have been reported. The drip of thawed meats should not be discarded: it contains up to 30% of the pantothenic acid and 10% of other B vitamins.

Meat products are permitted to contain most additives. Antioxidants (apart from vitamins C and E or their synthetic equivalents) may not be directly added but may be carried over when used in an ingredient. All meat products contain **salt** and most contain **monosodium glutamate**. Cured and pickled meats (like bacon, ham, luncheon meat, tongue, corned beef) may have added **nitrite**. All canned meats may be preserved with the **antibiotic** nisin. Sausages and other meat with cereal sold uncooked, like beefburgers, hamburgers, may be preserved with sulphur dioxide. This is important in preventing food poisoning, but they contain no vitamin B_1.

Some meat products have to contain minimum amounts of lean meat (see table). Mechanically recovered meat and offal is allowed to be counted as meat, although some offal, such as feet and brains are not allowed in uncooked meat products. These are only allowed to contain specified offal, such as head and tail meat, diaphragm and liver. Mechanically recovered meat is not normally taken off bones during hand trimming, but is scraped off by pressurised machinery, when the structure is lost. It is subsequently 'reformed' by the use of **soya** products or polyphosphates.

The minimum meat content of other meat products, such as meats in sauces, must be declared on the label. This will not all be lean and will include offal and recovered meat. Added water must also be declared in any product which looks like a cut, joint, or slice of meat by the amount it exceeds 10% in uncooked products or raw meat. This will include for example 'turkey roasts'. In cooked meats, like meats set in gelatine, all the added water has to be declared.

Animals have an important role in farming: they convert grass to a pleasant, nutritious and digestible food. However, it is impossible to satisfy present demands for meat from grazing alone and much of the world's food, for instance, cereals, fish and soya concentrates, that could be eaten by humans is given to animals. Although Britain produces sufficient food to feed all its population, paradoxically half of its food is imported. Even allowing for modern advances (like new breeds, the use of antibiotics), the conversion of plant foods into animal flesh is very inefficient: only one tenth of grain is returned as edible food. Famines in the rest of the world are aggravated by the disproportionately large quantity of the world's food supply consumed by developed countries. Anyone aware of this situation cannot justify large portions of meat.

Some examples of the minimum legal requirements for lean meat in meat products

Food	% lean meat	Comment
Corned beef	115[a]	Must contain only corned beef
Chopped meat	58	-
Beefburger, hamburger, luncheon meat	52	Beefburger must be 80% beef
Economy burger	36	Economy beefburger must be 60% beef
Sausages – pork	32	At least 80% of the meat must be pork
– beef	25	At least 50% of the meat must be beef
– liver	25	At least 30% of the meat must be liver
Meat spread	45	At least 70% must be the named meat
Pâté – liver or meat	35	-
Meat pie, pudding	10–12	} Total weight of the pie
		} higher value for cooked items
Pasties, sausage rolls	5–6	}

a – On a fresh weight basis. Corned beef loses water during processing

Melon

The melon species has many cultivated varieties, developed to suit varying climatic conditions worldwide. They are classified according to their skin, and colour of the flesh. 'Winter melons' are hard skinned and include the white skinned 'honeydew' and the dark-green skinned melon, mostly imported from Spain. The flesh is green and contains a little vitamin A, as carotene (see table).

Musk, cantaloupe and ogen melons have orange coloured flesh and contain about 300 micrograms of vitamin A per 100 grams. Otherwise the nutrient content of melons is very similar: they are 94% water.

Water melons are a different species with a slightly different nutrient composition, containing less vitamins C and A, and less potassium. They are also 94% water.

Average nutrients in 100 grams (3½ oz) Melons

	honeydew	water melon		honeydew	water melon
Energy kilojoules	90	92	Iron milligrams	0.2	0.3
kilocalories	21	21	Copper milligrams	0.04	0.03
Protein grams	0.6	0.4	Zinc milligrams	0.1	0.1
Total fat grams	0	0	Vitamin A micrograms	17	3
Saturated fat grams	0	0	Vitamin D micrograms	0	0
Polyunsaturated fat grams	0	0	Vitamin C milligrams	25	5
			Vitamin E milligrams	0.1	0.1 `
Cholesterol milligrams	0	0	B vitamins:		
Sugars grams	5.0	5.3	Thiamin (B$_1$) milligrams	0.05	0.02
Starch grams	0	0	Riboflavin (B$_2$) milligrams	0.03	0.02
Dietary fibre grams	0.9	–	Nicotinic acid milligrams	0.5	0.3
Sodium milligrams	20	4	Pyridoxine (B$_6$) milligrams	0.07	0.07
Potassium milligrams	220	120	Vitamin B$_{12}$ micrograms	0	0
Calcium milligrams	14	5	Folic acid micrograms	30	3
Magnesium milligrams	13	11	Pantothenic acid milligrams	0.23	1.55
			Biotin micrograms	–	–

(–) No information available   (0) Contains zero or trace amounts

Melon seeds

The values shown in the table below are for water melon seeds. They have a similar nutrient composition to **nuts**. Almost half their weight is **fat**, consequently they are high in energy. They also contain **iron** but this is probably poorly absorbed.

Average nutrients in 100 grams (3½ oz) Melon seeds

Energy kilojoules	2431	Iron milligrams		8.0
kilocalories	581	Copper milligrams		–
Protein grams	25.0	Zinc milligrams		–
Total fat grams	45.0	Vitamin A micrograms		0
Saturated fat grams	–	Vitamin D micrograms		0
Polyunsaturated fat grams	–	Vitamin C milligrams		0
		Vitamin E milligrams		–
Cholesterol milligrams	0	B vitamins:		
Sugars grams	} 19.0	Thiamin (B$_1$) milligrams		0.10
Starch grams		Riboflavin (B$_2$) milligrams		0.15
Dietary fibre grams	–	Nicotinic acid milligrams		–
Sodium milligrams	–	Pyridoxine (B$_6$) milligrams		–
Potassium milligrams	–	Vitamin B$_{12}$ micrograms		0
Calcium milligrams	50	Folic acid micrograms		–
Magnesium milligrams	–	Pantothenic acid milligrams		–
		Biotin micrograms		–

(–) No information available   (0) Contains zero or trace amounts

Metabolism

Life is an unstable process of unceasing chemical changes – metabolism – during which the energy released from breakdown of large molecules is used to make new molecules. Metabolism is derived from a Greek word meaning change. The speed at which **energy** in the body, ultimately derived from food, is being used can be measured as either the amount of heat produced or the amount of oxygen consumed and is called the **metabolic rate**.

Metabolic rate

The metabolic rate measures the speed at which **energy** from food or withdrawn from store is being used. It is measured as kilo**joules**, kilo**calories**, or watts.

The *basal metabolic rate* (BMR) is a measure of the amount of energy used in self maintenance – or the basic chemical changes necessary to maintain life. It includes the liberation of energy from **glucose** and **fatty acids** (see **lipid**) reactions, together with energy-using reactions such as the synthesis of new **proteins** needed for growth and repair; the elimination of waste products from the blood stream by the kidneys; the maintenance of the body temperature and **electrolyte** concentrations in cells; and the contraction of muscles in breathing and in the heart to maintain a constant supply of **nutrients** and oxygen in the blood stream. Children have a high basal metabolic rate because they are growing (synthesising new tissue); the rate of elderly people is less than young adults because the number of active cells declines with increasing age.

Average BMRs over the 24 hour period can be calculated from the equations given in the table below. A 55 kilogram (8½ stone) woman aged 65 years would have an average BMR of $0.04 \times 55 + 2.76$, or 4.85 Megajoules. During pregnancy an extra 0.8 to 1.2 Megajoules (200–285 kilocalories) is recommended on average to allow for the child's growth. Extra is also recommended for breast feeding, about 2 Megajoules, 500 kilocalories.

The standard BMRs predict the *average* needs for self maintenance over the whole 24 hour period and individuals can be expected to vary in their requirements by up to 20% greater or less than the average. Extra is also needed for moving about, because to do this muscular work is needed and this is also a chemical process requiring energy. Most people use about 1.4 times the BMR for both self maintenance and moving about – but over 1.5 is the recommended amount, see **energy**.

The body is only partially effective at converting one form of energy into another. Energy lost during energy using and energy liberating reactions is dissipated as heat and used to maintain the body temperature at or around 37°C, which is best suited to the activity of **enzymes**. Normally this heat is lost continually by radiation from the skin to the surrounding cooler air. In hot climates, less heat needs to be generated to maintain the body temperature and, to keep cool, most people further reduce their activity. The average man might have to reduce his food intake by 620 kilojoules (150 kilocalories) (in for instance two large slices of bread) or more if he moved from a temperate to a hot climate. In contrast, a very cold climate does not always increase the needs for energy to maintain the body temperature: the amount of heat lost from the skin is reduced by increased clothing and home heating.

Equations for calculating average metabolic rate in Megajoules per 24 hours

Note Body Weight (W) is in kilograms. To convert the result to kilocalories, divide by 4.2 and multiply by 1000.

Category	Average BMR equals	
	Male	**Female**
Children under 3 years	$0.25W - 0.13$	$0.24W - 0.13$
Children 3–10 years	$0.09W + 2.11$	$0.08W + 2.03$
Adolescents 10–18 years	$0.07W + 2.75$	$0.06W + 2.90$
Adults 18–30 years	$0.06W + 2.90$	$0.06W + 2.04$
Adults 30–60 years	$0.05W + 3.65$	$0.03W + 3.54$
Adults 60 years plus	$0.04W + 2.46$	$0.04W + 2.76$

Ref: Schofield et al *Hum. Nutr. Clin. Nutr.* 39C suppl. 1 1985

Methionine

Methionine is an essential **amino acid** – it cannot be made in the body and has to be obtained from **proteins** in food.

Cysteine is synthesised from methionine. It is also obtained from food proteins and reduces the daily needs for methionine: more is available for incorporation into new body proteins needed for growth and repair. Methionine is needed for the synthesis of other important substances, including **choline**. Cysteine, cystine, and methionine are the only amino acids which contain **sulphur**; the three are grouped together and called the sulphur amino acids.

The sulphur amino acids are usually the limiting amino acids in diets, determining the quality of the protein – or how much can be used for growth and repair. Although they are the limiting amino acids in British diets, there is no shortage: the estimated adult daily need is supplied, for example, by the 25 grams of protein in 80 grams (3 oz) of roast chicken. Excess intakes are used for energy purposes and the unwanted **nitrogen** is converted to urea. The kidney later filters waste urea and sulphur out of the blood stream.

Migraine

Severe migraine headaches affect about 8% of the population, often accompanied by nausea and vomiting. The precipitating factors are stress, hormonal changes, and diet. The foods most commonly involved in causing an attack are cheese, chocolate, citrus fruits and alcoholic drinks, and it is possible that the common factor in all of these foods is a substance called tyramine, formed from the amino acid **tyrosine**. Cheddar, Stilton and blue cheese contain the highest levels but the content depends on maturity and other factors so that one cheese may provoke an attack, whereas another will not. Chianti contains large amounts and another amine, octopamine, in citrus fruits may also be important.

The tyramine content of foods is not the only explanation since migraine sufferers given pure tyramine do not always respond with an attack. In a recent well controlled trial, nearly all of a group of children improved when given an elimination diet (see **allergy**) and developed migraine when various foods were introduced again. These included milk, eggs, chocolate, wheat, cheese, tomatoes, and squash containing **tartrazine** and benzoic acid (see **preservatives**). Many of the children reacted to several foods and to other factors such as emotional stress, exercise, cigarette smoke and perfume. When on the diet, only cigarette smoke and perfume triggered a migraine – which suggests that the children were allergic to these also.

Caffeine in tea and coffee may also provoke migraine in susceptible individuals.

Milk

Milk is an important source of **calcium, riboflavin, protein** and **zinc**. Cows' milk is a substitute for breast milk in infancy, and a convenient source of the extra essential **nutrients** needed in childhood, adolescence, pregnancy and breast feeding. Full cream and Channel Islands milks do however contain **fat**, mostly saturated **fatty acids**, and for this reason semi-skimmed or skimmed milks are recommended for adults and children over five. The nutritional value of skimmed milk is as good as whole milk, apart from the loss of vitamins A, D and E which are skimmed off with the cream, see table I. Because of the loss of these vitamins, skimmed milk (both dried and fresh) and semi-skimmed milk is not suitable for babies and children under the age of five.

Different milks are identified by different coloured bottle tops – silver for pasteurised, gold for Channel Islands, which contains more fat (see table), blue for skimmed, and red and silver for semi-skimmed. Homogenised red top, milk contains the same amount of fat as ordinary pasteurised milk and is treated to prevent fat rising to the top. Goats' milk has a similar composition to cows' but contains less **folic acid** (see table). **Anaemia** has sometimes occurred in babies fed boiled goats' milk.

Unless it is pasteurised, milk can be a dangerous carrier of micro-organisms, causing diseases like tuberculosis and scarlet fever. Unpasteurised milk is not permitted to be sold unless the herd is certified free of TB. Pasteurisation – heating the milk to above 61°C for 30 minutes – kills harmful bacteria, but a few harmless ones responsible for the eventual souring of milk remain. Pasteurisation causes minimal destruction of nutrients – see table II. During delivery (milk is about one day old when delivered) vitamin C decreases further – to about 10 milligrams per pint.

Riboflavin (vitamin B$_2$) is not sensitive to heat and is unaffected by pasteurisation but it is very sensitive to ultraviolet light. When left outside for only two hours, half the riboflavin is destroyed in bright sun, and one fifth on a dull day. Milk sold in shops in clear bottles exposed to fluorescent lighting for long periods is likely to contain much less riboflavin. There is no loss from milk in polyethylene-coated cartons. Riboflavin is converted to a substance which in turn quickly destroys any vitamin C. About one quarter of thiamin and any remaining vitamin C is lost when milk is boiled. If all the vitamin C has already been lost, boiling destroys folic acid.

Milk is preserved by evaporation or drying (to remove water) and by sterilisation (heating above boiling point). Sterilised milk is packed in sterile bottles or cartons and keeps for several months without the need for refrigeration. Ultra high temperature (longlife) milk has as good a nutrient content as pasteurised, but some of its vitamins are lost during storage – see Table II for nutrient losses in preserved milks and during storage. Riboflavin is unaffected by preservation, but may be lost during storage unless milk is kept in opaque containers.

Vegetable oils can be added to dried skimmed milk to make filled milks. These contain as much fat as ordinary (full cream) dried milks. Non dairy creamers are not a milk product. They are a mixture of fats, casein (milk protein) emulsifiers and other additives with hardly any nutritive value. See also **butter, cheese** and **yogurt**.

Milk is important in most welfare services. Table III shows the percentage of the recommended allowances for some nutrients supplied by one pint of milk. In Britain, a daily pint per person is supplied free of charge to low income families with pregnant and nursing mothers and children under school age. Although the elderly are not included in free milk schemes at least half a pint should be taken daily: milk is a cheap source of nutrients often lacking in an elderly person's diet.

In convalescence, milk, especially dried, is a useful way of enriching puddings and soups. It often relieves the pain of peptic **ulcers** but should not be taken to the exclusion of other foods. Its low content of iron and (when boiled) vitamin C and folic acid, predispose to **scurvy** and **anaemia**. Most races are unable to digest **lactose** in large quantities of milk: yogurt and cheese are better tolerated.

Baby feeding

Cows' milk – fresh, evaporated or dried – has been successfully used as a substitute for breast milk for millions of babies. Nevertheless, there are important differences in the protein and other nutrient contents of cows' and human milk. Some of the differences are overcome by diluting cows' milk – one part of water is mixed with two of fresh milk and a level teaspoon of sugar added for every 100 millilitres (3½ oz) of feed. The mixture must then be boiled to sterilise it. Instructions for the use of evaporated and sterilised milk are printed on the label of the tin and must be followed exactly. Welfare vitamin drops (containing vitamins A, D and C) are necessary for all babies, but the dose should be reduced for babies fed with powdered milks already fortified with vitamins.

When the mother's diet is adequate, breast feeding is preferable where possible, especially in the first fortnight after the birth. This is because breast milk contains proteins and immunoglobulin A which discourage the growth of harmful bacteria in the infant's digestive system, and may be important in **allergy**. After this time, the baby makes its own immunoglobulin A. However, allergy can occur in both breast and bottle fed babies because antigens are also found in human breast milk, when the mother may have to avoid the offending food. Nicotine, alcohol and caffeine also pass into breast milk and should be avoided during breast feeding.

Another important reason for encouraging breast feeding is that unless the cows' milk feed is hygienically prepared it is easily contaminated and diarrhoea may follow. Cows' milk, even when diluted, also contains more sodium and potassium and these require more water for the baby to excrete them, particularly in the case of powdered milk feeds which have been made up to be more concentrated than specified in the instructions. If the feed is too concentrated and no extra water is given, the baby becomes dehydrated and convulsions and brain damage may follow. Some powdered baby milks are adjusted to make their salt and fatty acid contents more like those of human milk but it is essential even with these that the instructions are followed exactly.

Whether the baby is breast fed or given artificial feeds or not, there is a consensus of opinion that solid foods should not be given to infants before the age of four months. This is to avoid the child becoming overweight, and possibly becoming prone to allergy – see for example **eczema**. The Department of Health and Social Security also recommend that mothers should avoid adding cereal foods to milk in the bottle feed, and sugar and salt to weaning foods and baby foods in general.

Table I
Average nutrients in 100 grams (3½ oz) Milks

	fresh skimmed cows'	fresh whole cows'	fresh whole goats'	dried skimmed	canned condensed	canned evaporated
Energy kilojoules	142	272	296	1512	1362	660
kilocalories	33	65	71	355	322	158
Protein grams	3.4	3.3	3.3	36.4	8.3	8.6
Total fat grams	0.1	3.8[a]	4.5	1.3[b]	9.0	9.0
Saturated fat grams	0	2.3	3.0	0.8	5.4	5.4
Polyunsaturated fat grams	0	0.1	0.1	0	0.3	0.2
Cholesterol milligrams	2	14	–	18	34	34
Sugars grams	5.0	4.7	4.6	52.8	55.5	11.3
Starch grams	0	0	0	0	0	0
Dietary fibre grams	0	0	0	0	0	0
Sodium milligrams	52	50	40	550	130	180
Potassium milligrams	150	150	180	1650	390	390
Calcium milligrams	130	120	130	1190	280	280
Magnesium milligrams	12	12	20	117	27	28
Iron milligrams	0.05	0.05	0.04	0.40	0.20	0.20
Copper milligrams	0.02	0.02	0.05	0.20	0.04	0.04
Zinc milligrams	0.36	0.35	0.30	4.1	1.0	1.1
Vitamin A micrograms	0	28–39	40	0	107	92
Vitamin D micrograms	0	0.01–0.03	0.06	0	0.09	2.8[c]
Vitamin C milligrams	1.6[d]	1.5[d]	1.5[d]	6.0	2.0	1.0
Vitamin E milligrams	0	0.10	–	0	0.42	0.56
B vitamins:						
Thiamin (B$_1$) milligrams	0.04	0.04	0.04	0.42	0.08	0.06
Riboflavin (B$_2$) milligrams	0.20[c]	0.19[c]	0.15[c]	1.6	0.48	0.51
Nicotinic acid milligrams	0.88	0.86	0.97	9.7	2.2	2.3
Pyridoxine (B$_6$) milligrams	0.04	0.04	0.04	0.25	0.02	0.04
Vitamin B$_{12}$ micrograms	0.3	0.3	0	3.0	0.5	0

	fresh skimmed cows'	fresh whole cows'	fresh whole goats'	dried skimmed	canned condensed	canned evaporated
Folic acid micrograms	5	5	1	21	8	7
Pantothenic acid milligrams	0.36	0.35	0.34	3.5	0.85	0.85
Biotin micrograms	2.0	2.0	2.0	16	3.0	3.0

(–) No information available   (0) Contains zero or trace amounts

aChannel Island (gold top) milk contains 4.8 grams, semi-skimmed 2.0 grams
bDried milks with vegetable fats contain 26 grams
cContains added vitamin D
dFalls to 0.5 milligrams in 24 hours
eIf kept out of sunlight (see text)

Table II
Nutrient losses in processing and storage of milk

Process	Nutrients lost	Comments
Pasteurisation	10% of the B vitamins: thiamin (B_1), pyridoxine (B_6), folic acid, vitamin B_{12}, 25% of vitamin C.	
Boiling	25% of vitamin B_1 (thiamin). Slight loss of riboflavin in open pan.	If all vitamin C lost, boiling destroys folic acid
UHT milk	Same as pasteurisation	50% of pyridoxine and vitamin B_{12} lost on 3 months' storage
Bottled sterilised	20% thiamin, B_{12} 30% folic acid 60% vitamin C	
Evaporated milk	80% vitamin B_{12} 50% vitamin C and B_6 20% vitamin A 20% vitamin B_1	Vitamin D is added but evaporation is most 'destructive' way of preserving milk
Condensed milk	10% vitamin B_1, B_6 25% vitamin C and folic acid 30% vitamin B_{12}	Less 'destructive' than evaporation: added sugar reduces the need for heat to sterilise the can. Skimmed or full cream milk can be used.
Dried milk	Same as pasteurisation	Only significant loss is when fat soluble vitamins are removed from skimmed milk.

Table III
Approximate percentage of recommended intake of some nutrients supplied by 600 millilitres (1 pint) milk

Nutrient	Pregnant woman	Breast feeding woman	6 year old child	16 year old girl	35 year old woman	65 year old woman
Calcium	60	60	145	120	145	145
Riboflavin	55	50	100	65	70	70
Protein	35	30	45	35	35	40
Energy	15	15	15	15	15	20

Millet

Millet contains the same **nutrients** as other **cereals**. It cannot support life when eaten alone because it is lacking in vitamins C, A and B_{12}, but is a valuable staple in the diet.

There are several varieties of millets, each with different local names. The three main varieties are pearl or bulrush millet; red or finger millet; and sorghum. Millets have similar nutritive values to wheat, but all are lacking in **gluten**. Millet is eaten whole as a kind of thick gruel, or ground by hand to flour for use in flat cakes. As it is not highly milled, millet retains all its nutritional value. No commercial millet foods are produced.

Millet has been grown in most arid areas and used as a staple in communities in Africa, Asia and South America. Its cultivation is declining in favour of new drought resistant varieties of wheat which can be made into leavened bread.

Average nutrients in 100 grams (3½ oz) Millet flour

Energy kilojoules	1481	Iron milligrams	–
kilocalories	354	Copper milligrams	–
Protein grams	5.8	Zinc milligrams	–
Total fat grams	1.7	Vitamin A micrograms	0
Saturated fat grams	–	Vitamin D micrograms	0
Polyunsaturated fat grams	–	Vitamin C milligrams	0
		Vitamin E milligrams	–
Cholesterol milligrams	0	B vitamins:	
Sugars grams	–	Thiamin (B_1) milligrams	0.68
Starch grams	75.4	Riboflavin (B_2) milligrams	0.19
Dietary fibre grams	–	Nicotinic acid milligrams	–
Sodium milligrams	21	Pyridoxine (B_6) milligrams	–
Potassium milligrams	365	Vitamin B_{12} micrograms	0
Calcium milligrams	40	Folic acid micrograms	–
Magnesium milligrams	–	Pantothenic acid milligrams	–
		Biotin micrograms	–

(–) No information available   (0) Contains zero or trace amounts

Mineral hydrocarbons

Mineral hydrocarbons are products derived from mineral oil. They are undesirable in food: they interfere with the absorption (see digestion) of the fat soluble vitamins A, D, E and K (large amounts of liquid paraffin can cause deficiency of these **nutrients**) and small amounts may be absorbed and deposited in the liver. Impurities are suspected carcinogens, consequently only high grade products are permitted in food.

The Mineral Hydrocarbons in Food Regulations 1966 prohibit their use in all except six foods, but allow for contamination of all processed food (to a maximum of 0.2%) with mineral oil used as release agents (see **Miscellaneous additives**) to processing apparatus. The six foods that are otherwise permitted to contain mineral hydrocarbons are:

Dried fruit: mineral oil can be added to a maximum of 0.5% (500 milligrams per 100 grams of food) to keep the fruit moist. The regulations assume that dried fruit is to be washed before eating.

Citrus fruit: mineral wax can be added to the skin to a maximum of 0.1%. The regulations assume that the skin is not eaten.

Sweets: used as a polish or glazing agent (see **additives**). Up to 0.2% is allowed.

Chewing gum: a maximum of 60% of mineral wax is permitted in the gum. Only very pure gum, subjected to a lengthy purification process, is allowed.

Eggs (must be marked 'sealed'): mineral wax can be used to coat hens' or duck egg shells, as a preservative.

Cheese: mineral wax may be used to coat hard, Edam and Gouda cheese. It is usually removed before sale from hard cheeses, and painted red in Edam.

Mineral water

Artificial

Water charged with the gas carbon dioxide. The effervescence is said to make the drink more refreshing than still water. Soda water must contain a minimum of 330 milligrams of sodium bicarbonate per pint.

Natural

Bottled spa waters. They have no proven benefits except that they may be drunk in preference to **alcohol**. Spa waters are usually alkaline and often have a strong smell or taste due to their mineral content. Some are charged with carbon dioxide. Under 1985 regulations, no reference to medicinal matters may be made in labelling or advertising natural mineral waters, to avoid misleading consumers.

Minerals

Minerals are essential **nutrients** which must be supplied in the diet. They may be incorporated into the body structure, or function as cofactors for **enzymes**, or are required as **electrolytes**.

Humans require at least fifteen minerals. The need for **calcium, phos-**

phorus, sodium, chlorine, iron, iodine, potassium and **magnesium** was recognised by the end of the nineteenth century, but knowledge of man's requirement for **copper, zinc, manganese, molybdenum, selenium,** and **chromium** has only been acquired with the development of more sensitive analytical methods and problems encountered in the maintenance of critically ill patients by intravenous feeding. **Cobalt** is required as **vitamin B_{12}**. The use of isolator cages and highly purified artificial diets has established the essentiality of six other elements (**silicon, tin, nickel, arsenic, vanadium** and **fluorine**) for animals and it is probable that these are also essential for humans.

Requirements for minerals in food and the amounts found in the body vary by factors of at least several hundred thousands. Seven minerals – calcium, magnesium, chlorine, phosphorus, potassium, sodium and sulphur occur in relatively large amounts. For example, adults contain about 1200 grams (over 2 lbs) of calcium, and the recommended intake for adults is 500 milligrams (one milligram is equal to one thousandth of a gram). Comparatively minute amounts of the **trace elements** – originally only measurable in foods and living tissues as 'traces', hence the term 'trace element' – are required and found in the body. For example, adults contain about 300 milligrams of iodine and probably need about 100 micrograms a day (one microgram is equal to one thousandth of a milligram). Iron and zinc are needed in intermediate amounts – a few milligrams.

Miscellaneous additives in food

The Miscellaneous Additives in Food Regulations 1980 permit about 150 substances in all foods. They are used for a variety of reasons and only a few examples are given in the list below. A full list of additives and their E numbers is shown in Appendix II. A few miscellaneous additives are permitted up to specified levels in certain foods only, and not all are numbered.

Acids are added to give an acid taste. They include acetic acid (E260), citric (E330) and malic acids (E350).

Buffers control acidity and are usually salts of weak acids, such as calcium lactate (E327).

Bases (alkalis) also control acidity. They include calcium hydroxide (526) and potassium carbonate (501).

Humectants keep foods like cakes soft by preventing the food from drying out. **Sorbitol** and **glycerol** (E420) and sodium potassium lactate (E325, E326) are examples of humectants.

Sequestrants inactivate stray minerals thus preventing deterioration from rancidity (see **antioxidants**). Include **glycine** and sodium calcium edetate in canned fish to prevent glass like crystals (struvite) forming. Citric acid (E330) and polyphosphates (E450) are also sequestrants.

Propellants used in aerosols like whipped cream. The gases nitrogen, carbon dioxide (E290) and nitrous oxide are permitted.

Glazing agents coated over food to give a shiny surface. Include beeswax, gelatin and shellac.

Anti-foaming agents prevent powders from clumping together, and foods from sticking to bags. Most dry powder foods contain them, such as salt, cake mixes and coffee whiteners. Also crisps. They include magnesium carbonate, sodium ferrocyanide in salt, and silicates.

Release agents prevent foods sticking to utensils. Include **glycerol** and **mineral hydrocarbons**.

Firming and crisping agents are calcium salts added to canned vegetables to give 'bite' – see **pectin**. Includes calcium chloride.

Packaging gas and liquid freezants are used to exclude air from packs and to freeze food, for example **nitrogen** and dichlorodifluomethane, permitted in all frozen food.

Bulking aids added to give 'mouth feel' to foods, such as **glucose** syrup.

Flavour modifiers such as **monosodium glutamate** (621).

Modified starches

Starch is used in cooking to thicken sauces and puddings, but normal starch requires heat, may form too hard a 'set', and the set can separate for example when foods are frozen. These problems can be overcome by chemically modifying starch in a variety of ways and these are used in most processed and convenience foods. Modified starches may also be used as **emulsifiers** and anti-caking agents (see **miscellaneous additives**). The average person eats about one gram of modified starch per day, or just over 0.5 lb per year.

At present modified starches are not subject to legal control but they are likely to be so in the future. In a recent government committee report, starches modified by heat, acids, alkalis and enzymes were recommended for use in food, and their probable E numbers will range from E1400 to E1404. For fourteen other starches (probable numbers E1410–1442) chemically treated to combine with, for example, **phosphorus** or **acetic acid** there was sufficient information to recommend their continued use over the short term, pending further safety tests.

Molybdenum

Molybdenum is an essential **nutrient** for animals and probably humans. It is a **trace element** and part of several **enzymes**, one of which is concerned in the formation of uric acid (see **gout**) and possibly in the utilisation of **iron**.

There are no well established values for molybdenum in food: the element is difficult to analyse and soil water and plant contents vary in different parts of the world. Leafy vegetables and pulses supply more than root vegetables. Plants grown in alkaline soils rich in humus absorb more than those grown in acid and sandy soils.

All diets supply some molybdenum. It is possible that the teeth of children living in a low molybdenum area may be less resistant to decay, but otherwise no disorder arising from lack of molybdenum is currently suspected.

In excess, molybdenum may possibly predispose to gout. Animals given feeds high in molybdenum become deficient in **copper**. A similar antagonistic effect of molybdenum is claimed to account for severe knock knees of humans living in a certain area of India, where the diet is very restricted and the soil is alkaline and high in molybdenum and **fluorine**.

Monosaccharides

Monosaccharides are simple sugars synthesised by plants, animals and microbes. There are many different monosaccharides in nature, but **fructose, glucose** and **galactose** are the most important in human nutrition. They are found only in small amounts naturally, but in abundance as combined forms – **disaccharides** and **polysaccharides**. During **digestion** the component monosaccharides of some combined forms in food are liberated and absorbed into the blood stream.

Monosodium glutamate (MSG) (621)

Monosodium glutamate is a **flavour** enhancer, which, like **salt**, intensifies the flavour of food. It also imparts a meaty taste. It is the sodium salt (in the same way that sodium chloride, common salt, is the salt of hydrochloric acid) of **glutamic acid**, an **amino acid** present in all food **proteins**. For instance, 100 grams (3 slices) of bread contains about 3 grams of glutamic acid, a medium sized (100 grams) grilled beefsteak about 4 grams. During **digestion**, proteins are dismantled and the amino acids absorbed into the blood stream.

MSG is manufactured from wheat **gluten** and is an accepted part of Chinese cuisine. It has also been added to Western processed foods for about 70 years. MSG contributes to the sodium content of the diet but when used in small amounts (100 to 200 milligrams per 100 grams of food) the MSG in processed foods is otherwise harmless for adults.

Excessive amounts of MSG are reported to cause unpleasant symptoms in some people; sweating, headache, numbness in the back of the neck, and chest pain have been reported after eating Chinese food. Between 2 and 12 grams of MSG (10 to 120 times that present in processed foods) are thought to be necessary before the unpleasant effects are felt. This effect of MSG is difficult to understand, given that large amounts are normally consumed in food, as glutamic acid, as described above. It may be absorbed more quickly when taken as clear soups on an empty stomach, or the effect may be due to the sodium (salt) content of such large amounts of MSG. Although the experience can be frightening for those who are thought to be sensitive to MSG, there is no evidence of permanent damage.

Animal experiments have shown that when young mice and rats are subjected to injections of very large doses of MSG, brain damage occurs, although other species such as monkeys are not affected. Ten times this level, or about 3000 times the equivalent amount eaten by humans, were necessary to cause damage to the young of pregnant mice. MSG is not added to baby foods, and pregnant women who like the taste of foods with added MSG are unlikely to damage the child by eating them. Foods with a high level of salt and containing MSG are however not generally regarded as healthy ones – see **diet**.

Muesli, see also breakfast cereals

Muesli is a blend of oats and other cereals, usually wheatflakes, together with nuts, dried fruit and, originally, fresh fruit, such as apple. It was devised as a breakfast dish by Dr Bircher Benner at the end of the nineteenth century but was only introduced as a branded product in 1972. Branded products contain added sugar (dried fruit flakes) and milk powder and are very variable in their nutrient and ingredient contents. The values shown in the table are from averages of four brands. Values from home-prepared muesli, containing rolled oats, toasted wheat flakes, sultanas, hazel nuts and fresh apple are also shown in the table.

Average nutrients in 100 grams (3½ oz) Muesli

	brand	home prepared[a]		brand	home prepared[a]
Energy kilojoules	1556	1240	Iron milligrams	4.6	4.0
kilocalories	368	295	Copper milligrams	0.41	0.3
Protein grams	12.9	8.0	Zinc milligrams	2.2	1.8
Total fat grams	7.5	7.2	Vitamin A micrograms	0	1
Saturated fat grams	1.3	1.0	Vitamin D micrograms	0	0
Polyunsaturated fat grams	3.0	1.9	Vitamin C milligrams	0	1
			Vitamin E milligrams	3.2	1.1
Cholesterol milligrams	0	0	B vitamins:		
Sugars grams	26.2	11.5	Thiamin (B₁) milligrams	0.33	0.5
Starch grams	40.0	42.0	Riboflavin (B₂) milligrams	0.27	0.8
Dietary fibre grams	7.4	7.6	Nicotinic acid milligrams	3.0	3.9
Sodium milligrams	180	136	Pyridoxine (B₆) milligrams	0.14	0.2
Potassium milligrams	600	382	Vitamin B₁₂ micrograms	0	0
Calcium milligrams	200	37	Folic acid micrograms	48	43
Magnesium milligrams	100	83	Pantothenic acid milligrams	–	0.4
			Biotin micrograms	–	6.1

(–) No information available   (0) Contains zero or trace amounts

[a]30% rolled oats
30% toasted wheat flakes
10% sultanas
10% flaked hazel nuts
20% fresh apple

Mushrooms

There are at least ten edible species of mushrooms and other fungi to be found in Britain, ranging from truffles to puff balls. Only one however, the field mushroom, is commonly eaten. Nutrient contents are shown in the table, together with some for the dried Chinese mushroom.

Average nutrients in 100 grams (3½ oz) Mushrooms

	raw field	dried Chinese		raw field	dried Chinese
Energy kilojoules	53	1188	Iron milligrams	1.0	11.7
kilocalories	13	284	Copper milligrams	0.64	–
Protein grams	1.8	10.0	Zinc milligrams	0.1	–
Total fat grams	0.6	1.8	Vitamin A micrograms	0	0
Saturated fat grams	0.1	–	Vitamin D micrograms	0	0
Polyunsaturated fat grams	0.3	–	Vitamin C milligrams	3	0
			Vitamin E milligrams	0	–
Cholesterol milligrams	0	0	B vitamins:		
Sugars grams	0	} 59.9	Thiamin (B_1) milligrams	0.10	0.37
Starch grams	0		Riboflavin (B_2) milligrams	0.40	1.32
Dietary fibre grams	2.5	–	Nicotinic acid milligrams	4.6	11.3
Sodium milligrams	9	38	Pyridoxine (B_6) milligrams	0.10	–
Potassium milligrams	470	1482	Vitamin B_{12} micrograms	0	0
Calcium milligrams	3	76	Folic acid micrograms	23	–
Magnesium milligrams	13	–	Pantothenic acid milligrams	2.0	–
			Biotin micrograms	–	–

(–) No information available   (0) Contains zero or trace amounts

Mussels

Mussels are nutritious foods, containing **protein, calcium** and well absorbed **iron** and **zinc**. They should be bought fresh from reputable fishmongers. Care should be taken not to gather wild mussels from polluted waters which may be contaminated with salmonella (see **poisons in food**), although the salmonella is destroyed by proper cooking. Occasionally, mussels contain a nerve toxin produced by a micro-organism which is not destroyed by cooking; this can cause paralysis and death.

Average nutrients in 100 grams (3½ oz) Mussels (boiled)

Energy kilojoules	366	Iron milligrams	7.7
kilocalories	87	Copper milligrams	0.48
Protein grams	17.2	Zinc milligrams	2.1
Total fat grams	2.0	Vitamin A micrograms	0
Saturated fat grams	0.4	Vitamin D micrograms	0
Polyunsaturated fat grams	0.5	Vitamin C milligrams	0
		Vitamin E milligrams	0.9
Cholesterol milligrams	100	B vitamins:	
Sugars grams	0	Thiamin (B_1) milligrams	–
Starch grams	0	Riboflavin (B_2) milligrams	–
Dietary fibre grams	0	Nicotinic acid milligrams	–
Sodium milligrams	210	Pyridoxine (B_6) milligrams	–
Potassium milligrams	92	Vitamin B_{12} micrograms	–
Calcium milligrams	200	Folic acid micrograms	–
Magnesium milligrams	25	Pantothenic acid milligrams	–
		Biotin micrograms	–

(–) No information available   (0) Contains zero or trace amounts

Mustard and cress

Seedlings eaten a few days old; the mustard seedling leaves are broader than the cress. They contain a good amount of **vitamin C** and minerals – though few analyses are available (see table). Mustard and cress are members of the *Cruciferae* family – see **cabbage**.

Average nutrients in 100 grams (3½ oz) Mustard and cress

Energy kilojoules	47	Iron milligrams	1.0
kilocalories	10	Copper milligrams	0.12
Protein grams	1.6	Zinc milligrams	–
Total fat grams	0	Vitamin A micrograms	83
Saturated fat grams	0	Vitamin D micrograms	0
Polyunsaturated fat grams	0	Vitamin C milligrams	40
		Vitamin E milligrams	0.7
Cholesterol milligrams	0	B vitamins:	
Sugars grams	0.9	Thiamin (B$_1$) milligrams	–
Starch grams	0	Riboflavin (B$_2$) milligrams	–
Dietary fibre grams	3.7	Nicotinic acid milligrams	–
Sodium milligrams	19	Pyridoxine (B$_6$) milligrams	–
Potassium milligrams	340	Vitamin B$_{12}$ micrograms	0
Calcium milligrams	66	Folic acid micrograms	–
Magnesium milligrams	27	Pantothenic acid milligrams	–
		Biotin micrograms	–

(–) No information available   (0) Contains zero or trace amounts

Nectarine

A variety of peach, with a richer flavour and colour and smooth skin. Its composition is very similar to the peach (see table).

Average nutrients in 100 grams (3½ oz) Nectarine

Energy kilojoules	214	Iron milligrams	0.5
kilocalories	50	Copper milligrams	0.06
Protein grams	0.9	Zinc milligrams	0.1
Total fat grams	0	Vitamin A micrograms	83
Saturated fat grams	0	Vitamin D micrograms	0
Polyunsaturated fat grams	0	Vitamin C milligrams	8
		Vitamin E milligrams	–
Cholesterol milligrams	0	B vitamins:	
Sugars grams	12.4	Thiamin (B_1) milligrams	0.02
Starch grams	0	Riboflavin (B_2) milligrams	0.05
Dietary fibre grams	2.4	Nicotinic acid milligrams	1.1
Sodium milligrams	9	Pyridoxine (B_6) milligrams	0.02
Potassium milligrams	270	Vitamin B_{12} micrograms	0
Calcium milligrams	4	Folic acid micrograms	5
Magnesium milligrams	13	Pantothenic acid milligrams	0.15
		Biotin micrograms	–

(–) No information available   (0) Contains zero or trace amounts

Nickel

Nickel is an essential **trace element** for some animals, and probably humans. In animals, it apparently helps to maintain the integrity of the liver. It is most unlikely that human diets would ever lack nickel: it is used as a catalyst for hydrogenating oils (see **margarine**) and for coating steel food processing equipment. Some is likely to be transferred to food.

Nicotinic acid

– other names, niacin, PP factor.
– group name for nicotinamide (also called niacinamide) plus nicotinic acid.

Nicotinic acid is part of the **vitamin B complex**. Insufficient nicotinic acid or tryptophan in the diet causes the deficiency disease **pellagra**.

The **amino acid**, **tryptophan**, which occurs in most **proteins** can be converted to nicotinic acid in the liver when sufficient tryptophan and vitamins B_1, B_2, and B_6 (**thiamin**, **riboflavin**, **pyridoxine**) are available. Consequently food contents and dietary requirements for the vitamin are expressed as nicotinic acid equivalents. One milligram equivalent is equal to 60 milligrams of tryptophan in food, or 1 milligram of available nicotinic acid.

Most foods, except sugar, fats and alcoholic spirits, contain some nicotinic acid equivalents, but foods rich in protein are the best sources. **Liver**, **peanuts** and **extracts** are good sources, as are **meats** followed by **fish**, **cheese**, **pulses**, **eggs**, other **vegetables**, **bread** and **milk**. Fruit is a poor source. During the roasting of **coffee**, nicotinic acid is released from trigonelline, and both instant and ground coffee are sources of the vitamin.

Cereals, except maize, contain tryptophan. Wholegrain cereals also contain nicotinic acid (it is removed when cereals are refined) but it is in a bound form, niacytin, not available to man unless treated with alkalis. Bicarbonate of soda (used to raise soda bread) may liberate some of the nicotinic acid in wholemeal and brown soda bread, but it also destroys thiamin. (vitamin B_1). Ordinary (leavened with yeast) white bread contains more nicotinic acid equivalents than wholemeal because nicotinic acid is added to all white flour by law – see **bread**. Some **breakfast cereals** also contain added nicotinic acid.

Nicotinic acid is one of the most stable of vitamins and there are little or no losses during storage, processing and cooking. Weight for weight, cooked **meat** may contain more than raw. However, the vitamin is water soluble and leaches out into cooking water. Vegetables lose about 40% of the vitamin when boiled in a large pan of water, but none when baked or fried. The vitamin can be recovered if the cooking water is used for sauce or gravy.

The **recommended intake** for women is 15 milligrams of nicotinic acid equivalents per day: the average British diet supplies nearly twice this amount. Men need slightly more than women (18 milligrams) and, to ensure an adequate supply for the growing child, a mother probably needs more than usual throughout pregnancy and breast feeding. Infants, children and adolescents need more in proportion to their weight than adults to allow for growth. See Appendix I for recommended intakes.

Nicotinic acid is the group name for two forms of the vitamin – nicotinic acid (also called niacin) and nicotinamide (also called niacinamide). Although nicotine in tobacco has a similar structure to nicotinic acid, the biochemical effects of the two are completely different. To avoid confusion, niacin is the preferred name for the vitamin in the USA. The vitamin is part of the B complex, but is not numbered in Britain for historical reasons (see **vitamin B**).

The two forms of the vitamin occur in food and are equally potent. In the body they are converted to two important co**Enzymes** involved in the liberation of **energy** within cells. Although there is no store of nicotinic acid in the body, it is widely distributed throughout all cells.

A diet totally lacking in both tryptophan and nicotinic acid takes about 50 days to deplete the tissues. The symptoms of pellagra – a sore tongue and diarrhoea; sunburn-like lesions on the skin; mental confusion and depression – are due to derangements of the digestive system, skin and brain cells. Death is usually hastened by an infection. Improvement of the condition results when the vitamin is given, but there are usually other deficiencies that must be treated before full health is restored. Pellagra is extremely rare in Britain but sometimes occurs when there is underlying disease, for example **malabsorption** and alcoholism.

Nicotinamide is harmless when taken in excess – it is filtered out of the blood stream by the kidneys – but supplements are unnecessary in balanced **diets**. Nicotinic acid however sometimes causes transient flushing and a burning sensation in the head, neck and arms. Its use – in powders dusted over meat to preserve its red colour – caused a public controversy in 1963. It was subsequently banned from meat (together with vitamin C) by the Meat (Treatment) Regulations 1964.

In pharmacological doses (much more than could be obtained from food) nicotinic acid (but not nicotinamide) may suppress the synthesis of **cholesterol** and daily doses of 3 grams have been used in the treatment of some inherited disorders (see **lipid**). Pharmacological doses of the vitamin are also used in two **inborn errors of metabolism** and may be of benefit in the treatment of schizophrenia.

Nitrite and nitrate (E249-252)

These are **preservatives** permitted in **cheese** (excluding Cheddar, Cheshire and soft cheeses), cured **meat** (including bacon, ham, luncheon meat) and pickled meat (like tongue, salt beef, corned beef, beef loaf, meat rolls, some sausages and pâté). They are the sodium or potassium salts of nitrous and nitric acids respectively (in the same way that sodium chloride (salt) is the salt of hydrochloric acid).

In cheese, nitrite prevents souring. In cured and pickled meat it prevents multiplication of bacteria responsible for botulism (a type of food poisoning that is usually fatal); contributes to the flavour; and combines with the pigment (myoglobin) in meat forming a stable pink colour. Unlike canned meats, bacon and ham cannot be heated to a sufficiently high temperature to kill the bacteria without spoiling the product. **Ascorbic acid** (vitamin C) is used in modern curing methods and sometimes enables less nitrite to be added. Nitrate (in salt petre) was the original curing substance and is converted to nitrite in the meat, partly by bacterial action. Since it was realised that nitrite is the active substance, it is usually added directly. The Preservatives in Food Regulations 1979 permit a maximum of 5 parts per million of nitrite in cheese, 50 in salami, and 200 parts per million in bacon, ham and other cured meats (1 part per million is equal to 0.1 milligrams per 100 grams of food).

Nitrates occur naturally in soil, water and some vegetables (they are the raw material of the protein made by plants). Abnormally high concentrations of nitrates in food and water can follow the excessive use of fertilisers. In itself this is harmless: nitrate is produced in the body and is toxic only in very large doses. However, **enzymes** from bacteria in vegetables and the human digestive system can convert the nitrate to nitrite. Spinach and lettuce seem to accumulate nitrate particularly.

Nitrite formation is more likely when little acid is secreted in the stomach, for example in infancy, and it combines with haemoglobin – the oxygen carrying pigment in red blood cells. Unlike adults, babies are not equipped with enzymes capable of reversing the effect of nitrite poisoning (methaemoglobinaemia) and the condition can be fatal. Special water is available in high nitrate areas for babies; nitrite and nitrate are not added to baby foods.

In 1965, it was realised that nitrite in food might have other more harmful effects. Under certain circumstances, it reacts with amines (in protein containing foods but especially cheese and fish) to form nitrosamines, which are known to cause **cancer** in animals. Over 100 different nitrosamines are known (they are formed from a variety of amines) and some cause cancer in many areas of animals' bodies, including liver, lungs, brain and digestive tract. One can cause cancer in offspring when given to pregnant animals.

Although nitrosamines have been found to be widespread in food, water, alcoholic drinks, cosmetics and tobacco, very sensitive equipment is necessary to detect them. Such small quantities may not cause cancer in humans (or, indeed, in animals) and in cured meats the additive is a necessary precaution against the fatal botulism. Nitrate is also found in saliva and nitrite (and therefore nitrosamines) is formed even if it is not added to food. Smokers form more than non-smokers. Vitamins C and E are able to inhibit the formation of some nitrosamines at least when taken with food. Vitamin C is added to some cured products, and there has been a fall in detectable nitrosamines in recent years. At present the general view is that nitrite used in processing meat presents only a low level of risk of cancer to the consumer. There are marked individual variations in the ability to both form and metabolise nitrosamines naturally from nitrite produced in the body and amines in protein foods, and this might turn out to be important in determining why some individuals are more susceptible to cancers in different parts of the body. Nevertheless, it is probably wise to eat plenty of vegetables and fruit containing vitamins E and C, and to limit to moderate portions all meat and other fatty food, including cured meats, as set out in **diet**. Smokers expose themselves to greater risks than others.

Nitrogen

Nitrogen is part of the structure of **amino acids**. The nitrogen content of a food is a measure of its **protein** content: proteins contain an average of 16% nitrogen. **Carbohydrates**, **fats** and **alcohol** contain no nitrogen.

Nitrogen is widespread in air (80% of the air is nitrogen gas); in combined forms in soil (including nitrates, ammonium salts); and in living matter (mainly protein). In excreta, nitrogen is mostly in the form of urea, the breakdown product of unwanted amino acids. Healthy adults are said to be in 'nitrogen balance' when the nitrogen eaten in food (mostly protein) is equal to the nitrogen losses (mostly urea) from the body.

Novel protein

Novel protein is artificial meat usually made from flavoured and coloured soya or, less commonly, field bean protein.

Two types of novel protein are manufactured. The textured (extruded) type – usually called textured vegetable protein (TVP) – is basically a dried foam, made from soya flour, relatively cheap to produce and mostly sold to caterers and food manufacturers as chunks or granules for addition to meat products (like pies, stews, curries, sausages). Some is sold as a mince extender. At present novel protein is not allowed to replace the legal minimum meat content in **meat** products, but can be used in addition if declared on the label.

Spun protein is more expensive. The protein is extracted, treated with alkalies, and spun through small holes into an acid solution. The fibres produced are stretched, combined with binders and shaped. Convincing steak, chicken and ham are made. Different layers can be made into bacon. The texture of spun protein is superior to extruded, but as yet the **flavour** of both types only resembles meat. If it is made clear that the product contains no meat, foods made entirely from novel protein can be sold.

When plants are processed directly into protein, by-passing the animal link, more food is produced from the same area of land. Novel proteins are thus cheaper than meat and may eventually play the same role as margarine in diets. Most contain as much or more protein, **minerals** and B **vitamins** (except zinc, and vitamins B_1, B_2 and B_{12}) as meat. Soya products contain little **fat**, though it is usually added to spun products, and about a third of the dry weight is **carbohydrate**. However novel protein is of poorer quality than meat (it is less efficiently used for growth and repair when eaten alone because it is relatively short of the essential amino acid **methionine**) and as it contains **phytic acid** its zinc and iron is less readily available to the body. The Food Standards Committee has recommended that the quality of novel proteins be improved by the addition of methionine and vitamins B_1, B_2 and B_{12}. It has also recommended minimum levels of protein and iron for novel proteins.

Protein could be extracted and made into novel protein from other sources, like the residue left after oil has been extracted from cotton seeds, sunflower seeds, peanuts and coconuts; wastes from meat and fish production; green leaves; and micro-organisms (fungi, bacteria, yeasts and algae). Different strains of these micro-organisms are being developed to grow on a variety of wastes from the oil, gas, paper, and food industries. If eventually accepted as safe, microbial sources are initially intended for animal feeding – perhaps the most palatable way of increasing supplies of meat by technological means.

Nutrients

Nutrients are substances, contained in foods, which provide **energy** and raw materials for the synthesis and maintenance of living matter. Human nutrients are **protein**, **carbohydrate**, **fat**, **minerals** and **vitamins**. **Alcohol** provides energy but is a drug rather than a nutrient. Those that cannot be made in sufficient quantities from raw materials in food in the body are called essential nutrients: vitamins, minerals, essential **amino acids** and **essential fatty acids**. Lack of an essential nutrient results in a specific deficiency disease. Excess quantities of some nutrients may cause ill health or reduce life span. Mixtures of foods that are thought to supply the optimum quantities of nutrients – so maintaining health – are called balanced **diets**.

Water and oxygen are also essential for human life, but are not usually classed as nutrients.

Nutrition

Nutrition is the requirement for food constituents for growth and **metabolism** in animals, plants and man. Human nutrition is classically associated with the discovery of constituents of food which must be supplied preformed in the diet, the essential **nutrients**, and the control of diseases caused by their absence. Indeed, the successful application of some 150 years of accumulated knowledge to public health measures during and after the Second World War led to the impression that the majority of human nutritional problems had been solved. This view has changed markedly in the last ten years.

The foundations of nutrition are generally attributed to the French scientist

Lavoisier (1734–94). Much of the work in establishing the chemical basis of **energy** and **protein** requirements can be traced to his influence and that of the vigorous school of chemistry that he left behind. Magendie (1783-1855) for example was led to interpret his feeding experiments in terms of the chemical composition of food and thus made the distinction between foods that contained **nitrogen** (azote) and those that did not. He was however a man of his time. It was his view that ". . . all parts of the body of man experience . . . movement, which has the double effect of expelling molecules that can or ought no longer to compose the organs, and replacing them with new molecules. This internal, intimate motion, constitutes nutrition." Furthermore, "Nutrition is more or less rapid according to the tissues". Munroe[1] has observed that "With Magendie we step out of primeval forests of mystery and speculation into the bright sunshine of scientific observation and deductive reasoning". Unfortunately Magendie did not found a school to carry on his teaching and his dynamic view of nutrition lapsed for 125 years.

In the interval, a visiting worker to the French school, a German scientist, Liebig (1803–73), later came to dominate events with his extensive chemical analyses of foods and biological materials. From his school emerged the majority of distinguished nutritionists and the era of meticulous observations using the techniques of the calorimeter and nitrogen balance. In fact, according to Drummond[2], "the nutrition experts were so busy at the end of the (nineteenth) century amassing quantitative data about the need for **protein** and **calories** that they seem to have had little time for any wider problems". It was however increasingly being recognised that it was impossible to keep animals alive on diets fulfilling the recommendations of the time. According to Pekelharing in 1905, they died of "deficiency" in the midst of "abundance". Only with the publication, in English, of the work of Hopkins and Funk in 1912, was the existence of the **vitamins** universally recognised, and spectacular demonstrations of their potential effectiveness in eradicating **scurvy**, **beriberi**, **rickets** and **pellagra** seen.

Also in the first half of the twentieth century, experiments with isolated **amino acids** established quantitative requirements for those which were essential. Research began to establish pathways in metabolism into which components of food, liberated during **digestion**, entered. The fundamental role of B vitamins, as co**Enzymes**, and some of the **minerals** as cofactors was established. The use of tracers, initiated by the American scientist Schoenheimer, also saw the end of the view, originating from Liebig's influence, of the body as a static entity, and a rebirth of the concept of turnover. In *The Dynamic State of Body Constituents* published in 1942, Schoenheimer stated, 'The protein must therefore have been involved in very rapid chemical reactions resulting in the fixation of at least half the added (dietary) amino acids. As the weight of the animals had remained constant, the processes in question must have been so balanced as to avoid ultimate change in the amount of protein'. Furthermore different organs turnover at different rates. 'The proteins of the internal organs, of serum, and of the intestinal tract are the most active; the proteins of the muscles show less activity . . . the proteins of the skin show least activity'.

Contemporary understanding of nutrition is therefore based on the concept of turnover, not only of proteins but of other essential nutrients within the cell, organs and body as a whole. Different turnover rates within the cell and mechanisms governing the absorption, transport to tissues and excretion from the body will dictate requirements of nutrients to sustain them. Faulty **diet** is of course the primary route by which metabolism can be disrupted, culminating in diverse clinical signs or disease. Requirements are greater during periods of growth, so that the groups most 'at risk' of dietary deficiencies are children and pregnant and lactating mothers, and shortage of food is quickly reflected in poor growth, so that the groups most 'at risk' of dietary deficiencies are children and pregnant and lactating mothers, and shortage of food is quickly reflected in poor growth rates and high infant mortality rates on a national level. The elderly have particular nutritional problems. The availability of nutrients from the gastroin – also cause too little or too much of nutrients to be available at the cellular level. The symptoms of a large number of diseases are now treated by modifications in diet to by-pass the faults concerned.

Many fundamental issues remain. The biochemical function of many vitamins remains to be established. For example, the role of **vitamin A** in vision is well known, but only 0.1% of the total body content (excluding liver stores) is found in the eye. The more fundamental role of vitamin A in the biosynthesis of cell membranes has yet to be elucidated. The importance of **folic acid** is recognised, but the amount required to possibly prevent spina bifida is uncertain. There are poorly understood apparent racial differences in the formation of **vitamin D** and hence in susceptibility to rickets. Another ten **trace elements** have only recently been identified, partly as a result of maintaining nutrition during surgery, intestinal disease, and in premature infants. The extent to which man is able to adapt to wide differences in the energy content of diets, thus maintaining **energy** balance remains poorly understood and is important in the aetiology of **obesity** and malnutrition in infancy and childhood. The amount of dietary **fibre** needed to maintain the health of the large bowel is under investigation. The control of **cholesterol** metabolism, **essential fatty acid** requirements, and **sodium** in the body, are subjects of intense interest in relation to **heart disease** and **stroke**. Developments have opened new avenues for the possible dietary treatment of some neurological disorders, and begun to define the metabolic pathways concerned in the nutrition of the brain. The importance of nutrients and food constituents in causing or preventing **cancer** now occupies a wide field of medical research. The spectrum of individual variation in food sensitivity and in nutrient requirements widens continually with increasing recognition of the importance of inheritance in the regulation of turnover and susceptibility to disease, and recent advances in the treatment of **allergy** and of rare inherited disturbances of nutrient supply and control (see **inborn errors of metabolism**).

Compared with the intricacies of nutrition research at the laboratory level, the application of nutrition to public health problems requires seemingly crude judgements based, usually, on no more than informed guesswork of the range of individual human requirements and studies of dietary intake in different populations which, due to the intimate association of dietary factors one with another and other environmental factors, may be inaccurate. However, there is ample evidence that even minimal standards are not reached in the Third World, where new estimates of the extent of malnutrition are almost overwhelming. Protein-energy malnutrition is estimated to contribute to the deaths of 5 million children each year, and at least 300 million suffer from **iodine** deficiency and the resultant impairment of both physical growth and mental capacity. Half a million children suffer from permanent blindness due to vitamin A deficiency. These deficiency diseases are not amenable to simple food fortification measures, such as vitamin A added to margarine, available to highly industrialised societies.

Of almost as great a magnitude are problems related to diet in the Western world. These include cancer, **osteoporosis**, heart disease, stroke, **diabetes**, obesity and most disorders of the large bowel, all major causes of ill health and premature death in Britain. All the diseases in question are multifactorial in which genetic susceptibility and other environmental factors, such as smoking and lack of exercise, confound attempts to gain clearcut estimates of risk in humans from diet, and neither is the causation of these diseases amenable to short term scientific investigation. Nevertheless, experimental and human physiological studies supported by population studies have stimulated radical changes in the treatment of, for example, high blood pressure, diabetes, and large bowel disorders.

The history of study of the science of nutrition thus extends over 200 years, but the present time is one of renewed enquiry and advance. This arousal of interest in nutrition from the cell to the whole body level has led to significant changes both in the treatment of disease and in our understanding of what **diet** best promotes the health of man.

[1] Munroe, H.N., Mammalian Protein Metabolism Vol. 1, 1964, Academic Press, New York
[2] Drummond, J.C. and Wilbraham, A. *The Englishman's Food.* Jonathan Cape: London, 1958

Nuts

Nuts are rich sources of **fat, protein, fibre** and some **minerals**. They cannot support life when eaten alone because they are lacking in vitamin B_{12} and usually vitamins C and A. **Peanuts** (botanically they are pulses), pine kernels, and **melon, sunflower** and **sesame seeds** are similar in nutritive value. **Chestnuts** differ from other nuts: they are low in protein and fat but high in **starch**.

Nuts contain more fat than fatty meat. **Hazelnuts** and **coconuts** contain about a third of their weight as fat: **walnuts, almonds** and peanuts about half; and brazils and desiccated coconut nearly two thirds. Walnuts and sunflower seeds contain the highest percentage of polyunsaturated **fatty acids** and coconuts and cashews the lowest.

Peanuts are richest in protein. Weight for weight they contain as much as Cheddar cheese; almonds, brazils and walnuts as much as eggs. However, when eaten alone, nut protein is used with less efficiency (i.e. is of poorer quality) than the protein in animal foods. Nuts are relatively lacking in the essential **amino acid lysine** and peanuts and almonds are also relatively lacking in **methionine**. These shortcomings are not important in normal mixed diets: the day's needs for essential amino acids are satisfied either by eating more nut protein, or by supplementing nuts with small quantities of animal protein (like cheese).

Nuts contain **calcium**, **zinc**, **magnesium** and **iron**. Some nuts are apparently better sources of these minerals than meat but peanuts contain **oxalic acid** and all nuts **phytic acid** which makes most of the calcium, iron, zinc and magnesium unavailable to the body. Nuts are rich in **potassium** which is well absorbed, and – unless salt is added during roasting – low in sodium.

Although nuts are deficient in vitamin B_{12}, they are at least as good a source as meat for others in the **vitamin B complex**. Brazils, peanuts, pine kernels, pistachios and sesame and sunflower seeds are as good sources of **thiamin** as pork, but about 75% is lost on roasting. Peanuts are exceptionally rich in **nicotinic acid**, containing about as much as liver. Almond and hazel nuts are richest in **vitamin E**; peanuts and brazils are also good sources. Pine kernels, pistachio nuts and sesame seeds contain a little **carotene**, but otherwise ripe nuts are lacking in vitamins A and C.

Nuts need to be thoroughly chewed for their protein and vitamins to be absorbed during digestion, or ground – as in ground almonds and nut butters. The iron in nuts will be better absorbed if a good source of **vitamin C** is taken at the same meal.

Oats – see also **muesli**

A hardy **cereal** with a similar nutrient content to whole wheat, except that it contains more fat and **biotin**. Only the husk is removed and oatmeal retains most of its **fibre** and all nutrients in the germ. Porridge oats are heat treated to inactivate a fat splitting **enzyme** in the germ which would otherwise free **fatty acids** that cause rancidity.

Oats have been found to lower blood **cholesterol** levels. This is usually attributed to the fibre in oats, but they also contain notable amounts of polyunsaturated fatty acids.

Average nutrients in 100 grams (3½ oz) Oats (dry) and porridge (made with water)

	oats	porridge		oats	porridge
Energy kilojoules	1698	188	Iron milligrams	4.1	0.5
kilocalories	401	44	Copper milligrams	0.2	0.03
Protein grams	12.4	1.4	Zinc milligrams	3.0	0.3
Total fat grams	8.7	0.9	Vitamin A micrograms	0	0
Saturated fat grams	1.5	0.1	Vitamin D micrograms	0	0
Polyunsaturated fat grams	3.5	0.4	Vitamin C milligrams	0	0
			Vitamin E milligrams	0.8	0.1
Cholesterol milligrams	0	0	B vitamins:		
Sugars grams	0	0	Thiamin (B_1) milligrams	0.5	0.05
Starch grams	73.0	8.2	Riboflavin (B_2) milligrams	0.1	0.01
Dietary fibre (NSP) grams	6.6	0.7	Nicotinic acid milligrams	2.8	0.3
Sodium milligrams	33	3	Pyridoxine (B_6) milligrams	0.1	0.01
Potassium milligrams	370	42	Vitamin B_{12} micrograms	0	0
Calcium milligrams	55	6	Folic acid micrograms	60	6
Magnesium milligrams	110	13	Pantothenic acid milligrams	1.0	0.1
			Biotin micrograms	20	2

(–) No information available   (0) Contains zero or trace amounts

Obesity – overweight

Obesity is inevitable when the **energy** (Calories) in food is regularly greater than energy needs. Only 200 kilojoules (50 kilocalories) a day, from an extra knob of butter (or 10 minutes less time spent walking) can result in a fat gain of 40 kilograms (6½ stones) in 20 years. The superfluous energy is stored in congregations of fat cells – **adipose tissue**, or 'fat' – around organs and under the skin. Layers of fat under the skin distort the normal body contours. It is the most common nutritional disorder in affluent countries – a third of the British adult population is estimated to be obese, despite the fact that national statistics show that the average person eats 10% less food now than 20 years ago.

Precise obesity tests measure the amount of fat in the body: normal women contain up to 30% of their weight as fat; men up to 20%. Most people however are judged obese if their weight is 10% or more above a desired weight (worked out by insurance companies) for their height and build. Anyone with a weight greater than that shown in the table on page 202 would almost certainly be obese. A critical look in a full length mirror and the ruler test (it should be possible to rest a ruler on both hip bones when lying flat) are alternative ways of confirming obesity.

Large fat deposits have been regarded as an asset in some societies, but now are unfashionable. More importantly, obesity reduces life span and causes much disability. Obese people are at much greater risk of **heart disease** for example, and in an obese person, the excessive weight that has to be supported against gravity strains the legs and feet and may cause flat feet, **arthritis** in the knees (and knock knees in children) and varicose veins. Fat around the lungs makes deep breathing difficult, contributing to bronchitis. Pendulous layers of fat are difficult to keep clean and dry, predisposing to infections, especially in the elderly. The heart enlarges to pump blood around the extra miles of blood vessels in adipose tissue and blood pressure may rise. Tiredness and lack of zest are due to fatigue – the extra weight that has to be carried around is often equivalent to a heavy suitcase. Overweight may precipitate **gout**, late onset **diabetes** and disorders of the blood **lipids**. These diseases are risk factors in heart disease.

Weight often accumulates gradually over the years, becoming obvious in middle life and after retirement, when it may be dismissed as 'middle age spread'. Men who were lean, active sportsmen when young may become obese without gaining much weight. Their gain of fat will be masked by loss of muscle.

Despite the 20 tons of food eaten in an average lifetime, gradual accumulation of weight is neither a natural or inevitable part of middle age. It is however more likely in those living a sedentary life and with modern diets high in fat and sugar – see **fat** and **energy**. Under these conditions it becomes difficult to match the body's relatively low needs for energy with sufficiently little food. The difficulties are further increased by the other roles played by food: it is a necessary part of social life and can be used as a palliative for boredom and unhappiness – sometimes as a result of habits formed in a childhood household particularly anxious about food.

An active job, or extra exercise, see **energy**, and a balanced **diet** are the best ways of maintaining fitness in middle life. Regular drinkers find it difficult to avoid obesity. Four pints of beer supply over a quarter of the recommended intake for a man living a sedentary life. Another worthwhile investment is a pair of bathroom scales. Weight should be checked every two months and a **slimming diet** begun immediately if more than about 2 kilograms (4 lbs) are gained. Most people find it easy to lose a few pounds of weight but lack the will power to lose more.

Many obese women attribute the start of their problem to their first pregnancy. There is a tendency, probably natural, to accumulate fat in pregnancy and the average is about 4 kilograms (9 lbs). This fat store is most easily lost by breast feeding, otherwise a slimming diet should be started as soon as possible after the birth. Successive gains of weight with each child can result in tenacious fat by middle age.

Obesity in infancy, childhood and adolescence is particularly harmful. If overweight develops during growth the child has a greater chance of becoming a grossly obese adult, possible because more fat cells are formed. Artifically fed babies are more likely to become plump: too many or over-concentrated feeds are easily given (see milk). Too early weaning (before four months) can also cause obesity.

It is better to slim children before they become fat adolescents (an unhappy adolescent who tries to slim may develop **anorexia**), but fat children should not be made to feel guilty about their weight. Parents who confuse the relationship between hunger and eating are often the root cause of a fat child. Tactful attempts should be made to encourage the child to eat less, and if possible the parents should also diet, so that no cakes, biscuits, sweets, pastry, soft drinks, puddings and fried food are in the home to tempt the child. Medical and qualified dietetic advice should be sought if this fails: a strict diet is usually necessary.

Obesity often runs in families and, although it is likely that attitudes to food learnt in the home are very important, there may be a genetic predisposition. Identical twins brought up by different sets of adoptive parents tend to reach an adult weight closer to each other than their adoptive parents. Genetic factors leading to natural variations in **metabolic rate** and the amount of activity taken may well be important together with diet in the development of obesity.

Grossly obese adults require an almost superhuman will power to lose all their fat – they may have up to 75 kilograms (12 stones) of fat to lose – and rarely manage to become permanently slim. They may also have an added handicap: the burden of weight causes fatigue and reduces activity, lowering the daily needs for energy below average. Thus obese people are not necessarily gluttons once they have become overweight. Nevertheless, at some time they have eaten more than their individual needs.

Exercise as a means of reducing weight has had much publicity recently. Whilst this is unlikely to be possible for the grossly obese person, an average of 20 minutes vigorous exercise each day is important for maintaining fitness and probably crucial for energy balance in people who have a sedentary job. Exercise alone in place of dieting, however, needs as much will power to keep up as dieting, and failure rates for both regimes are about the same. Prevention, by being aware of energy balance in childhood and adult life remains the only sure way of avoiding overweight.

Weights above which adults would be classified as obese

Height (no shoes)		Women[a]		Men[b]	
metres	ft/in	kilograms	st/lb	kilograms	st/lb
1.49	4.9	64	10.0		
1.48	4.10	65	10.3		
1.50	4.11	66	10.5		
1.52	5.0	68	10.10		
1.54	5.1	70	11.0		
1.56	5.2	70	11.0		
1.58	5.2	71	11.2	77	12.1
1.60	5.3	73	11.6	78	12.4
1.62	5.4	74	11.9	79	12.6
1.64	5.5	77	12.1	80	12.8
1.66	5.6	78	12.4	83	13.1
1.68	5.6	79	12.6	85	13.5
1.70	5.7	80	12.8	88	13.12
1.72	5.8	83	13.1	89	14.0
1.74	5.8	84	13.3	90	14.2

1.76	5.9	86	13.5	92	14.6
1.78	5.10	89	13.7	95	14.13
1.80	5.11			96	15.1
1.82	6.0			98	15.6
1.84	6.1			101	15.12
1.86	6.1			103	16.3
1.88	6.2			106	16.9
1.90	6.2			108	16.13
1.92	6.3			112	17.8

[a]Deduct 2 g(4 lb) if weighed with clothes, [b]Deduct 4g(9 llb) if weighed with clothes

Derived from WHO/FAO/UNO Tech. Rep. Ser. 724 1985

Octopus and squid

Octopus is a delicately flavoured mollusc, low in **fat**. The flesh contains some iron and vitamin A, but few analyses are available, (see table).

Squid, or calamary, a relative of the octopus, is considered a delicacy in Mediterranean cooking. It can be stuffed with onion, bread and egg, or spinach. Squid contains **protein** and a moderate supply of B **vitamins** and **minerals**.

Average nutrients in 100 grams (3½ oz) Octopus and Squid

	octopus	squid		octopus	squid
Energy kilojoules	285	278	Iron milligrams	0.9	0.2
kilocalories	68	66	Copper milligrams	–	0.68
Protein grams	13.5	13.1	Zinc milligrams	–	1.2
Total fat grams	1.1	1.5	Vitamin A micrograms	5	–
Saturated fat grams	–	–	Vitamin D micrograms	–	–
Polyunsaturated fat grams	–	–	Vitamin C milligrams	0	0
			Vitamin E milligrams	–	–
Cholesterol milligrams	–	–	B vitamins:		
Sugars grams	0	–	Thiamin (B₁) milligrams	0.12	0.05
Starch grams	0	–	Riboflavin (B₂) milligrams	0.11	0.02
Dietary fibre grams	0	–	Nicotinic acid milligrams	7.9	–
Sodium milligrams	–	185	Pyridoxine (B₆) milligrams	–	–
Potassium milligrams	–	145	Vitamin B₁₂ micrograms	–	2.5
Calcium milligrams	12	13	Folic acid micrograms	–	2
Magnesium milligrams	–	36	Pantothenic acid milligrams	–	–
			Biotin micrograms	–	–

(–) No information available   (0) Contains zero or trace amounts

Oils

Vegetable oils rank with cooking fats, butter and margarine as the richest source of **energy** (Calories) in the diet. They are 99.9% **fat**. Most are rich sources of **vitamin E** but oils contain no other vitamins or minerals (except for red palm oil which contains **carotene** (pro vitamin A)). Oils contain no **cholesterol**.

Most oils have a higher percentage of polyunsaturated **fatty acids** compared with animal fats and a low percentage of the saturated fatty acids known to raise the blood cholesterol. Safflower, sunflower, soya, corn and walnut oils are suitable for blood cholesterol lowering diets: they are low in saturated fatty acids and more than 50% of their fatty acids are polyunsaturated. Olive, peanut and rapeseed oils are low in both and probably have a neutral effect. Peanut oil is also called groundnut or arachis oil, and rapeseed is the most common constituent of oils sold as 'vegetable oil'. Palm and coconut oils are very low in polyunsaturated fats and high, especially palm oil, in saturated fats. They are mostly used in food manufacture – on food labels they will also be called vegetable oils or fats so the consumer has no way of telling from the ingredients whether or not a food is high or low in saturated fats.

Polyunsaturates in oils are more susceptible to rancidity than saturated fatty acids but vitamin E (a natural **antioxidant**) in fresh oils delays its onset. **Trace elements** (like copper) and free fatty acids which hasten rancidity are removed from most oils on sale. It is advisable to store oils in a dark cool place: light and warmth also promote rancidity.

Average nutrients in 100 grams (3½ oz) Oils

Energy kilojoules	3696	Iron milligrams	0
kilocalories	899	Copper milligrams	0
Protein grams	0	Zinc milligrams	0
Total fat grams	99.9	Vitamin A micrograms	0
Saturated fat grams	a	Vitamin D micrograms	0
Polyunsaturated fat grams	a	Vitamin C milligrams	0
		Vitamin E milligrams	a
Cholesterol milligrams	0	B vitamins:	
Sugars grams	0	Thiamin (B_1) milligrams	0
Starch grams	0	Riboflavin (B_2) milligrams	0
Dietary fibre grams	0	Nicotinic acid milligrams	0
Sodium milligrams	0	Pyridoxine (B_6) milligrams	0
Potassium milligrams	0	Vitamin B_{12} micrograms	0
Calcium milligrams	0	Folic acid micrograms	0
Magnesium milligrams	0	Pantothenic acid milligrams	0
		Biotin micrograms	0

[a]See table below

OILS RICH IN POLYUNSATURATED FATTY ACIDS

Type	Saturated fatty acids grams	Polyunsaturated fatty acids grams	Vitamin E micrograms
Safflower	10	72	39
Walnut	12	70	–
Soya	14	57	10
Sunflower	13	50	49
Maize (corn)	16	49	11
Cotton seed	26	48	39
OTHER OILS			
Rapeseed ('vegetable oil')	7	32	18
Peanut or arachis	18	28	13
Olive	14	11	5
Palm	45	8	26
Coconut	85	2	1

(–) No information available   (0) Contains zero or trace amounts

There is little loss of nutritive value when oils are used in baking but polyunsaturates decline when oils are heated for frying, and probably 10 to 20% are lost over a short period of frying. Over-heating or repeated use of oil for frying causes many decomposition products to develop, which are responsible for the unpleasant smell of burnt fat. Overheated fats have been shown to be toxic to laboratory animals, damaging the stomach, heart, liver and kidneys. Oils that smoke must never be reused, and foaming oils are definitely toxic.

Other oils

Essential oils are the flavours (or essences) extracted from plants, like oil of peppermint, oil of lemon, oil of almond – see **flavour**. They contain many complex substances and most are not digested. Fusel oils (congeners) are responsible for the flavour of alcoholic drinks.

Mineral oils have a different chemical structure to other oils and fats and cannot be digested, passing out of the system with other undigested food. Vitamins A, D, E and K dissolve in liquid paraffin (a laxative that lubricates the stools) and excessive use can cause deficiencies. Mineral oil is added to some food – see **mineral hydrocarbons**.

Castor oil extracted from the castor oil bean is composed of simple fat. It is digested in the normal way, but ricinoleic acid (a fatty acid) is liberated irritating the muscles of the digestive system, causing purgation.

Okra – Ladies' fingers

Okra or ladies' fingers belong to the hibiscus family. The immature pod is eaten, often to thicken soups and stews. It has a similar nutrient composition to most green vegetables (see table).

Average nutrients in 100 grams (3½ oz) Okra

Energy kilojoules	71	Iron milligrams	1.0
kilocalories	17	Copper milligrams	0.19
Protein grams	2.0	Zinc milligrams	–
Total fat grams	0	Vitamin A micrograms	15
Saturated fat grams	0	Vitamin D micrograms	0
Polyunsaturated fat grams	0	Vitamin C milligrams	25
		Vitamin E milligrams	–
Cholesterol milligrams	0	B vitamins:	
Sugars grams	2.3	Thiamin (B$_1$) milligrams	0.10
Starch grams	0	Riboflavin (B$_2$) milligrams	0.10
Dietary fibre grams	3.2	Nicotinic acid milligrams	1.3
Sodium milligrams	7	Pyridoxine (B$_6$) milligrams	0.08
Potassium milligrams	190	Vitamin B$_{12}$ micrograms	0
Calcium milligrams	70	Folic acid micrograms	100
Magnesium milligrams	60	Pantothenic acid milligrams	0.26
		Biotin micrograms	–

(–) No information available   (0) Contains zero or trace amounts

Olives

Olives are highly valued for their oil, see **oils**, and as a food. The values shown in the table are for olives salted in brine, hence the high **sodium** content. Olives in oil will contain less. Olives contain **fat** (mostly monounsaturated **fatty acids**), vitamin A (more in green than black olives) and some minerals. They contain virtually no vitamins B or C.

Average nutrients in 100 grams (3½ oz) Olives (in brine)

Energy kilojoules	422	Iron milligrams	1.0
kilocalories	103	Copper milligrams	0.2
Protein grams	0.9	Zinc milligrams	–
Total fat grams	11.0	Vitamin A micrograms	10–30
Saturated fat grams	1.5	Vitamin D micrograms	0
Polyunsaturated fat grams	1.2	Vitamin C milligrams	0
		Vitamin E milligrams	–
Cholesterol milligrams	0	B vitamins:	
Sugars grams	0	Thiamin (B₁) milligrams	0
Starch grams	0	Riboflavin (B₂) milligrams	0
Dietary fibre grams	4.4	Nicotinic acid milligrams	0
Sodium milligrams	2250	Pyridoxine (B₆) milligrams	0.02
Potassium milligrams	91	Vitamin B₁₂ micrograms	0
Calcium milligrams	61	Folic acid micrograms	–
Magnesium milligrams	22	Pantothenic acid milligrams	0.02
		Biotin micrograms	0

(–) No information available   (0) Contains zero or trace amounts

Onions

Onions are members of the *Allium* family, which also includes leeks and garlic. They have been used as a food and flavouring agent for at least 5000 years. The flavour and tear promoting chemical is released during cutting and slicing by the action of an **enzyme** allinase on a sulphur containing compound, allyl cysteine sulphoxide in the flesh.

Onions contain vitamin C, sugars and some B vitamins and minerals (see table). Spring onions contain rather more nutrients than mature onions.

Test meals of 75 grams of onions have been shown to reduce the tendency of the blood to clot, but the importance of this perhaps affording some protection against **heart disease** and **stroke** has not been investigated.

Average nutrients in 100 grams (3½ oz) Onion (raw)

	mature	spring		mature	spring
Energy kilojoules	99	151	Iron milligrams	0.3	1.2
kilocalories	23	35	Copper milligrams	0.08	0.13
Protein grams	0.9	0.9	Zinc milligrams	0.1	–
Total fat grams	0	0	Vitamin A micrograms	0	0
Saturated fat grams	0	0	Vitamin D micrograms	0	0
Polyunsaturated fat grams	0	0	Vitamin C milligrams	3–15	20–30
			Vitamin E milligrams	0	0
Cholesterol milligrams	0	0	B vitamins:		
Sugars grams	5.2	8.5	Thiamin (B₁) milligrams	0.03	0.03
Starch grams	0	0	Riboflavin (B₂) milligrams	0.05	0.05

Dietary fibre grams	1.3	3.1	Nicotinic acid milligrams	0.4	0.4
Sodium milligrams	10	13	Pyridoxine (B₆) milligrams	0.10	0.10
Potassium milligrams	140	230	Vitamin B₁₂ micrograms	0	0
Calcium milligrams	31	140	Folic acid micrograms	16	40
Magnesium milligrams	8	11	Pantothenic acid milligrams	0.14	0.14
			Biotin micrograms	0.9	0.9

(–) No information available   (0) Contains zero or trace amounts

Oranges – see also **fruit juices**

Oranges are a reliable source of **vitamin C**, though not as rich as **lemons**. Oranges were introduced into Europe, probably from China and South East Asia, about 2000 years ago, and are now grown in most areas of the world with a warm climate. Seville oranges are a different variety with a bitter taste, used particularly in Britain for marmalade.

Citrus fruit peel is likely to contain **preservatives** E230–232 to prevent mould and should be thoroughly washed before use in cooking and marmalade making.

Average nutrients in 100 grams (3½ oz) Oranges

Energy kilojoules	150	Iron milligrams	0.3
kilocalories	35	Copper milligrams	0.07
Protein grams	0.8	Zinc milligrams	0.2
Total fat grams	0	Vitamin A micrograms	8
Saturated fat grams	0	Vitamin D micrograms	0
Polyunsaturated fat grams	0	Vitamin C milligrams	40–60
		Vitamin E milligrams	0.2
Cholesterol milligrams	0	B vitamins:	
Sugars grams	8.5	Thiamin (B₁) milligrams	0.10
Starch grams	0	Riboflavin (B₂) milligrams	0.03
Dietary fibre grams	2.0	Nicotinic acid milligrams	0.3
Sodium milligrams	3	Pyridoxine (B₆) milligrams	0.06
Potassium milligrams	200	Vitamin B₁₂ micrograms	0
Calcium milligrams	41	Folic acid micrograms	37
Magnesium milligrams	13	Pantothenic acid milligrams	0.25
		Biotin micrograms	1.0

(–) No information available   (0) Contains zero or trace amounts

Organic foods

Foods grown under the principles of organic farming. Most people think of organic food as being free from pesticides and other farm chemicals (see **poisons in food**), but according to one definition, the main principle of organic farming is to feed the soil rather than the plant, thus maintaining soil structure. Most of the principles of organic farming are based on traditional practices and some pesticides, such as sulphur, copper, lime, derris and pyrethrum are permitted in organic produce. Organo-phosphorous and organochloride compounds however are not, and nor are weedkillers. Manures and other animal waste products, such as hoof and horn, which supply organic matter and **nitrogen** for plant growth are used for example, rather than the most commonly used non-organic fertiliser, ammonium nitrate, which acidifies the soil. Some non-acidifying nitrate, in small amounts, is permitted in organic farming in the form of nitrate of soda (sodium nitrate) extracted from deposits in Chile. Organic farmers also use limestone or chalk to keep the soil non-acid, rather than, for example, quicklime or slaked lime used in non-organic farming. The other major plant nutrient is **potassium**, and in organic farming wood ash for example is used, whereas muriate of potash (potassium choride) would mostly be used in non organic farming, sometimes raising the salt content of the soil to undesirably high levels.

Foods grown organically yield smaller harvests than when grown using present day methods, as little as two thirds for some crops. However, this loss to the farmer is offset by less outlay in agro-chemicals and up to a 50% greater commission. An intermediate, conservation grade, permitting for example hormone based weedkillers, has also recently been introduced.

It is often thought that organic food is nutritionally superior to ordinary but the few studies that have attempted to study this have not shown any difference. Breed, maturity, and the amount of sunshine a crop receives, influence vitamin and mineral contents more than the quality of the soil. Nevertheless, efforts to reduce the use of pesticides, particularly the chlorinated hydrocarbons (see **poisons in food**), are important. Intakes can be further reduced by avoiding large helpings of animal fats and by washing or throwing away the outside leaves and skins of fruits and vegetables. It should be remembered that organic food is not always pollutant free; fall out and polycyclic hydrocarbons from tractor and motor car exhausts can be deposited on both organic and ordinary food.

Osteomalacia

Osteomalacia is the adult form of rickets: both diseases are usually caused by lack of **vitamin D**. Insufficient **calcium** is absorbed from food, and, to maintain a normal blood level, calcium is withdrawn from the bones. The skeleton is weakened, resulting in persistant pain, deformity, and poor healing of fractures. If not corrected, muscular weakness and tetany (twitching) occur when the blood calcium falls.

In Britain, osteomalacia can complicate **malabsorption** syndromes and some kidney disease, but it is primarily a problem in the elderly and Asian immigrants. Confinement inside the house and heavy or traditional clothing when outside prevent sunlight from reaching the skin and initiating vitamin D synthesis. Once osteomalacia has developed, pain makes walking difficult and excursions from the house are even less frequent, completing a vicious circle. The elderly may require more vitamin D than young adults, perhaps due to the natural decline in the efficiency of the kidney (the kidney converts vitamin D to its active form).

If sunlight is not available, the needs for vitamin D are best met by using margarine, instead of butter or oil, and one multivitamin capsule a day. Excessive vitamin D is toxic.

Osteoporosis

Osteoporosis or loss of bone is a very common disease of old age. It is responsible for easily fractured bones and – due to compression of the backbone – loss of height. It is probably the most common cause of backache in the elderly (though many people experience no pain) and is often combined with **osteomalacia**.

Everyone begins to lose bone in early middle age, perhaps because the production of sex hormones begins to decline at this time. Those who have grown more bone by adulthood may lose the same percentage as others, but – because there is sufficient left in old age – do not develop severe symptoms. Women are at greater risk than men: they form less bone and lose it at a faster rate. Synthetic oestrogens given after the change of life may slow the rate of bone loss, but do not prevent it.

Improvement of diet in adults probably does not affect the course of the disease, but a childhood diet poor in **calcium**, and perhaps **fluorine**, may result in a less dense skeleton and greater likelihood of osteoporosis in old age. Immobilisation (for example confinement to bed) and probably a sedentary life increase the rate of bone loss. Vegetarians may be less affected than meat eaters perhaps because the acid residue of meat (see **ash**) increases the rate at which calcium is excreted by the kidney.

Oxalic acid

Oxalic acid is a simple acid in foods which forms insoluble salts with **calcium** and **magnesium** in the digestive system, rendering these minerals unavailable to the body. Rhubarb leaves contain toxic quantities.

Oxalic acid occurs in several fruits, vegetables and cereals, but the richest sources are tea (50-70 milligrams per cup), and beetroot, spinach and rhubarb, which contain over 600 milligrams per 100 grams. Peanuts contain about 150 milligrams per 100 grams. About 10 to 20% of the intake is absorbed and later excreted in the urine, together with oxalic acid made from **glycine** and **vitamin C**. The rest is passed out in the stools as insoluble salts.

In some people excessive oxalic acid can be made in the body from glycine and be passed out of the body in the urine. Unless the urine is kept very dilute (by drinking a lot of water) insoluble calcium oxalate crystals form and eventually solidify into kidney stones. Very large doses of vitamin C, excessive tea drinking, and spinach and other high oxalate foods are probably best avoided.

Oysters

The oyster has been used as a food from the earliest times; both the Greeks and Romans prized oysters highly. The Celts gathered oysters and up until about 1850 they were so plentiful and cheap they were associated with poverty. They are rich in **zinc** (see table) and some types contain vitamin C. After 1850, however, the price increased dramatically, due to overfishing of the natural beds. The oyster survived in Britain to become a luxury food, grown in artificial beds.

Average nutrients in 100 grams (3½ oz) Oysters

Energy kilojoules	217	Iron milligrams	6.0
kilocalories	51	Copper milligrams	7.6
Protein grams	10.8	Zinc milligrams	6–100
Total fat grams	0.9	Vitamin A micrograms	75
Saturated fat grams	0.1	Vitamin D micrograms	0
Polyunsaturated fat grams	0.3	Vitamin C milligrams	0–38
		Vitamin E milligrams	0.85
Cholesterol milligrams	50	B vitamins:	
Sugars grams	0	Thiamin (B_1) milligrams	0.10
Starch grams	0	Riboflavin (B_2) milligrams	0.20
Dietary fibre grams	0	Nicotinic acid milligrams	3.8
Sodium milligrams	510	Pyridoxine (B_6) milligrams	0.03
Potassium milligrams	260	Vitamin B_{12} micrograms	15
Calcium milligrams	190	Folic acid micrograms	10
Magnesium milligrams	42	Pantothenic acid milligrams	0.50
		Biotin micrograms	10

(–) No information available   (0) Contains zero or trace amounts

Pantothenic acid – obsolete name, vitamin B₃

Pantothenic acid is part of the **vitamin B complex**. It is however found in most foods – except sugar, fats and spirits, and human deficiency has only been induced under volunteer experimental conditions, using a synthetic diet.

The richest sources of the vitamin are yeast, yeast **extracts** and **liver** (which contains 5 – 8 milligrams per 100 grams (3½ oz). **Kidney**, **heart**, brains, **egg** yolk, **peanuts**, wheat **bran** and **mushrooms** are good sources, containing over 2 milligrams per 100 grams. The Royal jelly of bees contains 1 to 3 milligrams per 10 grams. Milk contains about 2 milligrams per pint, wholemeal **bread** and water **melon** about 1½ milligrams per 100 grams. Refined cereals are poorer than wholegrain – about half is lost when wheat is milled to white flour. Other foods (cheese, fish, other meat and vegetables, and fish) supply up to 1 milligram per 100 grams.

Pantothenic acid leaches out of foods into cooking water, like other B vitamins, and is also sensitive to dry heat, acids and alkalis. About a third is lost when meat and vegetables are cooked. Probably all the vitamin is retained during freezing, but a further third can be lost in the drip of thawed meats. Between one third and three quarters may be lost when foods are canned.

No **recommended intake** for the vitamin has been set, due to lack of information, but it is estimated that adults need between 5 and 10 milligrams per day, an amount contained in the average British daily diet.

Pantothenic acid is not stored, but it is present in all cells and a diet lacking in the vitamin takes about three months to deplete the body. As part of co**Enzyme** A (a vital link in the chain which liberates **energy** from food for synthesis of new substances needed for maintenance of life) pantothenic acid has a central role in **metabolism** and deficiency in animals and man results in a variety of symptoms. Human deficiency symptoms included headache; serious personality changes like irritability and restlessness; fatigue after very mild exercise; disordered sensation (pins and needles etc); stomach cramps; and difficulty in walking.

Despite its importance, there are no specific diseases attributed to lack of pantothenic acid. It has been used in the 'burning feet syndrome' – which develops in famine conditions and causes aching, throbbing feet and stabbing pains in the legs and feet – but there are usually other dietary deficiencies which must be treated before full health is restored. Lack of the vitamin causes grey hair in rats and mink, but pantothenic acid is ineffective in preventing greying of human hair.

Papaya or pawpaw

Pawpaw is a native of tropical America, now widely grown in tropical climates. The fresh fruit contains good amounts of **vitamin C**. Both fresh and canned contain vitamin A, as **carotene** in the orange flesh, minerals, sugars and B vitamins.

The **enzyme** papain is produced by the pawpaw and the dried powder or the fresh leaves can be used to tenderise meat, since it breaks down **proteins**. A recently much publicised dietary regime was based on the enzyme content of papaya, said to aid digestion. However, protein digestion in the human body is highly efficient. The success of such a diet in **slimming** would have been due to the fact that it contains much fruit, which is low in **energy** (Calories).

Average nutrients in 100 grams (3½ oz) Pawpaw

	fresh	canned		fresh	canned
Energy kilojoules	188	275	Iron milligrams	0.7	0.4
kilocalories	45	65	Copper milligrams	0.01	0.10
Protein grams	0.5	0.2	Zinc milligrams	0.4	0.3
Total fat grams	0.1	0	Vitamin A micrograms	118	83
Saturated fat grams	–	0	Vitamin D micrograms	0	0
Polyunsaturated fat grams	–	0	Vitamin C milligrams	73	15
			Vitamin E milligrams	–	–
Cholesterol milligrams	0	0	B vitamins:		
Sugars grams	11.3	17.0	Thiamin (B_1) milligrams	0.03	0.02
Starch grams	0	0	Riboflavin (B_2) milligrams	0.05	0.02
Dietary fibre grams	–	0.5	Nicotinic acid milligrams	0.4	0.2
Sodium milligrams	4	8	Pyridoxine (B_6) milligrams	–	–
Potassium milligrams	221	110	Vitamin B_{12} micrograms	0	0
Calcium milligrams	24	23	Folic acid micrograms	1	–
Magnesium milligrams	8	8	Pantothenic acid milligrams	–	0.20
			Biotin micrograms	–	–

(–) No information available   (0) Contains zero or trace amounts

Para amino benzoic acid (Paba)

Part of the vitamin **folic acid**, which is synthesised from paba by micro-organisms. Paba is therefore an essential **nutrient** for micro-organisms but not humans, who depend on a dietary supply of folic acid.

The sulphonamide drugs have a similar structure to paba and interfere with the formation of folic acid by bacteria, which cannot multiply in the absence of this vitamin. The curative effect of sulphonamides in diseases (like typhoid) caused by bacteria is negated if paba is also taken.

Lack of paba causes grey fur in black rats, but not grey hair in humans.

Parsley

Parsley has been grown in Britain since the sixteenth century; early cultivated forms, still grown in Europe, had uncurled leaves. Parsley is remarkably rich in most nutrients (see table) although the amount of calcium and iron available to the body is probably small. Nevertheless, a teaspoon (2 grams) of chopped parsley can supply most of the daily **recommended allowance** of vitamin C.

Average nutrients in 100 grams (3½ oz) Parsley

Energy kilojoules	88	Iron milligrams	8.0
kilocalories	21	Copper milligrams	0.52
Protein grams	5.2	Zinc milligrams	0.9
Total fat grams	0	Vitamin A micrograms	500–1670
Saturated fat grams	0	Vitamin D micrograms	0
Polyunsaturated fat grams	0	Vitamin C milligrams	100–200

		Vitamin E milligrams	1.8

Cholesterol milligrams	0	B vitamins:	
Sugars grams	0	Thiamin (B₁) milligrams	0.15
Starch grams	0	Riboflavin (B₂) milligrams	0.30
Dietary fibre grams	9.1	Nicotinic acid milligrams	1.8
Sodium milligrams	33	Pyridoxine (B₆) milligrams	0.20
Potassium milligrams	1080	Vitamin B₁₂ micrograms	0
Calcium milligrams	330	Folic acid micrograms	–
Magnesium milligrams	52	Pantothenic acid milligrams	0.30
		Biotin micrograms	0.4

(–) No information available   (0) Contains zero or trace amounts

Parsnips

Wild parsnip grows abundantly in Britain, but the fleshy rooted type only seems to have been developed in the Middle Ages. Parsnip contains starch and sugars, minerals, some B vitamins, vitamin E, and vitamin C. Apart from their use as vegetables, parsnips make a sweet wine.

Average nutrients in 100 grams (3½ oz) Parsnips (boiled)

Energy kilojoules	238	Iron milligrams	0.5
kilocalories	56	Copper milligrams	0.10
Protein grams	1.3	Zinc milligrams	0.1
Total fat grams	0	Vitamin A micrograms	0
Saturated fat grams	0	Vitamin D micrograms	0
Polyunsaturated fat grams	0	Vitamin C milligrams	5-20
		Vitamin E milligrams	1.0
Cholesterol milligrams	0	B vitamins:	
Sugars grams	2.7	Thiamin (B₁) milligrams	0.07
Starch grams	10.8	Riboflavin (B₂) milligrams	0.06
Dietary fibre grams	2.5	Nicotinic acid milligrams	0.9
Sodium milligrams	4	Pyridoxine (B₆) milligrams	0.06
Potassium milligrams	290	Vitamin B₁₂ micrograms	0
Calcium milligrams	36	Folic acid micrograms	30
Magnesium milligrams	13	Pantothenic acid milligrams	0.35
		Biotin micrograms	0

(–) No information available   (0) Contains zero or trace amounts

Passion fruit

A wrinkled, black, egg sized fruit, now grown in most warm climates, passion fruit has a distinctive and unusual flavour which transforms fresh fruit salad into a very special dessert. The pulp is inseparable from the black seeds – hence the high fibre content of passion fruit.

Average nutrients in 100 grams (3½ oz) Passion fruit

Energy kilojoules	147	Iron milligrams	1.1
kilocalories	34	Copper milligrams	0.12
Protein grams	2.8	Zinc milligrams	–
Total fat grams	0	Vitamin A micrograms	2
Saturated fat grams	0	Vitamin D micrograms	0
Polyunsaturated fat grams	0	Vitamin C milligrams	20
		Vitamin E milligrams	–

Average nutrients in 100 grams (3½ oz) Passion Fruit *(continued)*

Cholesterol milligrams	0	B vitamins:	
Sugars grams	6.2	Thiamin (B₁) milligrams	0
Starch grams	0	Riboflavin (B₂) milligrams	0.10
Dietary fibre grams	15.9	Nicotinic acid milligrams	1.9
Sodium milligrams	28	Pyridoxine (B₆) milligrams	–
Potassium milligrams	350	Vitamin B₁₂ micrograms	0
Calcium milligrams	16	Folic acid micrograms	–
Magnesium milligrams	39	Pantothenic acid milligrams	–
		Biotin micrograms	–

(–) No information available   (0) Contains zero or trace amounts

Pasta

Pasta is made from a stiff wheat dough, which is forced through perforated cylinders, and comes out in various shapes. The most well known are spaghetti, ravioli, macaroni, vermicelli, tagliatelli and lasagne. Traditionally the flour is white, from durum wheat, but wholemeal pasta has become available recently. It is more nutritious because it contains more **fibre**, **minerals** and B **vitamins** than white (see table). Canned pasta in tomato sauce contains about the same amount of vitamins and minerals as white cooked pasta.

Average nutrients in 100 grams (3½ oz) Pasta (cooked)

	white	wholemeal	canned in tomato sauce		white	wholemeal	canned in tomato sauce
Energy kilojoules	499	497	250	Iron milligrams	0.4	2.0	0.4
kilocalories	117	119	59	Copper milligrams	0.04	–	0.13
Protein grams	4.2	4.0	1.7	Zinc milligrams	0.3	–	–
Total fat grams	0.5	1.0	0.7	Vitamin A micrograms	0	0	0
Saturated fat grams	0.1	–	–	Vitamin D micrograms	0	0	0
Polyunsaturated fat grams	0.1	–	–	Vitamin C milligrams	0	0	0
				Vitamin E milligrams	0	0	–
Cholesterol milligrams	0	0	0	B vitamins:			
Sugars grams	0.4	–	3.4	Thiamin (B₁) milligrams	0.01	0.15	0.01
Starch grams	25.2	24.0	8.8	Riboflavin (B₂) milligrams	0.01	0.02	0.01
Dietary fibre (NSP) grams	1.0	3.0	0.6	Nicotinic acid milligrams	0.9	0.7	0.4
Sodium milligrams	6	2	500	Pyridoxine (B₆) milligrams	0.01	–	0.01
Potassium milligrams	58	14	130	Vitamin B₁₂ micrograms	0	–	0
Calcium milligrams	8	9	21	Folic acid micrograms	2	–	2
Magnesium milligrams	15	5	11	Pantothenic acid milligrams	0	–	0
				Biotin micrograms	0	–	0

(–) No information available   (0) Contains zero or trace amounts

Pastries

Pastry contains 30-50% of its weight as **fat**, which works out at 50-65% of **energy** (Calories) supplied by fat – nearly double the levels currently recommended for healthy eating. Puff pastry used in Danish pastry, croissants and sausage rolls, contains the most. The fat content is reduced when pastry is used as part of a recipe – fruit pies, for example, contain 15 grams of fat (see table) which works out at about 36% of total energy. If salt and baking powder are used, pastries are high in sodium. Bought pastries will also contain a variety of **additives** which are identifiable by their E number only if the food is prepacked.

Average nutrients in 100 grams (3½ oz) Pastries

	jam tarts	mince pies	fruit pies		jam tarts	mince pies	fruit pies
Energy kilojoules	1616	1826	1554	Iron milligrams	1.6	1.7	1.2
kilocalories	384	435	369	Copper milligrams	0.18	0.17	0.10
Protein grams	3.5	4.3	4.3	Zinc milligrams	–	0.4	0.5
Total fat grams	14.9	20.7	15.5	Vitamin A micrograms	70	90	0
Saturated fat grams	5.8	7.8	3.0	Vitamin D micrograms	0.6	0.8	0
Polyunsaturated fat grams	1.9	3.4	1.0	Vitamin C milligrams	4	0	0
				Vitamin E milligrams	0.6	0.8	–
Cholesterol milligrams	–	–	–	B vitamins:			
Sugars grams	37.5	30.0	30.9	Thiamin (B_1) milligrams	0.08	0.11	0.05
Starch grams	25.3	31.7	25.8	Riboflavin (B_2) milligrams	0.01	0.02	0.02
Dietary fibre grams	1.7	2.9	2.6	Nicotinic acid milligrams	1.3	1.7	0.9
Sodium milligrams	230	340	210	Pyridoxine (B_6) milligrams	0.04	0.08	0.03
Potassium milligrams	110	150	120	Vitamin B_{12} micrograms	0	0	0
Calcium milligrams	62	76	51	Folic acid micrograms	4	5	4
Magnesium milligrams	13	14	12	Pantothenic acid milligrams	0.1	0.1	0.1
				Biotin micrograms	1	1	0

(–) No information available   (0) Contains zero or trace amounts

Peaches

Peaches originated in China, and were introduced to Britain in 1562. The white-fleshed types are the hardiest in cold climates and are said to have the best flavour. Peaches contain little vitamin C, but the yellow flesh is a source of vitamin A, as **carotene**. Peaches contain moderate amounts of sugars, and some minerals and B vitamins. Canned peached, if sweetened, contain twice as much sugar, as sucrose, as fresh (see table).

Average nutrients in 100 grams (3½ oz) Peaches

	fresh	canned in syrup		fresh	canned in syrup
Energy kilojoules	156	373	Iron milligrams	0.4	0.4
kilocalories	37	87	Copper milligrams	0.05	0.06
Protein grams	0.6	0.4	Zinc milligrams	0.1	–
Total fat grams	0	0	Vitamin A micrograms	40-167	42
Saturated fat grams	0	0	Vitamin D micrograms	0	0
Polyunsaturated fat grams	0	0	Vitamin C milligrams	8	4
			Vitamin E milligrams	–	–
Cholesterol milligrams	0	0	B vitamins:		
Sugars grams	9.1	22.9	Thiamin (B_1) milligrams	0.02	0.01
Starch grams	0	0	Riboflavin (B_2) milligrams	0.05	0.02
Dietary fibre grams	1.4	1.0	Nicotinic acid milligrams	1.0	0.6
Sodium milligrams	3	1	Pyridoxine (B_6) milligrams	0.02	0.02

	fresh	canned in syrup		fresh	canned in syrup
Potassium milligrams	260	150	Vitamin B_{12} micrograms	0	0
Calcium milligrams	5	4	Folic acid micrograms	3	3
Magnesium milligrams	8	6	Pantothenic acid milligrams	0.15	0.05
			Biotin micrograms	0.2	0.2

(–) No information available   (0) Contains zero or trace amounts

Peanuts, also called groundnuts

A member of the *Leguminosae* (peas and beans) family, peanuts originated in South America and are now grown in most tropical regions – from the USA, Africa, India to China. They are a most important crop both for food and for processing into **oils** and cattle feed. In many communities, peanuts are ground and made into a sauce, adding a highly nutritious relish to the staple diet. Peanuts are rich in **protein**, **fat** and B **vitamins** (see table).

On roasting, 70% of the vitamin B_1 is lost, and **salt** is added. Peanuts contain zinc and iron, but also **phytic acid** which interferes with their absorption. Peanut butter is similar to roasted salted peanuts in its nutrient content.

Average nutrients in 100 grams (3½ oz) Peanuts

Energy kilojoules	2364	Iron milligrams	2.0
kilocalories	570	Copper milligrams	0.27
Protein grams	24.3	Zinc milligrams	3.0
Total fat grams	49.0	Vitamin A micrograms	0
Saturated fat grams	9.2	Vitamin D micrograms	0
Polyunsaturated fat grams	14.0	Vitamin C milligrams	0
		Vitamin E milligrams	8.1
Cholesterol milligrams	0	B vitamins:	
Sugars grams	3.1	Thiamin (B_1) milligrams	0.90
Starch grams	5.5	Riboflavin (B_2) milligrams	0.10
Dietary fibre grams	8.1	Nicotinic acid milligrams	21.3
Sodium milligrams	6	Pyridoxine (B_6) milligrams	0.5
Potassium milligrams	680	Vitamin B_{12} micrograms	0
Calcium milligrams	61	Folic acid micrograms	110
Magnesium milligrams	180	Pantothenic acid milligrams	2.7
		Biotin micrograms	–

(–) No information available   (0) Contains zero or trace amounts

Pears

Pears are indigenous to Europe, particularly the southern parts. Present day varieties were largely developed in the eighteenth century in Belgium and France, and the 'Conference' in Berkshire. Pears have an unremarkable composition (see table) with only a little vitamin C. Canned pears containing sugar, as sucrose, are mostly the 'Williams' or Bartlett variety.

Average nutrients in 100 grams (3½ oz) Pears

	fresh	canned in syrup		fresh	canned in syrup
Energy kilojoules	175	327	Iron milligrams	0.2	0.3
kilocalories	41	77	Copper milligrams	0.15	0.04
Protein grams	0.3	0.4	Zinc milligrams	0.1	–
Total fat grams	0	0	Vitamin A micrograms	2	2
Saturated fat grams	0	0	Vitamin D micrograms	0	0
Polyunsaturated fat grams	0	0	Vitamin C milligrams	3	1
			Vitamin E milligrams	0	0
Cholesterol milligrams	0	0	B vitamins:		
Sugars grams	10.6	20.0	Thiamin (B$_1$) milligrams	0.03	0.01
Starch grams	0	0	Riboflavin (B$_2$) milligrams	0.03	0.01
Dietary fibre grams	2.3	1.7	Nicotinic acid milligrams	0.2	0.3
Sodium milligrams	2	1	Pyridoxine (B$_6$) milligrams	0.02	0.01
Potassium milligrams	130	90	Vitamin B$_{12}$ micrograms	0	0
Calcium milligrams	8	5	Folic acid micrograms	11	5
Magnesium milligrams	7	6	Pantothenic acid milligrams	0.07	0.02
			Biotin micrograms	0.1	0

(–) No information available   (0) Contains zero or trace amounts

Peas

One of the most popular vegetables eaten in Britain; the average person consumed about 115 grams (4 oz) of peas per week in 1983. The largest purchases were of canned peas, 65 grams (2 oz) per person per week. Fresh and frozen peas are a good source of B vitamins, particularly **thiamin** and **folic acid**, and contain **protein**, **vitamins C** and **A**, and minerals (see table). Canned garden peas are almost as good as fresh or frozen, but canned processed (mushy peas) lose most of their vitamin C and B.

Dried peas, chick peas, and frozen peas are concentrated sources of most nutrients and, like other pulses, valuable sources of **protein** when mixed with cereals. Rice and peas is a particularly good combination of **amino acids**. Chick peas are the chief pulse crop in India, where they are known as 'Bengal gram'. Pigeon peas are the second most important, and are known as 'red gram'. They are unusual in that, unlike other pulses, the pigeon pea plant is a perennial shrub.

Mange tout, or sugar peas, have tender pods that can be eaten whole when young. No nutritional analyses are available, but they will be very similar to **runner beans**.

Average nutrients in 100 grams (3½ oz) Peas

	fresh and frozen, boiled	canned garden	canned processed	dried peas	dried chick peas	dried pigeon peas
Energy kilojoules	223	201	339	1215	1362	1278
kilocalories	52	47	80	286	320	301
Protein grams	5.0	4.6	6.2	21.6	20.2	20.0
Total fat grams	0.4	0.3	0.4	1.3	5.7	2.0
Saturated fat grams	0.1	0.1	0.1	0.5	–	–
Polyunsaturated fat grams	0	0	0	0.1	–	–
Cholesterol milligrams	0	0	0	0	0	0

	fresh and frozen, boiled	canned garden	canned processed	dried peas	dried chick peas	dried pigeon peas
Sugars grams	1.8	3.6	1.3	2.4	10.0	9.0
Starch grams	5.9	3.4	12.4	47.6	40.0	45.0
Dietary fibre grams	5.2	6.3	7.9	16.7	15.0	15.0
Sodium milligrams	0	230	330	38	40	29
Potassium milligrams	170	130	170	990	800	1100
Calcium milligrams	13	24	27	61	140	100
Magnesium milligrams	21	17	24	116	160	130
Iron milligrams	1.2	1.6	1.5	4.7	6.4	5.0
Copper milligrams	0.1	0.2	0.2	0.5	0.76	1.25
Zinc milligrams	0.5	0.7	0.8	3.5	–	–
Vitamin A micrograms	50	50	50	40	30	5
Vitamin D micrograms	0	0	0	0	0	0
Vitamin C milligrams	14	8	0	0	0	0
Vitamin E milligrams	0	0	0	0	0	0
B vitamins:						
Thiamin (B_1) milligrams	0.25	0.13	0.10	0.70	0.50	0.50
Riboflavin (B_2) milligrams	0.11	0.10	0.04	0.20	0.15	0.15
Nicotinic acid milligrams	2.3	2.8	1.5	6.7	4.2	3.9
Pyridoxine (B_6) milligrams	0.10	0.06	0.03	0.13	–	–
Vitamin B_{12} micrograms	0	0	0	0	0	0
Folic acid micrograms	78	52	3	33	180	100
Pantothenic acid milligrams	0.32	0.15	0.08	2.0	–	–
Biotin micrograms	0.4	0.4	0	–	–	–

(–) No information available   (0) Contains zero or trace amounts

Pectin (E440)

Pectin is a group of **polysaccharides** in fruits and vegetables which contributes to the dietary **fibre** in food. It is commercially extracted from apple pulp or citrus fruit pith and used as an **emulsifier** and stabiliser, and in the manufacture of jam (see **preserves**).

The cells of fruits and vegetables are held together by a layer of pectin with calcium attached. It is degraded as fruits ripen and by cooking; the cells separate, softening the food. Calcium and magnesium salts, which retard the breakdown, are added (and called firming agents – see **miscellaneous additives**) to fruits and vegetables like tomatoes and strawberries which would become very soft during canning and pickling. Some vegetables have to be canned in calcium free water, otherwise the food would be tough. Alkali (like bicarbonate of soda) softens vegetables (by hastening the breakdown of pectin) when added to cooking water, but also destroys **vitamin C** and **thiamin** (vitamin B_1).

Pellagra – (from Italian – pella = skin, agra = rough)

Pellagra is a deficiency disease caused by a diet lacking in **nicotinic acid** and the **amino acid tryptophan**. In Britain it occurs when there is underlying disease, like chronic alcoholism and **malabsorption**.

Initial symptoms are loss of weight, depression, weakness and inability to concentrate. The skin is red and itchy, later scaly, brown and infected, particularly over the face, neck and hands, but also in any areas of the the skin exposed to hot fires or sun. In chronic cases there are severe lesions of the brain and nervous system, causing dementia and difficulty in walking. A sore mouth and tongue makes eating difficult, and there may be diarrhoea or constipation. Only 24 hours after taking the vitamin, skin and digestive disorders are improved, though the nervous system may be irreversibly damaged. There are usually other deficiencies which must be remedied before full health is restored.

Nicotinic acid was known to chemists by 1840, but there was a 100 years delay in identifying its connection with pellagra, due to several confusing factors. As late as 1940, at least 2000 people died from pellagra in the USA. The disease was endemic in many communities subsisting on **maize** but chemical analyses revealed that maize was an apparently good source the vitamin. The disease could be prevented by **protein**, especially **milk** (which is not a particularly good source of the vitamin) and did not occur when the diet contained plenty of animal protein. However it was less common in communities subsisting on other cereals (like wheat) where no more animal protein was eaten than in those where pellagra was rife; in coffee drinking communities; and in those where maize was cooked with lime. The solution to the problem came in the 1930s with the realisation that nicotinic acid is a vitamin; that tryptophan (lacking in maize but adequate in other cereals and well supplied in animal protein) was converted to nicotinic acid in the body; and that nicotinic acid is in a bound form (niacytin) in all cereals and cannot be digested unless released by treatment with alkali, like lime. Other cereals were protective because they contained tryptophan. Coffee is a source of the vitamin. Despite understanding of the cause of pellagra, it remains endemic in parts of Africa and occurs sporadically in India in communities subsisting mainly on maize.

Peppercorns

Black and white peppercorns, which can be ground or kept whole, are spices obtained from the plant, *Piper nigrum*, which is a climbing vine, native to southern India. The black peppercorns are dried unripe seeds, and white peppercorns are obtained by soaking the ripe seed to remove the outer coat. About 5% of the peppercorn is made up of the active pungent chemical, piperine.

Peppers – capsicums

Sweet (green and red) peppers, pimentos and chilli peppers are members of the *Capsicum* family. When ripe the sweet pepper is coloured red or yellow, but it is most often eaten green. Sweet peppers are very good sources of vitamin C (see table). Paprika powder is made from the dried red pepper.

Chilli peppers are a much more pungent variety. They are generally sold partly dried, hence they are more concentrated sources of most nutrients, apart from vitamin C (see table). Chilli powder and cayenne are derived from the dried fruits. The pungency of the different kinds of both sweet and chilli peppers depends on their content of the chemicals dihydrocapsaicin and capsaicin.

Average nutrients in 100 grams (3½ oz) Peppers

	sweet	chilli		sweet	chilli
Energy kilojoules	65	485	Iron milligrams	0.4	3.6
kilocalories	15	116	Copper milligrams	0.07	0.10
Protein grams	0.9	6.3	Zinc milligrams	0.2	0.3
Total fat grams	0.4	1.4	Vitamin A micrograms	10-167	1100
Saturated fat grams	0.1	–	Vitamin D micrograms	0	0
Polyunsaturated fat grams	0.2	–	Vitamin C milligrams	60-170	96
			Vitamin E milligrams	0.8	–
Cholesterol milligrams	0	0	B vitamins:		
Sugars grams	2.2	} 9.8	Thiamin (B_1) milligrams	0	0.37
Starch grams	0		Riboflavin (B_2) milligrams	0.03	0.51
Dietary fibre grams	0.9	–	Nicotinic acid milligrams	0.9	–
Sodium milligrams	2	23	Pyridoxine (B_6) milligrams	0.17	–
Potassium milligrams	210	1286	Vitamin B_{12} micrograms	0	0
Calcium milligrams	9	86	Folic acid micrograms	11	16
Magnesium milligrams	11	19	Pantothenic acid milligrams	0.23	–
			Biotin micrograms	–	–

(–) No information available (0) Contains zero or trace amounts

Pheasant and partridge

Pheasant, named the 'Bird of Phasis' by the Romans from the Caspian region where it originated, is one of the most succulent of wild birds. It is similar to other game birds in nutritional composition (see table).

Partridge, like other game, is notable for its **iron** content but few other analyses are available.

Average nutrients in 100 grams (3½ oz) Pheasant and Partridge (roast)

	pheasant	partridge		pheasant	partridge
Energy kilojoules	892	890	Iron milligrams	8.4	7.7
kilocalories	213	212	Copper milligrams	–	–
Protein grams	32.2	36.7	Zinc milligrams	–	–
Total fat grams	9.3	7.2	Vitamin A micrograms	–	–
Saturated fat grams	3.1	1.9	Vitamin D micrograms	–	–
Polyunsaturated fat grams	1.1	1.7	Vitamin C milligrams	0	–
			Vitamin E milligrams	–	–
Cholesterol milligrams	–	–	B vitamins:		
Sugars grams	0	0	Thiamin (B_1) milligrams	0.04	–
Starch grams	0	0	Riboflavin (B_2) milligrams	0.15	–
Dietary fibre grams	0	0	Nicotinic acid milligrams	12.1	–
Sodium milligrams	100	100	Pyridoxine (B_6) milligrams	–	–
Potassium milligrams	410	410	Vitamin B_{12} micrograms	–	–
Calcium milligrams	49	46	Folic acid micrograms	–	–
Magnesium milligrams	35	36	Pantothenic acid milligrams	–	–
			Biotin micrograms	–	–

(–) No information available (0) Contains zero or trace amounts

Phenylalanine

Phenylalanine is an essential **amino acid** – it cannot be made in the body and has to be obtained from **proteins** in food. It is used for the synthesis of new body protein needed for growth and repair and is also the precursor of some hormones and the pigment melanin in hair, eyes and tanned skin. **Tyrosine**, made from phenylalanine can partially replace phenylalanine in the diet.

It is abundant in food proteins and deficiency of phenylalanine alone never occurs when a normal diet is eaten: four large slices of bread for example supply the estimated adult daily needs for phenylalanine and tyrosine. Excesses are converted to **glucose** or **fat** and used for **energy**. The **nitrogen** part is converted to urea, later filtered out of the blood stream by the kidneys.

Phenylketonuria is the commonest **inborn error of metabolism** successfully treated by diet. The absence of an **enzyme** in the liver blocks the normal metabolism of phenylalanine and the brain is irreversibly damaged unless a diet low in phenylalanine is given in the first few weeks of life. A synthetic diet, containing all nutrients except phenylalanine, is necessary together with low protein foods high in energy, like sugar, butter and low protein bread. The child's needs of phenylalanine for growth are given as small carefully calculated and weighed portions of normal foods, like milk. The diet is very specialised but the effort necessary to overcome the difficulties is well worthwhile. Treated phenylketonuric children are healthy and of normal intelligence. It is thought safe to discontinue the diet before adolescence (after the brain has matured). However it must be reinstated during pregnancy for women suffering from phenylketonuria to avoid damaging the growing child.

Phosphorus

Phosphorus is a **mineral**. It is a vital constituent of cells and, with **calcium**, needed for the hardening of bones and teeth.

All foods, with the exception of fats, sugar and spirits, contain some phosphorus, but good sources of calcium and protein (like milk, cheese, meat, fish and eggs) are richest. Cereals, nuts and pulses are apparently good sources but most of it is in the form of **phytic acid** unavailable to the body. Phosphorus is also added by food manufacturers as food **additives** (for example as **polyphosphates**, **raising agents**, and phosphoric acid in some **soft drinks**).

There is no **recommended intake** set for phosphorus: diets which supply the recommended intakes of **protein** and calcium contain sufficient. Adults eat between one and two grams a day, of which about two thirds is absorbed into the blood stream. An equivalent amount is later removed from the body in urine by the kidneys. However, infants, children and adolescents retain phosphorus for new cell and bone formation. It is also retained for the developing child in pregnancy and breast feeding.

When adulthood is reached, most people have accumulated more than 600 grams (over 1 lb) of phosphorus. Nearly all (80 to 85%) is in bone, combined with calcium, but it has other important roles, one of which is concerned with the transfer of energy (see **metabolism**) inside cells. Energy released from **glucose** and fats (see **lipid**) is transferred into a readily available form as 'high energy' phosphate bonds, most importantly in adenosine triphosphate (ATP). When energy is required – for example if muscles are to contract – **enzymes** break off the phosphorus and energy is liberated from the bond.

Lack of phosphorus alone from an inadequate diet does not occur in humans, although it is a problem in animals. Temporary inadequacies in the diet are counteracted by the kidneys, which cut down the quantity excreted in urine. However, despite conservation by the kidneys, phosphorus depletion has been caused by excessive quantities of some antacids used for digestive, and certain kidney, disorders. They bind phosphorus in food and none may be absorbed into the blood stream. Then phosphorus is withdrawn from the bones, which become so weak and painful that walking becomes very difficult. Lack of appetite, and severe tiredness and weakness follow and death is inevitable unless the antacids are changed.

Excess phosphorus is probably harmless for adults – it is either not absorbed or is eliminated by the kidneys. Phosphorus containing 'tonics' are of dubious value: weight for weight most foods are better sources. Many 'tonics' rely on their alcohol content for any apparent improvement in morale.

Phospholipids

Phospholipids are important substances concerned with the transport of fat (lipid) in the blood stream and probably with orderly organisation of molecules in the protoplasm of cells. Phospholipids form part of cell membranes and are especially abundant in nervous tissues, where they are incorporated into the myelin layer around fibres. This layer (or sheath) is an insulator – preventing leakage of nervous impulses from one nerve to another.

There are many different phospholipids, but their basic structure is a composition of **glycerol**, **phosphorus**, and up to two **fatty acids**. Some may have **choline** or serine (an amino acid) attached to the phosphorus part. **Lecithin** is the most common.

Phospholipids are abundant in both plant and animal foods – they are part of the structure of cells – but the body makes its own phospholipids and dietary supplies are unnecessary. The phospholipids (like glycerol phosphate) added to 'tonics' are of dubious value.

Phytic acid

Phytic acid is **inositol** combined with **phosphorus**. During **digestion** it forms insoluble salts with essential **minerals** (like calcium, iron, magnesium and zinc) in food, rendering them unavailable for absorption into the blood stream. Up to 80% of the phosphorus in **nuts**, wholegrain cereals and **pulses** is in the form of phytic acid, but nearly all is removed (with the bran) from white flour.

At one time, phytic acid was implicated as a cause of **rickets** but this is now thought unlikely. The body appears to adapt to the phytic acid in brown and wholemeal bread and other cereals, and eventually more calcium is absorbed out of food. It seems that an **enzyme**, secreted in digestive juices, is able to degrade phytic acid, splitting it to inositol and phosphorus. Phytic acid is also partially degraded by enzymes in yeast during proving of **bread**, and in pulses when they are soaked in water. Little is split during new bread making methods, which do not include a period of proving.

The extent to which phytic acid interferes with the absorption of other minerals – magnesium, iron and zinc – remains uncertain. A high phytic acid diet (from unleavened wholemeal breads) is though to be a cause of zinc deficiency.

The extraction rate of **flour** was increased during wartime, and calcium (as chalk) was added to all flour, except wholemeal, by law to overcome the then suspected rickets-producing effect of brown bread. These regulations are still in force and white flour now contains over three times more calcium than that needed to overcome the effect of phytic acid.

Pigeon

An inexpensive game bird, remarkably rich in well-absorbed **iron** (see table).

Average nutrients in 100 grams (3½ oz) Pigeon (roast)

Energy kilojoules	961	Iron milligrams	19.4
kilocalories	230	Copper milligrams	–
Protein grams	27.8	Zinc milligrams	–
Total fat grams	13.2	Vitamin A micrograms	–
Saturated fat grams	–	Vitamin D micrograms	–
Polyunsaturated fat grams	–	Vitamin C milligrams	0
		Vitamin E milligrams	0
Cholesterol milligrams	–	B vitamins:	
Sugars grams	0	Thiamin (B₁) milligrams	–
Starch grams	0	Riboflavin (B₂) milligrams	–
Dietary fibre grams	0	Nicotinic acid milligrams	14.1
Sodium milligrams	110	Pyridoxine (B₆) milligrams	–
Potassium milligrams	410	Vitamin B₁₂ micrograms	–
Calcium milligrams	16	Folic acid micrograms	–
Magnesium milligrams	34	Pantothenic acid milligrams	–
		Biotin micrograms	–

(–) No information available   (0) Contains zero or trace amounts

Pilchards

Unusually for a fatty **fish**, pilchards contain no vitamin A. They do however contain **vitamin D** and almost three times the **calcium** found in milk (from the small bones inseparable from the flesh). They are also good sources of **iron**, **zinc** and **vitamin B₁₂** (see table).

Average nutrients in 100 grams (3½ oz) Pilchards (canned in tomato sauce)

Energy kilojoules	531	Iron milligrams	2.7
kilocalories	126	Copper milligrams	0.19
Protein grams	18.8	Zinc milligrams	1.6
Total fat grams	5.4	Vitamin A micrograms	0
Saturated fat grams	1.7	Vitamin D micrograms	8
Polyunsaturated fat grams	1.8	Vitamin C milligrams	0

Average nutrients in 100 grams (3½ oz) Pilchards
(canned in tomato sauce)*(continued)*

		Vitamin E milligrams	0.70
Cholesterol milligrams	70	B vitamins:	
Sugars grams	0.7	Thiamin (B₁) milligrams	0.02
Starch grams	0	Riboflavin (B₂) milligrams	0.29
Dietary fibre grams	0	Nicotinic acid milligrams	11.1
Sodium milligrams	370	Pyridoxine (B₆) milligrams	–
Potassium milligrams	420	Vitamin B₁₂ micrograms	12
Calcium milligrams	300	Folic acid micrograms	–
Magnesium milligrams	39	Pantothenic acid milligrams	–
		Biotin micrograms	–

(–) No information available (0) Contains zero or trace amounts

Pineapple

Pineapple is a refreshing fruit which is somewhat unusual in that most of its sugars are composed of **sucrose** (7.9 grams per 100 grams). Pineapple also contains the **enzyme** bromelain used as a meat tenderiser since it breaks down **proteins**. It is sometimes recommended as an aid to **digestion** for this reason, but protein digestion is very efficient in man.

Average nutrients in 100 grams (3½ oz) Pineapple

	fresh	canned in syrup		fresh	canned in syrup
Energy kilojoules	194	328	Iron milligrams	0.4	0.4
kilocalories	46	77	Copper milligrams	0.08	0.05
Protein grams	0.5	0.3	Zinc milligrams	0.1	–
Total fat grams	0	0	Vitamin A micrograms	10	7
Saturated fat grams	0	0	Vitamin D micrograms	0	0
Polyunsaturated fat grams	0	0	Vitamin C milligrams	20–40	12
			Vitamin E milligrams	–	–
Cholesterol milligrams	0	0	B vitamins:		
Sugars grams	11.6	20.2	Thiamin (B₁) milligrams	0.08	0.05
Starch grams	0	0	Riboflavin (B₂) milligrams	0.02	0.02
Dietary fibre grams	1.2	0.9	Nicotinic acid milligrams	0.3	0.2
Sodium milligrams	2	1	Pyridoxine (B₆) milligrams	0.09	0.07
Potassium milligrams	250	94	Vitamin B₁₂ micrograms	0	0
Calcium milligrams	12	13	Folic acid micrograms	11	–
Magnesium milligrams	17	8	Pantothenic acid milligrams	0.16	0.10
			Biotin micrograms	0	0

(–) No information available (0) Contains zero or trace amounts

Pistachio

A highly prized **nut**, rich in **fat** (see table). Pistachios are native to the near East and central Asia and are used particularly in confectionery for their flavour and delicate green colour. They are also eaten roasted and salted.

Average nutrients in 100 grams (3½ oz) Pistachio nuts

Energy kilojoules	2619	Iron milligrams	14.0
kilocalories	626	Copper milligrams	–

Protein grams	20.0	Zinc milligrams	–
Total fat grams	54.0	Vitamin A micrograms	10
Saturated fat grams	–	Vitamin D micrograms	0
Polyunsaturated fat grams	–	Vitamin C milligrams	0
		Vitamin E milligrams	–
Cholesterol milligrams	0	B vitamins:	
Sugars grams	}15.0	Thiamin (B₁) milligrams	0.70
Starch grams		Riboflavin (B₂) milligrams	0.20
Dietary fibre grams	–	Nicotinic acid milligrams	–
Sodium milligrams	–	Pyridoxine (B₆) milligrams	–
Potassium milligrams	–	Vitamin B₁₂ micrograms	0
Calcium milligrams	140	Folic acid micrograms	–
Magnesium milligrams	–	Pantothenic acid milligrams	–
		Biotin micrograms	–

(–) No information available   (0) Contains zero or trace amounts

Plaice

A popular fish, with similar nutritional properties to other white **fish** (see table). The upper side of fresh plaice is dark, and the red and orange spots should be well marked. The colour of the spots fades as the fish becomes stale.

Average nutrients in 100 grams (3½ oz) Plaice (steamed)

Energy kilojoules	392	Iron milligrams	0.6
kilocalories	93	Copper milligrams	–
Protein grams	18.9	Zinc milligrams	–
Total fat grams	1.9	Vitamin A micrograms	0
Saturated fat grams	0.3	Vitamin D micrograms	0
Polyunsaturated fat grams	0.5	Vitamin C milligrams	0
		Vitamin E milligrams	–
Cholesterol milligrams	70	B vitamins:	
Sugars grams	0	Thiamin (B₁) milligrams	0.02–0.46
Starch grams	0	Riboflavin (B₂) milligrams	0.09–0.33
Dietary fibre grams	0	Nicotinic acid milligrams	6.5
Sodium milligrams	120	Pyridoxine (B₆) milligrams	0.43
Potassium milligrams	280	Vitamin B₁₂ micrograms	2
Calcium milligrams	38	Folic acid micrograms	10
Magnesium milligrams	24	Pantothenic acid milligrams	0.80
		Biotin micrograms	–

(–) No information available   (0) Contains zero or trace amounts

Plantain

A variety of **banana**, cooked and eaten when green in areas of the world, such as Uganda, where it is the staple food crop. It is a rich source of **starch** (see table). Some types are grown for steaming, others for roasting.

Average nutrients in 100 grams (3½ oz) Plantain (boiled)

Energy kilojoules	518	Iron milligrams	0.4
kilocalories	122	Copper milligrams	0.10
Protein grams	1.0	Zinc milligrams	0.2
Total fat grams	0.1	Vitamin A micrograms	10
Saturated fat grams	–	Vitamin D micrograms	0
Polyunsaturated fat grams	–	Vitamin C milligrams	3

Average nutrients in 100 grams (3½ oz) Plantain (boiled)*(continued)*

		Vitamin E milligrams	–
Cholesterol milligrams	0	B vitamins:	
Sugars grams	0.9	Thiamin (B₁) milligrams	0
Starch grams	30.2	Riboflavin (B₂) milligrams	0.01
Dietary fibre (NSP) grams	0.9	Nicotinic acid milligrams	0.5
Sodium milligrams	4	Pyridoxine (B₆) milligrams	0.3
Potassium milligrams	330	Vitamin B₁₂ micrograms	0
Calcium milligrams	9	Folic acid micrograms	18
Magnesium milligrams	34	Pantothenic acid milligrams	0.26
		Biotin micrograms	–

(–) No information available   (0) Contains zero or trace amounts

Plums

The many varieties of plums are hybrids of the common sloe and the cherry plum; 'Victoria' was found in a Sussex wood, in about 1840. Dessert varieties have a richer flavour and higher sugar content than the plums intended for cooking or canning. Plums contain very little vitamin C (see table).

Average nutrients in 100 grams (3½ oz) Plums

	dessert	stewed with sugar		dessert	stewed with sugar
Energy kilojoules	164	252	Iron milligrams	0.4	0.2
kilocalories	38	59	Copper milligrams	0.10	0.06
Protein grams	0.6	0.4	Zinc milligrams	0	0
Total fat grams	0	0	Vitamin A micrograms	37	28
Saturated fat grams	0	0	Vitamin D micrograms	0	0
Polyunsaturated fat grams	0	0	Vitamin C milligrams	3	2
			Vitamin E milligrams	0.7	0.4
Cholesterol milligrams	0	0	B vitamins:		
Sugars grams	9.6	15.1	Thiamin (B₁) milligrams	0.05	0.04
Starch grams	0	0	Riboflavin (B₂) milligrams	0.03	0.02
Dietary fibre grams	2.1	1.9	Nicotinic acid milligrams	0.6	0.5
Sodium milligrams	2	2	Pyridoxine (B₆) milligrams	0.05	0.03
Potassium milligrams	190	150	Vitamin B₁₂ micrograms	0	0
Calcium milligrams	11	11	Folic acid micrograms	3	1
Magnesium milligrams	7	5	Pantothenic acid milligrams	0.15	0.11
			Biotin micrograms	0	0

(–) No information available   (0) Contains zero or trace amounts

Poisons in food

A food may contain natural toxins, and is also liable to contamination with unwanted substances at several points before actually reaching the plate. Large doses of toxin can have an immediate (acute) effect, like vomiting or fits, but much smaller doses may be taken with no apparent harm and it is difficult to assess whether at these levels the substance is toxic. The body may be able to cope with a small regular intake, either eliminating it immediately or converting it to a harmless substance. Any damage that might have been done can then be repaired. The problems are greater when substances are eliminated with difficulty: they may be stored (for instance in body fat) and accumulate with increasing age.

The risks from carcinogens, mutagens and teratogens are even more difficult to establish. They react with DNA, the genetic blueprint in cells, causing a change in the genetic material. Carcinogens induce cancer: mutagens alter the germ cells (sperm and ova), when the change is passed on to succeeding generations. The mutation may be harmless, or at the other extreme be incompatible with life. Teratogens damage the growing child in the womb, and may cause severe mental or physical abnormalities. Thalidomide is an example of a teratogen. Other substances may contribute to other chronic diseases, like heart disease.

Acceptable daily intakes (or 'safe' limits) below which there is no measurable harmful effect can usually be established for individual toxicants. However, they are largely based on animal experiments which may not apply to the human situation and it is only possible to say with certainty that food intakes below the 'safe' limit *probably* carry no risks to health.

Natural toxins

A variety of plants contain known toxins, including thujone in wormwood (used in absinthe and vermouth) which in excess may cause convulsions; myristin in nutmeg which in excess can cause coma; solanine in **potatoes**; **oxalic acid** in spinach; arsenic in hops; and cyanide in bitter almonds and slivovitz. Comfrey, used in some herbal teas, contains alkaloids which have been known to cause liver cancer in animals. Chick **peas** also contain a neurotoxin (damaging to the nervous system) and in excess cause lathyrism – a disease which often results in spastic paraplegia – and sassafras, also used in some herbal teas, also contains a liver carcinogen. Raw or undercooked kidney, butter and runner **beans** contain lectins which can cause severe gastroenteritis with nausea, vomiting and diarrhoea. It is essential to boil dried beans for a minimum of 10 minutes before eating. Lectins are widespread in many other foods and those surviving cooking and **digestion** may be important in **allergy**. A lectin from castor oil seeds was probably used to assassinate Gyorgi Markov in 1978.

Perhaps the most insidious and dangerous natural toxins are made from fungi. Ergotism, caused by the fungus ergot growing on rye, is well known, but only recently has it been realised that one of the aflatoxins, formed by the mould **Aspergillus flavus** growing on poorly stored groundnuts and other food is a potent cause of liver cancer, at least for animals and almost certainly man. It is essential to avoid all mouldy food in the home because at least 100 other mycotoxins have been identified and many are suspected carcinogens. Trimming mould off the surface of food is not a sufficient precaution because the toxins migrate into the food. *All* of it should be thrown away.

Farm chemicals

At least 200 chemicals are available for use during farming, transport and storage of food, in addition to fertilisers such as **nitrate**. Of these, the majority are *herbicides* (about 80) including the translocated herbicides such as glyphosate and 2, 4, 5 T; contact herbicides such as paraquat; and soil acting herbicides such as isoproturon and tri-allate. About a further 60 are *pesticides* including the carbamates, such as aldicarb; the organophosphates, such as malathion; and the organochlorides such as aldrin and lindane (gamma HCH). Some pesticides are 'natural' substances used in organic farming (see **organic food**) such as derris. An important group is the *fungicides* (about 50) including captan, benomyl, sulphur, and thiabendazole. In addition, various growth regulators and sprout inhibitors, used for example on cereals and potatoes, such as technazene, may be used.

Agrochemicals as a whole have made a major contribution to efficient farming and hence increased yields of food. However, because they are high technology products, and some are potentially dangerous, their safe use requires a high degree of expertise by farmers and growers. Guidelines set by the Ministry of Agriculture, Fisheries and Food and the manufacturers are intended to prevent harm to consumers, handlers, and the environment. These include recommended minimum lengths of time between applying to crops and harvesting, prevention of pollution of water supplies, and specific advice on which product should be applied to particular crops. Some substances such as aldicarb and mercury containing compounds are also under the control of the Poisons Act 1984. The use of some persistent organochlorine compounds, such as aldrin, is subject to the Pesticides Safety Precautions Scheme, whereby their use is not advised or limited to a few crops only. Apart from the Poisons Act however, these schemes are not law, and are open to mistakes and abuse.

The dangers of mistakes are greatest in Third World countries and the largest outbreak of poisoning occurred in Iraq in 1972 when seed intended for planting, and therefore treated with a mercury containing fungicide, was consumed. Over 6000 people were admitted to hospital, and over 450 died. The herbicide 2, 4, 5 T was introduced in the 1940s and is not thought to be harmful for humans, but a contaminant, dioxin, is highly toxic. Dioxin levels are controlled to very low levels in UK supplies of 2, 4, 5 T but large amounts contaminated the environment after the chemical explosion in Seveso, Italy, in 1976. Supplies of 2, 4, 5 T used as Agent Orange in the Vietnam war were probably contaminated with dioxin. DDT was also introduced in the 1940s and was used extensively up until the 1970s and resulted in spectacular successes in controlling diseases carried by insects such as malaria, and in crop protection.

However, the chlorinated hydrocarbons, such as DDT, are particularly hazardous over the long term. They have a stable chemical structure, only slowly converted to harmless substances, and are continually recycled in the environment. Chlorinated hydrocarbons are stored in the body fat and excessive accumulations stimulate certain liver enzymes, hastening the breakdown of some drugs and oestrogens. Animals highest in the food chain, like predatory birds and humans, are at greatest risk of accumulating too much. Since the early 1960s – when it was realised that many birds were threatened with extinction – the use of DDT has been subject to a voluntary ban, under the Pesticides Safety Precautions Scheme. However, a survey by the Association of Public Analysts in 1983 showed that 10% of fruits and vegetables contained DDT. The 1985 Food and Environment Protection Act will introduce legal controls into the use of farm chemicals; the regulations banning DDT came into force in 1986.

Other pollutants

Many other industrial chemicals – including the very toxic polychlor-biphenyls, which, like DDT, are recycled in the environment – can pollute food. For instance, wood may be preserved with chlorophenols and these may contaminate food when the wood is used as poultry litter, or made into paper for packaging. Some chlorophenols have a disinfectant taste, even at almost undetectable levels. If wood is burnt, chlorodioxins, which are extremely toxic and suspected carcinogens, are formed from chlorophenols and contaminate food in contact with the smoke. Only fresh wood should be used for barbecuing and smoking food in the home, but even food smoked with fresh wood is not harmless. Smoke contains polycyclic hydrocarbons – the potent carcinogens in cigarette smoke and motor vehicle exhausts – which are deposited on smoked and barbequed food. Icelanders, who eat a lot of home smoked food, have one of the highest rates of stomach cancer. Polycyclic hydrocarbons are volatile and more are formed when high fat foods are barbecued. Fat should therefore be cut off meat, and the food should not be in contact with the flames.

In addition, food, particularly sea food, may be contaminated with cadmium, mercury, lead and arsenic, and accidents at nuclear power stations and atomic weapons testing bases cause contamination with radiation.

*Radiation.*Radiations are given off by radioactive substances – radioisotopes – as they decay to more stable forms. The radiations are carcinogens, mutagens and teratogens. There are many natural radioisotopes – for instance one of potassium (K 40), another of carbon (C 14), and uranium (U 236) – in the environment, which together with cosmic rays, contribute to "background radiation". Technology has also resulted in other sources of radiation, for instance X rays used in medicine and from TV sets, and radiation from artificial radioisotopes.

Artificial radioisotopes are formed in nuclear reactions, for instance, in atomic weapons and nuclear power stations. When there is an accident, artificial radioisotopes from power stations can significantly contaminate the environment, and they are released when atomic weapons are exploded in the atmosphere. They eventually return to the ground, mostly in rain, as fall out.

Both water and soil are contaminated with fall out, but as plants absorb relatively little from soil, the outer parts – in direct contact with rain – are the most radioactive. Thus outer leaves are more radioactive than inner, and wholemeal flour is more radioactive than white. Food from animals fed on contaminated pastures also contributes to the radioactivity of diets: local diets in hilly areas with west facing slopes (which have the most rainfall) are more contaminated than the average. Most radioactivity is filtered out in soil and in drinking water tends to be low. Fish are also relatively unpolluted with radioactivity because rain water is diluted by sea water.

The most important artificial radioisotopes likely to contaminate food are shown in Table I. Following the Chernobyl accident in the USSR in 1986, studies in Cambridge detected these isotopes in people who had not visited the area. However, the level of contamination was so low that extremely sensitive equipment was needed to detect it, and much less than the normal background radiation from potassium 40. Radiation increased 100 fold in milk, but the high levels still did not exceed the natural background radiation of the milk bottles.

Soft tissue, like the reproductive organs (which are also very sensitive to radiations) are likely to be damaged by caesium 137, but it is less dangerous than strontium 90. It is chemically similar to **potassium** and, like potassium, is eliminated fairly rapidly from the body. Foods high in potassium (like meat) are significant sources, but to some extent potassium is also protective against caesium 137. Although wholemeal flour contains more than white, less is absorbed into the blood stream because wholemeal flour is high in potassium.

Iodine 131, which like **iodine** is retained in the thyroid gland, is the most dangerous radioisotope after a nuclear power station accident or atomic explosion, but it is not hazardous over the long term. It nearly all decays (to iodine) within a month. In the event of an accident it contaminates the immediate vicinity of a power station, when local milk supplies are temporarily withdrawn (as happened at Windscale in 1957). The government has stocks of iodine 131-free milk in readiness for emergencies.

Strontium 90 is very hazardous over the long term because it has a long half life and – being chemically similar – is used almost as if it were **calcium** by the body. It is consequently retained in bone, increasing the risk of cancer of the bone marrow, which is one of the most radiation sensitive body tissues. Foods high in calcium contain the most strontium 90, but to some extent calcium is protective. Living things tend to use calcium in preference to strontium 90 so that plants grown in limed soil absorb less than others, and calcium added to white **bread** fortuitously reduces the amount of strontium 90 entering the blood stream.

Table I.
Artificial radioisotopes in food

Radioisotope	Half life[a]	Chemically similar to	Most damaging to	Main food source in the average diet
Iodine 131	8 days	Iodine	Thyroid gland	Milk (cheese and butter do not contain I 131 because it decays during their manufacture)
Strontium 90	28 years	Calcium	Bone marrow	Dairy products, cereals
Caesium 137	30 years	Potassium	Any soft tissue, but especially the germ cells	Dairy products, meat

[a] – the time taken for the radiations to decrease by half.

Trace elements. Traces of several elements not thought to be essential for health enter the body from food, water and air. Most appear to be harmless at low levels, but, like the essential **trace elements** (see for instance copper) high intakes of some are known to have toxic effects. Those most likely to contaminate food are arsenic, cadmium, lead and mercury.

Small amounts of arsenic occur naturally in most foods: shellfish, seaweed and hops contain more than most. Food contaminated with arsenic (for instance beer containing glucose made from impure sulphuric acid) has caused outbreaks of poisoning in the past, but food contents are now legally controlled and, at one tenth of the safe limit, the average dietary intake is well within the safe limit. At higher intakes, though still insufficient to cause poisoning, arsenic is a suspected carcinogen.

High intakes of cadmium cause kidney damage and animal experiments suggest that cadmium may be a cause of high blood pressure and possibly **heart disease**. It also appears to be antagonistic to the essential trace elements zinc, copper and selenium. In Japan, the disease "Itai Itai" is probably due to industrial contamination of water supplies with cadmium. In Britain the average intake is about one third of the probable safe limit. Other sources of cadmium are cigarette smoke (which may be a greater hazard because more is absorbed through the lungs than from food), soft water left standing in galvanised pipes, and some enamelled casseroles. A British Standard for cadmium in ceramic ware was introduced in 1972, but casseroles bought before then and enamelled red, yellow or orange on the inside (for instance on the inside of the lid) can be harmful, especially when used for cooking acid foods.

Excessive lead intakes cause anaemia and damage the kidneys and nervous system especially in children. Food is the main source, but although the average intake is about one third of the safe limit, extra can be added during cooking. For instance, lead dissolves out of pewter pots and from lead-containing glazes on some earthenware casseroles. Acid foods dissolve the most lead. Other sources of lead – water left standing in lead pipes (soft water dissolves out more than hard), air polluted with car exhausts (high octane fuel contains the most lead) and lead in old paint – can be more serious hazards. Several children used to die each year from eating chips of oil paint: modern paints contain much less lead. City dust also contains very high levels and can be dangerous if eaten by children. 1985 regulations for lead in food specify maximum permitted levels of 0.02 milligrams in most foods, and 0.1 milligrams per 100 grams for apples and pears and all canned foods. The limit is 0.002 milligrams in infant foods.

There are several forms of mercury (quicksilver), most of which are toxic in excess, but methyl mercury is the most dangerous. It damages the brain and nervous system irreversibly and is probably a carcinogen, mutagen and teratogen. Since 1953 at least 46 people have died in the Minamata Bay area of Japan from eating polluted fish. Mercury was discharged from local factories into the sea where it is converted by bacteria into methyl mercury. The fish were found to contain up to 50 micrograms per gram: only about 5 grams would have exceeded the safe limit. In Britain, nearly all fish landed is relatively unpolluted and the quantity of mercury in the average diet is about a quarter of the probable safe limit.

Cooking and processing of food

Further hazards await in the food factory, restaurant and kitchen. The brown colour of some cooked and stored foods, particularly milk, is due to the formation of complexes between proteins and sugars which are toxic in large amounts. Cholesterol can be oxidised in heated and stored foods to products which induce **atherosclerosis** and are carcinogenic. Overused or abused frying oils (for example in the home or small restaurants) contain many decomposition chemicals which are likely to damage the stomach, heart, liver and kidneys. Oils that smoke must never be reused and foaming oils are definitely toxic. Numerous mutagens and carcinogens have been found in meat and fish cooked at high heat, for instance grilling, in addition to nitrosamines and polycyclic hydrocarbons.

Lastly, careless cooking or handling can result in food poisoning by bacterial toxins that can be fatal. Salmonellas are responsible in at least half of traceable cases. Raw milk, eggs, meat and poultry can be contaminated on the farm or by droppings from pets or pests. They are destroyed by heat and freshly cooked food is theoretically safe. However meat (especially poultry, which is very likely to be contaminated) not properly thawed before cooking is dangerous because the inner part may not have reached a sufficiently high temperature to kill all the salmonella. In Sweden in 1953, 105 people died from salmonella in meat balls that had been inadequately cooked. Furthermore, salmonella can be transferred from one food to another by hands and equipment. Some outbreaks have been caused by portions of cooked chicken left out of the refrigerator after being cut up on a surface that had previously been used for preparing the raw chicken for the oven.

Clostridium welchii is responsible for up to a third of traceable cases. The spores of these bacteria are resistant to cooking and are found in dust and air: large joints of meat left to cool uncovered and partially reheated later may contain dangerous numbers. Meat – especially reheated meat and pies – is the usual source of infection.

About a further 5% of traceable cases are caused by staphylococci, but it is the toxins, and not the bacteria themselves, that cause poisoning. Most people have staphylococci in their noses and the bacteria are transferred to hair and hands. Handling food with unwashed hands, and sneezing, coughing and smoking over food can deposit the bacteria on it. They multiply – forming toxins – unless the food is refrigerated. The bacteria are destroyed by heat, but the toxins can withstand boiling for up to an hour – thus even thoroughly cooked food can be harmful if it has not been kept in a refrigerator. Foods that are not cooked after preparation, like trifles, custards, cream cakes and cold meat are, however, the most liable to be toxic.

Table II
Precautions against food poisoning

Precaution	Reason
1. High standard of hygiene (scrupulously clean hands, kitchen and equipment)	Unwashed hands, dirty equipment, flies and other pests (attracted by dirt and rubbish) can contaminate food. 2 and 3 are as important because it is difficult to eradicate food poisoning bacteria completely from hands and some equipment (like wooden chopping boards).

2. Food must always be cooled quickly after cooking, and always immediately stored in a refrigerator. Cold meat, pies, cream cakes, trifles, mayonnaise etc, which are not cooked before eating must never be left to stand in a warm place	Food poisoning bacteria cannot multiply below 4°C, the temperature of a well maintained refrigerator.
3. Food must always be cooked thoroughly	Heat kills most food poisoning bacteria
4. Frozen meat should always be completely thawed before cooking (but not fruits and vegetables)	Centre of frozen meat may not reach a sufficiently high temperature to kill bacteria
5. Avoid reheating meat and casseroles	Spores may survive cooking, germinate and multiply whilst the food is cooking or being reheated. If absolutely essential to reheat meat, it must be cooled quickly, refrigerated and quickly and thoroughly reheated
6. Keep raw and cooked foods separate, and avoid using the same surface for preparing raw and cooked food, unless thoroughly washed in very hot water and detergent	Avoids recontamination of cooked food
7. Rehydrated and food in opened cans should be treated as if it were fresh	Bacteria cannot multiply in dry food, and the sterile contents of cans are protected by the can. Once opened or rehydrated, these foods are as liable to contamination as other food.
8. Meat should never be bottled or canned in the home	Danger of botulism
9. Never taste suspect food	Food poisoning bacteria do not cause flavour deterioration

Clostridium botulinum – the cause of botulism – can only multiply in air-free non-acid foods, like canned and bottled meats and some vegetables, and smoked food. Nitrite added to cured and smoked meat inhibits its growth, and sea fish is unlikely to be contaminated. However, there is a risk from smoked trout unless it is kept refrigerated. All commercially canned food is heated to a temperature sufficiently high to kill spore forms but home canned and bottled meat is dangerous because it is difficult to reach the necessary temperature with domestic equipment. Spores which escape sterilisation germinate and multiply whilst the can is stored, forming a lethal nerve toxin. The consumer is severely ill within 3 days. Botulism is fortunately rare in Britain; it is fatal in about three-quarters of cases.

Of all the possible hazards of eating food, food poisoning is the most common and definite cause of ill health. It can however be prevented by simple measures. Table II lists precautions against food poisoning in the home.

Polyphosphates (E450)

Polyphosphates are legally permitted **miscellaneous additives** in food. They are classed as acids, and retard the growth of bacteria and moulds that would otherwise grow in foods like meat and fish. More importantly to the food industry, they prevent the normal loss of water that occurs on cooking, when proteins shrink, squeezing water out of food. The meat is more succulent, but also contains less nutrients, weight for weight than traditional products. Polyphosphates are also used to re-form mechanically recovered meat (see **meat**) into recognisable meat.

Polysaccharides

Polysaccharides are long chains of simple sugars (**monosaccharides**). Some, like **starch**, **dextrin** and **glycogen**, can be split to their constituent sugar, glucose, during digestion which is then absorbed into the blood stream and used for energy. Others, like **cellulose**, **edible gums**, **agar**, **alginates**, **pectin** and **inulin** cannot be digested and contribute to dietary **fibre**.

Pomegranate

Pomegranate is a tropical fruit, sufficiently hardy to be grown for its ornamental flowers in Britain – although the fruit rarely ripens. Pomegranates provide much entertainment for children although the juice is of only a moderate nutritional value (see table). Grenadine syrup, particularly popular in France, is made from pomegranate juice.

Average nutrients in 100 grams (3½ oz) Pomegranate juice

Energy kilojoules	189	Iron milligrams	0.2
kilocalories	44	Copper milligrams	0.07
Protein grams	0.2	Zinc milligrams	–
Total fat grams	0	Vitamin A micrograms	0
Saturated fat grams	0	Vitamin D micrograms	0
Polyunsaturated fat grams	0	Vitamin C milligrams	8
		Vitamin E milligrams	–
Cholesterol milligrams	0	B vitamins:	
Sugars grams	11.6	Thiamin (B_1) milligrams	0.02
Starch grams	0	Riboflavin (B_2) milligrams	0.03
Dietary fibre grams	0	Nicotinic acid milligrams	0.2
Sodium milligrams	1	Pyridoxine (B_6) milligrams	–
Potassium milligrams	200	Vitamin B_{12} micrograms	0
Calcium milligrams	3	Folic acid micrograms	–
Magnesium milligrams	3	Pantothenic acid milligrams	–
		Biotin micrograms	–

(–) No information available   (0) Contains zero or trace amounts

Pork

The nutritional value of pork varies considerably depending on how much **fat** to lean is eaten. Grilled belly of pork, for example, contains over three times as much fat and twice the **energy** of lean roast leg. The amount of **cholesterol** is the same in both fat and lean, but the fatty part of pork will raise blood cholesterol more than lean, due to its high content of saturated **fatty acids**. Pork is a good source of **zinc** and a rich source of **vitamin B_1** (see table). Pork fat contains vitamin E but there are only traces in the lean meat.

Average nutrients in 100 grams (3½ oz) Pork

	lean grilled chops	lean roast leg	grilled belly		lean grilled chops	lean roast leg	grilled belly
Energy kilojoules	945	777	1646	Iron milligrams	1.2	1.3	1.0
kilocalories	226	185	398	Copper milligrams	0.16	0.29	0.16

Protein grams	32.3	30.7	21.1	Zinc milligrams	3.5	3.5	2.6
Total fat grams	10.7	6.9	34.8	Vitamin A micrograms	0	0	0
Saturated fat grams	4.2	2.7	14.0	Vitamin D micrograms	0	0	0
Polyunsaturated fat grams	0.8	0.5	2.7	Vitamin C milligrams	0	0	0
				Vitamin E milligrams	0	0	0.05
Cholesterol milligrams	110	110	110	B vitamins:			
Sugars grams	0	0	0	Thiamin (B_1) milligrams	0.88	0.85	0.53
Starch grams	0	0	0	Riboflavin (B_2) milligrams	0.26	0.35	0.11
Dietary fibre grams	0	0	0	Nicotinic acid milligrams	13.6	12.3	8.1
Sodium milligrams	84	79	95	Pyridoxine (B_6) milligrams	0.41	0.41	0.23
Potassium milligrams	420	390	310	Vitamin B_{12} micrograms	2	2	1
Calcium milligrams	9	9	11	Folic acid micrograms	7	7	4
Magnesium milligrams	29	25	19	Pantothenic acid milligrams	1.3	1.3	0.7
				Biotin micrograms	3	3	2

(–) No information available   (0) Contains zero or trace amounts

Potassium

Potassium is an **electrolyte** in body fluids, necessary for the proper functioning of cells, including nerves. Adults contain between 100 and 150 grams (3½ to 5 oz), most of which is inside cells. It cannot be stored, and about 2½ grams are lost every day in the urine. This loss must be replaced by potassium absorbed from food.

Nearly all foods however contain potassium, except sugar, fats, oils and alcoholic spirits. Boiling of **vegetables** reduces their content by half, but the mineral can be recovered in the cooking water. None is lost on baking or steaming. Boiling vegetables with **salt** reverses the ratio of potassium to sodium and this has been linked with high blood pressure – see salt.

Potassium deficiency is rare in healthy adults and children. Nearly all of the 2 to 6 grams of potassium in the average diet is absorbed into the blood stream and amply replaces body losses. If deficiency is likely – when there are increased losses from the body, for example in chronic diarrhoea, vomiting, diabetes, some kidney diseases and from diuretics (drugs prescribed to increase the volume of urine) – the losses are counteracted by extra potassium, given as pills or intravenous fluids. The elderly, who frequently eat less than average quantities of potassium, are particularly at risk from the resultant weakness, mental confusion and – in severe cases – heart attack. Potatoes (each portion contains about ½ gram) and instant coffee are a convenient way of adding potassium to the diet.

In health, a high potassium diet is not harmful – the excess is eliminated by the kidneys, but in chronic kidney disease unwanted potassium accumulates in the blood stream, and can result in a heart attack.

Potatoes

When first introduced into Europe potatoes were thought to have weakening properties (or even be a cause of leprosy) and now they have an undeserved reputation as a purely fattening food. In fact, potatoes supply **vitamin** C, **minerals** and most B **vitamins**. Eighty per cent of their weight is (non fattening) water and 20% **starch**. However, as soon as **fat** is added, the energy

(Calorie) value rises dramatically – chips for example can contain up to four times the energy of boiled potatoes (see table), and crisps over six times. The amount of fat taken up depends on the thickness of the potato pieces so that roast potatoes contain less than chips, and thick cut chips less than thin ones. Oven ready chips contain less fat than fresh chips. Crisps contain over a third of their weight as fat, and low fat crisps one quarter.

Potatoes are an important source of **vitamin C** (especially in winter), supplying a fifth of the total in the average British diet. They are rich in **potassium** and supply moderate quantities of other **minerals**. They are lacking in vitamin B_{12} (like other vegetable foods), and are poor sources of vitamin B_2 (**riboflavin**), but are useful sources of other B **vitamins**. Potatoes contain **vitamin E** (crisps fried in oil are good sources) and yellow (but not white) sweet potatoes are sources of **carotene** (pro vitamin A). Potatoes supply small quantities of good quality **protein**.

Average nutrients in 100 grams (3½ oz) Potatoes (cooked without fat)

	boiled	baked	boiled new	instant powdered (no fat)
Energy kilojoules	343	448	324	299
kilocalories	80	105	76	70
Protein grams	1.4	2.6	1.6	2.0
Total fat grams	0.1	0.1	0.1	0.2
Saturated fat grams	0	0	0	0
Polyunsaturated fat grams	0	0	0	0
Cholesterol milligrams	0	0	0	0
Sugars grams	0.4	0.6	0.7	0.5
Starch grams	19.3	24.4	17.6	15.6
Dietary fibre (NSP) grams	1.0	1.0	1.0	–
Sodium milligrams	3	8	41	260
Potassium milligrams	330	680	330	340
Calcium milligrams	4	9	5	20
Magnesium milligrams	15	29	20	15
Iron milligrams	0.3	0.8	0.4	0.5
Copper milligrams	0.11	0.18	0.15	0.08
Zinc milligrams	0.2	0.3	0.3	0.2
Vitamin A micrograms	0	0	0	0
Vitamin D micrograms	0	0	0	0
Vitamin C milligrams	4-14	5-16	18	3
Vitamin E milligrams	0.1	0.1	0.1	1
B vitamins:				
Thiamin (B_1) milligrams	0.08	0.10	0.11	0.01
Riboflavin (B_2) milligrams	0.03	0.04	0.03	0.03
Nicotinic acid milligrams	1.1	1.8	1.6	1.7
Pyridoxine (B_6) milligrams	0.18	0.18	0.2	0.2
Vitamin B_{12} micrograms	0	0	0	0
Folic acid micrograms	10	10	10	5
Pantothenic acid milligrams	0.2	0.2	0.2	0.2
Biotin micrograms	0	0	0	0.1

(–) No information available   (0) Contains zero or trace amounts

Average nutrients in 100 grams (3½ oz) Potatoes (cooked with fat)

	roast	fresh chips	frozen chips	crisps
Energy kilojoules	662	1065	1214	2224
kilocalories	157	253	291	533
Protein grams	2.8	3.8	3.0	6.3
Total fat grams	4.8	7-15[a]	19.0	35.9[b]
Saturated fat grams	–	–	–	–
Polyunsaturated fat grams	–	–	–	–
Cholesterol milligrams	–	–	–	–
Sugars grams	–	–	0.5	0.7
Starch grams	27.3	37.3	28.5	48.6
Dietary fibre (NSP) grams	–	–	–	–
Sodium milligrams	9	12	34	550
Potassium milligrams	750	1020	540	1190
Calcium milligrams	10	14	11	37
Magnesium milligrams	32	43	27	56
Iron milligrams	0.7	0.9	1.0	2.1
Copper milligrams	0.2	0.3	0.15	0.2
Zinc milligrams	0.4	0.6	0.4	0.8
Vitamin A micrograms	0	0	0	0
Vitamin D micrograms	0	0	0	0
Vitamin C milligrams	5-16	5-16	4	17
Vitamin E milligrams	0.1	0.1	–	6.1
B vitamins:				
Thiamin (B_1) milligrams	0.1	0.1	0.09	0.19
Riboflavin (B_2) milligrams	0.04	0.04	0.02	0.07
Nicotinic acid milligrams	1.9	2.1	2.8	6.1
Pyridoxine (B_6) milligrams	0.18	0.18	0.39	0.89
Vitamin B_{12} micrograms	0	0	0	0
Folic acid micrograms	7	10	11	20
Pantothenic acid milligrams	0.2	0.2	–	–
Biotin micrograms	0	0	0	–

(–) No information available   (0) Contains zero or trace amounts

[a] Lower value, oven ready chips; higher value, deep fried chips
[b] Low fat crisps, 22-28 grams

It is often said that the skin of the potato should be eaten, for the extra **fibre**, vitamin C and protein, but if this is done the potatoes should be well washed to remove, for example, sprout inhibitors. Potatoes are not a notable source of fibre, and because of its small proportion of the whole, the skin does not add a great deal. On cooling some of the starch becomes resistant to the action of digestive **enzymes** and may act in a similar way to fibre. Cooked cooled potatoes, for example in potato salad, contain significant amounts of this starch.

Fresh potatoes are living, and vitamin C declines during storage. August and new potatoes contain about 30 milligrams of vitamin C per 100 grams, but by March the level has fallen to about 10 milligrams. Old potatoes eaten after May may contain no vitamin C. Bruised potatoes contain less than sound ones, and poor storage conditions will hasten its destruction. Ideally they should be kept in a dark, dry, cool (between 5 and 10°C) place. In light, they turn green and sprout, forming solanine, which can be toxic. The eyes and green parts should be cut out. Potatoes should be taken out of plastic bags, otherwise they become moist and start to rot. They quickly lose weight and vitamin C in warm places, but may become sweet (the starch is converted into sugar) if kept too cool, for example in a refrigerator.

Up to half of vitamin C and potassium can be lost when potatoes are boiled; less is lost if they are cooked in a small quantity of water for as short a time as possible. Stewed potatoes (for instance in soup) contain none. No potassium is lost during baking, frying and pressure cooking and only about a third of vitamin C is destroyed. After cooking, keeping potatoes hot further reduces vitamin C (by about half in two hours) but there is less destruction in boiled, rather than mashed, potato.

Instant potato contains less folic acid than fresh, and prepeeled potatoes and chips contain less vitamin B₁ than fresh because sulphur dioxide, a preservative, is added to prevent browning. Canned potatoes are similar to fresh.

Prawns and scampi

Prawns are native to British waters although most frozen ones are imported. The Italian scampi or Dublin Bay prawns are mid-way in size between prawns and Pacific prawns. All are low in fat, and, when cooked in salt water, high in salt (see table). The fat content is greatly increased when scampi are eaten fried. Prawns and scampi are good sources of **calcium** and, like all sea fish, **iodine**. They may contain the **preservative** sulphur dioxide, (E220-227).

Average nutrients in 100 grams (3½ oz) Prawns and Scampi

	boiled prawns	fried scampi		boiled prawns	fried scampi
Energy kilojoules	451	1321	Iron milligrams	1.1	1.1
kilocalories	107	316	Copper milligrams	0.7	0.22
Protein grams	22.6	12.2	Zinc milligrams	1.6	0.6
Total fat grams	1.8	17.6	Vitamin A micrograms	0	0
Saturated fat grams	0.3	–	Vitamin D micrograms	0	0
Polyunsaturated fat grams	0.7	–	Vitamin C milligrams	0	0
			Vitamin E milligrams	–	–
Cholesterol milligrams	200	–	B vitamins:		
Sugars grams	0	–	Thiamin (B₁) milligrams	–	0.08
Starch grams	0	28.9	Riboflavin (B₂) milligrams	–	0.05
Dietary fibre grams	0	–	Nicotinic acid milligrams	–	3.6
Sodium milligrams	1590	380	Pyridoxine (B₆) milligrams	–	–
Potassium milligrams	260	390	Vitamin B₁₂ micrograms	–	–
Calcium milligrams	150	99	Folic acid micrograms	–	–
Magnesium milligrams	42	30	Pantothenic acid milligrams	–	–
			Biotin micrograms	–	–

(–) No information available   (0) Contains zero or trace amounts

Preservatives

Preservatives are substances added to food to retard decay. Like other ways of preserving food (such as deep freezing, canning, dehydration) they inhibit the multiplication of micro-organisms (bacteria, yeasts and moulds) and may also inactivate **enzymes** in food which would otherwise cause deterioration of flavour and colour. Most micro-organisms cannot multiply in acid or very concentrated or dry foods. Cereals, dried fruits, and dried peas, beans and lentils, for example, keep well without added preservatives. **Acetic acid** in vinegar is used for pickling, and **lactic acid** (from bacteria) preserves milk products and sauerkraut to some extent. Lactic acid is also formed in meat after slaughter. When used in sufficient quantities, **sugar** and **salt** are effective preservatives, for example in preserves and salted meat and fish. Other natural preservatives are **alcohol** and substances in some **spices**, like cloves, hops, and smoke. In addition, some food **additives** are permitted in foods as preservatives.

Permitted preservatives

The Preservatives in Food Regulations 1979 permit the addition of eight groups of chemical preservatives in specified amounts to foods, including some fresh foods (see table).

Sulphur dioxide (E220) and its alternative forms (E221-227) is the most commonly used preservative. It is an effective steriliser (kills bacteria) and is especially useful in fruits and vegetables because it prevents browning and preserves **vitamin C**. It is permitted in 52 kinds of food, including fresh grapes and canned garden peas. However it destroys vitamin B_1 (thiamin) and is only permitted in meat products (an important source of thiamin) that would otherwise be a dangerous source of food poisoning, like sausages. It is used in most wines and beers and regular drinkers probably consume the most. At high doses it has been found to be a mutagen (see **poisons in food**) in bacteria, and it may react with fats stored for several months, causing toxic compounds.

Foods Allowed To Contain Preservatives

Food group	Foods	Preservative	E number
Meat and fish	Cured meats, salami, bacon, pepperoni, ham	Sodium nitrite & nitrate	E250,251
	Sausages, hamburger, or any other mixture of meat and cereal	Sulphur dioxide	E220-227
	Prawn, shrimps, scampi, canned crab meat	Sulphur dioxide	E220-227
	Marinated herrings and mackerel	Benzoates or hexamine	E210-219 E239
Vegetables	Dehydrated vegetables, canned garden peas, canned cauliflower, frozen mushrooms, fresh peeled potatoes	Sulphur dioxide	E220-227
	Beetroot	Benzoates	E210-219
Fresh fruit	Bananas, citrus fruit	Biphenyls	E230-233
	Grapes	Sulphur dioxide	E220-227
Fruit products	Fruit juice, dried fruit	Sulphur dioxide	E220-227
	Frozen fruit pulp	Sulphur dioxide or benzoates	E220-227 E210-219

Food group	Foods	Preservative	E number
	Figs, prunes, candied peel, fruit based desserts	Sulphur dioxide or sorbic acid	E220-227 E200-203
	Crystallised or glacé fruit, jams, pie fillings	Sulphur dioxide or sorbic acid or benzoates	E220-227 E200-203 E210-219
Dairy products	Cheese	Nisin, sorbic acid	E200-203
	Any cheese except cheddar, cheshire, soft, provolone	Sodium nitrite and nitrate	E250,251
	Provolone cheese	Hexamine	E239
	Fruit yogurt	Sulphur dioxide or benzoates or sorbic acid	E220-227 E210-219 E200-203
	Bread, Christmas Pudding	Propionic acid	E280-283
Flour products	Flour used for biscuits or pastry	Sulphur dioxide	E220-227
	Cakes, pastry, crumpets etc	Propionic acid or sorbic acid	E280-283 E200-203
	Beer	Sulphur dioxide or benzoates	E220-227 E210-219
Alcoholic drinks	Wine, cider, perry	Sulphur dioxide or sorbic acid	E220-227 E200-203
	Coffee and chicory essence	Benzoates	E210-219
Other drinks	Frozen drinks, soft drinks	Sulphur dioxide or benzoates or sorbic acid	E220-227 E210-219 E200-203
	Vinegar	Sulphur dioxide	E220-227
Pickles	Olives, pickles, mayonnaise, salad cream, sauces	Sulphur dioxide or benzoates or sorbic acid	E220-227 E210-219 E200-203
	All canned food	Nisin	–
Miscellaneous	Dried snack meals, soups	Benzoates or sorbic acid	E210-219 E200-203
	Desiccated coconut	Sulphur dioxide	E220-227
	Concentrated food additives eg. flavours, colours, enzymes, some miscellaneous additives	Sulphur dioxide or benzoates	E220-227 E210-219

Benzoic acid (E210) is found naturally in some foods, such as cranberries and loganberries. It and its alternate forms (E211, 212, 213) are permitted in 24 kinds of food, either solely, or as an alternative to other preservatives. Because, like sulphur dioxide, it is permitted in additives such as flavours and colours, it may be carried over into any food in which they are used. Foods containing both naturally occurring benzoates and added benzoates as preservatives may have to be avoided by people sensitized to benzoates, sometimes by sunscreen lotions or drugs – see **allergy**. In one study for example, 11% of a group of people with **urticaria** reacted to benzoates.

Nitrites and nitrates (E250-251) are added to bacon, ham, and other cured meats and some cheeses. By virtue of this they may find their way into foods such as turkey and ham loaf, or pizza. They are used partly also for colour and because they are a very efficient preservative against *Clostridium botulinum*, see nitrates and nitrites and poisons in food.

Nisin is an **antibiotic** that occurs naturally in some cheeses, and is allowed to be added to cheese, and to any canned foods.

Propionic acid (E280–283) is produced by bacteria in the human large bowel (see **fibre**) and is an effective preservative against moulds. It is permitted in several flour products, including **bread**.

Sorbic acid (E200–203) also prevents the growth of moulds and occurs naturally. It is permitted in foods such as dairy products, alcoholic drinks, pizza and cakes (see table).

Citrus fruits and bananas may have phenyls on the skin to prevent mould. These have been implicated in some allergies and when used in cooking or to make marmalade the skin of citrus fruit should be well washed. The regulations also allow small amounts of formaldehyde (used to make some wrappings), but do not control substances such as sprout inhibitors or preservatives added whilst the food is held in bulk storage, for example fungicides or insecticides, see **poisons in food**.

Preserves

Jam and marmalade making is the traditional way of preserving excess fruit. The fruit is sterilised by boiling, and sugar (**sucrose**) acts as a **preservative**. Both sugar and **pectin** are necessary for the jam to set. Pectin is degraded as fruits ripen: overripe fruit (or those naturally low) require added pectin or are combined with a fruit high in pectin, like apples or plums.

About 70% of the weight of preserves is sugar. 25 grams of jam or marmalade doubles the **energy** (Calorie) content of a thin (30 gram) slice of bread. Yellow fruit (like apricots, marmalade) preserves contain **carotene**. Although the B vitamins are destroyed, some vitamin C in fruits which are rich sources, like blackcurrants, survives the boiling process in jam and in marmalade (see table).

Jams and marmalade are manufactured from imperfect fruit unsuitable for canning or freezing. Legally they must contain not less than 60% of sugar and fruit solids, and at least 20% of fruit in marmalade (35% in jam) must be used in the recipe.

Jams may also contain **preservatives**, **colour** (dark marmalades may be coloured with caramel), flavours and fruit acids (see **miscellaneous additives**). Small quantities of **mineral hydrocarbon** and **antioxidant**, added to some fruits, may also remain in the jam.

Average nutrients in 100 grams (3½ oz) Jam and Marmalade

	jam	marmalade		jam	marmalade
Energy kilojoules	1114	1114	Iron milligrams	1.5	0.6
kilocalories	261	261	Copper milligrams	0.2	0.1
Protein grams	0.6	0.1	Zinc milligrams	–	–
Total fat grams	0	0	Vitamin A micrograms	0	8
Saturated fat grams	0	0	Vitamin D micrograms	0	0
Polyunsaturated fat grams	0	0	Vitamin C milligrams	0–24	10
			Vitamin E milligrams	0	0
Cholesterol milligrams	0	0	B vitamins:		
Sugars grams	69.0	69.5	Thiamin (B$_1$) milligrams	0	0

	jam	marmalade		jam	marmalade
Starch grams	0	0	Riboflavin (B₂) milligrams	0	0
Dietary fibre grams	1.0	0.7	Nicotinic acid milligrams	0	0
Sodium milligrams	16	18	Pyridoxine (B₆) milligrams	0	0
Potassium milligrams	110	44	Vitamin B₁₂ micrograms	0	0
Calcium milligrams	24	35	Folic acid micrograms	0	5
Magnesium milligrams	10	4	Pantothenic acid milligrams	0	0
			Biotin micrograms	0	0

(–) No information available   (0) Contains zero or trace amounts

Protein

Protein is part of the structure of each of the millions of cells in the human body. It is constantly being broken down and remade; cells are constantly dying, and in most cases, being replaced. Some of the proteins are discarded in the daily turnover, and an equivalent amount must be provided in the diet. Babies, children and adolescents need more protein in proportion to their weight than adults because they are growing and making many new cells. Pregnant and nursing mothers also need more than usual to ensure adequate supplies for the growing child.

No natural food is pure protein. Even low fat soya flour – the most concentrated natural source – only contains half its weight (45%) as protein. Meat, fish, cheese, eggs, most nuts (particularly peanuts), dried peas, beans and lentils however contain a high proportion – between 10 and 30%. Cereals contain 10%. Fresh milk, because it is mainly water, contains a low percentage but it is taken in larger quantities and contributes a significant quantity to the diet. Dried skimmed milk contains 34% of protein. Other vegetables contain varying amounts but never more than 5%. Fruits contain very little; sugar, fats and alcoholic spirits none.

Most adults eat about 70 grams of protein a day, of which nearly ⅔ (63%) is derived from meat, fish, cheese, eggs and milk. Cereals, including bread, contribute another ¼ (25%), and vegetables a further 10%. The table below demonstrates the approximate protein content of some average portions of food. Three thin slices of bread contains as much protein as an egg, but see also **amino acids**.

Type of food	Grams of protein	Average portion
Fish	18	100 grams (3½ oz) steamed cod
Meat and poultry	13	50 grams lean roast beef
Cheese	12	50 grams (two thick slices) cheddar
Milk	10	300 millilitres (½ pint)
Egg	7	60 grams (1 standard)
Nuts	14	50 grams peanuts
Pulses	8	150 grams (1 small tin) baked beans
Cereals	8	100 grams (3 thin slices) bread
Vegetables	2	150 grams (moderate portion) boiled potatoes
Fruit	½	One medium apple

Structure of proteins

There are many different proteins but all are composed of long chains of amino acids. Each protein contains its own specific number (sometimes thousands) of amino acids in a specific sequence in the chain. The chain is folded and twisted into complex structures, dictated by the amino acid sequence, which in turn is determined by the individual genetic template (DNA) in the nucleus of cells. Most foods contain several different proteins – for instance there are at least 5 different proteins in meat, and 3 in milk – but it is the total sum of individual amino acids that determines the protein quality of a food.

Heat alters the structure of proteins, causing the chains to unfold partially. Acids, such as lemon juice, can have the same but limited effect. Changes in the protein structure (coagulation) occur when most food proteins are cooked. For instance, the proteins in raw egg white are dissolved in water, but when cooked they are coagulated and made insoluble. The white hardens and becomes opaque. The temperature at which proteins coagulate varies: egg white proteins coagulate at 60°C, egg yolk proteins at 65°C, and milk proteins at 100°C. If the heating is prolonged, proteins are toughened and shrink, squeezing water out of the food – thus overcooked scrambled egg and meat and fish is dry and tough.

Usually cooking and processing do not affect the nutritional value of protein, and light cooking may improve digestibility (the amino acids in an unfolded, coagulated, chain are more accessible to digestive enzymes). Tough overcooked proteins are however less digestible, and toasting and puffing of breakfast cereals such as cornflakes, may reduce the quality of their protein. Amino acids, particularly **lysine**, are destroyed by dry heat. Lysine is also inactivated when sugars react with it, forming a brown coloured substance, in foods like dried milk.

Protein in the human body

A 70 kilogram (11 stone) man contains about 13 kilograms (2 stones) of protein, distributed, in different types, throughout all cells. Nearly all parts of the body contain collagen, a protein especially abundant in bones, skin and muscles. Keratin is in nails and hair, elastin in tendons and arteries. In muscles, which contain 40% of the total body protein, there are two special proteins able to move together and apart when muscles contract and relax. The thousands of **enzymes** and some of the hormones – like insulin – are also proteins. In blood, proteins like the oxygen-carrying, red pigment haemoglobin, are used to carry nutrients from one part of the body to another. Other blood proteins are involved in protecting the body against infection. All these proteins are continually replaced at different rates: enzymes are exchanged very quickly, but bone collagen very slowly. Most of the constituent amino acids from the dismantled proteins are recycled, but some are discarded every day and must be replaced by amino acids derived from proteins in food.

Proteins in food, from both animal and plant sources, except the very tightly coiled keratin, are split to their component amino acids by enzymes during **digestion** and transported, in the blood stream, to the liver. Amino acids are then used to synthesise new protein, and amounts in excess of requirements are used for **energy**, as **fat** or **glucose**.

Protein requirements

The minimum requirement for protein for adults depends on the number of active cells in the body. Men have more muscle cells, and therefore require slightly more than women and the elderly. Current World Health Organisation estimates allowing for individual variation are 0.75 grams of protein per kilogram body weight, or about 50 grams per day for a 70 kilogram man. This does not allow for the mixture of proteins eaten in normal diets and current British **recommended intakes** vary from 55 to 90 grams per day for adult men and women. During growth, pregnancy and breast feeding amounts in excess of that needed for replacement are needed, see Appendix 1 for details.

For some, as yet unexplained, reason more proteins are lost from the body in times of stress such as during recovery from operations, burns or accidents. The requirements for protein are therefore greater during convalescence when the 'stress' reaction ceases, and losses can be replaced.

Excess/deficiency of protein in the diet

Protein eaten in excess of the daily requirement cannot be stored. The potentially toxic **nitrogen** is removed from amino acids and converted to urea and other relatively harmless substances, later filtered out of the blood by the kidneys and excreted in the urine. The other part of amino acids is converted into fat or glucose, and stored or used immediately for energy (Calories). Protein can thus be as fattening as carbohydrates or fats.

A high protein diet per se is not thought to be harmful for adults, although large intakes of meat have been associated with **osteoporosis** and large bowel **cancer**. Too much protein is harmful for babies. The kidneys are immature during the first few months of life and unless infants are given sufficient water, the extra urea formed from excess protein is not excreted and accumulates in the blood stream, making the baby thirsty and nauseated.

The body can become depleted of protein both by diets low in protein (for instance in alcoholism) and in **starvation**, when amino acids are diverted away from repair and used for energy. Children are more readily affected – see **kwashiorkor** and **marasmus**. All bodily processes are interrupted but initially non-essential protein replacement, in hair and nails, and growth are checked. Later muscles are wasted away to supply amino acids for more vital proteins like enzymes; the liver accumulates fat and blood proteins are not replaced. Eventually the heart and digestive tract degenerate, and death results from heart or liver failure.

Protein and special diets

The liver has a central role in protein metabolism, forming for example, blood proteins and converting unwanted amino acids into urea. The kidneys are responsible for conserving blood proteins and eliminating urea and other waste products from the body. The level of blood proteins may fall in the early stages of liver or kidney disease: water then seeps out of the blood stream and body fluids accumulate, causing oedema (waterlogging). Extra protein may be necessary and, as the diets are sometimes restricted in **sodium**, may be given in the form of special high protein, low salt drinks.

In later stages, low protein high energy diets are necessary to minimise the work of the diseased liver or kidneys and to avoid accumulation of urea and other waste products which are toxic in excess. To meet the bodily needs for essential amino acids, most of the small quantity allowed is taken as carefully calculated and weighed portions of animal protein (eggs, milk, meat or fish). In very low protein diets (20 grams per day) used for kidney failure; cereal, nut, pulse and other sources of vegetable protein are almost entirely excluded. **Gluten**-free flour (wheat starch) is used in place of ordinary for bread, cakes, pastries and biscuits. The benefits of low protein diets are not felt if the diet contains insufficient energy. Plenty of butter, double cream, other fats, sugar and preserves are essential, otherwise wasting (and production of urea) continue. Special glucose drinks and other low protein high calorie foods are available on prescription when necessary.

Prunes

Prunes are red or purple plums, dried on the tree or artificially. They keep well for a long time. Californian prunes are well known, but most prunes will dry successfully. Prunes contain a laxative, diphenylisatin.

Average nutrients in 100 grams (3½ oz) Prunes (stewed)

	with sugar	without sugar		with sugar	without sugar
Energy kilojoules	444	349	Iron milligrams	1.4	1.4
kilocalories	104	82	Copper milligrams	0.08	0.08
Protein grams	1.2	1.3	Zinc milligrams	–	–
Total fat grams	0	0	Vitamin A micrograms	78	85
Saturated fat grams	0	0	Vitamin D micrograms	0	0
Polyunsaturated fat grams	0	0	Vitamin C milligrams	0	0
			Vitamin E milligrams	–	–
Cholesterol milligrams	0	0	B vitamins:		
Sugars grams	26.5	20.4	Thiamin (B₁) milligrams	0.04	0.04
Starch grams	0	0	Riboflavin (B₂) milligrams	0.09	0.09
Dietary fibre grams	7.7	8.1	Nicotinic acid milligrams	0.9	1.0
Sodium milligrams	5	7	Pyridoxine (B₆) milligrams	0.10	0.10
Potassium milligrams	420	440	Vitamin B₁₂ micrograms	0	0
Calcium milligrams	18	19	Folic acid micrograms	0	0
Magnesium milligrams	13	13	Pantothenic acid milligrams	0.20	0.21
			Biotin micrograms	0	0

(–) No information available   (0) Contains zero or trace amounts

Pulses – also called legumes

Pulses are **peas**, **beans** and **lentils**. All are good sources of **protein, vitamin B, fibre**, and **minerals**. All except **soya** are low in fat and all are a valuable addition to **diets**, especially **vegetarian diets**.

Pumpkin, and pumpkin seeds

Pumpkin has a similar nutrient composition to cucumbers, melons and marrows – all members of the *Cucurbita* family. 94% of pumpkin is water –

hence its low content of most nutrients except **vitamin A**, as carotene, in the yellow flesh.

Pumpkin seeds are rich in **fat** and **protein** and are eaten deep fried and salted.

Average nutrients in 100 grams (3½ oz) Pumpkin and pumpkin seeds

	pumpkin	seeds		pumpkin	seeds
Energy kilojoules	65	2562	Iron milligrams	0.4	10
kilocalories	15	610	Copper milligrams	0.08	–
Protein grams	0.6	30.0	Zinc milligrams	0.2	-
Total fat grams	0	50.0	Vitamin A micrograms	115-330	15-50
Saturated fat grams	0	–	Vitamin D micrograms	0	0
Polyunsaturated fat grams	0	–	Vitamin C milligrams	5	0
			Vitamin E milligrams	0	–
Cholesterol milligrams	0	0	B vitamins:		
Sugars grams	2.7	} 10.0	Thiamin (B₁) milligrams	0.04	0.2
Starch grams	0.7		Riboflavin (B₂) milligrams	0.04	0.2
Dietary fibre grams	0.5	–	Nicotinic acid milligrams	0.5	–
Sodium milligrams	1	–	Pyridoxine (B₆) milligrams	0.06	–
Potassium milligrams	310	–	Vitamin B₁₂ micrograms	0	–
Calcium milligrams	39	40	Folic acid micrograms	13	–
Magnesium milligrams	8	–	Pantothenic acid milligrams	0.4	–
			Biotin micrograms	0.4	–

(–) No information available   (0) Contains zero or trace amounts

Pyridoxine

– or vitamin B₆ – group name for pyridoxine (also called pyridoxol and pyridoxamine).

– obsolete names, adermin, factor I and factor Y

Part of the **vitamin B complex**, pyridoxine is essential for growth, blood formation, protection against infection and healthy skin and nerves, but there is no adult disease specifically attributed to dietary lack of the vitamin.

Good sources of pyridoxine are **meats**, **cheese**, **liver**, **fish**; wholegrain cereals, such as some breakfast cereals, and **wholemeal bread**; vegetables, especially **peas**, **beans**, **lentils**, **broccoli**, **cauliflower** and **brussel sprouts**; nuts especially **walnuts**, **peanuts**, and **hazel nuts**; and **bananas** and **avocado pears**.' During cooking, pyridoxine leaches out of foods cooked in water, and it is also sensitive to heat, light and alkalis. Vegetables can lose up to 40% and are best steamed or microwaved rather than boiled. Meats lose from 30 to 60% if stewed, and fish from 10 to 20% – but the vitamin can be recovered to some extent if the gravy or stock is used.

Vitamin B₆, or pyridoxine, is the group name for three, equally potent, forms of the vitamin – pyridoxine, pyridoxal and pyridoxamine. Pyridoxine is found mainly in cereals and vegetable foods, and others in animal foods. During **digestion**, nearly all the vitamin is transferred to the blood stream and transported to all cells of the body, where it is converted to its active form.

As part of a co**Enzyme**, pyridoxine has a vital role in the formation of new body **proteins** needed for growth and repair. It is needed to activate enzymes which recycle **amino acids** forming proteins (including haemoglobin – the oxygen carrying pigment in blood); regulatory substances in the brain (like dopamine, serotonin, noradrenaline); **nicotinic acid** and **histamine** (from **histidine**). It also takes part in the release of glucose from **glycogen** and possibly the conversion of **linoleic acid** into other essential **fatty acids**.

Pyridoxine is not stored, but it is contained in all cells and a diet totally lacking in the vitamin takes one to two months to deplete the body. Animals depleted of pyridoxine suffer a variety of disorders (including in monkeys a type of **atherosclerosis** and dental caries, which may be of relevance in human **heart disease** and tooth decay); but the only well established effect of a deficient diet occurred when babies were fed a proprietary baby milk which had been subjected to severe heat treatment (oven drying). The babies suffered convulsions due to insufficient formation of GABA (a brain regulator). Fortunately the convulsions were cured by injections of pyridoxine.

Other adult deficiency symptoms have occurred when a diet lacking in pyridoxine has been augmented with an antagonistic drug. Additional symptoms include eczema around the eyes, mouth, scalp, neck and groin; a sore mouth, irritability, depression, drowsiness, nausea and sometimes neuritis. Similar symptoms of neuritis (and the 'burning feet syndrome' – see **pantothenic acid**) often occur as a side effect of drugs used to treat tuberculosis.

Between 1 and 1 ½ milligrams of pyridoxine are needed each day, but more is required (and eaten) when the diet contains more than 100 grams of protein. There are no British **recommended intakes** set for pyridoxine (due to lack of information) but the average daily intake of 1 to 2 milligrams is presumed to be sufficient for most people.

Large doses (10 to 100 milligrams daily) are used in the treatment of two rare **inborn errors of metabolism**: in adults a special type of anaemia can be cured, and in children (if the disorder is detected in time) epilepsy and mental retardation can be avoided.

Even larger doses than this, of several grams per day, have resulted in severe damage to the nervous system, possibly permanent, in people who have been given or taken the vitamin in an attempt to treat a variety of problems. The metabolism of pyridoxine is altered in women using the contraceptive pill, but this does not mean that supplements are needed in the diet, particularly if the guidelines on a healthy **diet** are followed. In 1983, for example, seven people were reported in the medical press to have been taking pyridoxine supplements for various reasons, including depression and premenstrual tension. All were severely disabled with an unstable gait and loss of sensation in the hands, legs and feet. All improved after they stopped taking the vitamin, but some of the symptoms persisted for several months afterwards.

Quince

A hard and acid fruit which turns pink on cooking with sugar, quince contains a lot of **pectin** and is used mainly for jam and jellies. The fruits of the flowering shrub Japonica are similar to quince and give a pleasant flavour when cooked with apple or pear.

Average nutrients in 100 grams (3½ oz) Quince (fresh)

Energy kilojoules	106	Iron milligrams	0.3
kilocalories	25	Copper milligrams	0.13
Protein grams	0.3	Zinc milligrams	–
Total fat grams	0	Vitamin A micrograms	0
Saturated fat grams	0	Vitamin D micrograms	0
Polyunsaturated fat grams	0	Vitamin C milligrams	15
		Vitamin E milligrams	–
Cholesterol milligrams	0	B vitamins:	
Sugars grams	6.3	Thiamin (B_1) milligrams	0.02
Starch grams	0	Riboflavin (B_2) milligrams	0.02
Dietary fibre grams	6.4	Nicotinic acid milligrams	0.2
Sodium milligrams	3	Pyridoxine (B_6) milligrams	–
Potassium milligrams	200	Vitamin B_{12} micrograms	0
Calcium milligrams	14	Folic acid micrograms	–
Magnesium milligrams	6	Pantothenic acid milligrams	–
		Biotin micrograms	–

(–) No information available   (0) Contains zero or trace amounts

Rabbit

Rabbit is an inexpensive food, with a nutritional composition similar to that of dark chicken meat.

Average nutrients in 100 grams (3½ oz) Rabbit (stewed)

Energy kilojoules	749	Iron milligrams	1.9
kilocalories	179	Copper milligrams	–
Protein grams	27.3	Zinc milligrams	–
Total fat grams	7.7	Vitamin A micrograms	–
Saturated fat grams	3.1	Vitamin D micrograms	–
Polyunsaturated fat grams	2.5	Vitamin C milligrams	0
		Vitamin E milligrams	–
Cholesterol milligrams	71	B vitamins:	
Sugars grams	0	Thiamin (B_1) milligrams	0.07
Starch grams	0	Riboflavin (B_2) milligrams	0.28
Dietary fibre grams	0	Nicotinic acid milligrams	13.6
Sodium milligrams	32	Pyridoxine (B_6) milligrams	0.5
Potassium milligrams	210	Vitamin B_{12} micrograms	12
Calcium milligrams	11	Folic acid micrograms	4
Magnesium milligrams	22	Pantothenic acid milligrams	0.8
		Biotin micrograms	1

(–) No information available   (0) Contains zero or trace amounts

Radish and mooli

Radishes were known to the Egyptians, although their origin is uncertain. Red radishes are most common in Britain, although many other types are grown, such as the long, large, white type called mooli. There are slight differences in their composition (see table).

Radishes are part of the *Cruciferae* family and are valued for their pungency, liberated due to an **enzyme** released during cutting – see **cabbage**.

Average nutrients in 100 grams (3½ oz) Radish and Mooli

	Radish	Mooli		Radish	Mooli
Energy kilojoules	62	100	Iron milligrams	1.9	0.4
kilocalories	15	24	Copper milligrams	0.13	0.15
Protein grams	1.0	1.0	Zinc milligrams	0.1	0.2
Total fat grams	0	0.1	Vitamin A micrograms	0	0
Saturated fat grams	0	–	Vitamin D micrograms	0	0
Polyunsaturated fat grams	0	–	Vitamin C milligrams	10–35	42
			Vitamin E milligrams	0	–
Cholesterol milligrams	0	0	B vitamins:		
Sugars grams	2.8	}4.3	Thiamin (B_1) milligrams	0.04	0.02
Starch grams	0		Riboflavin (B_2) milligrams	0.02	0.03
Dietary fibre grams	1.0	–	Nicotinic acid milligrams	0.4	0.7
Sodium milligrams	59	27	Pyridoxine (B_6) milligrams	0.10	–
Potassium milligrams	240	228	Vitamin B_{12} micrograms	0	0
Calcium milligrams	44	27	Folic acid micrograms	24	–
Magnesium milligrams	11	15	Pantothenic acid milligrams	0.18	–
			Biotin micrograms	–	–

(–) No information available   (0) Contains zero or trace amounts

Raffinose

Raffinose is a sugar, one quarter as sweet as **sucrose**, found in beet, molasses, beans, leeks, cabbage and peas. It contains three simple sugars (glucose, fructose and galactose) and is not broken down during **digestion**. It is however fermented in the large gut by bacteria, like **fibre**.

Raising agents - see Miscellaneous additives

Bicarbonate of soda and an acid (cream of tartar, tartaric acid, acid calcium phosphate, acid sodium phosphate) added to cakes, scones and soda bread. When mixed with water or put into a hot oven, the gas carbon dioxide is released and expands, raising the mixture. In the baking industry raising agents are mixed just before baking. Baking powders are ready mixed and have **starch** added to separate the ingredients. They become less effective once the tin is opened. Golden baking powders contain added yellow colour (originally to simulate eggs) and release slightly less carbon dioxide than white ones. Self raising flour also contains baking powder: it should be stored in a dry, cool place.

Bicarbonate of soda destroys **thiamin** (vitamin B_1). The greater the amount used, the greater the destruction. Soda bread, (and some bread mixes), cakes and scones are very unreliable sources of vitamin B_1. Where possible, bread should be leavened with yeast.

Raisins

Raisins are dried grapes, which are very rich in **sugars**, mostly glucose and fructose. The finest raisins are dried on the vines. Raisins usually have **mineral hydrocarbons** (905) added to them; they should be well washed before eating.

Average nutrients in 100 grams (3½ oz) Raisins

Energy kilojoules	246	Iron milligrams	1.6
kilocalories	1049	Copper milligrams	0.24
Protein grams	1.1	Zinc milligrams	0.1
Total fat grams	0	Vitamin A micrograms	5
Saturated fat grams	0	Vitamin D micrograms	0
Polyunsaturated fat grams	0	Vitamin C milligrams	0
		Vitamin E milligrams	–
Cholesterol milligrams	0	B vitamins:	
Sugars grams	64.4	Thiamin (B_1) milligrams	0.10
Starch grams	0	Riboflavin (B_2) milligrams	0.08
Dietary fibre grams	6.8	Nicotinic acid milligrams	0.6
Sodium milligrams	52	Pyridoxine (B_6) milligrams	0.30
Potassium milligrams	860	Vitamin B_{12} micrograms	0
Calcium milligrams	61	Folic acid micrograms	4
Magnesium milligrams	42	Pantothenic acid milligrams	0.10
		Biotin micrograms	–

(–) No information available   (0) Contains zero or trace amounts

Raspberries

Raspberries are a fruit of the *Rubus* species, containing significant amounts of **vitamin C** and **minerals**. They contain less sugar than most other fruits. Frozen raspberries are as good nutritionally as fresh, containing 20 milligrams of vitamin C per 100 grams. Canned raspberries contain added sugar, and rather less vitamin C (see table).

Average nutrients in 100 grams (3½ oz) Raspberries

	raw	canned in syrup		raw	canned in syrup
Energy kilojoules	105	370	Iron milligrams	1.2	1.7
kilocalories	25	87	Copper milligrams	0.21	0.10
Protein grams	0.9	0.6	Zinc milligrams	–	–
Total fat grams	0	0	Vitamin A micrograms	13	13
Saturated fat grams	0	0	Vitamin D micrograms	0	0
Polyunsaturated fat grams	0	0	Vitamin C milligrams	14–35	7
			Vitamin E milligrams	0.3	–
Cholesterol milligrams	0	0	B vitamins:		
Sugars grams	5.6	22.5	Thiamin (B$_1$) milligrams	0.02	0.01
Starch grams	0	0	Riboflavin (B$_2$) milligrams	0.03	0.03
Dietary fibre grams	7.4	5.0	Nicotinic acid milligrams	0.5	0.4
Sodium milligrams	3	4	Pyridoxine (B$_6$) milligrams	0.06	0.04
Potassium milligrams	220	100	Vitamin B$_{12}$ micrograms	0	0
Calcium milligrams	41	14	Folic acid micrograms	–	–
Magnesium milligrams	22	11	Pantothenic acid milligrams	0.24	0.17
			Biotin micrograms	1.9	–

(–) No information available   (0) Contains zero or trace amounts

Recommended intake – or allowance

Recommended daily allowances (RDAs) are published by most governments and the World Health Organisation for the major essential nutrients (**protein, energy, vitamins, minerals**). Appendix I shows the current British RDAs.

Except in the case of energy, British RDAs are based on human experimental studies designed to assess the minimum requirement of each nutrient necessary to avoid the clinical manifestation of deficiency diseases such as **scurvy, beriberi, anaemia** and **pellagra**. Allowances are made for the bio-availability of nutrients in food and for the range of individual variation in requirements in order to arrive at 'safe' or 'recommended' levels for the majority of individuals in a population.

Whilst RDAs are important in both planning and judging the adequacy of the diet of a particular population (for example, a nation or institution as a whole) they do not cover pathological variations in individual requirements due for example to either inherited or acquired disease. During infection and surgery, requirements may be very much increased – as is the case with vitamin C, or the capacity to excrete excess amounts of nutrients can be markedly reduced in some disorders, such as some **inborn errors of metabolism**.

Less than 2% of individuals within a population would, in theory, be at risk of deficiency disease when consuming intakes of protein, vitamins and minerals at or above the RDA. The requirement of the majority of individuals would be lower than this, and a diet containing less than the RDA is not necessarily 'deficient' in a particular nutrient. Nevertheless, it is prudent to follow the guidelines set out in **diet** to make sure that all the RDAs are fulfilled. Good nutrition is not just a question of vitamins and it is a far better health insurance to make the right choice of food than to rely on supplements from pills or tonics. In some cases these can be harmful - see for example **pyridoxine** and **vitamin A**.

Recommendations for **energy** (Calories) are based on the assumed average requirement for the class of the population concerned, taking account of activity levels, body weight, age and sex. Because it is an average, half the class is expected to require more than the RDA for energy and half less. To find out more precisely what your own requirements for energy might be, see the entries on **energy** and **metabolic rate**.

Perhaps surprisingly, there is a lack of research material on which to base recommended allowances for many nutrients, usually because the minute quantities required are found in most foods and deficiencies caused by diet alone are unknown or extremely rare. Experts may also differ on the level which should be taken as a minimum - sufficient to prevent deficiency disease or enough to maintain full saturation of the body. The Americans tend to take the latter view so that American RDAs are usually higher than the British, despite the fact that few Americans actually manage to achieve the high levels set and yet are in no worse health. Where there is lack of information the recommendations have to be a consensus of opinion which may change, either with more information or a different committee. The World Health Organisation recommendations for protein have changed radically from time to time over the past twenty years for example. Sometimes a consensus is not possible and recommendations cannot be made, as is the case for some nutrients in Britain. Due to lack of agreement, new American RDAs for most nutrients scheduled for 1985 have been delayed for an unspecified period.

Redcurrants

Redcurrants are a member of the *Ribes* family, which includes gooseberries and blackcurrants. White currants are seedlings of the redcurrant with a slightly different flavour, and no vitamin A activity. Redcurrants are a useful source of **vitamin C**, although they contain only one fifth of that in blackcurrants.

Average nutrients in 100 grams (3½ oz) Redcurrants (fresh)

Energy kilojoules	89	Iron milligrams	1.2
kilocalories	21	Copper milligrams	0.12
Protein grams	1.1	Zinc milligrams	–
Total fat grams	0	Vitamin A micrograms	12
Saturated fat grams	0	Vitamin D micrograms	0
Polyunsaturated fat grams	0	Vitamin C milligrams	40
		Vitamin E milligrams	0.1
Cholesterol milligrams	0	B vitamins:	
Sugars grams	4.4	Thiamin (B_1) milligrams	0.04
Starch grams	0	Riboflavin (B_2) milligrams	0.06
Dietary fibre grams	8.2	Nicotinic acid milligrams	0.3
Sodium milligrams	2	Pyridoxine (B_6) milligrams	0.05
Potassium milligrams	280	Vitamin B_{12} micrograms	0

Calcium milligrams	36	Folic acid micrograms		–
Magnesium milligrams	13	Pantothenic acid milligrams		0.06
		Biotin micrograms		2.6

(–) No information available   (0) Contains zero or trace amounts

Rhubarb

Rhubarb is a sour stem eaten as fruit. It contains only small amounts of vitamin C, but relatively large amounts of calcium, however this is combined with **oxalic acid** preventing good absorption. Rhubarb leaves contain toxic amounts of oxalic acid.

Average nutrients in 100 grams (3½ oz) Rhubarb (stewed)

	with sugar	without sugar		with sugar	without sugar
Energy kilojoules	191	25	Iron milligrams	0.3	0.4
kilocalories	45	6	Copper milligrams	0.11	0.12
Protein grams	0.5	0.6	Zinc milligrams	–	–
Total fat grams	0	0	Vitamin A micrograms	9	9
Saturated fat grams	0	0	Vitamin D micrograms	0	0
Polyunsaturated fat grams	0	0	Vitamin C milligrams	7	8
			Vitamin E milligrams	0.2	0.2
Cholesterol milligrams	0	0	B vitamins:		
Sugars grams	11.4	0.9	Thiamin (B_1) milligrams	0	0
Starch grams	0	0	Riboflavin (B_2) milligrams	0.03	0.03
Dietary fibre grams	2.2	2.4	Nicotinic acid milligrams	0.3	0.3
Sodium milligrams	2	2	Pyridoxine (B_6) milligrams	0.02	0.02
Potassium milligrams	360	400	Vitamin B_{12} micrograms	0	0
Calcium milligrams	84	93	Folic acid micrograms	4	4
Magnesium milligrams	12	13	Pantothenic acid milligrams	0.05	0.06
			Biotin micrograms	–	–

(–) No information available   (0) Contains zero or trace amounts

Riboflavin

– other name vitamin B_2
– obsolete names vitamin G and lactoflavin

Riboflavin is part of the **vitamin B complex** and needed for growth in children and to maintain a healthy skin and eyes. It is present in nearly all foods except sugar, fats and spirits.

Liver, kidney, heart, almonds and **extracts** are rich sources of riboflavin; and **cheese, eggs, milk,** yogurt, fatty fish like **sardines, mackerel, roes** and **mushrooms**, some **breakfast cereals**, and chocolate are good sources, as are dark green vegetables like **broccoli, spinach** and **spring greens, peas, Kiwi fruits, nuts, avocado pears** and **prunes**. Wholemeal **bread** and other meats and fishes are also good sources. In the average diet, 40% of the total intake of 1.76 milligrams is derived from milk, cheese and yogurt, 10% from vegetables, and 20% from meat.

In cooked and processed foods, riboflavin is fairly stable to heat, but it is destroyed by ultra violet light, is sensitive to alkalis, and, like other B vitamins, leaches out of foods cooked in water.

The most drastic losses of riboflavin occur when milk is exposed to light. Half the vitamin is lost in two hours' exposure to bright sunlight, and one fifth in dull light. Milk on sale in clear containers under fluorescent lighting is likely to contain none. Slight losses occur when eggs and milk are cooked in an open pan.

Some riboflavin is lost when meat and fish are cooked, but nearly all can be recovered if the liquor is used for sauce or gravy. Canned and frozen meats retain most of the vitamin: there are no losses in stored canned meats, but it may decline (by up to 30% in 8 months) in frozen meats. There may also be slight losses in the drip of frozen meats. A third of riboflavin also leaches out of vegetables but provided bicarbonate of soda is not used (bicarbonate is an alkali) the vitamin can be recovered in the cooking water. Bicarbonate of soda in baking powder may also destroy some riboflavin in soda bread and cakes.

Needs for riboflavin are related to the number of active cells (all except fat) in the body. Athletes and other people with highly developed muscles will need more than others. The minimum daily needs for a man are about 1.1 milligrams, but to allow for individual variation, the daily **recommended intake** for men is 1.7 milligrams. The recommended intake for women (who have less muscle than men) is less - 1.3 milligrams. The table below shows portions of food supplying this amount. Children, infants and adolescents need more in proportion to their weight than adults to allow for growth, and women need more than usual during pregnancy and breast feeding to ensure adequate supplies for the child.

Source	Food	Average content milligrams per 100 grams	Quantity supplying 1.3 milligrams	Approximate measure
Rich	Liver	3	45 grams	1½ oz
	Kidney	2	65 grams	2½ oz
Good	Cheddar cheese	0.5	260 grams	½ lb
	Egg	0.35	370 grams	6 large
	Milk	0.15	870 mls	1½ pints
Moderate	Roast beef	0.22	600 grams	1¼ lb
	Boiled broccoli tops	0.2	650 grams	1½ lb

Nearly all riboflavin is absorbed out of food during **digestion** and transferred to the blood stream. As part of two very important co**Enzymes** in cells, riboflavin is essential for many body processes, particularly the release of energy from food. Lack of the vitamin checks growth in children, but surprisingly does not appear to have very serious effects in adults. In adults the main symptoms are a sore magenta tongue; a type of eczema round the nose, chin and groin, and painful fissures (angular stomatitis) around the mouth. The eyes may become blood shot and itchy. However, none of these symptoms are specific for riboflavin deficiency – for instance, angular stomatitis can be caused by poorly fitting dentures.

Larger intakes of riboflavin in the levels found in most vitamin pills are probably harmless because the excess is filtered into the urine. Megadoses turn the urine bright yellow and their safety is not established. An improvement in

diet is preferable to vitamin pills and tonics. The elderly are perhaps most vulnerable to riboflavin deficiency and should include at least a half pint of milk in their daily diet.

Rice

Like other **cereals**, rice is low in fat, and contains **protein** and most B **vitamins** but cannot support life when eaten alone because it is lacking in vitamins A, C and B$_{12}$. It contains rather less protein than other cereals, and no **gluten**.

Brown rice has only the outer husk removed and contains all the nutrients in the germ and outer layers of the grain. White rice is a very poor source of B vitamins: for instance 80% of the **thiamin** is removed. Glossy, polished rice is produced by a further rubbing in leather lined drums - sometimes with talc and glucose. Parboiling before milling and polishing, when the B vitamins diffuse into the centre of the grain, causes less loss of thiamin - between 30 and 60%, depending on the extent of polishing.

Most people in Britain eat so little rice that losses in milling do not affect the quality of the diet as a whole. It is normally eaten - as **breakfast cereal** or pudding - with milk, a good source of essential nutrients. Puffed rice is low in B vitamins, but some manufacturers add thiamin, riboflavin and nicotinic acid. When rice is used as an alternative to potatoes, brown rice is preferable. Weight for weight, boiled brown rice provides about as much thiamin as boiled **potatoes** (and slightly more energy). It is not however particularly rich in dietary **fibre** (see table).

Average nutrients in 100 grams (3½ oz) Rice (boiled)

	white	brown		white	brown
Energy kilojoules	522	505	Iron milligrams	0.2	0.7
kilocalories	123	120	Copper milligrams	0.02	–
Protein grams	2.2	2.7	Zinc milligrams	0.4	–
Total fat grams	0.3	0.5	Vitamin A micrograms	0	0
Saturated fat grams	0.1	–	Vitamin D micrograms	0	0
Polyunsaturated fat grams	0.1	–	Vitamin C milligrams	0	0
			Vitamin E milligrams	0.1	–
Cholesterol milligrams	0	0	B vitamins:		
Sugars grams	0	–	Thiamin (B$_1$) milligrams	0.01	0.08
Starch grams	29.6	26.0	Riboflavin (B$_2$) milligrams	0.01	0.02
Dietary fibre (NSP) grams	0.2	0.6	Nicotinic acid milligrams	0.5	–
Sodium milligrams	2	–	Pyridoxine (B$_6$) milligrams	0.05	–
Potassium milligrams	38	–	Vitamin B$_{12}$ micrograms	0	–
Calcium milligrams	1	3	Folic acid micrograms	6	–
Magnesium milligrams	4	–	Pantothenic acid milligrams	0.2	–
			Biotin micrograms	1	–

(–) No information available   (0) Contains zero or trace amounts

Rickets

Rickets is usually caused by lack of **vitamin D**, normally made in the skin after exposure to ultra violet or sunlight. Most food supplies too little vitamin D for children's needs – for instance, a child would have to drink 35 pints of milk or eat 1¾ lbs butter or 11 eggs or a half packet of margarine to fulfil the daily **recommended intake**. Fatty fish are the only good sources (125 grams supplies a child's recommended intake).

When there is lack of vitamin D, insufficient **calcium** is absorbed from food and the growing child's bones are not hardened and become deformed. The skull is 'bossed' instead of round; there may be a pigeon chest and a line of bumps on the ribs; and the wrist, knee and ankle joints are enlarged. When the child begins to walk, the long bones in the legs bend (resulting in bow legs) and the backbone and pelvis are twisted. The deformities in the chest carry a greater susceptibility to bronchitis, and in the pelvis later difficulties in bearing children.

Rickets is thought to have been recognised in the sixteenth century, and was well known in the seventeenth century. It was particularly common in the darkest days of the industrial revolution, and, at the beginning of the twentieth century 75% of children living in cities are said to have been affected. After the cause was elucidated, Clean Air Acts, better housing, fortification of margarine and baby milks, and distribution of welfare cod liver oil almost eliminated the disease.

However, rickets is still a problem in Britain, occurring most frequently in toddlers (Asians and children confined to high rise flats are particularly at risk). Some children, whose mothers have **osteomalacia**, are born with it. All children require a daily supplement of vitamin D (as welfare vitamin drops or cod liver oil) up to the age of five. Failure to give the supplements, coupled with inadequate exposure to sunshine is thought to be the explanation of the continuing, and increasing, problem. Schoolchildren are also affected and any child who has little sunshine will benefit from extra vitamin D (as margarine, cod liver oil or malt) until growth is completed. Excessive doses are toxic.

Other types of rickets, caused by inherited abnormalities, and kidney disorders, are not responsive to the usual dose of dietary vitamin D.

Roe and taramasalata

Roe is a rich source of **vitamin A** and **E, biotin** and **thiamin**, and probably **copper**. It also contains vitamins D and C and is very high in **cholesterol**.

Taramasalata is a pâté of smoked cod or mullet roe, made with bread, olive oil and garlic; it is high in **fat** but few nutritional analyses are available (see table).

No analyses are available for caviar.

Average nutrients in 100 grams (3½ oz) Roe and Taramasalata

	fried cod roe	taramasalata		fried cod roe	taramasalata
Energy kilojoules	844	1837	Iron milligrams	1.6	0.4
kilocalories	202	446	Copper milligrams	–	5.8
Protein grams	20.9	3.2	Zinc milligrams	–	0.4
Total fat grams	11.9	46.4	Vitamin A micrograms	150	–
Saturated fat grams	–	–	Vitamin D micrograms	2.2	–
Polyunsaturated fat grams	–	–	Vitamin C milligrams	26	1
			Vitamin E milligrams	6.9	–

Cholesterol milligrams	500	–	B vitamins:			
Sugars grams	} 3.0	} 4.1	Thiamin (B_1) milligrams	1.3	0.08
Starch grams			Riboflavin (B_2) milligrams	0.9	0.10
Dietary fibre grams	–	–	Nicotinic acid milligrams	5.2	–
Sodium milligrams	130	650	Pyridoxine (B_6) milligrams	0.28	–
Potassium milligrams	260	60	Vitamin B_{12} micrograms	11	2.9
Calcium milligrams	17	21	Folic acid micrograms	–	4
Magnesium milligrams	11	6	Pantothenic acid milligrams	2.6	–
			Biotin micrograms	15	–

(–) No information available   (0) Contains zero or trace amounts

Runner, French and broad beans

Runner and French beans are generally eaten as the immature pods and have a similar nutrient composition. Unlike the dried beans they contain **vitamins A and C** (see table). The beans of runner and haricot (French) beans have been shown to contain lectins and it is advisable to cook the pods (and immature beans) before eating them; see **Beans**. Frozen runner and French beans usually contain as much vitamin C as fresh but canned green beans contain almost half – 2 milligrams per 100 grams.

Broad beans (*Vicia faba*) originated in the Mediterranean region. Although they can be eaten after drying they are usually eaten fresh, frozen or canned and contain vitamins A and C. Canned broad beans contain about half the vitamin C of fresh boiled beans – 6 milligrams per 100 grams. Broad beans do not contain lectins. However, 35% of people in some Mediterranean populations and 10% of Africans, Indians and Chinese, are known to have a hereditary defect of an **enzyme** and because of this are likely to develop a particular type of **anaemia**, called favism, after eating broad beans or inhaling the pollen.

Average nutrients in 100 grams (3½ oz) Runner and Broad Beans (boiled)

	runner beans	broad beans		runner beans	broad beans
Energy kilojoules	83	206	Iron milligrams	0.7	1.0
kilocalories	19	48	Copper milligrams	0.05	0.43
Protein grams	1.9	4.1	Zinc milligrams	0.3	–
Total fat grams	0.2	0.6	Vitamin A micrograms	67	42
Saturated fat grams	–	–	Vitamin D micrograms	0	0
Polyunsaturated fat grams	–	–	Vitamin C milligrams	5	15
			Vitamin E milligrams	0.2	0
Cholesterol milligrams	0	0	B vitamins:		
Sugars grams	1.3	0.6	Thiamin (B_1) milligrams	0.03	0.10
Starch grams	1.4	6.5	Riboflavin (B_2) milligrams	0.07	0.04
Dietary fibre grams	3.4	4.2	Nicotinic acid milligrams	0.8	3.7
Sodium milligrams	1	20	Pyridoxine (B_6) milligrams	0.04	–
Potassium milligrams	150	230	Vitamin B_{12} micrograms	0	0
Calcium milligrams	22	21	Folic acid micrograms	28	–
Magnesium milligrams	17	28	Pantothenic acid milligrams	0.04	3.8
			Biotin micrograms	0.5	2.1

(–) No information available   (0) Contains zero or trace amounts

Rye

Rye is a **cereal**, with similar nutritive properties to wheat, that will grow in cold climates and is an important crop in Scandinavia, Russia and north Germany. It contains a small quantity of **gluten**, and rye flour can be made into bread. Rye bread has a sour taste from **lactic acid** (made by bacteria in the yeast mixture) and sometimes added **citric acid**. Pumpernickel and black breads are made entirely from rye, but others contain 40 to 80% wheat flour. Nutrient contents depend on the proportion of wheat, and the extraction rates of the **flours** used. Coarse (heavy dark) rye flour is similar to wholemeal flour, light similar to white, unenriched wheat flour. Rye bread may be coloured with caramel, and darker loaves are not necessarily higher in nutritive value.

In Britain, most rye is eaten as crispbreads, which are very dry and consequently 'light', but weight for weight contain more **energy** (Calories) than wholemeal bread. In slimming diets, not more than two medium or three thin crispbreads should be exchanged for each slice of bread.

Average nutrients in 100 grams (3½ oz) Rye flour and crispbreads

	crispbreads	rye flour		crispbreads	rye flour
Energy kilojoules	1367	1428	Iron milligrams	3.7	2.7
kilocalories	321	335	Copper milligrams	0.4	0.4
Protein grams	9.4	8.2	Zinc milligrams	3.1	2.8
Total fat grams	2.1	2.0	Vitamin A micrograms	0	0
Saturated fat grams	0.3	0.3	Vitamin D micrograms	0	0
Polyunsaturated fat grams	1.0	1.0	Vitamin C milligrams	0	0
			Vitamin E milligrams	0.5	0.8
Cholesterol milligrams	0	0	B vitamins:		
Sugars grams	3.2	0	Thiamin (B_1) milligrams	0.28	0.4
Starch grams	67.4	75.9	Riboflavin (B_2) milligrams	0.14	0.2
Dietary fibre (NSP) grams	–	11.9	Nicotinic acid milligrams	1.8	1.6
Sodium milligrams	220	1	Pyridoxine (B_6) milligrams	0.3	0.3
Potassium milligrams	500	410	Vitamin B_{12} micrograms	0	0
Calcium milligrams	50	32	Folic acid micrograms	40	78
Magnesium milligrams	100	92	Pantothenic acid milligrams	1.1	1.0
			Biotin micrograms	7	6

(–) No information available   (0) Contains zero or trace amounts

Sago

Extracted from the pith of the sago palm and sold as "pearls". Its poor nutritional value – it is virtually pure **starch**, yielding **energy** but little other nutrients – is improved when cooked with milk.

Average nutrients in 100 grams (3½ oz) Sago (dry)

Energy kilojoules	1515	Iron milligrams	1.2
kilocalories	355	Copper milligrams	0.03
Protein grams	0.2	Zinc milligrams	–
Total fat grams	0.2	Vitamin A micrograms	0
Saturated fat grams	–	Vitamin D micrograms	0
Polyunsaturated fat grams	–	Vitamin C milligrams	0
		Vitamin E milligrams	0
Cholesterol milligrams	0	B vitamins:	
Sugars grams	0	Thiamin (B_1) milligrams	0
Starch grams	94.0	Riboflavin (B_2) milligrams	0
Dietary fibre (NSP) grams	0.5	Nicotinic acid milligrams	0
Sodium milligrams	3	Pyridoxine (B_6) milligrams	0
Potassium milligrams	5	Vitamin B_{12} micrograms	0
Calcium milligrams	10	Folic acid micrograms	0
Magnesium milligrams	3	Pantothenic acid milligrams	0
		Biotin micrograms	0

(–) No information available   (0) Contains zero or trace amounts

Salicylates

Salicylates are substances with a similar chemical structure to aspirin found naturally in many foods and also used to **flavour** chewing gums, ice cream, soft drinks and cake mixes. People who have an **allergy** to aspirin (usually taking the form of **urticaria**) are often also allergic to salicylates.

Recent analyses[1] show that most fruits contain salicylates, dried fruits (**prunes**, **raisins**, **currants** and **sultanas**) and **raspberries** containing the most. Apricots, oranges, loganberries, strawberries, and pineapple also contain fairly large amounts. Of the vegetables, **chicory**, **endive**, **mushrooms**, green **olives**, green **peppers**, **radishes** and **courgettes** contain the most. Many **herbs and spices** contain large quantities – notably curry, paprika, thyme, and Worcestershire sauce. Teas and some coffees contain salicylates, although decaffeinated coffee contains none. **Liquorice**, some **honeys**, and mints may also contain large quantities, and they are also found in **beers**, **wines**, liqueurs (especially Benedictine) and some **spirits**. Cereals, legumes, dairy foods and meat however have virtually none.

[1] Swain, A.R. Dutton, S.P., Truswell, A.S. (1985) *J. Am. Diet. Ass*, **85** 9950-959

Salmon

The gourmet's delight, containing moderate amounts of **fat** and much **protein**. Salmon contains useful amounts of minerals and B vitamins. Atlantic salmon contains no vitamin A and D but Pacific may contain as much as the values shown for canned salmon in the table.

Average nutrients in 100 grams (3½ oz) Salmon

	steamed fresh	smoked	canned		steamed fresh	smoked	canned
Energy kilojoules	823	598	649	Iron milligrams	0.8	0.6	1.4
kilocalories	197	142	155	Copper milligrams	–	0.09	0.09
Protein grams	20.1	25.4	20.3	Zinc milligrams	–	0.4	0.9
Total fat grams	13.0	4.5	8.2	Vitamin A micrograms	0	0	20-150
Saturated fat grams	3.2	1.1	2.0	Vitamin D micrograms	0	0	5-20
Polyunsaturated fat grams	3.3	1.1	2.1	Vitamin C milligrams	0	0	0
				Vitamin E milligrams	–	–	1.5
Cholesterol milligrams	80	70	90	B vitamins:			
Sugars grams	0	0	0	Thiamin (B$_1$) milligrams	0.20	0.16	0.04
Starch grams	0	0	0	Riboflavin (B$_2$) milligrams	0.11	0.17	0.18
Dietary fibre grams	0	0	0	Nicotinic acid milligrams	10.8	13.5	10.8
Sodium milligrams	110	1880	570	Pyridoxine (B$_6$) milligrams	0.83	–	0.45
Potassium milligrams	330	420	300	Vitamin B$_{12}$ micrograms	6	–	4
Calcium milligrams	29	19	93	Folic acid micrograms	29	–	12
Magnesium milligrams	29	32	30	Pantothenic acid milligrams	1.8	–	0.50
				Biotin micrograms	4	–	5

(–) No information available   (0) Contains zero or trace amounts

Salsify

A root vegetable, rarely found on sale in Britain but commonly eaten in Europe. The flavour has been likened to oysters – hence the name 'oyster plant root'. Scorzonera is very similar, except that the skin is black. Care has to be taken when preparing these vegetables because the white exudate tends to make a brown stain which is difficult to remove. Salsify and scorzonera contain no starch or sugars, instead they contain **inulin** a polysaccharide of **fructose** which acts in a similar way to dietary **fibre**.

Average nutrients in 100 grams (3½ oz) Salsify (boiled)

Energy kilojoules	77	Iron milligrams	1.2
kilocalories	18	Copper milligrams	0.12
Protein grams	1.9	Zinc milligrams	–
Total fat grams	0	Vitamin A micrograms	0
Saturated fat grams	0	Vitamin D micrograms	0
Polyunsaturated fat grams	0	Vitamin C milligrams	4
		Vitamin E milligrams	–
Cholesterol milligrams	0	B vitamins:	
Sugars grams	0	Thiamin (B$_1$) milligrams	0.03
Starch grams	a	Riboflavin (B$_2$) milligrams	–
Dietary fibre grams	–	Nicotinic acid milligrams	–
Sodium milligrams	8	Pyridoxine (B$_6$) milligrams	–
Potassium milligrams	180	Vitamin B$_{12}$ micrograms	0
Calcium milligrams	60	Folic acid micrograms	–
Magnesium milligrams	14	Pantothenic acid milligrams	–
		Biotin micrograms	–

(–) No information available   (0) Contains zero or trace amounts

a Contains 5.6 grams **inulin**

Salt – chemical name sodium chloride

The main source of **sodium** in the diet, salt is used as a **preservative** and flavour enhancer in food.

A normal diet, containing salty foods and salt in cooking supplies about 10 grams of salt. Table salt may contribute another 4 to 10 grams per day. A high sodium diet is associated with high blood pressure, **stroke** and stomach **cancer**, see **sodium**.

Much of the daily intake is obtained from cereals (it is an ingredient in **bread** and **breakfast cereals**) but table salt does not have to be added to food. Vegetables cooked without salt taste better if they are steamed, rather than boiled.

Sea salt rather than ordinary salt is sometimes recommended as being healthier, but in fact sea salt mills produce larger granules so that more is likely to be added to food. Unless iodised, sea salt contains only small quantities of iodine, in an unstable form. Free running salt contains anticaking agents – see **Miscellaneous additives**.

Sardines

Sardines are nutritious foods, containing well absorbed **iron**, **zinc** and (from the bones) **calcium**. They also contain **vitamin D** and are good sources of **vitamin B$_{12}$** (see table).

Average nutrients in 100 grams (3½ oz) Sardines (canned)

	in oil[a]	in tomato[b] sauce		in oil[a]	in tomato[b] sauce
Energy kilojoules	906	740	Iron milligrams	2.9	4.6
kilocalories	217	177	Copper milligrams	0.19	0.23
Protein grams	23.7	17.8	Zinc milligrams	3.0	2.7
Total fat grams	13.6	11.6	Vitamin A micrograms	0	0
Saturated fat grams	2.6	3.3	Vitamin D micrograms	7.5	7.5
Polyunsaturated fat grams	2.7	3.7	Vitamin C milligrams	0	0
			Vitamin E milligrams	0.3	0.5
Cholesterol milligrams	100	100	B vitamins:		
Sugars grams	0	0.5	Thiamin (B$_1$) milligrams	0.04	0.02
Starch grams	0	0	Riboflavin (B$_2$) milligrams	0.36	0.28
Dietary fibre grams	0	0	Nicotinic acid milligrams	12.6	8.8
Sodium milligrams	650	700	Pyridoxine (B$_6$) milligrams	0.48	0.35
Potassium milligrams	430	410	Vitamin B$_{12}$ micrograms	28	14
Calcium milligrams	550	460	Folic acid micrograms	8	13
Magnesium milligrams	52	51	Pantothenic acid milligrams	0.50	0.50
			Biotin micrograms	5	5

(–) No information available   (0) Contains zero or trace amounts

[a] Fish only   [b] Total contents of can

Sausages

Sausages are mixtures of meat, fat and cereals. All are high in **fat**, particularly salami (see table) and the method of cooking makes little difference to the fat content. Fried and grilled beef sausages for example contain 18.0 and 17.3 grams of fat, which is at least half the **energy** content.

Sausages must legally contain a certain amount of meat to be called sausages – this is 32% lean pork in pork sausages and 25% lean beef in beef sausages – see **Meat**. Some of this meat may well be mechanically recovered meat, reformed with polyphosphates and soya. Sausages also contain a variety of other **additives**, including **colours**, **monosodium glutamate**, **antioxidants** and the **preservative** sulphur dioxide which results in the loss of vitamin B_1 (thiamin).

Sausage skins used to be made from the intestines of sheeps and pigs but these are no longer allowed for hygiene reasons. Present day skins are made from collagen, a protein in cattle hide, which is extruded into a tube and then set usually with **alginates**; inedible skins are made from **cellulose** or plastics.

Average nutrients in 100 grams (3½ oz) Sausages

	fried beef	grilled pork	frankfurters	salami
Energy kilojoules	1124	1320	1135	2031
kilocalories	269	318	274	491
Protein grams	12.9	13.3	9.5	19.3
Total fat grams	18.0	24.6	25.0	45.2
Saturated fat grams	7.3	10.0	9.9	17.9
Polyunsaturated fat grams	0.8	2.0	1.9	3.5
Cholesterol milligrams	42	53	46	79
Sugars grams	0	0	0	0
Starch grams	14.9	11.5	3.0	1.9
Dietary fibre grams	–	–	–	–
Sodium milligrams	1090	1000	980	1850
Potassium milligrams	180	200	98	160
Calcium milligrams	64	53	34	10
Magnesium milligrams	16	15	9	10
Iron milligrams	1.6	1.6	1.3	1.0
Copper milligrams	0.36	0.34	0.24	0.24
Zinc milligrams	1.6	1.6	1.4	1.7
Vitamin A micrograms	0	0	0	0
Vitamin D micrograms	0	0	0	0
Vitamin C milligrams	0	0	0	0
Vitamin E milligrams	0.28	0.22	0.25	0.28
B vitamins:				
Thiamin (B_1) milligrams	0	0.02	0.08	0.21
Riboflavin (B_2) milligrams	0.14	0.15	0.12	0.23
Nicotinic acid milligrams	8.2	6.8	3.0	8.2
Pyridoxine (B_6) milligrams	0.07	0.06	0.03	0.15
Vitamin B_{12} micrograms	1	1	1	1
Folic acid micrograms	2	3	1	3
Pantothenic acid milligrams	0.5	0.6	0.4	0.8
Biotin micrograms	2	3	2	3

(–) No information available   (0) Contains zero or trace amounts

Scallops

Like all seafood, scallops are low in fat, and contain good amounts of **iron** and **calcium**. Few analyses are available however (see table). Scallops should be well cooked before eating; see **mussels**.

Average nutrients in 100 grams (3½ oz) Scallops (steamed)

Energy kilojoules	446	Iron milligrams	3.0
kilocalories	105	Copper milligrams	–
Protein grams	23.2	Zinc milligrams	–
Total fat grams	1.4	Vitamin A micrograms	0
Saturated fat grams	0.3	Vitamin D micrograms	0
Polyunsaturated fat grams	0.3	Vitamin C milligrams	0
		Vitamin E milligrams	–
Cholesterol milligrams	40	B vitamins:	
Sugars grams	0	Thiamin (B_1) milligrams	–
Starch grams	0	Riboflavin (B_2) milligrams	–
Dietary fibre grams	0	Nicotinic acid milligrams	–
Sodium milligrams	270	Pyridoxine (B_6) milligrams	–
Potassium milligrams	480	Vitamin B_{12} micrograms	–
Calcium milligrams	120	Folic acid micrograms	17
Magnesium milligrams	38	Pantothenic acid milligrams	0.14
		Biotin micrograms	0

(–) No information available   (0) Contains zero or trace amounts

Scampi see **prawns**

Scurvy

Scurvy is the result of a diet totally lacking in **vitamin C**, necessary for the integrity of collagen, the main **protein** in connective tissue which 'holds' the body together.

Tiredness and depression precede the characteristic features of scurvy – haemorrhages – which are first noticed as bruises on the skin. The gums swell, ulcerate and bleed, and the teeth loosen and fall out. Old wounds, which are knitted together with connective (scar) tissue, reopen and the legs become blue and swollen. Death follows rapidly from internal haemorrhage unless vitamin C is given, when there is a dramatic improvement in health and vigour.

In Britain, scurvy is rare but occasionally occurs in babies. Bottled, evaporated and some dried milks contain virtually no vitamin C and it must be given as welfare vitamin drops or orange juice (not boiled). Breast milk may be an inadequate source if the mother's diet is low in vitamin C. In adults, any diet lacking in fruit or vegetables (like the 'higher' levels of **macrobiotic diets**) is dangerous. Scurvy has also occasionally resulted from other very restricted diets, for instance milk regimes for ulcers. Many elderly people – subsisting on meals containing overcooked vegetables and fruits poor in vitamin C may be on the borderline of scurvy.

Scurvy was common in medieval North Europe (particularly in early Spring) but declined after the introduction of the potato. However as late as the early twentieth century military campaigns, sea voyages and expeditions were all liable to be jeopardised by scurvy. Florence Nightingale believed that more men died from it in the Crimea than from any other cause, and at least one member of Scott's last journey to Antarctica is thought to have died from scurvy. Not until the discovery of the vitamin in the 1920s was it fully realised that the disease was a result of deficiency in food, rather than infection, salt, poisons, or the many other factors associated with it. See also **lemons and limes**.

Selenium

Selenium is a **trace element** which is part of a self defence system in cells of the body. Selenium deficiency is common in farm animals in some parts of the world and recent studies have confirmed that it is an essential nutrient for humans. Like other trace elements, selenium is toxic in excess.

Plants take up selenium from the soil and soil contents determine the selenium content of local diets. The selenium content of soils varies markedly from one part of the world to another and from one area of a country to another. In the USA both selenium excess and deficiency used to occur in livestock before the cause was established. New Zealand is well known to be a selenium deficient area, with resultant problems with livestock, and human diets contain half that found in Britain, and less than a quarter of that of North East America. Blood levels reflect these variations in dietary intake, and blood levels in visitors fall within three months to match those of their New Zealand hosts.

The average diet in Britain contains 60 micrograms of selenium of which half is derived from cereals, especially bread. Bread flour is largely imported from the USA and Canada which are high selenium areas, and as more home grown flour is used (see **bread**) selenium levels may well decline. Some values for the selenium content of British foods are shown in the table. Foods containing more protein, such as fish, liver, pork, cheese, eggs, walnuts and brazil nuts contain good amounts, but other foods, including vegetables contain very little.

Content of selenium in foods in micrograms per 100 grams

Cereals	White breadmaking flour	42
	Wholemeal flour	53
	Plain white flour[a]	4
	Macaroni	16
	Rice	10
	Cornflakes	2
Meat	Beef, lamb, pork, heart	1 – 14
	Liver	6 – 20
	Kidney	60 – 280
Fish	Cod	10
	Kipper, herring, mackerel	32 – 76
Dairy products	Cheddar cheese	12
	Eggs	12
	Milk	1
Vegetables	Mushrooms	8 – 10
	Other vegetables	1 – 2
	Fruits	1
Nuts	Brazils	2 – 5300
	Walnuts	19
	Cashews	30 – 40
	Peanuts	4 – 66
	Hazel nuts, chestnuts, almonds	1 – 4

Ref: Thorn et al *B. J. Nut.* **39** p. 391, 1978

[a] Probably home produced

In the body, selenium is a cofactor for the **enzyme** glutathione peroxidase which is part of the **antioxidant** system within cells responsible for preserving the structure and function of cell membranes. Another glutathione enzyme and **vitamin E** are also part of this system. The biosynthesis of prostaglandins from **essential fatty acids** and possibly DNA, the genetic blue print in cells, may also be protected by glutathione peroxidase.

The human requirements for selenium are uncertain. Farm animals feeding on low selenium pastures develop a type of muscular dystrophy and so far the only reports of human deficiencies have been from the low selenium areas of China and New Zealand. In New Zealand muscle pain and tenderness in a person unable to take food by mouth and fed intravenously was relieved by selenium, and in China a type of muscular disease in the heart has responded to selenium.

Because of its role in maintaining cell structure and in blood clotting, too little selenium has been associated with **heart disease** in Finland (another low selenium area) and in the USA the regional variations in the selenium content of soil have been associated with some **cancers**. More detailed studies have not however confirmed whether or not high intakes of selenium confer protection against cancer. Studies from New Zealand suggest that selenium is conserved by the body when intakes are low. The selenium glutathione system is not the only antioxidant mechanism of cells.

The safety of supplements, particularly megadoses, taken as a precaution against possibly developing cancer or for arthritis is uncertain – especially in areas like Britain that are not low in selenium. Selenium is toxic in excess, and in farm animals the symptoms of alkali disease caused by selenium toxicity include loss of hair and deformed hooves. According to the American National Research Council, increasing the selenium intake to more than 200 micrograms per day with supplements should be 'regarded as an experimental procedure requiring strict medical supervision and is not recommended for use by the public'.

Sesame seeds

Sesame seeds are used primarily for flavouring bread and cakes in temperate climates; they may also be ground to make a spread, or stewed whole. They are rich in fat, and the **oil** can be extracted. Sesame seed oil is high in polyunsaturated **fatty acids**. The seeds also contain **protein**, and iron, calcium and magnesium – but little of these minerals is available for digestion – see **nuts**.

Average nutrients in 100 grams (3½ oz) Sesame seeds

Energy kilojoules	2460	Iron milligrams	7.8
kilocalories	588	Copper milligrams	–
Protein grams	26.4	Zinc milligrams	10.3
Total fat grams	54.8	Vitamin A micrograms	7
Saturated fat grams	–	Vitamin D micrograms	0
Polyunsaturated fat grams	–	Vitamin C milligrams	–
		Vitamin E milligrams	–
Cholesterol milligrams	0	B vitamins:	

Sugars grams	} 6.4	Thiamin (B₁) milligrams	0.72
Starch grams		Riboflavin (B₂) milligrams	0.09
Dietary fibre grams	–	Nicotinic acid milligrams	12.6
Sodium milligrams	40	Pyridoxine (B₆) milligrams	–
Potassium milligrams	407	Vitamin B₁₂ micrograms	0
Calcium milligrams	131	Folic acid micrograms	–
Magnesium milligrams	347	Pantothenic acid milligrams	–
		Biotin micrograms	–

(–) No information available   (0) Contains zero or trace amounts

Shrimps

A low fat food, ideal for slimmers, shrimps are a good source of **calcium**, **iron**, **iodine** and **zinc**. Shrimps boiled in sea water are very high in sodium (see table).

Average nutrients in 100 grams (3½ oz) Shrimps

	boiled in sea water	canned		boiled in sea water	canned
Energy kilojoules	493	398	Iron milligrams	1.8	5.1
kilocalories	117	94	Copper milligrams	0.8	0.2
Protein grams	23.8	20.8	Zinc milligrams	5.3	2.4
Total fat grams	2.4	1.2	Vitamin A micrograms	0	0
Saturated fat grams	0.4	0.2	Vitamin D micrograms	0	0
Polyunsaturated fat grams	0.8	0.4	Vitamin C milligrams	0	0
			Vitamin E milligrams	–	–
Cholesterol milligrams	200	200	B vitamins:		
Sugars grams	0	0	Thiamin (B₁) milligrams	0.03	0.01
Starch grams	0	0	Riboflavin (B₂) milligrams	0.03	0.02
Dietary fibre grams	0	0	Nicotinic acid milligrams	7.4	4.7
Sodium milligrams	3840	980	Pyridoxine (B₆) milligrams	0.10	0.03
Potassium milligrams	400	100	Vitamin B₁₂ micrograms	1	2
Calcium milligrams	320	110	Folic acid micrograms	–	15
Magnesium milligrams	110	49	Pantothenic acid milligrams	0.30	0.35
			Biotin micrograms	1	1

(–) No information available   (0) Contains zero or trace amounts

Silicon

The second most abundant element: one quarter of the earth's crust is silicon. It is found in the human body, and studies of animals reared on highly purified diets have shown that it is an essential nutrient. It is probably also essential for humans.

Some forms of silicon are permitted in food as **miscellaneous additives**, for example calcium silicate, aluminium silicate (kaolin) and magnesium trisilicate are permitted anticaking agents. Dimethylpolysiloxane – an organic (carbon containing) polymer of silicon – is a permitted anti-foaming agent: it prevents foam when, for example, fruit juices are canned.

Skate – ray

Skate, or ray, is the only fish which is said to gain in flavour by being slightly 'high'. It is ready to eat about ten hours after catching – when the glutinous coating which adheres to the skin no longer forms. It is generally eaten fried (see table) or poached.

Average nutrients in 100 grams (3½ oz) Skate (fried in batter)

Energy kilojoules	830	Iron milligrams	1.0
kilocalories	199	Copper milligrams	0.09
Protein grams	17.9	Zinc milligrams	0.9
Total fat grams	12.1	Vitamin A micrograms	–
Saturated fat grams	–	Vitamin D micrograms	–
Polyunsaturated fat grams	–	Vitamin C milligrams	0
		Vitamin E milligrams	1.2
Cholesterol milligrams	–	B vitamins:	
Sugars grams	4.9ª	Thiamin (B₁) milligrams	0.03
Starch grams		Riboflavin (B₂) milligrams	0.10
Dietary fibre grams	–	Nicotinic acid milligrams	–
Sodium milligrams	140	Pyridoxine (B₆) milligrams	–
Potassium milligrams	240	Vitamin B₁₂ micrograms	–
Calcium milligrams	50	Folic acid micrograms	–
Magnesium milligrams	27	Pantothenic acid milligrams	–
		Biotin micrograms	–

(–) No information available   (0) Contains zero or trace amounts

ª from batter

Slimming diets

The principle behind *all* slimming regimens is the same. There are no slimming foods or combinations. If a diet contains less than daily needs, **energy**, is withdrawn from stores, mostly **adipose tissue**, and weight decreases. Each kilogram (2.2 lbs) adipose tissue contains about 30 Mega**joules** (7000 kilo**calories**). If a slimming diet contains 4 Megajoules (1000 kilocalories) less than daily needs, over the week there is an energy deficit of 30 Megajoules. The weekly expected weight loss (the amount of fat used from stores) will be 30/30 – which is equal to one kilogram.

Anyone can reduce their weight simply by keeping to a definite plan, or slimming diet. A sample menu and variations recommended by the *Companion* is shown on (page 268). It allows plenty of food but will not deplete the body of essential nutrients. It is high in vitamins, minerals and protein and extra vitamin tablets are not necessary. The diet contains about 6 Megajoules (1500 kilocalories), sufficient for most people to lose weight, at varying rates depending on their **metabolic rate** and activity pattern. It is important not to limit energy to less than 5 Megajoules (1200 kilocalories) except under close medical supervision because this is below the basal metabolic rate, or minimum survival needs, for the average person.

The *Companion* diet allows any vegetable freely, and plenty of fruit, but the **fat** containing foods, and those with **starch** must be weighed out. Over estimations are very easily made, especially when hungry. A set of bathroom scales and a notebook should also be bought, and weight checked no more than once a week at the same time of the day. If weight is not lost over three consecutive weeks, weights of food eaten should first be checked, so that the diet is closely followed. A record of all food and drink for a week often shows up where the problem lies. Day to day energy intake can be calculated for foods using the *Companion*. If these show that the average energy content of the daily diet is 6 Megajoules or less, then energy expenditure needs to be increased. Starting off with five minutes a day for five days a week, most people are able to cycle, swim or jog for thirty minutes continuously after gradual training of five minutes extra each week over a six week period. Over five days a week, this level of activity reaches the World Health Organisation recommendations, see **energy**. Good shoes and stretching exercises are however essential to avoid jogging injuries, especially in obese people.

Once ideal **body weight** has been reached, great care is needed to prevent weight returning. It is best to replace energy slowly, in weekly steps of 0.5 Megajoules, 120 kilocalories, up to the average basal metabolic rate for the (new) weight, times 1.4 or 1.5 (depending on the amount of vigorous exercise). This is about 10 Megajoules (2400 kilocalories) for a 70 kilogram (11 stone) man or 7.5 Megajoules (1800 kilocalories) for a 55 kilogram (8½ stone) woman. In replacing the weekly steps of 0.5 Megajoules, alternate adding in more starch, as bread (50 grams) or potato (150 grams) in the first week, then add an extra fat score in the second, up to a total of 6 or 7 depending on ideal body weight.

The Companion Diet – sample menu

Meal	Megajoules	Fat score	Kilocalories
BREAKFAST, breakfast cereal			
Large helping any non-sugared breakfast cereal, 50 grams	0.7	–	165
Fresh or frozen fruit – strawberries, melon, apple	0.2	–	50
Milk, using allowance (below)			
LUNCH, sandwiches and fruit			
3 slices wholemeal bread, 100 grams	0.9	–	215
Filling of low fat spread, 12 grams	0.2	½	40
and 1 hard boiled egg	0.3	½	75
with cress	–	–	–
Fresh fruit 1 or 2 apples	0.4	–	100
EVENING MEAL, chicken cordon bleu			
Poached chicken breast, no skin, 185 grams	1.1	1	270
with melted gruyère cheese, 20 grams	0.3	1	80
steamed broccoli	–	–	–
boiled potato, 150 grams	0.5	–	120
Fresh fruit, e.g. grapes or banana	0.4	–	100

DRINKS
For tea, coffee, breakfast cereal			
1 pint semi-skimmed milk	1.2	1	300
Sugar free soft drinks, mineral water	–	–	–
TOTAL	6.2	5	1500

Variations

– Eat any fresh or frozen vegetable you like, as much as you like – but only raw, baked, steamed, boiled or microwaved, with no added fat – unless this is counted in the fat exchange system.

– The diet allows a total of 5 fat scores a day. Three of these must be meat, cheese, eggs, fish, milk, soya or nuts. Otherwise, any combination is possible, using the list on pp. 104-5.

– You will have more to eat if you choose variations from the right hand columns of this list. Other food not on the list can be eaten (like 'Lean Cuisine' meals) provided the label tells you how much fat is in it. Each fat score contains 10 grams fat.

– Use yogurt as an alternative to fruit, and in cooking. Only buy low or fat free yogurt, not Greek or whole milk (unless you count these as fat exchanges). One plain yogurt is equivalent to a piece of fresh fruit (100 grams), and a fruit yogurt is equivalent to two pieces. Otherwise eat up to 500 grams fresh or frozen fruit or fruit juice a day. Avoid canned fruit with added sugar or dried fruit. Use **sweeteners** rather than sugar for cooking.

– Use fat-free stock for cooking, and plenty of herbs and spices.

– If you like dried beans or peas, pasta or rice, exchange them for bread or potato. 150 grams potato equals 30 grams peas, beans, pasta or rice (uncooked weight), 200 grams baked beans, or 50 grams bread. Soya contains fat and has to be counted into the fat score system.

– No added sugar is included in this diet. Neither is alcohol. An occasional glass of wine or half pint of beer can be exchanged for two pieces of fruit – otherwise drink sugar free **soft drinks**, or **mineral water**.

Other ways of slimming

The most popular books on slimming diets all include a 'wonder' factor, guaranteed to speed up weight loss for the beguiled. The ones that work do so by restricting choice of food to a very narrow range, or eliminate it completely, so that total energy intake is reduced. Of these, the F Plan diet is varied, safe, and allows plenty to eat. Although based on the supposed slimming properties of fibre it actually works because it is low in fat and sugar (as is the *Companion* diet on page 268. Some other regimens however are an uncertain risk to health.

Very low carbohydrate diets

These include the Dr Atkins Diet Revolution, the Air Force Diet, the Quick Weight Loss Diet, the Eat Fat and Get Slim Diet, the Grapefruit Diet and some so called 'Mayo Clinic' Diets. All are very low carbohydrate regimes (0 to 20 grams per day) unrestricted in protein and sometimes fat. They force the body to release large quantities of fat from adipose tissue, which can only be partly used for energy. The unused part (ketones) accumulate in the blood stream, causing nausea. Appetite is said to be reduced and less food is eaten. Some of these diets include strict instructions to eat particular combinations of foods, claimed to hasten fat loss. It should be remembered however that there are no known slimming combinations of food: all the diets rely on this basic (ketogenic) action. Any diet containing too little carbohydrate will cause excessive fatty acid release: diets which encourage plenty of fat on food (like the Atkins regime) make ketone production more likely. This 'Diet Revolution' has been severely criticised by the American Medical Association: **diabetes** and **gout** may be precipitated and blood **cholesterol** may rise, increasing the risk of a heart attack. Fluid (released as **glycogen**) accounts for weight losses of about 4 kilograms claimed for 'ten day' diets – for example the Grapefruit Diet. As soon as former eating habits are resumed after the diet, glycogen and water reaccumulate and weight returns.

Very low calorie, liquid formula and protein diets

Liquid protein diets caused mayhem in the USA in the late 1970s. They consisted of protein (from collagen in cattle hide) in a tin, containing only 1.7 Megajoules (400 kilocalories), and were marketed as the sole source of food. About 37,000 overweight people used these diets for several months. In effect they were **starvation** diets, and probably because the heart muscle wastes away also during starvation, 58 people using these diets died suddenly. Ironically, some of these were marketed as the 'Last Chance Diet'. A number of Very Low Calorie Diets are on the British Market. They also contain about 400 Calories but are based on milk powder with added vitamins and minerals. The cost of a week's supply is more than normal food, although the ingredients cost only a few pence. The formula of these diets is different from the liquid protein diets, but in view of the problems with liquid protein diets, the safety of Very Low Calorie Diets has been discussed and reviewed at several expert meetings. So far, the safety of these diets for people who are only moderately overweight is uncertain and it is generally agreed that they should not be sold to people who have a ratio of (weight in kilograms) over (height in metres^2) of less than 25. This would mean, for example, a 1.64m (5'5") tall woman weighing less than 66 Kg (10st. 5lb). In general, Very Low Calorie Diets are thought to be safer for very obese people who probably lose proportionately less body protein to fat when their food intake is restricted in this way. However, they require close medical supervision if the diet is prolonged beyond 3-4 weeks and the diets do not help very obese people to remedy poor eating habits over the long term. The diets are not suitable for children or infants under any circumstances, and only for adolescents under medical supervision. Neither are they safe for pregnant or breast feeding women, the elderly, people with heart disease, high blood pressure, diabetes and various other medical conditions. Anyone contemplating starting these diets should think very carefully before doing so, and only after having first consulted with their doctor.

Slimmer's special foods

Slimmer's meals, puddings, soups, snacks, biscuits, sweets and breads marketed as being 'part of a Calorie (energy) controlled diet' are often no lower in energy, weight for weight, than normal foods. Good fresh food is better for controlling weight over the long term.

Acids and other fallacies

Acids (grapefruit, lemon juice, cider vinegar) have all been claimed to 'burn up fat' at one time or another. This is a fallacy, based on imagination. Even more imaginative was the best seller with the wonder ingredient of **enzymes** in fruits like pineapple and pawpaw. Diets containing only fruit will reduce weight, but not because of their enzyme content. Other diets rely on restricting salt and fruit, but this causes weight loss by losing water, not fat, and is not recommended.

Sodium

An **electrolyte**, sodium is of importance in maintaining a constant body **water** content. Most sodium in the diet is derived from **salt** (sodium chloride).

Some foods – meat, fish, eggs, and milk – naturally contain small amounts of sodium. Shell fish contain slightly more than ordinary fish. A daily diet to which **no** salt is added supplies about 0.5 grams of sodium. Flour, unsalted butter, cream, oil, fruits, fresh vegetables, and unsalted nuts contain virtually none. Salt, added in cooking, at the table, and to many foods, causes wide variation in the sodium content of individual diets.

The table below shows portions of salted foods supplying approximately 0.5 grams of sodium. Other sources of sodium are **monosodium glutamate** and bicarbonate of soda in mineral waters and baking powder.

Food		Approximate portion supplying 0.5 grams of sodium
Meat	Fried bacon	15 grams (1 rasher)
	Corned beef	35 grams (1 ¼ oz)
	Fried pork sausages	50 grams (1 ⅔oz)
Fish	Prawns boiled in salt water	30 grams (1 oz)
	Tinned sardines	60 grams (2 oz)
Dairy foods	Cheddar cheese	85 grams (3 oz)
	Salted butter	85 grams (3 oz)
Cereals	Cornflakes	50 grams (1 ⅔ oz)
	Bread	100 grams (3 slices)
Miscellaneous	Table salt	1.3 grams (small pinch)
	Marmite	10 grams (⅓ oz)
	Tomato ketchup	50 grams

Foods to which salt is added include all cured meats and fish; sausages; pickles; sauces; canned and bottled meats, vegetables and fish; most breakfast cereals;

crisps; olives; roasted nuts; bread; salted butter; margarine; shell fish; extracts; packet soups; tinned soups.

Adults contain between 75 and 100 grams of sodium. Over half is in the blood plasma and fluids surrounding cells (interstitial fluids); 10% is held inside cells; and the rest forms part of the structure of bones.

Sodium in the diet is avidly absorbed and the excess of needs excreted in the urine. In most societies, several grams are both eaten and excreted each day in the urine. Worldwide variations in the amount eaten, and variations in **blood pressure** have prompted very large research programmes into the relationship between the two.

The probable needs for sodium are comparatively small. There are a number of primitive cultures in isolated parts of the world, such as the Yanomamo Indians in Brazil, the !Kung bushmen of Northern Botswana, and the Masai in Tanzania, where blood pressure does not rise with age. In these populations, salt is not available and consequently their intakes are very low, less than 1 gram per day. In Britain, the average intake is about 4 grams per day and probably similar to most other countries, where blood pressure does increase with age. In Japan intakes are higher, about 5 grams per day on average although in some areas they are as high as 9 grams. Japan has one of the highest rates of death from **stroke** and high blood pressure is very common. The regional variations in rates of death from stroke have been related within Japan to the regional variations in sodium intake, and national efforts to reduce the amount of sodium (as salt) used in cooking have resulted in recent years to a fall in the death rate from stroke. It is also possible to show that blood pressure rises when people from communities unaccustomed to salt are given it – as happened to Samburu nomadic warriors serving in the Kenyan army.

Within a population such as Britain where sodium intakes are comparatively high, many studies have failed to show a relationship between salt intake and blood pressure, even in people with a family history of high blood pressure, who might be thought to be more susceptible to a high salt diet. It is however extremely difficult to measure how much salt people actually consume. If sodium is involved, via an increase in heart output which both increases blood pressure and flow through the kidney in an effort to excrete excess sodium and its associated water, then intakes in childhood and adolescence are likely to set the scene for middle age – when blood pressure begins to rise. Whether a lower salt diet can prevent high blood pressure is therefore uncertain at present, but most authorities recommend a reduction.

The first step is not to add salt to food at the table, and to gradually reduce salt used in cooking. Vegetables for example taste much better if they are steamed without salt than if they are boiled in water – which also leaches out **potassium** which in itself has been linked to blood pressure. However, it is difficult to reduce levels much lower than this because sodium, as salt, baking powder and monosodium glutamate, is added to bread, breakfast cereals, and most other processed foods, (although at a lower level than those which are traditionally salty, such as bacon and ham). As a result about 40% of the average intake of salt is derived from these foods. Meats, margarine, butter and cheese supply about another 30%. Salted foods, including **extracts** should not be given to babies because their immature kidneys require more water than adults to eliminate the excess.

Over the short term, high intakes of sodium are eliminated by the kidney, provided sufficient water is drunk. Sodium poisoning only occurs when sea water is drunk in the absence of fresh water. In people unaccustomed to hot climates, losses of salt in sweat can be substantial, when the amounts excreted in urine fall to very low levels. However, this only occurs for the first few days, and after that the amount of salt in sweat is reduced. Mild symptoms – muscular cramps – can occur in miners working in hot pits. Severe deficiency from a loss of 8 grams or more can occur as a result of heat exhaustion and in patients with hormonal or kidney disorders, and if sodium is not absorbed from the gut, due to diarrhoea, vomiting, or removal of the large bowel. Water and sodium are transferred out of the blood stream (to maintain the concentration of sodium in interstitial fluid) when blood pressure falls, causing tiredness, nausea and dizziness. If thirst is satisfied with water the body fluids are diluted, resulting in convulsions and coma. Salt should always be taken together with water under these conditions.

Low sodium diets are part of the treatment of some heart and kidney disorders. In severe heart failure, blood is not pumped around the body with sufficient force, and the kidneys become less effective. Sodium accumulates and the body becomes waterlogged (oedematous). Diuretics (which increase the flow of urine) and a low sodium diet may be necessary.

All low sodium diets exclude table salt (salt added after food is cooked) and very salty foods like cured and pickled meats and fish; bottled sauces; cheese; sausages; bacon; ham; tinned meats and fish; salted nuts and extracts, but usually allow a small amount of salt in cooking. Stricter diets may exclude certain breakfast cereals; cakes made with bicarbonate of soda or baking powder; and salted butter. Further restriction such as no salt at all in cooking, salt free bread and special milk is avoided if possible because at this level the diet becomes very unpalatable.

Soft drinks

Squashes, cordials, fruit drinks and carbonated drinks are of poor nutritive value: their main ingredients are **water** and **sugar**. Soft drinks are unlikely to contain **vitamin C**, unless it is added and declared on the label.

Legally, all soft drinks (except diabetic and low calorie drinks) must contain specified minimum contents of **sucrose** (sugar). Saccharin is permitted, up to specified amounts, but must be declared on the label. There are also specified minimum contents of fruit: those that contain no fruit (and are essentially flavoured and coloured water) must be called '. . . flavour' or '. . . ade', and no picture of fruit is allowed on the label. Comminuted fruit drinks (usually described as made from whole fresh . . .) made from finely macerated pulp and peel, are allowed to contain less fruit than squashes, crushes and cordials. Citrus fruit and barley drinks like lemon and barley water may also contain less fruit than squashes.

Carbonated drinks have to comply with similar standards. Tonic water must contain a minimum quantity of quinine (which is usually the bitter ingredient in bitter orange and lemon). Glucose drinks like Lucozade contain glucose syrup in place of sugar. Cola drinks contain sugar, caramel (to colour brown), phosphoric acid, flavouring oils, carbon dioxide and usually **caffeine**.

All soft drinks are permitted to contain **preservatives** (either sulphur dioxide or benzoic acid), **emulsifiers** (to prevent particles of fruit clumping together and forming sediment), **colours**, **flavours** and miscellaneous **additives**. Only citric, malic, tartaric, ascorbic and nicotinic acids (added to give a tart flavour) are permitted in fruit drinks. Non-fruit drinks may also contain acetic and phosphoric acids.

Low calorie drinks must legally contain not more than 7½ kilocalories per fluid ounce (or 1½ kilocalories per fluid ounce when sold ready diluted). "Diabetic" soft drinks must not contain sugar: they contain **sweeteners** and are virtually free of energy.

Average nutrients in 100 grams (½ glass) Soft drinks

	colas	lemonade	lime[a] cordial	Lucozade	orange[a] squash	Ribena[a]
Energy kilojoules	168	90	479	288	456	976
kilocalories	39	21	112	68	107	229
Protein grams	0	0	0.1	0	0	0.1
Total fat grams	0	0	0	0	0	0
Saturated fat grams	0	0	0	0	0	0
Polyunsaturated fat grams	0	0	0	0	0	0
Cholesterol milligrams	0	0	0	0	0	0
Sugars grams	10.5	5.6	24.8	18.0	28.5	60.9
Starch grams	0	0	0	0	0	0
Dietary fibre grams	0	0	0	0	0	0
Sodium milligrams	8	7	8	29	21	20
Potassium milligrams	1	1	49	1	17	86
Calcium milligrams	4	5	9	5	8	9
Magnesium milligrams	1	0	4	1	3	5
Iron milligrams	0	0	0.3	0.1	0.1	0.5
Copper milligrams	0.03	0.01	0.07	0.04	0.01	0.02
Zinc milligrams	0	–	–	–	–	–
Vitamin A micrograms	0	0	0	0	–	–
Vitamin D micrograms	0	0	0	0	0	0
Vitamin C milligrams	0	0–15	0	3	0–60	210
Vitamin E milligrams	0	0	0	0	0	–
B vitamins:						
Thiamin (B$_1$) milligrams	0	0	0	0	0	–
Riboflavin (B$_2$) milligrams	0	0	0	0	0	–
Nicotinic acid milligrams	0	0	0	0	0	–
Pyridoxine (B$_6$) milligrams	0	0	0	0	0	–
Vitamin B$_{12}$ micrograms	0	0	0	0	0	0
Folic acid micrograms	0	0	0	0	0	–
Pantothenic acid milligrams	0	0	0	0	0	–
Biotin micrograms	0	0	0	0	0	–

(–) No information available   (0) Contains zero or trace amounts

[a] Undiluted

Sole

Dover sole is considered the best of the flat white fish with white, delicately flavoured firm flesh that can be prepared in an infinite number of recipes. No nutritional analyses are available for Dover sole, but lemon sole is likely to be similar (see table). Like all white fish, it is a rich, fat-free source of **protein** ideally suited to current concepts of a healthy **diet**.

Average nutrients in 100 grams (3½ oz) Lemon Sole (steamed)

Energy kilojoules	384	Iron milligrams	0.6
kilocalories	91	Copper milligrams	0.1
Protein grams	20.6	Zinc milligrams	–
Total fat grams	0.9	Vitamin A micrograms	0
Saturated fat grams	0.1	Vitamin D micrograms	0
Polyunsaturated fat grams	0.3	Vitamin C milligrams	0
		Vitamin E milligrams	–
Cholesterol milligrams	60	B vitamins:	
Sugars grams	0	Thiamin (B$_1$) milligrams	0.09
Starch grams	0	Riboflavin (B$_2$) milligrams	0.09
Dietary fibre grams	0	Nicotinic acid milligrams	7.4
Sodium milligrams	120	Pyridoxine (B$_6$) milligrams	–
Potassium milligrams	280	Vitamin B$_{12}$ micrograms	1
Calcium milligrams	21	Folic acid micrograms	13
Magnesium milligrams	20	Pantothenic acid milligrams	0.31
		Biotin micrograms	5

(–) No information available   (0) Contains zero or trace amounts

Solvents – (no additive numbers)

Solvents are used for the incorporation of **flavours**, **colours** and other food **additives** into food. Nine are permitted by the Solvents in Food Regulations 1967:
Ethanol (alcohol)
Ethyl acetate (combination of alcohol and acetic acid)
Diethyl ether (ether)
Glycerol
Mono, di and tri acetin (combinations of acetic acid and glycerol)
Iso propyl alcohol (another type of alcohol, one of the congeners in alcoholic beverages)
Propylene glycol (converted to **glycogen** in the body)

Sorbitol

Sorbitol is a **sweetener** used in diabetic foods and a humectant (see **miscellaneous additives**). It is found naturally in small amounts in some fruits – for instance cherries – but commercial supplies are made from **glucose**.

Sorbitol, 60% as sweet as **sucrose**, is absorbed at a very slow rate into the blood stream during **digestion**. Though the precise way in which it is used by the body is uncertain sorbitol does not appear to raise the blood glucose level (see **diabetes**) appreciably, and is a useful substitute for sucrose in diabetic diets. It is added to foods like diabetic jams, tinned fruits, chocolates, marmalade and sweets. However it cannot be used freely in slimming diets: it contains 16 kilojoules (4 kilocalories) per gram – the same as sucrose.

Soups

Perhaps surprisingly, soups are not especially nourishing: 75 to 95% of their weight is **water**. Their nutrient content depends on the ingredients used, but in general soups contain less than 5% **protein** and only small amounts of **minerals** and **vitamins**. 'Cream' soups usually contain more **energy** than other soups: clear soups are very low in energy. A clear soup, made from **extracts** or stock (left overnight in a refrigerator and the fat removed) with a few diced vegetables is suitable for slimmers. In sickness and convalescence, dried skimmed milk enriches vegetable soups. Broths are a good appetite stimulant, but of little value (see **gelatine**) by themselves.

Canned soups, though standards are not controlled by law, are of similar value to home made. Manufacturers follow a Code of Practice (not law, but it can be used as evidence in legal proceedings): meat soups must contain a minimum of 6% meat; scotch broth a minimum of 3%. Brown, Windsor and Eton soups (made from a brown roux and meat stock) and minestrone do not have to contain meat. Unless otherwise stated, consommé should be made from meat stock. In vegetable soups, a single vegetable (like tomato) should contain more of the named vegetable than others; mixed vegetable soup should contain at least four different vegetables; and green pea should be made from fresh or frozen peas. Cream soups must contain butter fat.

Dehydrated soups are not subject to regulations or a Code of Practice, though, like canned soups, their ingredients must be stated on the **label**. They tend to be lower in protein and energy than canned soups: some, especially the 'instant' kind, are a mixture of **additives** – **flavours**, **colours**, **emulsifiers**, and **preservatives** and **antioxidants** 'carried over' in ingredients – with little or no food value.

Average nutrients in 100 grams (½ bowl) Soups

	canned cream[a]	canned oxtail	canned vegetable	packet[b]	condensed[c]
Energy kilojoules	242	185	159	84	407
kilocalories	58	44	37	20	98
Protein grams	1.7	2.4	1.5	0.8	2.6
Total fat grams	3.8	1.7	0.7	0.3	7.2
Saturated fat grams	–	–	–	–	–
Polyunsaturated fat grams	–	–	–	–	–
Cholesterol milligrams	–	–	–	–	–
Sugars grams	1.1	0.9	2.5	0.6	1.4
Starch grams	3.3	4.2	4.2	3.1	4.6
Dietary fibre grams	–	–	–	–	–
Sodium milligrams	460	440	500	370	710
Potassium milligrams	41	93	140	16	62
Calcium milligrams	27	40	17	3	41
Magnesium milligrams	5	6	10	3	7
Iron milligrams	0.4	1.0	0.6	0.2	0.5
Copper milligrams	0.02	0.04	0.06	0.02	0.03

Zinc milligrams	0.3	0.4	0.3	0.1	0.5
Vitamin A micrograms	0-35	0	0	0	0-65
Vitamin D micrograms	0	0	0	0	0
Vitamin C milligrams	0	0	0	0	0
Vitamin E milligrams	–	–	–	–	–
B vitamins:					
Thiamin (B_1) milligrams	0.01	0.02	0.03	0.01	0.02
Riboflavin (B_2) milligrams	0.03	0.03	0.02	0	0.04
Nicotinic acid milligrams	0.5	1.2	0.6	0.3	1.1
Pyridoxine (B_6) milligrams	0.01	0.03	0.05	–	–
Vitamin B_{12} micrograms	0	0	0	0	0
Folic acid micrograms	0-12	–	10	–	–
Pantothenic acid milligrams	–	–	–	–	–
Biotin micrograms	–	–	–	–	–

(–) No information available   (0) Contains zero or trace amounts

a Tomato, chicken, mushroom, celery etc
b Minestrone, chicken etc, made up
c Undiluted chicken, tomato etc

Soya

Soya is unique in the plant foods in that it is probably a good source of well-absorbed **iron**. It is therefore particularly beneficial in **vegetarian diets**. The beans also supply high quality **protein, fat**, mostly as polyunsaturated **fatty acids**, other **minerals** and B **vitamins**.

Soya is an important ingredient in traditional Japanese and Chinese cuisine: the beans are eaten whole or processed into sauce (like soy sauce) or into soya milk, soup, or curd (Tofu). Modern varieties of the soya bean contain 20% fat (originally soya was fat free) and are an important crop in the USA. The residue left after **oil** has been extracted is used for soya flour (added to many foods), **novel proteins** and cattle fodder. As yet, soya is not cultivated in Britain.

Average nutrients in 100 grams (3½ oz) Soya

	cooked beans	tofu	milk	soy sauce	flour
Energy kilojoules	648	291	164	268	1871
kilocalories	155	70	39	64	447
Protein grams	13.1	7.4	1.2	5.2	36.8
Total fat grams	6.8	4.2	–	0.5	23.5
Saturated fat grams	1.0	–	–	–	3.3
Polyunsaturated fat grams	3.8	–	–	–	13.3
Cholesterol milligrams	0	0	0	0	0
Sugars grams	4.5	} 0.6	} 9.0	} 8.3	11.2
Starch grams	4.5				12.3
Dietary fibre grams	4.6	0.3	–	–	11.9
Sodium milligrams	2	4	3	–	1
Potassium milligrams	645	63	54	–	1660
Calcium milligrams	87	507	5	65	210
Magnesium milligrams	102	23	8	–	240
Iron milligrams	3.2	1.2	0.3	4.8	6.9
Copper milligrams	–	1.7	0.05	–	–
Zinc milligrams	–	0.7	0.1	–	–
Vitamin A micrograms	1	–	–	0	0
Vitamin D micrograms	0	0	0	0	0
Vitamin C milligrams	–	0	0	0	0

	cooked beans	tofu	milk	soy sauce	flour
Vitamin E milligrams	–	–	–	–	–
B vitamins:					
Thiamin (B_1) milligrams	0.4	0.06	0.02	0.04	0.75
Riboflavin (B_2) milligrams	0.01	0.02	0	0.17	0.31
Nicotinic acid milligrams	–	–	–	–	10.6
Pyridoxine (B_6) milligrams	–	–	–	–	0.57
Vitamin B_{12} micrograms	0	0	0	0	0
Folic acid micrograms	38	–	–	–	–
Pantothenic acid milligrams	–	–	–	–	1.8
Biotin micrograms	–	–	–	–	–

(–) No information available   (0) Contains zero or trace amounts

Spices

Spices are barks, flowers, seeds and roots of plants used to enhance and blend with the **flavour** of food, and probably in the past to mask tainted meat and fish. They are eaten in tiny quantities and consequently are of no direct nutritional value (except red pepper and curry powder – see below). However they stimulate appetite and are part of good cuisine. Some, like cloves, cinnamon and mustard have a preservative action.

Most spices contain no vitamins C or A. Red paprika and cayenne peppers however contain 30 to 60 vitamin A micrograms per gram, as **carotene**. Some of the colour in other spices is due to orange yellow pigments chemically related to carotene but with no vitamin activity – for instance curcumin in turmeric. Fresh horseradish contains 10 milligrams of vitamin C per 10 grams. Spices contain small amounts of B vitamins, calcium (0 – 10 milligrams per 1 gram) and other **minerals**, for instance 0.2 – 0.05 milligrams of iron per gram. Curry powder contains **iron**, 3 milligrams in an average portion of 10 grams, but very little of this is absorbed.

Spice products

Curry powder should contain at least 85% spices and not more than 15% salt. Different blends are made from fenugreek with three to four of the following spices: turmeric, cinnamon, cassia, coriander, fennel, ginger, red pepper, pepper, mustard, allspice, cardamom, mace, cummin, dill and a piece of bay leaf.

Black pepper is the unripe fruit, white the ripe fruit with the outer coat removed. It is more pungent freshly ground, and black is more pungent than white.

Mustards are a mixture of brown and yellow (black and white) varieties. If it has added starch it must be called mustard condiment or compound mustard. Prepared mustards (French, etc) are a mixture of the ground seeds with vinegar (or wine), salt, sugar and other spices.

Mixed spice contains five ground spices selected from cloves, ginger, coriander, fennel, cinnamon, cassia, red pepper and turmeric.

Pickling spices are selected from whole coriander, allspice, chillies, ginger, white mustard, cloves, mace, cinnamon, black mustard and white pepper.

Sausage seasonings contain sage, pepper, cloves, ginger, nutmeg, allspice, red pepper. Herbs, ginger, pepper, mace, allspice and cloves are used in delicatessen meats.

Spice extracts are the essential oils (see **flavour**) dissolved in alcohol and preserved in sulphur dioxide or benzoic acid. Ginger and horseradish are also allowed to contain preservative.

Spinach

The legendary nutritional qualities of spinach are to some extent well-founded, because when compared with other **vegetables**, spinach does contain more **protein**, **iron** and **vitamin A** (as **carotene**). It is also an apparently rich source of calcium, but little of this is absorbed into the body, because spinach is known to contain large amounts of **oxalic acid**. The iron is also poorly absorbed and at least ten times the weight of spinach would have to be eaten for the same amount of iron to be absorbed as from meat.

Average nutrients in 100 grams (3½ oz) Spinach (boiled)

Energy kilojoules	128	Iron milligrams	4.0
kilocalories	30	Copper milligrams	0.26
Protein grams	5.1	Zinc milligrams	0.4
Total fat grams	0.5	Vitamin A micrograms	670–1670
Saturated fat grams	0.1	Vitamin D micrograms	0
Polyunsaturated fat grams	0.3	Vitamin C milligrams	10–60
		Vitamin E milligrams	2.0
Cholesterol milligrams	0	B vitamins:	
Sugars grams	1.2	Thiamin (B_1) milligrams	0.07
Starch grams	0.2	Riboflavin (B_2) milligrams	0.15
Dietary fibre grams	6.3	Nicotinic acid milligrams	1.8
Sodium milligrams	120	Pyridoxine (B_6) milligrams	0.18
Potassium milligrams	490	Vitamin B_{12} micrograms	0
Calcium milligrams	600	Folic acid micrograms	140
Magnesium milligrams	59	Pantothenic acid milligrams	0.21
		Biotin micrograms	0.1

(–) No information available   (0) Contains zero or trace amounts

Spirits and liqueurs

Spirits are concentrated sources of **alcohol**: they supply **energy** (Calories) but are deficient in all other **nutrients**. A half bottle of 70° proof spirit contains 3.5 Megajoules (840 kilo**calories**) – nearly one third of the **recommended intake** for energy for most men.

Spirits can be distilled from any fermented carbohydrate – for instance whisky and gin are made from cereals; vodka from rye or potatoes; brandy from grapes; rum from molasses; and calvados from apples. Fusel oils (congeners) which distil across with alcohol contribute to the flavour. Fusel oils are responsible for some of the unpleasant side effects of alcoholic drinks, but are virtually removed during redistillation of vodka and gin. Juniper berries and coriander are added when gin is redistilled.

All spirits sold in Britain must be at least 65° proof (contain at least 65% of proof spirit) unless otherwise stated on the label. The original way of measuring proof was to mix a sample of alcohol with a small quantity of gunpowder and set light to it. 'Proof' spirit contained sufficient alcohol to ignite the gunpowder: in an underproof sample the alcohol would burn but the relative excess of water made the gunpowder too damp to explode. The modern definition of proof spirit (in the UK) is that it contains approximately 50% of alcohol by weight and 57% by volume. For instance, 70° proof gin contains 70% of proof spirit by volume – i.e. $70/100 \times 57 = 40$ mls of alcohol per 100 mls of gin (or approximately $40 \times 0.8 = 32$ grams of alcohol per 100 mls of gin).

Liqueurs contain more alcohol (30 to 40 grams per 100 millilitres) than spirits, are sweetened with sugar, and flavoured with herbs and spices.

Average nutrients in 100 mls (3 measures) Spirits and Liqueurs

	spirits	liqueurs		spirits	liqueurs
Energy kilojoules	919	1303	Iron milligrams	0	0
kilocalories	222	311	Copper milligrams	0	0
Protein grams	0	0	Zinc milligrams	0	0
Total fat grams	0	0	Vitamin A micrograms	0	0
Alcohol grams	32	30	Vitamin D micrograms	0	0
			Vitamin C milligrams	0	0
			Vitamin E milligrams	0	0
			B vitamins:		
Sugars grams	0	28.3	Thiamin (B₁) milligrams	0	0
Starch grams	0	0	Riboflavin (B₂) milligrams	0	0
Dietary fibre (NSP) grams	0	0	Nicotinic acid milligrams	0	0
Sodium milligrams	0	0	Pyridoxine (B₆) milligrams	0	0
Potassium milligrams	0	0	Vitamin B₁₂ micrograms	0	0
Calcium milligrams	0	0	Folic acid micrograms	0	0
Magnesium milligrams	0	0	Pantothenic acid milligrams	0	0
			Biotin micrograms	0	0

(–) No information available   (0) Contains zero or trace amounts

Sprats

Sprats are a small silvery fish, related to the herring. Young sprats, called brislings, are sometimes tinned in oil or tomato sauce. Sprats, both fresh and smoked, are good sources of **iron** and **calcium** but few other nutritional analyses are available.

Average nutrients in 100 grams (3½ oz) Sprats (fried)

Energy kilojoules	1826	Iron milligrams	4.5
kilocalories	441	Copper milligrams	–
Protein grams	24.9	Zinc milligrams	–
Total fat grams	37.9	Vitamin A micrograms	–
Saturated fat grams	–	Vitamin D micrograms	–
Polyunsaturated fat grams	–	Vitamin C milligrams	0
		Vitamin E milligrams	
Cholesterol milligrams	–	B vitamins:	
Sugars grams	0	Thiamin (B₁) milligrams	–
Starch grams	0	Riboflavin (B₂) milligrams	–
Dietary fibre grams	0	Nicotinic acid milligrams	–
Sodium milligrams	130	Pyridoxine (B₆) milligrams	–

Potassium milligrams	410	Vitamin B_{12} micrograms	–
Calcium milligrams	710	Folic acid micrograms	–
Magnesium milligrams	46	Pantothenic acid milligrams	–
		Biotin micrograms	–

(–) No information available   (0) Contains zero or trace amounts

Spring greens see cabbage

Squid see octopus

Starch

Starch is an important **energy** yielding constituent of food. It is found mostly in seeds. Cereals contain about 70%, bread 50%, chestnuts 30%, potatoes 20%, sweetcorn and peas, beans and lentils 10 to 15%, and nuts and parsnips about 5%. Other vegetables and most fruits contain traces, but unripe bananas are 15% starch. Arrowroot, sago, tapioca and cornflour are virtually pure starch. Pure starch, extracted from any food, is extensively used by the food industry and called edible or **modified starch**.

Although starch should provide most of the energy in the diet, consumption of bread and potatoes has gradually fallen over the past century, so that the 110 grams of starch in the average British diet now only provides 20% of total energy. This is probably too little when compared with nearly 40% from **fat** and 13% from sugar. Partly because starchy foods are low in fat, but also because unrefined starch foods contain **vitamins**, **minerals**, **protein** and **fibre**, good health is more likely with a diet that includes starch in an unrefined form, such as potato, rice, pasta and bread (preferably wholemeal) rather than one in which potatoes and bread are avoided but foods high in fat and sugar (cakes, sweets, puddings and biscuits) are eaten instead. See **fat** and **diet** for ways of increasing unrefined starch in the diet.

Starch – a **polysaccharide** composed of many molecules of **glucose** linked together in chains – is stored in characteristic granules in plants. Uncooked starch does not dissolve in water easily and is poorly digested. Grinding into flour breaks down cell walls, but only partially damages starch granules. When added to water, starch takes up a small quantity of water but does not dissolve until the mixture is heated, when the granules eventually burst (gelatinise) thickening the food. Sauces are smoother and thicker if they are stirred, which helps to rupture the granules. Dry heat has a different effect – the starch is broken down to **dextrins** (for example in toast and breakfast cereals). Prolonged heat chars starch, rendering it useless for food.

Most starch is dismantled during **digestion** by **enzymes** and the liberated glucose absorbed into the blood stream. Starch therefore yields the same energy (about 16 kilojoules or 4 kilo**calories** per gram) as glucose and other carbohydrates. Some starch, particularly in unripe bananas, escapes digestion and enters the large bowel, where it acts in a similar way to fibre.

Starvation – see also **marasmus**

Severe loss of weight caused by insufficient food for bodily needs. Starvation is usually associated with famine, but can be self imposed, for example for political reasons or in **anorexia nervosa**, a serious mental condition affecting adolescent girls in particular. Loss of weight – caused by lack of appetite, fever, **malabsorption**, and some feeding régimes (for example low fat or protein diets) inadvertently low in **energy** – is also a feature of many other diseases.

Normal adults can survive with no food for about six weeks, thin people for less. As fat stores (**adipose tissue**) are depleted, energy expenditure is usually decreased (starving people are listless and apathetic) but sufferers from anorexia nervosa are often very active, giving a false impression of good health. The body proteins are also wasted away, first to supply essential **amino acids**, then, as fat stores are exhausted, for energy. As muscles shrink, the skin becomes lax, though the accumulation of water may give a superficial well fed appearance.

Few people can survive a loss of more than one third of their normal body weight: death is usually precipitated by a heart failure or diarrhoea. In the early stages, recovery is complete once food is made available, but the outlook is less good if the digestive tract has degenerated. Specialist treatment, including very dilute feeds of skimmed milk and glucose or intravenous fluids are necessary until the digestive tract has regenerated.

When weight has been lost after illness, small frequent meals are advisable until appetite has recovered sufficiently for normal meals (with extra helpings) to be taken. Fruit juices with glucose, or proprietary glucose and milk based drinks are useful ways of increasing energy intake. Treatment of the underlying disease sometimes requires a **therapeutic diet**.

Strawberries

Apart from the European alpine strawberry, modern cultivated strawberries are derived from two American varieties, introduced into Europe in 1600 and 1800.

Strawberries are one of the most popular fruits. They are also good sources of **vitamin C** (values for fresh strawberries are shown in the table). Frozen strawberries contain 50 milligrams per 100 grams, only slightly less than the average of 60 milligrams in fresh strawberries. Canned contain rather less (see table).

Most strawberry products contain added flavour and colour. The synthetic **colours** likely to be used are E124 in sweets, ice cream and canned fruit, and E122 and E110 in soft drinks. As in all natural **flavours** strawberry is composed of many complex chemicals, which are difficult to identify and blend in the correct proportions, although modern mixes are an almost exact match. Flavours do not have additive numbers, for reasons set out in the entry on **flavour**.

Average nutrients in 100 grams (3½ oz) Strawberries

	fresh	canned in syrup		fresh	canned in syrup
Energy kilojoules	109	344	Iron milligrams	0.7	0.9
kilocalories	26	81	Copper milligrams	0.13	0.03
Protein grams	0.6	0.4	Zinc milligrams	0.1	0.2
Total fat grams	0	0	Vitamin A micrograms	5	0
Saturated fat grams	0	0	Vitamin D micrograms	0	0
Polyunsaturated fat grams	0	0	Vitamin C milligrams	40-90	21
			Vitamin E milligrams	0.2	–
Cholesterol milligrams	0	0	B vitamins:		
Sugars grams	6.2	21.1	Thiamin (B$_1$) milligrams	0.02	0.01
Starch grams	0	0	Riboflavin (B$_2$) milligrams	0.03	0.02
Dietary fibre grams	2.2	1.0	Nicotinic acid milligrams	0.5	0.4
Sodium milligrams	2	7	Pyridoxine (B$_6$) milligrams	0.06	0.03
Potassium milligrams	160	97	Vitamin B$_{12}$ micrograms	0	0
Calcium milligrams	22	14	Folic acid micrograms	20	20
Magnesium milligrams	12	7	Pantothenic acid milligrams	0.34	0.21
			Biotin micrograms	1.1	1.0

(–) No information available   (0) Contains zero or trace amounts

Stroke – cerebrovascular disease

A stroke is damage to the brain usually caused by an obstruction (for example a clot) in an artery, or by bleeding from a ruptured artery. It usually causes paralysis or disablement on one side of the body depending on which part of the brain is affected, and problems with speech are common.

High **blood pressure** and **atherosclerosis** are the underlying causes of most strokes. Death rates have been declining since the 1950s, possibly because of greater consumption of vegetables and less **sodium**, but more probably because of better treatment of high blood pressure. Nevertheless, 100,000 people suffer strokes every year and of these 30,000 are permanently disabled. Stroke still accounts for 9% of all deaths in men in Britain, and 15% in women.

Sucrose – common name sugar

Sugar is commercially produced from beet, cane, and to a lesser extent, maple. The chemical composition of sucrose is identical from all sources: each molecule of sucrose contains one of **glucose** and one of **fructose**. Most plants contain traces, but nearly all sucrose in the diet is derived from commercially produced white sugar; a highly purified substance containing 99.5% sucrose and no other nutrient. Sucrose supplies the same **energy** (approximately 16 kilojoules or 4 kilo**calories** per gram) as other pure **carbohydrates**.

Pure crystals of sucrose (white sugar) are produced from cane or beet by a complex process of extraction. Different size crystals – caster, granulated or preserving – can be made by modification of the final processing. Icing sugar tastes sweeter because the ground powder dissolves quickly on the tongue. Demerara retains some of the colour and flavour of raw cane sugar, but it is little better than white as a source of nutrients. Other brown sugars are made by mixing refined sugar with syrup.

Molasses, which remains when sugar has been crystallised out of cane or beet sugar solutions, is used to make treacle and golden syrup. These contain **minerals** (see table). Some of the iron and calcium are derived from machinery and lime used in purification. The table shows nutrient contents in 100 grams of sugars and syrups; one to two teaspoons of syrup or two teaspoons of sugar weigh 10 grams. Glucose (corn) syrup is made from starch, usually **maize**.

Sugar is a **preservative** and is necessary for 'lightness' in cakes, but it is valued primarily for its taste. After about 1850, it became a common article of food in Britain, and, apart from restrictions during war and post war shortages, consumption increased markedly up to 1956. In 1855, average total daily consumption per person was about (35 grams 1¼ ounces) but (140 grams 5 ounces) in 1956. A similar pattern is emerging as underdeveloped countries become urbanised. A level of just over 2 lb total per person per week seems to be the saturation point, probably because then income has increased sufficiently for other, more satisfying foods, like meat to be bought. In Britain, daily consumption of sugar has been falling since 1956 to 75 – 100 grams total sugar per person, which provides 13% of the total energy in the adult diet.

About half of the average total sugar is used in cooking and in sweetening tea and coffee. People who do not take sugar in drinks will of course consume less. Others, who take 2 teaspoons of sugar (10 grams) or more in drinks will exceed the average. The rest of the average intake is eaten in **preserves** like jam, sweets, **cakes**, **biscuits**, **soft drinks**, **chocolate** and sweets, and **ice cream**. Boiled sweets contain 90% sugar, toffees, jams and marmalades 70%, and chocolates 50%. Cakes and soft drinks vary.

During **digestion**, sugar is split to glucose and fructose which are absorbed into the blood stream and transported to the liver. In very large quantities fructose tends to be used in a different way from glucose, raising the level of some of the blood **lipids**. Very large quantities increase the blood cholesterol level in animals, but in men, women past the menopause, and some women taking the contraceptive pill, the blood triglycerides (or simple fats) are raised. The effect is not seen with normal quantities or if the diet is also high in polyunsaturated **fatty acids** (from sunflower seed oil), and low in saturated fats. It is likely to be a subsidiary risk factor in **heart disease**: a high intake of sugar alone probably does not affect mortality (in some countries where consumption of sucrose is high, such as Jamaica and Cuba, there is a low rate of death from heart disease), but in conjunction with other risk factors – for example a diet high in saturated fats – the risk is increased.

Heart disease apart, sugar is a food of poor nutritional value for people living sedentary lives. It contains energy (Calories) but no other nutrient and can safely be discarded from the diet without risk of depleting the body of essential protein, vitamins and minerals. Sucrose is also known to be important in **tooth decay**, particularly when it is eaten in a sticky form (like toffee), and may raise the level of triglycerides on the skin. The advice to those who suffer from a greasy skin and spots to avoid sugar is probably well founded.

Average nutrients in 100 grams (3½ oz) Sugar and Syrups

	white	demerara	golden syrup	black treacle
Energy kilojoules	1680	1681	1269	1096
kilocalories	394	394	298	257
Protein grams	0	0.5	0.3	1.2
Total fat grams	0	0	0	0
Saturated fat grams	0	0	0	0
Polyunsaturated fat grams	0	0	0	0
Cholesterol milligrams	0	0	0	0
Sugars grams	105.0	104.5	79.0	67.2
Starch grams	0	0	0	0
Dietary fibre grams	0	0	0	0
Sodium milligrams	0	6	270	96
Potassium milligrams	2	89	240	1470
Calcium milligrams	2	53	26	500
Magnesium milligrams	0	15	10	140
Iron milligrams	0	0.9	1.5	9.2
Copper milligrams	0.02	0.06	0.09	0.43
Zinc milligrams	0	–	–	–
Vitamin A micrograms	0	0	0	0
Vitamin D micrograms	0	0	0	0
Vitamin C milligrams	0	0	0	0
Vitamin E milligrams	0	0	0	0
B vitamins:				
Thiamin (B_1) milligrams	0	0	0	0
Riboflavin (B_2) milligrams	0	0	0	0
Nicotinic acid milligrams	0	0	0	0
Pyridoxine (B_6) milligrams	0	0	0	0
Vitamin B_{12} micrograms	0	0	0	0
Folic acid micrograms	0	0	0	0
Pantothenic acid milligrams	0	0	0	0
Biotin micrograms	0	0	0	0

(–) No information available   (0) Contains zero or trace amounts

Sugar – see Sucrose

Sugar is synonymous with **sucrose** but there are many other sugars in food. After sucrose, the most common are **glucose**, **fructose**, **maltose** and **lactose**. Mannose is found in manna – the gummy sap of the tamarisk tree eaten in a sweet with nuts. They are all chemically related (as **carbohydrates**), converted to glucose in the body, and taste sweet. They have different sweetening powers: compared with sucrose, fructose is the sweetest (1.7 times) and lactose the least sweet (0.2 times).

Other substances that taste sweet but are not sugars are called artificial **sweeteners**.

Sulphur

Sulphur is part of the essential **amino acid**, **methionine**, and of **cysteine** and **cystine**. Nearly all dietary sulphur is derived from **proteins** containing these amino acids, though two B vitamins (**thiamin** and biotin) also contain small amounts. Apart from the needs for these essential nutrients, humans are not thought to require extra sulphur.

Adults contain about 120 grams of sulphur, mostly in proteins. Daily diets contain 600 – 1600 milligrams, depending on the quantity and quality of protein. An equivalent amount is filtered out daily from the blood by the kidney, mostly as salts of sulphuric acid (sulphates).

Sultanas

Sultanas are small, seedless raisins, produced by drying grapes. They are rich sources of **sugars** (mostly glucose and fructose) and contain some vitamins and minerals (see table).

Average nutrients in 100 grams (3½ oz) Sultanas

Energy kilojoules	1066	Iron milligrams	1.8
kilocalories	250	Copper milligrams	0.35
Protein grams	1.8	Zinc milligrams	0.1
Total fat grams	0	Vitamin A micrograms	5
Saturated fat grams	0	Vitamin D micrograms	0
Polyunsaturated fat grams	0	Vitamin C milligrams	0
		Vitamin E milligrams	0.7
Cholesterol milligrams	0	B vitamins:	
Sugars grams	64.7	Thiamin (B$_1$) milligrams	0.10
Starch grams	0	Riboflavin (B$_2$) milligrams	0.08
Dietary fibre grams	7.0	Nicotinic acid milligrams	0.6
Sodium milligrams	53	Pyridoxine (B$_6$) milligrams	0.30
Potassium milligrams	860	Vitamin B$_{12}$ micrograms	0
Calcium milligrams	52	Folic acid micrograms	4
Magnesium milligrams	35	Pantothenic acid milligrams	0.10
		Biotin micrograms	–

(–) No information available   (0) Contains zero or trace amounts

Sunflower seeds

The majority of sunflower seeds are grown for their **oil** and the cake which is left is used for cattle fodder. Some are eaten whole, and they have a similar composition to **nuts**. A few nutritional analyses are shown in the table.

Average nutrients in 100 grams (3½ oz) Sunflower seeds

Energy kilojoules	2200	Iron milligrams	7.0
kilocalories	524	Copper milligrams	–
Protein grams	27.0	Zinc milligrams	–
Total fat grams	36.0	Vitamin A micrograms	0 .
Saturated fat grams	–	Vitamin D micrograms	0
Polyunsaturated fat grams	–	Vitamin C milligrams	–
		Vitamin E milligrams	–
Cholesterol milligrams	0	B vitamins:	
Sugars grams	} 23	Thiamin (B$_1$) milligrams	1.9
Starch grams		Riboflavin (B$_2$) milligrams	0.2
Dietary fibre grams	–	Nicotinic acid milligrams	–
Sodium milligrams	–	Pyridoxine (B$_6$) milligrams	–
Potassium milligrams	–	Vitamin B$_{12}$ micrograms	–
Calcium milligrams	100	Folic acid micrograms	–
Magnesium milligrams	–	Pantothenic acid milligrams	–
		Biotin micrograms	–

(–) No information available   (0) Contains zero or trace amounts

Swedes

Swedes are probably a hybrid of turnips and cabbage. They are of minor nutritional value, containing no starch or vitamin A, and moderate amounts of B vitamins and vitamin C.

Average nutrients in 100 grams (3½ oz) Swede (boiled)

Energy kilojoules	76	Iron milligrams	0.3
kilocalories	18	Copper milligrams	0.04
Protein grams	0.9	Zinc milligrams	–
Total fat grams	0	Vitamin A micrograms	0
Saturated fat grams	0	Vitamin D micrograms	0
Polyunsaturated fat grams	0	Vitamin C milligrams	8-25
		Vitamin E milligrams	0
Cholesterol milligrams	0	B vitamins:	
Sugars grams	3.7	Thiamin (B$_1$) milligrams	0.04
Starch grams	0.1	Riboflavin (B$_2$) milligrams	0.03
Dietary fibre grams	2.8	Nicotinic acid milligrams	1.0
Sodium milligrams	14	Pyridoxine (B$_6$) milligrams	0.12
Potassium milligrams	100	Vitamin B$_{12}$ micrograms	0
Calcium milligrams	42	Folic acid micrograms	21
Magnesium milligrams	7	Pantothenic acid milligrams	0.07
		Biotin micrograms	0

(–) No information available   (0) Contains zero or trace amounts

Sweetcorn

The head of **maize** boiled and eaten when fresh as a vegetable, rather than as the dried grain. Depending on the maturity and variety, sweetcorn may contain some sugar and less starch than the harvested grain. Canned kernels are particularly tender and low in starch (see table).

Average nutrients in 100 grams (3½ oz) Sweetcorn

	boiled on the cob	canned		boiled on the cob	canned
Energy kilojoules	520	325	Iron milligrams	0.9	0.6
kilocalories	123	76	Copper milligrams	0.1	0.05
Protein grams	4.1	2.9	Zinc milligrams	1.0	0.6
Total fat grams	2.3	0.5	Vitamin A micrograms	40	35
Saturated fat grams	0.4	0.1	Vitamin D micrograms	0	0
Polyunsaturated fat grams	1.1	0.2	Vitamin C milligrams	9	5
			Vitamin E milligrams	0.5	0.5
Cholesterol milligrams	0	0	B vitamins:		
Sugars grams	1.7	8.9	Thiamin (B$_1$) milligrams	0.20	0.05
Starch grams	21.1	7.2	Riboflavin (B$_2$) milligrams	0.08	0.08
Dietary fibre grams	4.7	5.7	Nicotinic acid milligrams	0.4	0.3
Sodium milligrams	1	310	Pyridoxine (B$_6$) milligrams	0.16	0.16
Potassium milligrams	280	200	Vitamin B$_{12}$ micrograms	0	0
Calcium milligrams	4	3	Folic acid micrograms	33	32
Magnesium milligrams	45	23	Pantothenic acid milligrams	0.38	0.22
			Biotin micrograms	–	–

(–) No information available   (0) Contains zero or trace amounts

Sweeteners

Sweeteners are substances which, like **sugars**, stimulate the sweet sensitive taste buds of the tongue. Artificial sweeteners, however, usually contain no energy (Calories) and are much sweeter than sugars. Other substances in food also taste sweet – for instance **glycerol** and glycine (0.7 times as sweet as **sucrose**) but they are not generally used solely as sweeteners.

Nine non-sucrose sweeteners are permitted in foods such as **soft drinks** by the 1983 Sweeteners in Food Regulations. They are acesulfame potassium (K), aspartame, hydrogenated **glucose** syrup, isomalt, mannitol (E421), saccharin, **sorbitol** (E420), thaumatin, and xylitol.

Compared with sucrose, saccharin is 400 times as sweet, but it has a bitter aftertaste, which intensifies when it is used in cooking. Many studies have been carried out on its safety and in 1972 two American studies found that in very high doses it caused bladder cancer in rats. These studies have not been confirmed in man, but it is probably wise to limit adult intake to about 12 tablets of saccharin per day. The safety limit would be exceeded by children drinking more than one large bottle of a fizzy drink per day sweetened entirely with saccharin.

Aspartame, trade name NutraSweet, is composed of two **amino acids** (**phenylalanine** and aspartic acid) and is nearly 200 times sweeter than sucrose. Like saccharin this sweetener is of limited value in cooking because it breaks down when heated. It is however added to many soft drinks and is available in tablets and granulated form as Canderel. In 1983 it was suggested by an American expert that large doses of aspartame in soft drinks might cause mental problems because phenylalanine is involved in the metabolism of the brain. The British committee on Toxicity of Food reviewed this and reiterated its view that aspartame is safe for use.

No safety problems have been reported for acesulfame K which is 200 times sweeter than sucrose, or for thaumatin, a protein 3000 times sweeter than sucrose. Thaumatin breaks down on cooking and it produces a delayed sense of sweetness, so its usefulness is also limited. Acesulfame K is however stable to cooking and is available under several brand names, such as Diamin, Hermesetas Gold and Sweetex Plus.

The other sweeteners permitted are used partly to give a sensation of bulk to foods – as sucrose does. Glucose syrup and sorbitol offer no advantages to slimmers because they have the same **energy** (Calorie) content as sucrose. Mannitol, sorbitol and xylitol are derivatives of sugars, and isomalt a combination of mannitol and another derivative, glucitol.

Other interesting proteins which are intensely sweet are miraculin and monellin which are extracted from plants originally found in West Africa. Miracullin causes sour foods to taste sweet several hours after being spread on the tongue. Neither of these is commercially viable.

Tangerines

Tangerines are a citrus fruit, containing useful amounts of **vitamin C** (see table). They originated in the Far East, becoming known to Europeans in the 18th century. Mandarin orange is another name, denoting its origin. Although these, and satsumas, may be different types, all these names are used synonymously. Canned mandarin oranges contain more sugar and rather less vitamin C than fresh.

Average nutrients in 100 grams (3½ oz) Tangerines and mandarin oranges

	fresh tangerines	canned mandarin oranges		fresh tangerines	canned mandarin oranges
Energy kilojoules	143	237	Iron milligrams	0.3	0.4
kilocalories	34	56	Copper milligrams	0.09	0.05
Protein grams	0.9	0.6	Zinc milligrams	0.1	0.4
Total fat grams	0	0	Vitamin A micrograms	17	8
Saturated fat grams	0	0	Vitamin D micrograms	0	0
Polyunsaturated fat grams	0	0	Vitamin C milligrams	30	14
			Vitamin E milligrams	–	0
Cholesterol milligrams	0	0	B vitamins:		
Sugars grams	8.0	14.2	Thiamin (B_1) milligrams	0.07	0.07
Starch grams	0	0	Riboflavin (B_2) milligrams	0.02	0.02
Dietary fibre (NSP) grams	1.9	0.3	Nicotinic acid milligrams	0.3	0.3
Sodium milligrams	2	9	Pyridoxine (B_6) milligrams	0.07	0.03
Potassium milligrams	160	88	Vitamin B_{12} micrograms	0	0
Calcium milligrams	42	18	Folic acid micrograms	21	8
Magnesium milligrams	11	9	Pantothenic acid milligrams	0.20	0.15
			Biotin micrograms	–	0.8

(–) No information available   (0) Contains zero or trace amounts

Tannins

Tannins are flavanoids (see **bioflavonoids**) responsible for the astringency of red **wine** and **tea**. As red wine ages it becomes less astringent, owing to a complex series of chemical changes in tannins and the **colour** pigments of **grapes** called anthocyanins. In tea, tannins may interfere with **iron** absorption and cause the **anaemia** reported to affect some people who drink a lot of tea.

Tapioca

Tapioca is extracted from cassava (manioc) roots, partially cooked and sold as pearls (which resemble sago) or flakes. Untreated cassava from some sources is poisonous, containing cyanide.

The nutritional deficiencies of tapioca – it is virtually pure **starch**, yielding **energy** but few other nutrients – are overcome when it is cooked with milk. However, it is easily grown and has become the staple food in many communities, often where milk is in short supply. Children weaned onto cassava (but not given milk or other sources of protein) are at risk from the protein deficiency disease **kwashiorkor**.

Average nutrients in 100 grams (3½ oz) Tapioca and Cassava flour

	tapioca	cassava		tapioca	cassava
Energy kilojoules	1531	1436	Iron milligrams	0.3	2.0
kilocalories	359	342	Copper milligrams	0.07	–
Protein grams	0.4	1.5	Zinc milligrams	–	–
Total fat grams	0.1	0	Vitamin A micrograms	0	–
Saturated fat grams	–	0	Vitamin D micrograms	0	–
Polyunsaturated fat grams	–	0	Vitamin C milligrams	0	0
			Vitamin E milligrams	0	–
Cholesterol milligrams	0	0	B vitamins:		
Sugars grams	0	0	Thiamin (B₁) milligrams	0	0.04
Starch grams	95.0	84.0	Riboflavin (B₂) milligrams	0	0.04
Dietary fibre (NSP) grams	0.5	–	Nicotinic acid milligrams	0	–
Sodium milligrams	4	–	Pyridoxine (B₆) milligrams	0	–
Potassium milligrams	20	–	Vitamin B₁₂ micrograms	0	–
Calcium milligrams	8	55	Folic acid micrograms	0	–
Magnesium milligrams	2	–	Pantothenic acid milligrams	0	–
			Biotin micrograms	0	–

(–) No information available   (0) Contains zero or trace amounts

Taro

A root crop, used as a staple food in some tropical islands and parts of Africa and Asia. Like other starchy tubers – such as cassava and potato – it is a valuable source of **energy** but its low **protein** content makes it less satisfactory nutritionally than cereals – particularly to children who require a greater proportion of nutrients than adults to allow for growth.

Average nutrients in 100 grams (3½ oz) Taro (raw)

Energy kilojoules	393	Iron milligrams	1.2
kilocalories	94	Copper milligrams	–
Protein grams	2.2	Zinc milligrams	–
Total fat grams	0.4	Vitamin A micrograms	0
Saturated fat grams	–	Vitamin D micrograms	0
Polyunsaturated fat grams	–	Vitamin C milligrams	8
		Vitamin E milligrams	–
Cholesterol milligrams	0	B vitamins:	
Sugars grams	} 20.2	Thiamin (B₁) milligrams	0.12
Starch grams		Riboflavin (B₂) milligrams	0.04
Dietary fibre grams	–	Nicotinic acid milligrams	1.4
Sodium milligrams	10	Pyridoxine (B₆) milligrams	–
Potassium milligrams	448	Vitamin B₁₂ micrograms	0
Calcium milligrams	34	Folic acid micrograms	–
Magnesium milligrams	33	Pantothenic acid milligrams	–
		Biotin micrograms	–

(–) No information available   (0) Contains zero or trace amounts

Tartaric acid (E334–337)

Tartaric acid is found in grapes, and is partly responsible for the acid taste of young wine. Little is absorbed from food. It is used to give a sharp taste to some soft drinks and jams. Cream of tartar and tartaric acid are the acid ingredients in some **raising agents**.

Tartrazine

A yellow food **colouring** (E102), added to many foods, drugs and drinks, which has attracted particular attention because of the suggestion by Feingold in the mid-seventies that this was one of a number of food **additives** causing **hyperactivity** in children. This has not been borne out by subsequent careful investigations but, nevertheless, tartrazine has been found to provoke some types of allergic (see **allergy**) attacks – including **urticaria, asthma** and **eczema** when used to colour medicines and pills, particularly in people who are sensitised to aspirin and **salicylates**. So far, tartrazine per se is not thought to provoke the main type of food allergic reaction (type 1), although it is metabolised by bacteria in the gut and the resulting product may be responsible for a type IV reaction. From three in 10,000 to one in 1000 people are currently thought to be sensitive to tartrazine.

Tea

Tea originated in China and became a popular drink in Britain in the middle of the eighteenth century. Indian and Ceylonese supplies virtually replaced Chinese towards the end of the nineteenth century. The shoots from the tea bushes are withered, rolled, fermented and dried. Green teas are not fermented.

Teas contain flavouring oils, **caffeine** and **tannin**, an astringent. Indian and Ceylon teas contain more tannin than Chinese, and green teas contain more than black. Caffeine contents are about the same. Blends contain about twenty different types, selected for flavour and astringency. Caffeine is extracted out of tea more readily than tannin, so that first cups contain more of the stimulant and less of the astringent than second cups.

Tea is a good source of two **trace elements, manganese** and **fluorine** – and contains small amounts of two B vitamins, **riboflavin** and **nicotinic acid**. Too much tea however interferes with **iron** absorption, and several cases of **anaemia** in people drinking large amounts have been reported. Tea also contains aluminium.

The table below shows the contents of a 150 millilitre (5 oz) cup of tea, made with 5 grams of tea and no milk.

Caffeine	Fluorine	Manganese	Riboflavin	Nicotinic acid
50–80 milligrams	0.2–0.5 milligrams	1 milligram	0.02 milligrams	0.2 milligrams

Textured vegetable protein see novel proteins

Therapeutic diets

Therapeutic diets are normal diets altered – usually in their content of one or more **nutrients**, but also in their texture – for medical purposes. Because indisposition is often attributed to food they were one of the first treatments used in medicine. Unfortunately many diets used in the past were based on unfounded beliefs, and some present day claims for dietetic 'cures' are based on equally uncertain evidence. Nevertheless, therapeutic diets are an important part of modern treatments of many medical conditions.

Therapeutic diets are most commonly needed for weight reduction. All **slimming diets**, despite hundreds of 'different' regimes, are designed to contain less **energy** (Calories), than normal food. No food has special slimming properties.

Fat, protein, carbohydrate, fibre, calcium, salt (sodium), **potassium** and some **vitamin** modified diets may be necessary for the treatment of many conditions, see individual entries. See also **coeliac disease, diabetes, inborn errors of metabolism, gout, heart disease, dyspepsia, ulcers, allergy**.

Substantial alteration of the diet carries with it the risk of unsuspected deficiency diseases – for instance, scurvy has occasionally resulted from some types of ulcer regimes. Self treatment with very restricted diets is inadvisable – medical and qualified dietetic assistance should be sought.

Thiamin – other name vitamin B_1, obsolete name, aneurine

Thiamin, part of the **vitamin B complex**, is essential for growth and life. The nervous system is first affected by a diet lacking in the vitamin, but deficiency diseases – **beriberi** and other nervous disorders – are now rare except amongst alcoholics.

Wholegrain **cereals, pork, bacon, ham, heart, liver, kidney**, cod **roe**, most **nuts** and pulses (**peas** and **beans**) are good sources of thiamin (see also yeast). Most other fresh foods contain thiamin, but it is readily destroyed during cooking and processing – see below. Although it is removed in wheat germ (a rich source) and bran during milling, white flour is legally required to have added thiamin. Sugar, fats, refined starches and alcoholic spirits contain none.

Needs for thiamin depend on the amount of **carbohydrate** (sugar and starch) in the diet, but daily **recommended intakes** (twice the usual minimum needs) are related to **energy** requirements and are greater for men (1.1–1.4 milligrams) than women (0.9-1.0 milligrams). The table on page 294 shows portions of food supplying 0.9 milligrams, the allowance for most women. Requirements are decreased when little carbohydrate is eaten, and may be increased by large intakes of alcohol. See Appendix I for other recommended intakes.

Allowing for cooking and processing losses, the average British diet contains about 30% more thiamin than the average recommended intake. Nearly half the average intake is supplied by bread and other cereal products; vegetables and meat contribute a further third.

Thiamin is vulnerable to heat, particularly when alkalis, such as bicarbonate of soda, are used and – like other B vitamins – leaches out of foods cooked in water.

Alkalis and sulphur dioxide are the most destructive. In soda bread, cakes and greens cooked with baking powder or bicarbonate of soda, losses are increased proportionally to the amount used. Bright green vegetables or yellow scones (alkalis cause yellowing of flour) will contain no thiamin. Self raising flour and some bread mixes also contain bicarbonate of soda. To conserve thiamin, bread should always be leavened with **yeast**. Sulphur dioxide is a permitted **preservative** and foods containing it cannot be relied on as sources of thiamin.

All cooking destroys some thiamin. In general, grilled, fried or roast meat loses less (0–40%) than stewed or braised meat (40–70%): little is left in the gravy. Fish loses 10–30%, peas, beans and potatoes up to 30%, and roasted nuts up to 75%. Large volumes of water increases losses in boiled vegetables by up to 60%. Keeping food hot causes further destruction.

No thiamin is lost when meat and fish are frozen, but losses can occur in storage: 20 to 40% can be lost when meat is stored in a deep freeze for six months. Losses will be greater if temperatures are allowed to rise above −18°C. Canning causes losses of between 50 and 75%, and there are further losses on storage if cans are not kept cool – up to 40% at warm (20°C) temperatures over a year. Canned sardines and corned beef contain no thiamin. Less heat is required to sterilise acid fruit and so canned orange juice retains most of the vitamin. Cured meats (which are preserved with **nitrite**) retain most of the vitamin, but smoking causes a 20% loss. Bloaters and kippers contain no thiamin.

Thiamin is also destroyed during toasting and puffing of breakfast cereals, which usually contain negligible amounts unless it is added by manufacturers (when it will be declared on the label). Bread loses up to 30% when toasted for a minute.

The human body contains about 25 milligrams of thiamin, fairly evenly distributed thoughout all cells. As part of a co**Enzyme** thiamin is necessary for many metabolic (see **metabolism**) processes, most importantly the release of energy from **glucose**. Nervous tissue is especially dependent on glucose as a source of energy and is markedly affected by a diet containing minimal amounts after about three weeks. Initial symptoms are loss of weight, due to nausea and vomiting, sleeplessness, depression, irritability, and failure to concentrate. Later changes include degeneration of the nerves and atrophy of the muscles they supply – causing loss of sensation and weakness, particularly in the legs, and loss of memory – and sometimes enlargement of the heart and accumulations of body fluids, see also **beriberi**. Underlying disease, such as **malabsorption**, cancer and vomiting in pregnancy may also cause deficiency.

Thiamin cannot be stored and excesses as pills or tonics are filtered out of the blood stream by the kidneys. Although often prescribed as a tonic in the past, thiamin alone is now thought to be of limited value: a diet needing supplements of thiamin, is also likely to be lacking in other B vitamins and occasionally large doses of thiamin have precipitated other B vitamin deficiencies. A balanced **diet** is a better safeguard of health than vitamin pills and tonics.

Thiamin contents of food

Food		Grams containing an average of 0.9 milligrams
Rich	Cod roe	60
	Wheat germ	70
	Brazil nuts	90
	Fresh peanuts	100
	Roast pork[a]	110
Good	Oatmeal	180
	Fried bacon, braised heart	220
	Kidney, liver	300
	Boiled peas[a] roasted peanuts	370
	Wholemeal bread[b]	450
	White bread[b]	500
Moderate	Eggs	
	Oranges, raisins, avocado pears	
	Boiled potatoes[a]	1–2 kg
	Roast beef	
	Milk	
	Cheddar cheese	2–3 kg
	Boiled cabbage	

[a] – Sulphur dioxide is added to hamburgers, sold uncooked, prepeeled potatoes and chips (used in most restaurants and canteens) sausages and (if declared on the label) dehydrated peas and vegetables. At permitted levels, about half the thiamin in meat may be destroyed (subsequent frying leads to total destruction) and probably all in vegetables.

[b] – At least 20% lost with baking powder or soda. Nearly 90% destruction with excessive quantities (sufficient to yellow the flour)

Threonine

Threonine is an essential **amino acid** needed in the daily diet for replacement (repair) of body **proteins** lost through daily wear and tear, and for new proteins made during growth. All food proteins supply threonine: the estimated daily adult needs are supplied by, for example, the 11 grams of protein in 330 grams (just over ½ pint) of milk. Excesses not needed for new body proteins are converted to glucose and used for energy purposes. The **nitrogen** part is converted to urea, later filtered out of the blood stream by the kidneys.

Tin

Tin is probably an essential **trace element** for animals. If it is also essential for humans, the normal daily intake of 1 to 4 milligrams would be more than adequate. Canned foods and foods wrapped in tin foil contain more than unprocessed foods.

Excess tin in food causes a metallic taste and can be toxic. Legally, foods should not contain more than 250 parts per million (2.5 milligrams per 100 grams of food). Some cans are lined with lacquer to prevent erosion by acid contents. Other foods do not cause erosion in unopened cans, but once in contact with the oxygen in air, tin is rapidly dissolved. Food should not be stored in open cans.

Tomatoes

Tomatoes are native to South America and were introduced to Europe in the 16th century. They are greatly valued for their flavour, colour and versatility in cooking. They also supply appreciable amounts of **vitamin A** and **C** (see table).

Average nutrients in 100 grams (3½ oz) Tomatoes

	fresh	canned		fresh	canned
Energy kilojoules	60	51	Iron milligrams	0.4	0.9
kilocalories	14	12	Copper milligrams	0.1	0.1
Protein grams	0.9	1.1	Zinc milligrams	0.2	0.3
Total fat grams	0	0	Vitamin A micrograms	33–167	50–100
Saturated fat grams	0	0	Vitamin D micrograms	0	–
Polyunsaturated fat grams	0	0	Vitamin C milligrams	10–30	18
			Vitamin E milligrams	1.2	1.2
Cholesterol milligrams	0	0	B vitamins:		
Sugars grams	2.8	2.0	Thiamin (B₁) milligrams	0.06	0.06
Starch grams	0	0	Riboflavin (B₂) milligrams	0.04	0.03
Dietary fibre grams	1.5	0.9	Nicotinic acid milligrams	0.8	0.8
Sodium milligrams	3	29	Pyridoxine (B₆) milligrams	0.11	0.11
Potassium milligrams	290	270	Vitamin B₁₂ micrograms	0	0
Calcium milligrams	13	9	Folic acid micrograms	28	25
Magnesium milligrams	11	11	Pantothenic acid milligrams	0.33	0.20
			Biotin micrograms	1.5	1.5

(–) No information available   (0) Contains zero or trace amounts

Tongue

Tongue is a good source of well-absorbed **iron**, although high in **fat**, mostly saturated. Pickled tongue is high in salt (and therefore **sodium**) and contains the **preservatives nitrate** and **nitrite**.

Average nutrients in 100 grams (3½ oz) Tongue

	sheep	ox		sheep	ox
Energy kilojoules	1197	1216	Iron milligrams	3.4	3.0
kilocalories	289	293	Copper milligrams	–	–
Protein grams	18.2	19.5	Zinc milligrams	–	–
Total fat grams	24.0	23.9	Vitamin A micrograms	0	0
Saturated fat grams	7.8	–	Vitamin D micrograms	0	0
Polyunsaturated fat grams	1.4	–	Vitamin C milligrams	6	2
			Vitamin E milligrams	0.3	0.35
Cholesterol milligrams	270	100	B vitamins:		
Sugars grams	0	0	Thiamin (B₁) milligrams	0.13	0.06
Starch grams	0	0	Riboflavin (B₂) milligrams	0.45	0.29
Dietary fibre grams	0	0	Nicotinic acid milligrams	7.6	8.3
Sodium milligrams	80	1000	Pyridoxine (B₆) milligrams	0.10	0.09
Potassium milligrams	110	150	Vitamin B₁₂ micrograms	7	4
Calcium milligrams	11	31	Folic acid micrograms	4	5
Magnesium milligrams	13	16	Pantothenic acid milligrams	0.8	0.5
			Biotin micrograms	2	3

(–) No information available   (0) Contains zero or trace amounts

Tooth decay and gum disease

Tooth decay (dental caries) is most active up to the age of twenty years. In adults, gum disease is more likely to cause loss of teeth.

Dental caries

The accumulation of bacteria in deposits (plaque) on the teeth is the most widely accepted cause of decay. The bacteria multiply on **carbohydrate** in food, producing **lactic acid** which dissolves out the protective enamel on the tooth. Unless the resultant cavity is filled, bacteria infect the inside of the tooth, causing toothache and eventual loss of the tooth.

Rarely, vitamin deficiencies before teeth erupt result in defective enamel, which is more easily eroded. Once the teeth have erupted they cannot be improved by extra vitamins or a high **calcium** diet. There is an unknown hereditary factor in tooth decay: some people have more resistant tooth enamel than others. Other **trace elements** (vanadium, molybdenum and selenium), besides **fluorine**, in water may affect the resistance of the enamel.

The most effective preventative measure against dental caries is a high standard of mouth hygiene. Teeth should be cleaned at least after breakfast and before bed. If there are no facilities for brushing teeth after other meals, the mouth should be rinsed with water. Frequent use of dental floss is important, especially for faultily aligned teeth which are more difficult to keep clean. There is no necessity for fluorine-containing toothpastes in an area where the water has a good content.

Sucrose (sugar) is thought to be particularly important in dental decay because bacteria manufacture a sticky deposit from it which is necessary for their adherence to the tooth surface. Once bacteria are established on the tooth surface, the acidity at which enamel begins to be dissolved is reached within five minutes of eating sugar. The alkalinity of saliva protects to some extent. Apples, crisp foods and fibrous foods help maintain the health of the gums, but do not always prevent caries.

Very acid foods are capable of dissolving away the enamel and the front teeth may be particularly affected. Acid cola and carbonated drinks are best taken with a straw, and other acid foods – citrus fruits, pickles in vinegar and acid drops – should not be retained in the mouth.

Gum disease

Most adults, even with well cared for mouths, have some gingivitis – the most frequent cause of tooth loss in adult life. It is usually caused by accumulated plaque on the teeth. Bacteria invade the margin between the gum and the tooth, causing inflammation and bleeding. If untreated, ulcers develop and the teeth loosen and fall out or have to be extracted. Frequent effective flossing and tooth brushing – which removes plaque and stimulates the blood supply in the gums – is the most important preventative factor.

Trace elements

Trace elements are **minerals** needed in tiny amounts in the diet for health. They are so called because older methods of analysis could detect only unmeasurable traces in food and living tissues. With modern methods of chemical analysis the needs for trace elements are becoming known more precisely, especially for animals, but accurate estimations of quantities are still lacking.

Eight trace elements are presently known to be essential nutrients for humans: iodine, copper, manganese, cobalt, molybdenum, selenium, chromium and vanadium. Silicon, tin, nickel, arsenic, and fluorine are essential nutrients for animals, and probably humans. Many other elements occur in traces in the body, food and water, but are not thought to be essential for life or health.

Excess quantities of trace elements are poisonous and there is often only a small difference between the quantity needed for health or safety and the quantity which is toxic. Relative excess of some trace elements can cause deficiency of others. The risk of obtaining too little or too much in food is minimised by eating a wide variety of foods in moderation (see **diet**).

Triglycerides

Triglycerides are simple **fats** (sometimes also called neutral fats). Each molecule of triglyceride contains one of **glycerol** and three **fatty acids**. In food, triglycerides always have different fatty acids. The hardness (melting temperature) and other characteristics of a fat are determined by its content of fatty acids.

Triglycerides can be modified in many ways to make **emulsifiers** and stabilisers. The simplest modified fats, superglycerinated fats (E475), contain less than three fatty acids for each molecule of glycerol (these are also formed in **digestion**). Glycerol monostearate, for example, contains one fatty acid (stearic acid) for each molecule of glycerol. Other emulsifiers have organic acids (like tartaric, lactic and acetic acids (E472)) or **sorbitol** substituted for fatty acids, or glycerol (491–495). E473 and 474 have sucrose substituted instead.

Tripe

The lining of the stomach of the ox. It is usually cooked in milk and provides some nutrients – although it has a distinctive taste, difficult for many to enjoy. Most tripe goes into pet food manufacture.

Average nutrients in 100 grams (3½ oz) Tripe (stewed in milk)

Energy kilojoules	418	Iron milligrams	0.7
kilocalories	100	Copper milligrams	0.14
Protein grams	14.8	Zinc milligrams	2.3
Total fat grams	4.5	Vitamin A micrograms	0
Saturated fat grams	2.2	Vitamin D micrograms	0
Polyunsaturated fat grams	0.1	Vitamin C milligrams	3
		Vitamin E milligrams	0.1
Cholesterol milligrams	160	B vitamins:	
Sugars grams	0	Thiamin (B_1) milligrams	0
Starch grams	0	Riboflavin (B_2) milligrams	0.08

Dietary fibre grams	0	Nicotinic acid milligrams	3.2
Sodium milligrams	73	Pyridoxine (B$_6$) milligrams	0.02
Potassium milligrams	100	Vitamin B$_{12}$ micrograms	0
Calcium milligrams	150	Folic acid micrograms	1
Magnesium milligrams	15	Pantothenic acid milligrams	0.2
		Biotin micrograms	2

(–) No information available   (0) Contains zero or trace amounts

Trout

The flesh of trout is rich in **protein**, and it contains some fat and minerals, including **iron** (see table). Sea trout contains more sodium than brown (river) trout, or rainbow trout. No analyses for vitamins are available.

Average nutrients in 100 grams (3½ oz) Trout (steamed)

Energy kilojoules	566	Iron milligrams	1.0
kilocalories	135	Copper milligrams	–
Protein grams	23.5	Zinc milligrams	–
Total fat grams	4.5	Vitamin A micrograms	–
Saturated fat grams	–	Vitamin D micrograms	–
Polyunsaturated fat grams	–	Vitamin C milligrams	0
		Vitamin E milligrams	–
Cholesterol milligrams	80	B vitamins:	
Sugars grams	0	Thiamin (B$_1$) milligrams	–
Starch grams	0	Riboflavin (B$_2$) milligrams	–
Dietary fibre grams	0	Nicotinic acid milligrams	–
Sodium milligrams	88	Pyridoxine (B$_6$) milligrams	–
Potassium milligrams	370	Vitamin B$_{12}$ micrograms	–
Calcium milligrams	36	Folic acid micrograms	–
Magnesium milligrams	31	Pantothenic acid milligrams	–
		Biotin micrograms	–

(–) No information available   (0) Contains zero or trace amounts

Tryptophan

Tryptophan is an essential **amino acid**, needed in the daily diet for the rebuilding (repair) of **proteins** lost through daily wear and tear, and for new proteins made during growth.

Tryptophan is limiting in **maize** protein, but most other food proteins contain adequate amounts. The estimated adult needs are supplied by, for example, the 25 grams of protein in 310 grams (7 large slices) of bread, or the 15 grams of protein in 140 grams (2 large) eggs.

If the diet contains sufficient **pyridoxine** tryptophan is converted to **nicotinic acid** and to serotonin. Serotonin, also called 5-hydroxytryptamine, is a brain regulator (neuro transmitter) and a potent substance causing blood vessels to contract when a blood clot forms. In the brain, serotonin induces sleepiness and sedation. Recent work suggests that large doses of tryptophan raise blood levels of serotonin which, in the absence or lower supplies of other amino acids, enter the brain. High protein meals contain other amino acids which compete for admission to the brain, so that in theory high protein meals should promote wakefulness, whereas high sugar or starch meals, by increasing the amount of tryptophan and therefore serotonin levels, should have a calming effect. This is interesting and may suggest that some carbohydrate before bedtime may help insomniacs – unfortunately blood levels were only noticed to be changed in the morning, and not in the evening. See also **caffeine**.

Tuna

A meaty, fatty **fish**, containing **vitamins D** and **E** and **vitamin B$_6$**. The fat is mostly composed of polyunsaturated **fatty acids**, and grilled fresh tuna can be included in a healthy **diet**. Most tuna is sold canned.

Average nutrients in 100 grams (3½ oz) Tuna (canned)

Energy kilojoules	1202	Iron milligrams	1.1
kilocalories	289	Copper milligrams	0.09
Protein grams	22.8	Zinc milligrams	0.8
Total fat grams	22.0	Vitamin A micrograms	–
Saturated fat grams	3.9	Vitamin D micrograms	5.8
Polyunsaturated fat grams	8.0	Vitamin C milligrams	0
		Vitamin E milligrams	6.3
Cholesterol milligrams	65	B vitamins:	
Sugars grams	0	Thiamin (B$_1$) milligrams	0.04
Starch grams	0	Riboflavin (B$_2$) milligrams	0.11
Dietary fibre grams	0	Nicotinic acid milligrams	17.2
Sodium milligrams	420	Pyridoxine (B$_6$) milligrams	0.44
Potassium milligrams	280	Vitamin B$_{12}$ micrograms	5
Calcium milligrams	7	Folic acid micrograms	15
Magnesium milligrams	28	Pantothenic acid milligrams	0.42
		Biotin micrograms	3

(–) No information available   (0) Contains zero or trace amounts

Turnips

A member of the *Brassica* family (see **cabbage**), mostly grown for the swollen roots. These contain some vitamin C (see table). The leaves of turnips can also be eaten and are a good source of **vitamins A, C** and **E**, and the B vitamins **riboflavin** and **folic acid** (see table).

Average nutrients in 100 grams (3½ oz) Turnips (boiled)

	turnips	turnip tops (leaves)		turnips	turnip tops (leaves)
Energy kilojoules	60	48	Iron milligrams	0.4	3.1
kilocalories	14	11	Copper milligrams	0.04	0.09
Protein grams	0.7	2.7	Zinc milligrams	–	0.4
Total fat grams	0.3	0	Vitamin A micrograms	0	667–2000
Saturated fat grams	0	0	Vitamin D micrograms	0	0
Polyunsaturated fat grams	0.2	0	Vitamin C milligrams	8–25	20–70
			Vitamin E milligrams	0	1.0
Cholesterol milligrams	0	0	B vitamins:		
Sugars grams	2.3	0	Thiamin (B$_1$) milligrams	0.03	0.06

	turnips	turnip tops (leaves)			turnips	turnip tops (leaves)
Starch grams	0	0.1	Riboflavin (B$_2$) milligrams	0.04	0.20
Dietary fibre grams	2.2	3.9	Nicotinic acid milligrams	0.6	0.9
Sodium milligrams	28	7	Pyridoxine (B$_6$) milligrams	0.06	0.16
Potassium milligrams	160	78	Vitamin B$_{12}$ micrograms	0	0
Calcium milligrams	55	98	Folic acid micrograms	10	110
Magnesium milligrams	7	10	Pantothenic acid milligrams	0.14	0.30
			Biotin micrograms	0	0.4

(–) No information available   (0) Contains zero or trace amounts

Turkey

One of the largest poultry birds. Weights varying from 6 to 40 lb. Turkey is low in fat, and supplies some well absorbed **iron** and **zinc** (more in dark meat than white). The low fat content of turkey makes it difficult to keep succulent during roasting; it helps to roast the bird for part of the time on its breast.

Average nutrients in 100 grams (3½ oz) Turkey (roast)

Energy kilojoules	590	Iron milligrams	0.9
kilocalories	140	Copper milligrams	0.15
Protein grams	28.8	Zinc milligrams	2.4
Total fat grams	2.7	Vitamin A micrograms	0
Saturated fat grams	1.0	Vitamin D micrograms	0
Polyunsaturated fat grams	0.9	Vitamin C milligrams	0
		Vitamin E milligrams	0
Cholesterol milligrams	80	B vitamins:	
Sugars grams	0	Thiamin (B$_1$) milligrams	0.07
Starch grams	0	Riboflavin (B$_2$) milligrams	0.21
Dietary fibre grams	0	Nicotinic acid milligrams	13.9
Sodium milligrams	57	Pyridoxine (B$_6$) milligrams	0.32
Potassium milligrams	310	Vitamin B$_{12}$ micrograms	2
Calcium milligrams	9	Folic acid micrograms	15
Magnesium milligrams	27	Pantothenic acid milligrams	0.8
		Biotin micrograms	2

(–) No information available   (0) Contains zero or trace amounts

Tyrosine

Tyrosine is an **amino acid** made in the body from phenylalanine. It is required for the formation of new **proteins** needed for growth and repair and is the precursor of some hormones (like adrenalin and the thyroid hormones) and the brown pigment melanin formed in hair, eyes and tanned skin. Tyrosine is found in all food proteins and reduces the requirement of phenylalanine. Excess quantities are converted to **glucose** or **fat** and used for **energy**: the **nitrogen** part is converted to urea, later filtered out of the blood stream by the kidneys.

High levels of tyrosine – due to a temporary insufficiency of an **enzyme** necessary for its normal **metabolism** – sometimes accumulate in the blood stream of newborn babies. The disorder is made worse by lack of vitamin C (necessary for the action of the enzyme) and artificial milk (cows' milk contains more phenylalanine and tyrosine than breast milk). This is one important reason for giving Vitamin C supplements, as orange juice or welfare vitamin drops. Permanent deficiency of the enzyme – hypertyrosinaemia, a rare **inborn error of metabolism** – can cause liver and kidney failure unless treated with a synthetic diet low in phenylalanine and tyrosine.

Foods containing tyramine, a derivative of tyrosine, must be avoided when certain tranquilisers are taken – see **cheese**.

Ulcers (peptic) – see also **digestion**

Ulcers are open sores in the walls of the digestive system in contact with digestive (peptic) juices secreted by the stomach. They usually occur in the duodenum, which connects the stomach to the small intestine, sometimes in the stomach itself (gastric ulcers) and rarely at the bottom of the oesophagus.

Peptic juices contain two potent substances – hydrochloric acid and pepsin, a protein splitting **enzyme** – and it is surprising that ulcers do not occur more commonly. Normally however the walls of the stomach and duodenum are resistant to erosion: a sticky mucous substance is also secreted and probably acts as a barrier. The underlying cause is unknown but, in duodenal ulcers, worry, stress and overwork are important predisposing factors. There is also a familial tendency and men, and people in blood group O, are more commonly affected. Gastric ulcers are thought to occur less frequently now: this decrease may reflect improvements in the general standard of nutrition over the past 30 years.

Pain – when acid comes into contact with the raw surface – from gastic ulcers is usually felt shortly after eating, and from duodenal ulcers when the stomach is empty. The pain is relieved by milk or other antacids (alkalis that neutralise the acid in the stomach) and a bland diet (see **dyspepsia**). Most ulcers heal spontaneously, but rest in bed and some drugs accelerate healing. Complicated dietary regimes are now thought to have little effect on healing, though they are occasionally necessary as part of hospital treatment if an ulcer haemorrhages by penetrating a blood vessel. Those prone to ulcers should however avoid irritants like smoking, **caffeine** and **alcohol** in excess (particularly when no food is eaten) and highly spiced and fried foods. Rest, both before and after small meals, spaced regularly through the day, is also advisable.

Ulcers that perforate or do not heal are surgically removed, which sometimes results in **malabsorption**.

Urticaria

An itchy rash, sometimes with swelling of the lips, face, tongue and occasionally mouth and throat. It is a common symptom of **allergy** to food, drugs, pollen etc., but there are other causes, for example exercise, **histamine** in food, and infections.

The protein foods most commonly involved in allergic urticaria are nuts, fish and eggs. In rare cases, fruit, peas, beans, garlic and mushrooms may be responsible. Attacks may also be provoked by **salicylates** and benzoic acid (see **preservatives**) in people allergic to aspirin, and **colours** such as annatto, a natural colouring used in butter. People allergic to yeast (candida) may have to avoid a wide selection of foods including bread, cheese and wine.

Valine

Valine is an essential **amino acid** needed in the daily diet for the rebuilding (repair) of body **proteins** lost through daily wear and tear, and for new proteins formed during growth. It is found in all food proteins: the estimated daily adult needs are supplied by, for example, the 14 grams of protein in 50 grams (nearly 2 oz) of roast beef. Excesses eaten, and not needed for growth and repair, are converted to glucose and used for energy purposes. The nitrogen part is converted to urea, later filtered out of the blood stream by the kidneys.

Valine is restricted in the treatment of maple syrup urine diseases, see **isoleucine**.

Vanadium

Vanadium is a **trace element** only recently found to be an essential nutrient for some animals and thought to be essential for man, although food contents and normal intakes are uncertain. Supplements of vanadium affect blood **lipids** and the rate of dental decay in animals, but the relevance of these findings to human **heart disease** and dental decay is unknown.

Excess vanadium in fumes or dust from certain industrial processes can be harmful but there is little risk of toxic levels in food.

Veal

This is not food for the squeamish, given some current methods of production. It is the flesh of the young calf, not more than three months old, fed exclusively on milk or other foods low in iron. It contains about half the iron content of beef.

Average nutrients in 100 grams (3½ oz) Veal (lean roast fillet)

Energy kilojoules	963	Iron milligrams	1.6
kilocalories	230	Copper milligrams	–
Protein grams	31.6	Zinc milligrams	–
Total fat grams	11.5	Vitamin A micrograms	0
Saturated fat grams	4.8	Vitamin D micrograms	0
Polyunsaturated fat grams	0.5	Vitamin C milligrams	0
		Vitamin E milligrams	–
Cholesterol milligrams	–	B vitamins:	
Sugars grams	0	Thiamin (B_1) milligrams	0.06
Starch grams	0	Riboflavin (B_2) milligrams	0.27
Dietary fibre grams	0	Nicotinic acid milligrams	13.7
Sodium milligrams	97	Pyridoxine (B_6) milligrams	0.32
Potassium milligrams	430	Vitamin B_{12} micrograms	1
Calcium milligrams	14	Folic acid micrograms	4
Magnesium milligrams	28	Pantothenic acid milligrams	0.5
		Biotin micrograms	0

(–) No information available   (0) Contains zero or trace amounts

Vegetables – see also **potatoes**

Large helpings of fresh vegetables are a vital part of a healthy **diet**. They are particularly important for their content of two B vitamins, **folic acid** and **riboflavin**, and for **vitamin A** (as carotene) and **vitamin C**.

Dark green vegetables such as **broccoli, Brussels sprouts, cabbage, endive, spring greens, peas, beans, lettuce, spinach, turnip** tops, **peppers** and **watercress** are a rich or very good source of all four nutrients. **Carrots** are rich in vitamin A, and **mushrooms** in riboflavin. Vitamins C and folic acid are however easily lost by poor cooking practices. Steaming or microwave cooking conserve the most and the table below shows how best to conserve these nutrients.

Vegetables also supply **minerals** especially **potassium** and **trace elements**, if they are not overcooked. They also contain small amounts of **protein**, and **vitamin E** and **fibre**, mostly as **pectin** and **cellulose**. Although cooking does not reduce fibre content appreciably, cellulose is softened and pectin partially degraded so that nutrients inside cells become more accessible for digestion. Overcooked vegetables are however unpleasant to eat and will have lost most of their vitamin C and folic acid.

Many studies have shown that people who eat plenty of vegetables and fruit are at less risk of some types of **cancer** and possibly **stroke**. The reason for this is unknown but vegetables contain a wide variety of natural substances, including the **bioflavonoids** and **essential fatty acids**, as well as vitamin C, riboflavin, folic acid and **carotene** which are felt to be particularly important. They are also low in **energy** and people who put plenty of vegetables on their plate (but without **fat**) are likely to be less prone to **obesity**.

Salads are not superior to properly cooked vegetables in their content of nutrients, although because they are eaten raw there is less chance of total destruction – as can happen in canteen cooked food. Vitamin C and folic acid decrease immediately vegetables are sliced, chopped and dressed, and wilted lettuce leaves are likely to contain none. Bright green or soft boiled vegetables (indicating that bicarbonate of soda has been used) are also likely to contain none.

Most of the information about the effect of processing on vitamin contents of vegetables relates to vitamin C, partly because the importance of folic acid has been recognised comparatively recently, and it is difficult to analyse. However, losses of folic acid are proportional to those of vitamin C.

Conservation of folic acid and vitamin C

Agents and processes that destroy folic acid and vitamin C	To conserve folic acid and vitamin C in food
Loss during storage	Use fresh foods when possible. Keep foods in a cool dark place. Do not allow to wilt.
Waste during preparation	Prepare immediately prior to cooking

Heat from	(a) cooking	Steam or microwave, or boil cooking water before putting vegetables in the pan. Do not cook whole vegetables - (slice immediately before cooking) because small pieces take less time to cook. Cook for the shortest possible time; vegetables should have 'bite' after cooking.
	(b) keeping hot	Serve vegetables immediately they are cooked.
Leaching into water during	(a) cooking	Steam or microwave, or use the minimum amount of water for cooking.
	(b) washing	Use as little water as possible and do not allow to soak. Wash intact leaves quickly.
Enzyme released from damaged cells after frost, bruising, pounding or chopping		Enzyme inactivated at 65°C. Slice and peel vegetables with a sharp knife, then drop into boiling (100°C) water immediately.
Oxygen in air		Do not leave vegetables to stand or soak. Boil water to expel air before putting vegetables in to cook. Use a lid on the pan to keep air out. Do not store cooked vegetables or liquor – even in a refrigerator.
Alkali in bicarbonate of soda		Do not use. Lemon juice and vinegar are acids and will help to preserve vitamin C.
Iron from rusty implements		Do not use.
Copper from copper pans		Do not use.

Storage of fresh vegetables

Vitamin C begins to decline as soon as vegetables are harvested. Any damage, like wilting or bruising destroys it, and the losses are accelerated in warm temperatures. Greens can lose up to 50%, beans 20% in a day when kept at room temperature. Losses are minimal when whole vegetables are kept covered in a cool place, preferably in the salad drawer of a refrigerator, but there can be severe losses if vegetables are allowed to be frost bitten.

Frozen vegetables

Before processing all vegetables are blanched (dipped in hot water to reduce bacterial contamination and to inactivate enzymes that would otherwise cause loss of vitamin C and flavour) and this causes losses of 10 to 30% of vitamin C. However, vegetables are blanched when their vitamin content is at a maximum and blanching losses may be less than those encountered in transport and storage in shops.

Freezing does not affect vitamin C, but it gradually declines during storage. There is hardly any loss at very low temperatures (−30°C) but at normal deep freeze temperatures (−18°C), up to 30% can be lost over a year. If they are not thawed before cooking, cooked frozen peas may contain as much vitamin C as cooked fresh peas bought from a shop: peas are frozen immediately after harvesting when their vitamin C content is at its highest and are cooked for a shorter time than fresh peas, so less vitamin C is lost. Frozen peas lose little vitamin C in a well maintained deep freeze (about 10% over a year), but there can be considerable losses at higher temperatures (25% in four months, and 80% in a year, in a freezing compartment of a refrigerator). Finely chopped foods – like spinach – will lose more (up to 50%). There are severe losses at higher temperatures (at −12°C, 50% can be lost in four months). Vegetables should never be thawed before cooking and must always be cooked according to the manufacturers' instructions, otherwise there will be further losses: vegetables that have been allowed to defrost (shown by ice crystals in the pack) should be rejected. Vitamin A is stable to freezing, but vitamin E may decline during storage.

Canned vegetables

Canned vegetables have to be sterilised by heat, causing further loss of vitamin C. Overall, most canned vegetables lose between 40 and 60%, but acid tomatoes retain most of the vitamin. Canned foods should be stored in cool (10 to 15°C) conditions, when they retain most of their vitamin C. Losses are accelerated in warm temperatures – up to 15% can be lost over a year when cans are stored at 27°C. Canned vegetables must be reheated according to manufacturers' instructions and must not be stored in open containers, otherwise all vitamin C may be lost. There may be severe losses of vitamin E on canning but vitamin A is stable. Although there are losses of vitamin C in canning, canned *garden* peas require little cooking (and are also canned immediately after harvesting): cooked canned garden peas may contain only slightly less vitamin C than cooked fresh bought peas. Canned *processed* peas however are dried before canning and may contain no vitamin C. About half the thiamin is destroyed during canning, but there are no losses of vitamin A. Little vitamin C is lost when canned peas are stored at room temperature, but 20% can be lost over a year when the cans are kept in a hot (80°F) store cupboard.

Dehydrated vegetables

Dehydrated vegetables that have retained their colour will probably have retained half their vitamin C, but losses are very variable. Sulphur dioxide (a **preservative** declared on **labels**) preserves vitamin C, but destroys thiamin. Dehydrated vegetables kept cool (10°C) lose little vitamin C, but there can be severe losses at higher temperatures (up to 50% in four months at 30°C). Carrots lose 20 to 40% of vitamin A when dehydrated.

Other ways of preserving vegetables

Other methods of preserving vegetables are pickling and fermenting. Sauerkraut, preserved in salt and **lactic acid** formed by bacterial action, is a very variable source of vitamin C, but most samples can be expected to contain half the vitamin C of properly cooked cabbage. Other pickles are preserved in salt and **vinegar**, sometimes with added lactic or acetic acids, and the permitted preservatives sulphur dioxide or benzoic acid. Thick pickles are a mixture of vegetables, spices, sugar, salt and vinegar, thickened with **edible gum** or starch. They can be coloured, for example brown with caramel, yellow with tartrazine. Pickles are of little nutritional value in themselves, but they can add variety and flavour to, for example, sandwiches spread with less margarine or butter to reduce the fat contents of diets.

Vegetarianism

Vegetarianism is avoidance of meat and fish, but not dairy products or, usually, eggs.

Nuts, pulses and dairy products supply the same range of essential **nutrients** as meat and fish and most vegetarians are able to eat a balanced **diet**. In fact, several studies have shown that vegetarians tend to be less **obese**, have a lower blood **cholesterol**, and are thought to be less susceptible to **heart disease**. They may also be less prone to **osteoporosis**. However, meat and fish are the best sources of **iron** and vegetarian diets may supply too little for vegetarian women, children and adolescents without careful planning to include for example **soya** products. Cheese is a good source of well absorbed **zinc**.

Vegetarians are sometimes advised to plan their menus so that the **amino acids** complement each other. This is probably unnecessary because foods such as peas, lentils, beans and nuts are sufficiently good sources of protein to supply enough essential amino acids. Soya is a particularly good value protein, its biological value approaching that of cheese. Nevertheless, the table below shows limiting amino acids for various foods. Peanuts for example would be a good supplementary alternative to peas with rice.

Vegan diets, which exclude all animal products, may be low in **vitamin B_{12}** and incur a greater risk of pernicious **anaemia**.

Qualities of various proteins

Protein	Limiting amino acid	% Adequacy[a] compared with reference protein[b]	Biological tests[c]
Egg	None	100	94
Cod	None	100	83
Milk, cows'	S aa[d]	95	82
Beef	None	100	70
Cheese	S aa	98	70
Soya beans	S aa	74	65
Rice, polished	Lysine	67	59
Wheat, whole	Lysine	53	48
Maize	Lysine	49	52
Peas	S aa	57	50
Potatoes	S aa	54	60
Peanuts	S aa	65	47
Gelatine	Tryptophan	0	2

a   or score, calculated from *Amino Acid Contents of Foods and Biological Data on Proteins*, FAO 1970
b   using new scoring pattern – FAO/WHO 1973, *Energy and Protein Requirements*, WHO Tech. Rep. Ser. 522
c   Net Protein Utilisation, taken from reference a. Values for Biological Value (which do not take into account undigested protein) are slightly higher
d   Sulphur amino acids – methionine and cysteine.

Venison

A game meat thought to have been hunted by man as early as 18,000 BC. It is a low **fat** meat, rich in **iron** and containing good amounts of **vitamin B₁**.

Average nutrients in 100 grams (3½ oz) Venison (roast)

Energy kilojoules	832	Iron milligrams	7.8
kilocalories	198	Copper milligrams	–
Protein grams	35.0	Zinc milligrams	–
Total fat grams	6.4	Vitamin A micrograms	–
Saturated fat grams	–	Vitamin D micrograms	–
Polyunsaturated fat grams	–	Vitamin C milligrams	0
		Vitamin E milligrams	–
Cholesterol milligrams	–	B vitamins:	
Sugars grams	0	Thiamin (B₁) milligrams	0.22
Starch grams	0	Riboflavin (B₂) milligrams	–
Dietary fibre grams	0	Nicotinic acid milligrams	–
Sodium milligrams	86	Pyridoxine (B₆) milligrams	–
Potassium milligrams	360	Vitamin B₁₂ micrograms	–
Calcium milligrams	29	Folic acid micrograms	–
Magnesium milligrams	33	Pantothenic acid milligrams	–
		Biotin micrograms	–

(–) No information available   (0) Contains zero or trace amounts

Vine leaves

Vine leaves stuffed with rice and lamb are well known as dolmades in Greek and Turkish cookery. They can also be used to give an unusual flavour when partridges are poached, wrapped in vine leaves. Most vine leaves available are sold canned (see table) and contain a lot of salt, as **sodium**. Vine leaves, like other green vegetables, are also good sources of **vitamin A** and B₂ (**riboflavin**).

Average nutrients in 100 grams (3½ oz) Vine leaves (canned)

Energy kilojoules	64	Iron milligrams	2.3
kilocalories	15	Copper milligrams	1.6
Protein grams	3.6	Zinc milligrams	0.3
Total fat grams	–	Vitamin A micrograms	383
Saturated fat grams	–	Vitamin D micrograms	0
Polyunsaturated fat grams	–	Vitamin C milligrams	15
		Vitamin E milligrams	–
Cholesterol milligrams	0	B vitamins:	
Sugars grams	0.2	Thiamin (B₁) milligrams	0.08
Starch grams	0	Riboflavin (B₂) milligrams	0.24
Dietary fibre grams	5.0	Nicotinic acid milligrams	–
Sodium milligrams	2210	Pyridoxine (B₆) milligrams	–
Potassium milligrams	45	Vitamin B₁₂ micrograms	0
Calcium milligrams	391	Folic acid micrograms	–
Magnesium milligrams	41	Pantothenic acid milligrams	–
		Biotin micrograms	–

(–) No information available   (0) Contains zero or trace amounts

Vinegar

Vinegar contains **acetic acid**, a strong acid which is an effective **preservative**, formed from alcohol by bacteria. Vinegar is made from malted barley (malt vinegar); grape juice or wine (wine vinegar); cider; or spirits. Colourless vinegars are usually distilled from malt vinegar. Vinegar should not contain less than 4% acetic acid and may contain caramel, to colour brown, and sulphur dioxide (a preservative). Non-fermented vinegars, made from synthetic acid, must be called 'non brewed condiment'.

Vinegar has no slimming properties, but it contains virtually no **energy** and is therefore permitted freely in slimming diets. Cider, wine and malt vinegars contain traces of B vitamins and minerals.

Vitamins

The vitamins are a diverse organic group of substances (that are made by bacteria, plants or animals) needed for growth and **metabolism** and therefore health. They cannot be made in the human body in sufficient amounts to satisfy needs, and must be supplied preformed in the **diet**.

Diseases such as **scurvy, beriberi, pellagra** and **rickets** are ancient ones. Scurvy was feared for centuries at sea, where it inflicted more deaths than all other causes combined, including shipwreck and battle. Together with beriberi, scurvy was a contributory factor to the tragic outcomes of many campaigns and expeditions, including Scott's last journey to Antarctica. It had been suspected for some time that these diseases had something to do with diet, but according to Sharman,[1] Funk was the first person to group them all together and postulate that they all had a common cause, namely a deficiency of some constituents in the diet. In 1912, in coining the term 'vital amine' or 'vitamine' Funk saw that 'it was necessary for me to choose a name that would sound well and serve as a catchword' even though he was 'well aware that these substances might later prove not to be of an amine nature'.

In the same year, F.G. Hopkins introduced the concept of 'accessory food factors' necessary to support growth, showing that rats given 'an astonishingly small amount' of milk would thrive on artifical diets that would otherwise cause loss of weight. Later, when it was shown that there were at least two 'growth factors', water soluble B and fat soluble A, and that factor B behaved as though it contained Funk's anti-beriberi vitamine, it was realised that the 'accessory food factors' necessary for growth, and the 'vitamines' necessary to cure deficiency diseases were in fact the same. The 'e' of vitamines was dropped in 1920.

Since that time, humans have been shown to require fifteen different vitamins which have different functions and chemical structures and occur in different foods (see table). Requirements vary from a few micrograms to several milligrams per day, and differ between species. Man for example is one of the few known to lack the necessary **enzymes** to synthesise vitamin C from **glucose**. **Para amino benzoic acid, inositol**, and **lipoic acid** are essential vitamins for micro-organisms and some animals but have not been shown to be essential for man. **Choline** and **carnitine** are also essential for some animals and micro-organisms but are usually synthesised from other materials in humans, although deficiency may occur on rare occasions when these are in short supply. The **bioflavonoids** (including rutin) are not proven essential nutrients for microorganisms, animals or man.

Vitamins are sometimes divided into fat soluble (A, D, E and K) and water soluble (B and C) groups. Although vitamins A and D were first isolated from dairy (fatty) foods, the division is largely of historical interest: E and K occur in fruits and vegetables. However, fat soluble vitamins are more stable to cooking and processing than vitamins B and C. Water soluble vitamins leach out of foods into cooking water and most are readily destroyed by heat. They are consequently more vulnerable to cooking and processing.

Vitamins were initially lettered from A to P as they were identified, but F, G, H, L, M and P were later found not to be vitamins or to be misidentifications of substances that had previously been discovered. Similarly only four B complex vitamins are still numbered. Vitamin B_{12} was the last vitamin to be isolated in 1948.

[1] I. M. Sharman, *Endeavour* 1, 97-102

Vitamins known to be essential for humans:

Vitamin	Chemical name	Discussed under
A	Retinol and carotene	Vitamin A
B	(Eight different)	See vitamin B complex
C	Ascorbic acid	Vitamin C
D	Cholecalciferol and ergocalciferol	Vitamin D
E	Tocopherol and tocotrienol	Vitamin E
K	Phylloquinone and menaquinone	Vitamin K

Vitamin A – chemical name, retinol

Vitamin A maintains the health of the skin; is necessary for colour and night vision; and is probably involved in the senses of taste and balance.

Liver is the richest source of vitamin A. Other good sources are **margarine, eels, eggs, butter** and **cheese**; **milk** and **cream** contain slightly more in summer than winter. **Carrots**, and dark green **vegetables** are also good sources: they contain **carotene**, a precursor of vitamin A. **Salmon, herring** and **mackerel** also contain vitamin A.

Cereals, nuts, meat, white fish, white vegetables and fruits, oils (except red palm oil) and white fats contain virtually no vitamin A. Fish liver oils, which used to be used as dietary supplements are very rich sources.

The daily adult **recommended intake** for vitamin A (more than twice the average minimum needs to allow for individual variation) is 750 micrograms. The table on page 311 shows portions of foods that will meet the adult daily allowance. Women need more throughout breast feeding to ensure adequate supplies for the growing child, and children need more in proportion to their weight than adults, to allow for growth (see Appendix 1). The average British diet supplies more than the average recommended allowance – 1300 micrograms in 1983.

Vitamin A is fairly stable to heat, and does not leach out of foods cooked in water. There are minimal losses in cooking and processing, but the vitamin is sensitive to light and oxygen, and is destroyed by rancid fats. **Antioxidants** added to most fats prevent rancidity and loss of vitamin A, but fish liver oils left in clear glass bottles are likely to be less potent than those kept in dark glass. See also carotene. Retinol is sometimes called vitamin A_1 to distinguish it from another form, vitamin A_2 (dehydroretinol), which has only half the potency of retinol and is rarely eaten (it is found in the liver of some fresh water fish).

Average portion of foods supplying the recommended adult daily intake of vitamin A

	Food	Portion supplying an average of 750 microgram equivalents of vitamin A
Rich sources	Liver, ox	5 grams (⅙ oz)
	calves	5 grams (⅙ oz)
	lamb	5 grams (⅙ oz)
	chicken	10 grams (⅓ oz)
	pig	10 grams (⅓ oz)
	Old carrots	40 grams (1⅓ oz)
	Eels[a]	60 grams (2 oz)
	New carrots, spinach, butter, margarine	75 grams (2½ oz)
Good sources	Cheddar cheese, double cream, broccoli	180 grams (6 oz)
	Eggs	250 grams (4 standard)
Moderate sources	Tinned apricots	450 grams (1 lb)
	Milk	2000 grams (3½ pints)
	Herring	1650 grams (3½ lb)

a – Based on an average content of 1200 micrograms per 100 grams, but may vary from 250 to 2500 micrograms

Adults eating the recommended intake have usually accumulated about 150,000 micrograms of vitamin A, of which 90% is stored in the liver. In the eye, vitamin A is attached to a protein in the cells of the retina (light sensitive part) responsible for perceiving dim and red or green light. Light slightly alters the structure of the vitamin A molecule, stimulating nerve receptors in the cells. An impulse is transmitted to the brain, which registers light. The vitamin may act in a similar way in other sense organs responsible for smell, taste and balance. One of the first symptoms of vitamin A deficiency is an inability to see in dim light (night blindness) but there are many other causes – including anxiety – which are not affected by vitamin A. The eye contains less than 10 micrograms of vitamin A, and this role is subsidiary to the remaining 15,000 micrograms found in the rest of the body, excluding the liver.

By an as yet unknown mechanism vitamin A is involved in the synthesis of proteins which are constituents of membranes and have a key role in many biological processes, including the growth, communication and adhesion of cells. In deficiency, skin and other cells lining many internal surfaces (including the trachea, bronchus, vagina and the lubricating skin and tear ducts) lose their specialised function and proliferate. These 'linings' (epithelial tissues) are the body's main defence against infection, and this property of vitamin A to reinforce the proper functioning of cells may be important in avoiding **cancer** (see below). More immediately, however, in the absence of vitamin A, the epithelial cells of the tear ducts become hard and flake off, blocking the ducts, with eventual infection, scarring, and permanent blindness. Worldwide, the number of children with diseases of the eye attributable to vitamin A deficiency is estimated to be 1 million and 30 to 50% of them will lose their sight.

In animals deficient in vitamin A the bronchial tubes become blocked with cells from the lining of the tubes, causing broncho-pneumonia. Animals also appear to need vitamin A for reproduction, the development of sound teeth and prevention of some types of kidney stones but the relevance of these findings to human health is uncertain. In humans fed a vitamin A deficient diet the skin becomes dry and may develop a 'toad skin' appearance but permanent goose-flesh (folliculosis) often seen in well nourished people is not due to vitamin A deficiency. Night blindness and other symptoms of vitamin A deficiency only occur when the liver stores are exhausted. Except in some medical conditions, like **malabsorption**, people living in prosperous communities have stores sufficient to last for several months or years.

Vitamin A is toxic and dangerous in excess. Except under medical advice, no more than one supplement shown in the table below should be taken each day.

Over dosage (when 100 times or more the recommended allowance is given) results in poor appetite, loss of hair, headache and peeling itching skin. The symptoms disappear when the vitamin is stopped, but in children excessive vitamin A may cause permanent deformities of bones. Intoxication never arises from diet alone (unless polar bear, whale, or shark liver is eaten – polar bear liver contains 60,000 micrograms per 10 grams) but teaspoons of halibut oil and vitamin pills have caused poisoning in children. The death of a man from liver failure in 1974 caused by a daily intake of 2,000,000 micrograms of vitamin A was given wide publicity.

Supplements of vitamin A

Supplement	Dose	Vitamin A content in micrograms
Cod liver oil BP	1 teaspoon	900
Halibut liver oil BP	1 drop	900
Malt with cod liver oil	60 grams (1 dessertspoon)	1350
Welfare vitamin drops for babies	7 drops	300
Haliborange capsules	1 capsule	750
Multivite tablets[a]	1 tablet	700
Welfare mothers' vitamin tablets	1 tablet	1200

[a] Others vary; vitamin potencies listed on box (100 i.u.s = 30 micrograms).

Vitamin A and cancer

Vitamin A is felt to be important in cancer for a number of reasons. Animals fed a diet containing no vitamin A develop changes in the epithelial cells which resemble changes in cancerous cells. In animals given known carcinogens, vitamin A appears to protect against tumours in the epithelial cells of the mouth, lung, skin, bladder, and large bowel. In humans living in prosperous communities, it is difficult to eat a diet that will provoke deficiency outright and consequently liver stores are comparatively high. Nevertheless, blood levels of vitamin A have been found to be lower in patients who later develop cancer, including lung cancer. Cancer patients also report eating less vitamin A containing foods than normal healthy controls. These findings are difficult to explain because, as vitamin A is toxic, most of the dietary supply has to be stored in the liver so that blood levels are held relatively constant, except when the stores are exhausted and night blindness develops. One possibility, certainly for the diet findings, is that carotene is the protective factor, rather than vitamin A, see **carotene**.

As a consequence of these findings, non toxic vitamin A compounds and carotene are undergoing trials to see if they can be useful in the treatment of cancer, or precancerous conditions, or in preventing it. Meanwhile, for this and other reasons, good helpings of vegetables are important for a healthy **diet**.

Vitamin B complex

These vitamins all occur in yeast, cereal germ and liver (except vitamin B_{12} which is mostly found in animal foods), but also in varying amounts in other foods including meat. Ten are known to be essential nutrients for human health (see table below) and all have different chemical structures and different, though related, functions in the body.

B complex vitamins known to be essential nutrients
for humans
– see individual entries

Thiamin (B_1)	Folic acid
Riboflavin (B_2)	Biotin
Pyridoxine (B_6)	Pantothenic acid
Vitamin B_{12}	Choline
Nicotinic acid	Carnitine

Originally the germ of cereals was thought to contain only one vitamin – the anti-beriberi vitamin or vitamin B. Others were later discovered and numbered vitamins B_2 to vitamin B_{15}. However, some were later found not to be vitamins or had already been discovered. Consequently only four B complex vitamins are still numbered – B_1 thiamin, B_2 riboflavin, B_6 pyridoxine, and vitamin B_{12}.

Very large supplements of B vitamins are often promoted by enthusiasts on the basis that more can only do good, and the excess of needs are harmlessly eliminated. This has turned out not to be true, certainly in the case of pyridoxine. A prudent **diet** is a safer way of safeguarding health than unnaturally high doses of vitamins.

Vitamin B$_{12}$ – group name for several forms of the vitamin, including cyanocobalamin and hydroxycobalamin

Part of the **vitamin B complex** necessary for protection against pernicious **anaemia**. It is plentifully supplied in animal foods, but almost entirely absent from plants: vegans (who eat no animal foods) are likely to become deficient, but most vegans supplement their diet with vitamin B$_{12}$. There are other medical causes of pernicious anaemia.

Although liver is the richest source, all animal foods – heart, kidney, fatty fish, shell fish, meat, cheese, white fish, eggs and milk – supply vitamin B$_{12}$. Most British diets supply at least 4 micrograms each day, which is probably more than double the adult requirement. The table on page 315 shows vitamin B$_{12}$ contents of non-flesh foods; eggs, cheese and milk are quite good sources; only 2 eggs, just over 1 pint of milk, or about 150 grams (5 oz) cheese supplying 2 micrograms. Other non-meat foods contain vitamin B$_{12}$, such as beer, Marmite and comfrey but in insufficient amounts to meet requirements without severe risks to health. Comfrey contains liver carcinogens for example and 400 grams would have to be eaten to obtain 2 micrograms.

Vitamin B$_{12}$ is fairly stable to heat, but, like other B vitamins, leaches out of foods cooked in water. Up to half can be lost when meat is cooked, but little is known of the losses incurred in food processing.

During **digestion** vitamin B$_{12}$ is transferred from the small intestine into the blood stream. Intrinsic factor – a substance made in the lining of the stomach – is essential for adequate absorption of the vitamin. Once in the blood stream, the vitamin is stored in the liver or taken up by cells and converted to co**Enzymes** involved, with **folic acid**, in the replication of cells during division. Very active cells, continuously dividing, need more than others. The vitamin is also needed for growth and to maintain the integrity of the insulating (myelin) sheath of nerves, and possibly the reproductive system. Supplements are particularly important for breast feeding or pregnant vegan mothers, in order to ensure the needs of the growing child.

Otherwise, liver stores tide the body over when insufficient vitamin B$_{12}$ is absorbed from food. Most people have stores to last for at least two years, but if they are eventually exhausted, blood levels fall and pernicious **anaemia** develops. The bone marrow produces fewer blood cells and they are immature. The disease causes pallor and tiredness, the tongue becomes bright red and occasionally diarrhoea develops. More seriously, nerves lose their myelin sheath and degenerate, causing a variety of symptoms, including mental disturbance and spasticity. Folic acid – plentifully supplied in vegan diets – can mask the anaemia but not prevent gradual degeneration of the nervous system which is sometimes irreversibly damaged.

Pernicious anaemia mostly develops in middle age, probably as a result of an inherited defect in the immune system. No intrinsic factor is formed and in its absence, vitamin B$_{12}$ cannot be absorbed into the blood stream. Capacity to absorb the vitamin may also be lost following surgery (removal of parts of the stomach or small bowel); infections (fish tape worm or bacteria in the small intestine sequester the vitamin); and some drug treatments. The disease used to be fatal but is now treated with injections of vitamin B_{12} (formerly raw liver) which cause a remarkable improvement in well being.

Vitamin B_{12} content of some foods

Food	Micrograms vitamin B_{12} per 100 grams food
Eggs, free range	2.9
Breakfast cereals with added vitamin B_{12}[1]	1.7–2.5
Cheese	1.2–1.5
Milk	0.3
Yogurt	0
Strong ale (Barley wine)	0.4
Other beers	0.1–0.2
Marmite	0.5
Comfrey leaves [2]	0.5
Comfrey tea [2]	0.3

[1] Kellogg's Corn Flakes, Frosties, Special K and Start
[2] Briggs, D.R. et al. *J. Plant Foods* (1983) **5**, 143–147.

Vitamin C - chemical name **ascorbic acid**

Small amounts of vitamin C in the diet are essential to allow growth in children and to protect against the deficiency disease **scurvy**. Requirements are increased during recovery from surgery or severe accidents, but it is controversial whether large intakes are otherwise conducive to improved health and resistance to infection.

Fruits and **vegetables** supply almost all the vitamin C in the diet. Cereals, eggs, fats, and most dairy foods, fish, nuts and meat contain none. Exceptions are liver, kidney, fresh fish roe, some oysters, unripe walnuts and some cured meats (like tinned ham) which have ascorbic acid added during curing. **Milk** and freshly killed meat contain a little, but it quickly disappears during storage. In the average British diet, nearly half of the total intake is derived from vegetables and potatoes, and half from fruit, especially **fruit juices**.

Of the fruits, citrus are the most reliable source of vitamin C, followed by berries. Other rich sources are blackcurrant and rosehip syrups. Apples, plums, peaches and pears contain little; dried fruits none. Of the vegetables, green peppers, sprouts, cresses and dark green leaves are the best source, but overcooked vegetables may contain none by the time they are eaten. Root and blanched vegetables (like celery) contain little: dried (not dehydrated) vegetables contain none, but it is formed in intact pulses (peas, beans and lentils) which are allowed to sprout, see **bean shoots**.

The British daily **recommended intake** for adults for vitamin C is 30 milligrams. More vitamin C is required during pregnancy and breast feeding to ensure adequate supplies for the child (see Appendix I, Ascorbic acid). The table below shows average portions of foods containing sufficient to meet the adult intake, but it is important to remember that vitamin C contents are greatly affected by the type and variety of plant grown, and the climate and maturity when harvested. Green peppers for instance can vary three-fold.

Storage time and method of cooking however, cause the most important variations in vitamin C contents of fruits and vegetables, see **vegetables** and individual entries.

Fresh fruits and vegetables contain more vitamin C than those that have been stored because the soft tissues of harvested plants are alive and continue to use up the vitamin C accumulated during growth of the plant. Thus, the vitamin C content of potatoes falls from 30 milligrams per 100 grams when harvested to 10 milligrams per 100 grams after six months' storage. Losses are increased if vegetables are allowed to wilt, or if they are damaged by frost or bruising.

Vitamin C is the nutrient most vulnerable to cooking and processing. It leaches out of foods cooked in water and is rapidly destroyed by oxygen (in air); heat; (especially if alkalis, iron or copper are also present); and the enzyme (ascorbic acid oxidase) released from vegetable cells during peeling and chopping. Some or all of these are in contact with vitamin C when food is cooked, and losses are unavoidable. For this reason, citrus fruits and tomatoes, which can be eaten without preparation, are the most reliable sources.

There are further losses when vegetables are kept hot after cooking. Vegetables eaten in canteens and restaurants are unreliable sources and in these situations, tomato or cress salads are a better alternative. Lettuce (especially if wilted), cucumber, chicory, celery contain little vitamin C -in an average portion.

The proportion of vitamin C lost during processing and preservation depends on the amount of heat to which the food is subjected. Acid fruits lose less than vegetables. A comparison between processed and foods freshly prepared in the home shows, perhaps surprisingly, that differences in vitamin C may be minor. In some cases preserved vegetables may contain more vitamin C than stored, unpreserved ones because they are processed when the vitamin C content is at a maximum.

The three most common methods of preservation are freezing, canning and dehydration, all of which begin by blanching (dipping in hot water) when 10 to 30% of the vitamin is lost. There is no further loss on freezing, but canned foods are sterilised by another period of heat when more vitamin C is destroyed. Dehydrated foods are also subjected to heat, but in modern processes, losses of vitamin C are minimal. Foods that have been dried by prolonged exposure to heat or sun will contain none. Processed foods should be stored at the lowest temperature possible and cooked according to the manufacturers' instructions, otherwise further losses of vitamin C may occur. Frozen vegetables for example should be cooked from the frozen state, and fruit juices should not be stored once the can or tin is opened. See **potatoes, vegetables** and **fruit** for more information.

Nearly all animals studied synthesise sufficient vitamin C for daily needs from **glucose**. Humans and guinea pigs are two exceptions: they lack one of the **enzymes** in the vitamin C synthesising chain and must obtain the vitamin from food. Within about four months a diet totally lacking in vitamin C results in the breakdown of connective tissue, a cementing substance that binds cells together (the vitamin takes part in the formation of the main proteins in connective tissue). The symptoms of scurvy – bruising (from leakage of blood into surrounding tissues), loss of teeth, weakening of bones – are due to loss of binding substance between cells. If given in time vitamin C restores full health; otherwise, sudden death is likely from internal haemorrhage. For most adults, a daily intake of 10 milligrams of vitamin C will prevent scurvy, but recommended allowances (30 milligrams for most adults) are greater to allow for individual variation. It is claimed that some women are able to synthesise small quantities of the vitamin and are better able to withstand scurvy.

Requirements for vitamin C are increased by wounds – incurred during surgery, burns or severe accidents which are repaired by scars, a form of connective tissue. Increased requirements are temporarily met by withdrawal from the blood, but these reserves are small. Hospital diets and intravenous fluids often contain insufficient vitamin C and supplements may be necessary for adequate healing. Babies may also develop scurvy unless given vitamin C (as welfare vitamin drops or orange juice, not boiled), see also **tyrosine**.

Recommended intakes are more than adequate to prevent scurvy, but it is often proposed that – for full health – humans require additional vitamin C. These proposals stem partly from animal experiments and partly from uncertainties about other roles of vitamin C. It is implicated in many body processes (including brain activity, formation of red blood cells and cholesterol synthesis) and may be essential for normal **metabolism** of all cells. Needs may be increased by stress. However, apart from its role in the formation of one hormone, its fundamental action remains elusive. Until this problem is resolved it will be difficult to establish whether or not raised intakes are beneficial to otherwise healthy people – see also below. Smokers have greater requirements for vitamin C than normal.

Vitamin C cannot be stored, but large doses are retained in the body until cells are saturated. A fully saturated 70 kilogram (11 stone) man contains about 5 grams of vitamin C. Once the cells are saturated intakes in excess of needs are eliminated in the urine. For full health, guinea pigs need enough for saturation, but most authorities remain unconvinced that recommended intakes should ensure saturation of human tissues. In Britain the recommended intake would then be unrealistically high: 60 to 100 milligrams daily are necessary for saturation but the average British diet only supplies 60 milligrams. Nevertheless, an intake of 100 milligrams can easily be achieved in a healthy **diet** with plenty of properly cooked vegetables.

Average portions of foods supplying the adult recommended intake of vitamin C

Food		Average portion supplying 30 milligrams vitamin C
Rich sources	Blackcurrants, strawberries, rosehip syrup, blackcurrant syrup, kiwi fruit, watercress, mustard and cress, green peppers, pea shoots, broccoli tops[a], brussels sprouts[a], cabbage[a], cauliflower[a], horseradish[a], kale[a], parsley[a], spinach[a], turnip tops[a]	15 to 30 grams (½ to 1 ¾ oz)

Food	Average portion supplying 30 milligrams vitamin C
Good sources Oranges, lemons, grapefruit, tangerines redcurrants, gooseberries, blackcurrant jam, bean sprouts, new potatoes[a], broad beans[a], beet greens[a], seakale[a], turnip tops[a], asparagus[a]	50 to 100 grams (3½ oz)
Blackberries, limes, melon, pineapple (fresh), raspberries, canned grapefruit, avocado pears, runner beans[a], leeks[a], lettuce, spring onions, parsnips[a], peas[a], radishes, swedes[a], tomatoes, turnips[a], potatoes[a] up to 6 months old, liver, roe, some cured meats	100 to 200 grams (7 oz)
Poor sources Apples, apricots, bananas, cherries, grapes, peaches, pears, plums, canned pineapple, rhubarb, most jam, marmalade, artichokes[a], beetroot, carrot[a], celery, cucumber, endive, marrow[a], mushrooms[a], onions[a], potatoes older than 6 months, milk	200 grams to 1 kilogram (2¼ lbs)

Processed peas, dried pulses, (peas, beans, lentils), dried fruits (currants, dates, figs, prunes, raisins, sultanas, peaches, apricots), olives and jams made with fruits poor in vitamin C contain none.

[a] – There are considerable losses in cooking, see vegetables

Vitamin C, colds, and orthomolecular medicine

Even larger doses – 2 to 10 grams daily (equivalent to the quantities synthesised by animals not dependent on food for vitamin C) – have been suggested by Linus Pauling, a Nobel prizewinner for peace and chemistry, to enhance resistance to infections from the cold virus, and from bacteria which later infect the damaged membranes of the sinuses, nose and lungs. A group of white blood cells, the body's main defence against infection, are less efficient when they are depleted of vitamin C, and their vitamin C content decreases with the onset of a cold. This fall can be prevented by a large dose (6 grams, or 1 teaspoon of powdered vitamin C) taken immediately symptoms are noticed, though not by a regular daily dose of 1 gram of vitamin C. Small doses (30 to 50 milligrams contained in most cold remedies are unlikely to confer any benefit, but a number of trials using both daily doses in different amounts to see if colds can be prevented, and large doses taken at the onset of symptoms have been carried out. The first have shown a slight (but not significant) reduction in the number of days attributable to cold infection but large doses (in excess of 1 gram per day) do not appear to confer any greater benefit than amounts that can be obtained from a diet containing plenty of fruit and vegetables, that is 100–150 milligrams per day. This would be beneficial for other reasons (see diet). Large doses (1–5 grams) taken at the onset of a cold also lessened the symptoms, but again, the findings were marginal and not significant.

Similar pharmacological doses of vitamin C, far greater than could be obtained from food, have also been suggested by Pauling and others to be of benefit in the treatment of **cancer, heart disease**, and mental disease, for example schizophrenia. So far, these have not been born out, except in the treatment of rare **inborn errors of metabolism** where diet has been used for many years to treat or prevent brain and nervous tissue dysfunction. Many studies which have attempted to use large doses of vitamins have been criticised because a control (placebo) group have not been studied as well. In one of the most recent, from the Mayo Clinic, patients with cancer were given approximately 10 grams of vitamin C, and the results were compared with those from a control group, not given vitamin C. There was no difference in survival or well being between the two groups.

The value of high dose vitamins has also been extensively investigated by psychiatrists because the possibility that mental disease is largely curable by seemingly innocuous vitamins is obviously attractive. However, a task force convened by the American Psychiatric Association in 1975 concluded after thorough investigation that trials of vitamins in psychiatry were either inconclusive, because no controls, or other factors, like drugs, had been included, or that no beneficial effects had been found and in some cases there were hazards, for example with **nicotinic acid** and **pyridoxine**.

Up to 500 milligrams of vitamin C is probably a harmless daily intake, but larger doses should be taken with care. **Oxalic acid** formed partly from vitamin C is excreted in urine: excess amounts passing through the kidney may result in kidney stones.

Vitamin D – chemical names cholecalciferol, ergocalciferol

Vitamin D – formed in the skin exposed to sunlight – is necessary for the absorption of **calcium** from food, and the hardening of bones with calcium and **phosphorus**. Insufficient vitamin D causes **rickets** in childhood and **osteomalacia** in adulthood.

Vitamin D is also found in foods but confined to very few. The only notable sources are some fatty **fish, margarine** and **eggs**. Dairy foods (butter, milk, cheese) and liver contain very small quantities. Other foods (fruits, vegetables, cereals, other fish, fats, oils and meat) contain none. Fish liver oils, which used to be used as dietary supplements, are rich sources. Vitamin D is stable to heat and does not leach out of foods cooked in water. The only losses thought to occur in cooking and processing are with fat when milk is skimmed and fatty fish are grilled.

There are several forms of vitamin D, but only two – vitamin D_2 (ergocalciferol) and D_3 (cholecalciferol) – are important to humans. Vitamin D_3 is the 'natural' vitamin found in food and formed in the skin. Vitamin D_2 is made when yeast is treated with ultra violet light: it is used for vitamin D supplements (for example in pills and margarine) and is thought to be as potent as D_3 for humans (though not for some animals).

Dietary vitamin D is transferred with **fat** into the blood stream after **digestion** into the liver. In the skin, a derivative of **cholesterol** is transformed to vitamin D by ultra-violet light from sunlight or ultraviolet lamps. This is stored until needed in the skin, and slowly diffuses into the blood stream when it is converted into active hormone – like forms in the liver, and then the kidney. The active form stimulates the production of a **protein** necessary for the absorption of calcium out of food. There is a separate mechanism which controls the absorption of phosphorus. When little of the skin is exposed to sunlight, and liver stores are reduced from insufficient in food, little calcium is available to the body. For unexplained reasons, Asians seem to be more susceptible to the results of vitamin D deficiency – rickets and osteomalacia. Skin pigmentation is not the answer because West Indians are no more susceptible than Caucasians. Diseases which interfere with the absorption of fat (**malabsorption**), kidney failure, congenital diseases, and some drugs used for the treatment of epilepsy can also cause rickets and osteomalacia.

Although adults derive sufficient from sunlight, extra vitamin D – for example as welfare vitamin tablets – may be necessary in pregnancy and breast feeding, otherwise calcium is withdrawn from the mother's bones to meet the needs of the growing child. With increasing age the kidneys may not convert vitamin D to its active form so efficiently: osteomalacia is therefore also likely in elderly people. Substitution of margarine in place of butter and extra calcium (in at least half a pint of milk a day) is advisable, together with one multivitamin tablet daily for those confined indoors. The table on page 321 shows amounts of food containing 10 micrograms of vitamin D.

Mothers who are exposed to sunlight or take sufficient vitamin D as tablets or food are probably able to allow the developing child to lay down sufficient liver stores of vitamin D until the baby is exposed to sunlight. Milk – both breast and bottle – contains very little. Otherwise, to prevent rickets babies need vitamin D, as welfare vitamin drops or cod liver oil. After weaning, vitamin drops, cod liver oil (or malt with cod liver oil) should be continued up to the age of five years: children and adolescents infrequently exposed to sunlight are likely to benefit from supplements until they stop growing.

Excessive vitamin D is toxic. As little as ten times the recommended intake has caused ill health in some infants. Extra calcium is absorbed from food, resulting in a dangerously high level of calcium in the blood stream. Death may result from kidney failure following the deposition of calcium in the blood vessels. For this reason, no more than the recommended dose of vitamin drops or pills (or no more than a daily teaspoon of cod liver oil) should be given to children or taken in pregnancy. Adults are less susceptible to overdosage than children: doses in excess of twenty five times the recommended intake have proved toxic.

Sources of vitamin D[a]

Food or supplement	Quantity supplying an average of 10 micrograms vitamin D
Cod liver oil	1 teaspoon
Welfare vitamin drops for children	7 drops
Welfare vitamin tablets for mothers	1 tablet
Other vitamin tablets[b]	

Rich sources	Fatty fish, eels	10 to 40 grams (⅓ to 1⅓ oz)
	brislings	40 to 20 grams (⅓ to ⅔ oz)
	herrings, kippers	45 grams (1½ oz)
	mackerel	55 grams (2 oz)
	salmon, canned	80 grams (2¾ oz)
	sardines, canned	135 grams (4¾ oz)
	Cod liver oil and malt	45 grams (1 dessertspoon)
Moderate sources	Margarine	125 grams (4½ oz)
	Eggs	665 grams (11 standard)
	Fortified dried milk	115 grams (4 oz)
	Fortified evaporated milk	345 grams (12 oz)
Poor sources	Butter	800 grams (28 oz)
	Liver; cheese, cream; unfortified dried, evaporated and condensed milk; milk	more than 1 kilogram (2¼ lb)

[a]Some plants are reported to contain vitamin D. Apart from alfalfa sprouts treated with u.v. light, these are not commonly eaten by humans.
[b]Potencies listed on box – 100 i.u. = 2.5 micrograms.

Vitamin E – group name for several substances (the tocopherols and tocotrienols) in food, and synthetic forms

Vitamin E has had a chequered career. Since 1922 it has been known to be necessary for normal reproduction and to prevent a variety of disorders in animals, but its exact role in human health has remained an enigma. Partly as a result of this and the animal findings, vitamin E has misleadingly been promoted as a 'miracle' vitamin, able to cure a variety of conditions ranging from wrinkles to impotency. Recently new studies have however shown that vitamin E is critically important for maintaining the structure of cell membranes. As such, lack of vitamin E can have profound effects, most noticeably in the nervous system.

Vitamin E is widespread in foods. **Oils** are the richest sources, particularly sunflower seed oil. **Almonds** and **hazel nuts** are also very rich sources. Wholegrain **breakfast cereals**, wholemeal **bread**, dark green **vegetables**, such as broccoli, **eggs, margarine, cheese**, and dairy products are all notable sources. In the average British diet, about one fifth is derived from vegetables and fruit, and nearly two-thirds from meat, dairy products, fish, eggs, and fats. The rest is found in cereals.

There are probably minimal losses of vitamin E in cooking – it is fairly stable to heat and does not leach out of foods cooked in water – but there may be severe losses in processing and storage. For example, although wholemeal bread is a good source of vitamin E, much is removed, with the germ, during milling. Bleaching agents, used in white **flour** destroy any remaining vitamin. Refined breakfast cereals also contain little or no vitamin E. In fats, vitamin E is removed when milk is skimmed so that skimmed milk contains none, and yogurt comparatively little. About 20% may be lost in fat when meat is cooked. Canned and frozen vegetables contain about the same as fresh, although there may be severe losses on prolonged storage of frozen food.

There are at least eight substances in food which have vitamin E activity. Potencies are assessed from experiments with rats – the animal first found to be susceptible to lack of vitamin E. α tocopherol is the most potent: other forms, although they contribute to the total vitamin E contents of diets and are antioxidants in food, are much less potent – at least for rats. The vitamin can also be synthesised: dl α tocopherol acetate is the synthetic stable form commonly added to food and vitamin E tablets.

Adults probably need a minimum of 3 milligrams of α tocopherol daily, but British authorities feel unable to specify reliable **recommended intakes**. There are uncertainties about the potencies of the different forms of vitamin E for humans and lack of extensive information about vitamin E contents of normal diets. Attempts to establish requirements are made difficult by the rare occurrence of deficiency and further complicated by other constituents of food. Polyunsaturated **fatty acids** increase requirements for vitamin E and **selenium** and sulphur amino acids (like **cystine**) may decrease them. Allowances of at least 12 micrograms per day for American diets – which contain more polyunsaturated fatty acids – are almost certainly more than is necessary. The average British diet contains 6 micrograms.

Vitamin E is held in the membranes of cells and is essential to maintain their orderly structure – precise organisation of molecules within cell membranes is necessary for normal **metabolism**. It also acts as an **antioxidant** of polyunsaturated fatty acids, particularly the **essential fatty acids**, in cell membranes and the blood stream. Nervous tissue and the brain contain large amounts of essential fatty acids and symptoms of deficiency include difficulty in walking, changes in the eye, loss of touch or pain senses and muscle weakness. Because body stores are so large, these deficiency symptoms are very rare, only occurring with some types of **inborn errors of metabolism** or difficulty in absorbing fat from food (**malabsorption**). Premature infants however do develop a type of **anaemia** which is associated with low blood levels and is remedied by vitamin E.

Based on the fact that similar diseases occur in animals made deficient in vitamin E, large doses – 200 milligrams or more daily – of α tocopherol have been tried in the treatment of many conditions, including habitual abortion, sterility and muscular dystrophy. Despite adequate blood levels before treatment (and therefore absence of deficiency) some doctors claim the vitamin to be of benefit to their patients. However, most doctors have found no benefits. Large doses are also given to athletes. The assumed antioxidant effect of vitamin E is believed to aid muscular efficiency – but this is unlikely. The performance of schoolboy swimmers given supplements of vitamin E for several weeks was no better than that of boys given placebo tablets of exactly the same appearance.

Equally well controlled experiments would probably confirm that vitamin E does not revitalise sexual powers, nor prolong life or remove wrinkles. It may however accelerate wound healing from burns or accidents in people who have low blood levels, and by virtue of its effect on essential fatty acids be important in lessening the risk of **stroke** or **heart disease**. A healthy **diet** containing plenty of fresh vegetables and wholegrain cereals supplies more than the average amount.

Compared with vitamins A and D, vitamin E is said to be harmless in large doses for man, but animals are reported to become infertile. One hundred milligrams daily (30 times minimum needs) is thought to be safe for those who believe in the reputed benefits of vitamin E.

Vitamin K

Vitamin K is necessary for the formation of proteins responsible for clotting of blood. In its absence, prolonged bleeding can lead to death, but humans are not entirely dependent on dietary supplies. It is synthesised by bacteria inhabiting the digestive system, and at least half the daily requirement is thought to be obtained from this source.

Although a fat soluble vitamin, most vitamin K in the diet is supplied by vegetables: other foods (apart from liver) contain hardly any. Adult daily requirements – about 100 micrograms – are easily met by a helping of vegetables. Cabbage, sprouts, cauliflower, and spinach are probably the richest sources, containing up to 4 milligrams (4000 micrograms) in each 100 grams. Beans, peas, potatoes, carrots and liver contain up to 400 micrograms per 100 grams. Losses of vitamin K in cooking and processing are thought to be minor: it does not leach out of foods cooked in water and is relatively stable to heat.

In food, the vitamin has a slightly different structure (vitamin K_1, called phylloquinone or phytomenadione) from that made by bacteria in the digestive system (vitamin K_2, called menaquinone). Putrid food, infected with bacteria, also contains vitamin K_2. Many other forms have been manufactured, including K_3 (called menadione) which is more potent than K_1 and K_2. Natural forms are absorbed out of food dissolved in fat, which must be finely divided (emulsified) by bile salts before it can be transferred to the blood stream. Once in the blood stream, vitamin K is transported to the liver, where blood clotting proteins are formed. Antagonists of vitamin K – like Warfarin – are used medicinally to inhibit unwanted blood clotting. It is uncertain whether vitamin K has any other functions in the body.

Newborn babies are susceptible to vitamin K deficiency: in the first few days of life they have no bacteria inhabiting the digestive system, and milk is a poor source. Supplements are sometimes necessary to avoid death from haemorrhage. Adult deficiency is unlikely, except when the bile duct is blocked by gall stones – a cause of jaundice. The body is quickly depleted of vitamin K (unlike other fat soluble vitamins there are no large stores) and injections are necessary before operations to remove stones, otherwise there is a risk of prolonged bleeding. Other causes of **malabsorption** can also result in deficiency.

Natural forms of vitamin K are not thought to be toxic when taken in excess, but some synthetic forms are soluble in water. They are useful for the treatment of vitamin K deficiency (being absorbed in the absence of bile) but in amounts greater than 100 times the minimum requirement can cause brain damage.

Walnuts

The walnut tree is valued both for its nuts, and the quality of the wood. It is native to Europe, Asia and China. The nuts are rich in **fat**, mostly as polyunsaturated **fatty acids**, which can be extracted and used as edible **oil**.

Average nutrients in 100 grams (3½ oz) Walnuts

Energy kilojoules	2166	Iron milligrams	2.4
kilocalories	525	Copper milligrams	0.31
Protein grams	10.6	Zinc milligrams	3.0
Total fat grams	51.5	Vitamin A micrograms	0
Saturated fat grams	5.6	Vitamin D micrograms	0
Polyunsaturated fat grams	35.2	Vitamin C milligrams	0
		Vitamin E milligrams	0.8
Cholesterol milligrams	0	B vitamins:	
Sugars grams	3.2	Thiamin (B_1) milligrams	0.30
Starch grams	1.8	Riboflavin (B_2) milligrams	0.13
Dietary fibre grams	5.2	Nicotinic acid milligrams	3.0
Sodium milligrams	3	Pyridoxine (B_6) milligrams	0.73
Potassium milligrams	690	Vitamin B_{12} micrograms	0
Calcium milligrams	61	Folic acid micrograms	66
Magnesium milligrams	130	Pantothenic acid milligrams	0.90
		Biotin micrograms	2.0

(–) No information available   (0) Contains zero or trace amounts

Water

Though not strictly a **nutrient**, water is essential for life. In temperate climates, most adults need to drink at least 1 litre (6 cups) of water or **beverages** daily. In hard water areas, drinking water is a significant source of **calcium** – London water for instance contains 200 parts per million of calcium (or about 200 milligrams in an average intake of 1 litre). Hard waters are associated with a lower risk of mortality from **heart disease**, but the reason for this is unknown. Calcium or other minerals in hard water may be protective, or there may be harmful factors in soft water – which is more acidic and tends to dissolve lead and other unwanted trace elements (see poisons in food) out of pipes and containers.

Perhaps surprisingly, over half (60%) of the weight of an adult man is water. Most is held inside cells: relatively little (about 2½ litres (4½ pints) in a 70 kilograms (11 stone) man) is in the blood stream. Women contain less water than men: they have more fat which is drier (10% water) than muscle (80% water). Babies contain more water than adults, and the elderly slightly less.

Water is needed, from drink and food, to balance losses of water in urine and from the skin, lungs and faeces. Normally losses are almost exactly balanced by gains; the table below shows an approximate water balance for adults:

Approximate water balance for adults living in a temperate climate

Gains (millilitres)	are balanced by	Losses (millilitres)
1000 from drink		1000 from urine
1000 from food		900 from skin
300 from metabolism		400 from faeces & lungs
2300	Total	2300

In temperate climates, drinking water usually balances the water needed by the kidney for elimination of waste products in urine. A minimum of 900 millilitres (1½ pints) is usually required, but more in old age and infancy (when the kidneys are unable to concentrate waste products as efficiently) and if the diet is high in **protein** and **salt**. Requirements for drinking water are also increased in hot conditions and feverish illnesses to make good losses necessary to cool the body, in perspiration.

In cool conditions, losses of water from faeces, lungs and skin (losses from the skin continue even when there is no obvious perspiration) are balanced by gains from food. Daily diets supply at least 750 millilitres of water. Milk, fruit and vegetables contain the most (75 to 95%). Meat, fish and eggs contain 50 to 75%; cheese and bread 40%; flour, cereals and nuts 5 to 15%. Sugar and fats contain little or no water. Metabolic water (released when fats, carbohydrates and proteins are used for energy) and water in soups, gravies and sauces also contribute to the total.

When losses are greater than gains, body fluids are concentrated, triggering a thirst response in the brain. Normally the desire to drink prevents dehydration when water is freely available, but the elderly may suppress thirst for fear of incontinence. Babies – who cannot ask for water – are also susceptible to dehydration.

When thirst is not satisfied, losses (a minimum of 1 litre a day in adults) continue. A loss of 2 litres is harmless but may contribute to confusion in the elderly. When more than 4 litres is lost however, water is withdrawn from cells, causing weakness and collapse. Few people would survive a loss of more than 8 litres of water. Survival time is greatly reduced in hot climates when perspiration losses are at least ½ litre per hour.

Excess water is eliminated – as dilute (pale) urine – by the kidneys. Water in food and drink is severely restricted in kidney failure, but drinking plenty of water is otherwise harmless, and may benefit some people. Some type of kidney stones (see **calcium**) are less likely to form if urine is kept dilute by drinking at least 2 litres of water daily, and water with meals helps satiety in slimming diets. Water intoxication (really **sodium** depletion) is only likely when severe perspiration losses are replaced with salt free beverages.

Water chestnut (Chinese)

The tuber of a sedge plant which grows at the edge of shallow lakes and marshes. It is valued for its crisp texture in Chinese cookery; canned water chestnuts (see table) are imported from Hong Kong to the West.

Average nutrients in 100 grams (3½ oz) Water chestnuts

Energy kilojoules	205	Iron milligrams	0.5
kilocalories	49	Copper milligrams	–
Protein grams	0.9	Zinc milligrams	–
Total fat grams	0	Vitamin A micrograms	0
Saturated fat grams	0	Vitamin D micrograms	0
Polyunsaturated fat grams	0	Vitamin C milligrams	6
		Vitamin E milligrams	–
Cholesterol milligrams	0	B vitamins:	
Sugars grams	}12.5	Thiamin (B_1) milligrams	0.01
Starch grams		Riboflavin (B_2) milligrams	0.03
Dietary fibre grams	–	Nicotinic acid milligrams	–
Sodium milligrams	14	Pyridoxine (B_6) milligrams	–
Potassium milligrams	154	Vitamin B_{12} micrograms	0
Calcium milligrams	18	Folic acid micrograms	–
Magnesium milligrams	6	Pantothenic acid milligrams	–
		Biotin micrograms	–

(–) No information available (0) Contains zero or trace amounts

Watercress

Watercress is rich in **vitamins A, folic acid, riboflavin** and **vitamin C**. It is a member of the *Nasturtium* species; nasturtium flowers and leaves make an attractive and edible garnish, with a flavour similar to watercress.

Average nutrients in 100 grams (3½ oz) Watercress

Energy kilojoules	61	Iron milligrams	1.6
kilocalories	14	Copper milligrams	0.14
Protein grams	2.9	Zinc milligrams	0.2
Total fat grams	0	Vitamin A micrograms	250–580
Saturated fat grams	0	Vitamin D micrograms	0
Polyunsaturated fat grams	0	Vitamin C milligrams	40–80
		Vitamin E milligrams	1.0
Cholesterol milligrams	0	B vitamins:	
Sugars grams	0.6	Thiamin (B_1) milligrams	0.10
Starch grams	0.1	Riboflavin (B_2) milligrams	0.10
Dietary fibre grams	3.3	Nicotinic acid milligrams	1.1
Sodium milligrams	60	Pyridoxine (B_6) milligrams	0.13
Potassium milligrams	310	Vitamin B_{12} micrograms	0
Calcium milligrams	220	Folic acid micrograms	200
Magnesium milligrams	17	Pantothenic acid milligrams	0.10
		Biotin micrograms	0.4

(–) No information available (0) Contains zero or trace amounts

Wheat – see also **bread, flour, pasta, breakfast cereals, bran**

Wheat is a valuable staple food, providing **energy**, **protein**, B **vitamins** and **minerals**. In the average British diet, it supplies a third of the total energy and a quarter of the total protein. Like other **cereals** however, it cannot support life when eaten alone because it is deficient in vitamins A, C and B_{12}.

Wheat germ, recovered when white flour is milled, is a rich source of B complex vitamins and vitamin E. It has a high unsaturated **fatty acid** content and is liable to become rancid unless kept under refrigeration. Processed germ (Bemax) is treated to prevent rancidity: virtually all nutrients are retained.

Average nutrients in 100 grams (3½ oz) Bemax

Energy kilojoules	1465	Iron milligrams	10.0
kilocalories	347	Copper milligrams	1.2
Protein grams	26.5	Zinc milligrams	–
Total fat grams	8.1	Vitamin A micrograms	0
Saturated fat grams	1.1	Vitamin D micrograms	0
Polyunsaturated fat grams	3.6	Vitamin C milligrams	0
		Vitamin E milligrams	11.0
Cholesterol milligrams	0	B vitamins:	
Sugars grams	16.0	Thiamin (B$_1$) milligrams	1.45
Starch grams	28.7	Riboflavin (B$_2$) milligrams	0.61
Dietary fibre grams	–	Nicotinic acid milligrams	5.3
Sodium milligrams	4	Pyridoxine (B$_6$) milligrams	0.95
Potassium milligrams	1000	Vitamin B$_{12}$ micrograms	0
Calcium milligrams	17	Folic acid micrograms	330
Magnesium milligrams	300	Pantothenic acid milligrams	1.7
		Biotin micrograms	–

(–) No information available   (0) Contains zero or trace amounts

Whitebait

Whitebait are the young of herrings and sprats. The usual method of cooking is to coat them in flour, fry and eat whole when freshly cooked. Fried whitebait contain plenty of **calcium** (from the bones) and are good sources of **iron**, but they are very rich in **fat**.

Average nutrients in 100 grams (3½ oz) Whitebait (fried in batter)

Energy kilojoules	2174	Iron milligrams	5.1
kilocalories	525	Copper milligrams	–
Protein grams	19.5	Zinc milligrams	–
Total fat grams	47.5	Vitamin A micrograms	–
Saturated fat grams	–	Vitamin D micrograms	–
Polyunsaturated fat grams	–	Vitamin C milligrams	0
		Vitamin E milligrams	–
Cholesterol milligrams	–	B vitamins:	
Sugars grams	0	Thiamin (B$_1$) milligrams	–
Starch grams	5.3[a]	Riboflavin (B$_2$) milligrams	–
Dietary fibre grams	–	Nicotinic acid milligrams	–
Sodium milligrams	230	Pyridoxine (B$_6$) milligrams	–
Potassium milligrams	110	Vitamin B$_{12}$ micrograms	–
Calcium milligrams	860	Folic acid micrograms	–
Magnesium milligrams	50	Pantothenic acid milligrams	–
		Biotin micrograms	–

(–) No information available   (0) Contains zero or trace amounts

[a] From batter

Whiting

Whiting is related to the **cod**, and has the same nutritional characteristics; low in fat and hence in energy (Calories) but is a poor source of iron when compared with fatty fish, like **sardines**.

Average nutrients in 100 grams (3½ oz) Whiting (steamed)

Energy kilojoules	389	Iron milligrams	1.0
kilocalories	92	Copper milligrams	–
Protein grams	20.9	Zinc milligrams	–
Total fat grams	0.9	Vitamin A micrograms	0
Saturated fat grams	0.1	Vitamin D micrograms	0
Polyunsaturated fat grams	0.2	Vitamin C milligrams	0
		Vitamin E milligrams	–
Cholesterol milligrams	110	B vitamins:	
Sugars grams	0	Thiamin (B$_1$) milligrams	–
Starch grams	0	Riboflavin (B$_2$) milligrams	–
Dietary fibre grams	0	Nicotinic acid milligrams	–
Sodium milligrams	130	Pyridoxine (B$_6$) milligrams	–
Potassium milligrams	300	Vitamin B$_{12}$ micrograms	–
Calcium milligrams	42	Folic acid micrograms	–
Magnesium milligrams	28	Pantothenic acid milligrams	–
		Biotin micrograms	–

(–) No information available   (0) Contains zero or trace amounts

Wine and cider

Although wine is strictly prepared from grapes, a variety of other vegetables and fruits are used to make country wines and cider. All have a similar nutritional value: they contain **alcohol**, **sugars**, both are sources of **energy** (Calories), and small quantities of B vitamins and minerals.

All table wines contain less than 12 grams of alcohol per 100 millilitre (a small glass): fermentation stops when this level is reached. There is some sugar left in sweet wine, but very dry wines are virtually sugar free. Wines contain many other substances in small amounts – for instance, acids, tannins, higher alcohols (congeners), gums, pectin, flavouring oils, glycerol, and esters (combinations of acids and alcohols) – which are responsible for colour, flavour and body. Sulphur dioxide is a permitted **preservative** in wine.

Sherry, port, madeira, and marsala, fortified with spirit to preserve them, contain up to 17 grams of alcohol per 100 millilitres. Sherry is basically a very dry wine (it is fortified after fermentation is complete) and some sherries are almost sugar free. Most however are later blended with sugar. Vermouths – wines flavoured with bitter ingredients and sugar – are similar in alcoholic strength to the fortified wines.

Cider is less alcoholic than wine. Most contain 4 grams of alcohol per 100 millilitres, though vintage ciders may have twice this amount. Most bottled ciders contain between 2½ to 4 grams of sugars per 100 millilitres, but others vary from 1 to 8 grams per 100 millilitres. Some ciders are as acid as young wine: though lacking in tartaric acid (the chief acid in grapes) they contain malic acid.

Red wine, sometimes thought to be good for blood formation, does not necessarily contain more **iron** than white but the iron in both is well absorbed and large intakes (2 litres or more), coupled with a low protein diet, may cause excessive absorption and result in liver damage.

Average nutrients in 100 grams (½ large glass) Wines and cider

	red wine	dry white wine	sweet white wine	dry cider	dry sherry	port
Energy kilojoules	284	275	394	152	481	655
kilocalories	68	66	94	36	116	157
Protein grams	0.2	0.1	0.2	0	0.2	0.1
Total fat grams	0	0	0	0	0	0
Alcohol grams	9.5	9.1	10.2	3.8	15.7	15.9
Sugars grams	0.3	0.6	5.9	2.6	1.4	12.0
Starch grams	0	0	0	0	0	0
Dietary fibre grams	0	0	0	0	0	0
Sodium milligrams	10	4	13	7	10	4
Potassium milligrams	130	61	110	72	57	97
Calcium milligrams	7	9	14	8	7	4
Magnesium milligrams	11	8	11	3	13	11
Iron milligrams	0.9	0.5	0.6	0.5	0.4	0.4
Copper milligrams	0.12	0.01	0.05	0.04	0.03	0.1
Zinc milligrams	–	0.01	–	–	–	–
Vitamin A micrograms	0	0	0	0	0	0
Vitamin D micrograms	0	0	0	0	0	0
Vitamin C milligrams	0	0	0	0	0	0
Vitamin E milligrams	0	0	0	0	0	0
B vitamins:						
Thiamin (B_1) milligrams	0	0	0	0	0	0
Riboflavin (B_2) milligrams	0.02	0.01	0.01	0	0.01	0.01
Nicotinic acid milligrams	0.09	0.06	0.08	0.01	0.10	0.06
Pyridoxine (B_6) milligrams	0.02	0.02	0.01	0.01	0.01	0.01
Vitamin B_{12} micrograms	0	0	0	–	0	0
Folic acid micrograms	0.2	0.2	0.1	–	0.1	0.1
Pantothenic acid milligrams	0.04	0.03	0.03	0.04	–	–
Biotin micrograms	–	–	–	0.6	–	–

(–) No information available   (0) Contains zero or trace amounts

Winkles

Winkles, or periwinkles, are molluscs commonly found on British beaches. They are rich sources of well absorbed **iron** and **zinc**. They also contain **protein**, a little fat, and are good sources of **calcium**. They are generally cooked in sea water – hence their high sodium content.

Average nutrients in 100 grams (3½ oz) Winkles (boiled in sea water)

Energy kilojoules	312	Iron milligrams	15.0
kilocalories	74	Copper milligrams	1.3
Protein grams	15.3	Zinc milligrams	5.7
Total fat grams	1.4	Vitamin A micrograms	0
Saturated fat grams	–	Vitamin D micrograms	0
Polyunsaturated fat grams	–	Vitamin C milligrams	0

		Vitamin E milligrams	–
Cholesterol milligrams	100	B vitamins:	
Sugars grams	0	Thiamin (B$_1$) milligrams	–
Starch grams	0	Riboflavin (B$_2$) milligrams	–
Dietary fibre grams	0	Nicotinic acid milligrams	–
Sodium milligrams	1140	Pyridoxine (B$_6$) milligrams	–
Potassium milligrams	150	Vitamin B$_{12}$ micrograms	–
Calcium milligrams	140	Folic acid micrograms	–
Magnesium milligrams	360	Pantothenic acid milligrams	–
		Biotin micrograms	–

(–) No information available   (0) Contains zero or trace amounts

Yam

A starchy tuber, containing about one third of its weight as **starch** (see table). It is used as a staple food in parts of West Africa but its low protein content makes it a less suitable food for children than cereals, such as **millet**.

Average nutrients in 100 grams (3½ oz) Yam (boiled)

Energy kilojoules	508	Iron milligrams	0.3
kilocalories	119	Copper milligrams	0.15
Protein grams	1.6	Zinc milligrams	0.4
Total fat grams	0.1	Vitamin A micrograms	2
Saturated fat grams	–	Vitamin D micrograms	0
Polyunsaturated fat grams	–	Vitamin C milligrams	2
		Vitamin E milligrams	–
Cholesterol milligrams	0	B vitamins:	
Sugars grams	0.2	Thiamin (B_1) milligrams	0.05
Starch grams	29.6	Riboflavin (B_2) milligrams	0.01
Dietary fibre grams	3.9	Nicotinic acid milligrams	0.8
Sodium milligrams	17	Pyridoxine (B_6) milligrams	–
Potassium milligrams	300	Vitamin B_{12} micrograms	0
Calcium milligrams	9	Folic acid micrograms	6
Magnesium milligrams	14	Pantothenic acid milligrams	0.4
		Biotin micrograms	–

(–) No information available   (0) Contains zero or trace amounts

Yeast

Yeast is notable for its contribution to the social life of man, via its ability to ferment **carbohydrate** to **alcohol**. Various other types are propagated for animal feeds, baking, yeast extract manufacture, and ergosterol (vitamin D) production. Yeasts are rich in B complex **vitamins** from which these were first isolated, but their nutritional properties vary between the types. Dried brewers' yeast for example contains much more vitamin B, than bakers' yeast (see table).

Average nutrients in 100 grams (3½ oz) Yeast

	fresh	dried		fresh	dried
Energy kilojoules	226	717	Iron milligrams	5.0	20.0
kilocalories	53	169	Copper milligrams	1.6	5.0
Protein grams	11.4	35.6	Zinc milligrams	2.6	8.0
Total fat grams	0.4	1.5	Vitamin A micrograms	0	0
Saturated fat grams	–	–	Vitamin D micrograms	0	0
Polyunsaturated fat grams	–	–	Vitamin C milligrams	0	0
			Vitamin E milligrams	0	0
Cholesterol milligrams	0	0	B vitamins:		
Sugars grams	0	0	Thiamin (B_1) milligrams	0.71	2.33[a]
Starch grams	1.1	3.5	Riboflavin (B_2) milligrams	1.7	4.0
Dietary fibre grams	–	–	Nicotinic acid milligrams	13	43
Sodium milligrams	16	50	Pyridoxine (B_6) milligrams	0.6	2.0
Potassium milligrams	610	2000	Vitamin B_{12} micrograms	0	0

Calcium milligrams	25	80	Folic acid micrograms	1250	4000
Magnesium milligrams	59	230	Pantothenic acid milligrams	3.5	11.0
			Biotin micrograms	60	200

(–) No information available   (0) Contains zero or trace amounts

ᵃ Value for bakers' yeast; brewers' yeast contains 15.6 milligrams

Yogurt

Yogurt is a useful low fat alternative to cream or other desserts. The main difference between fruit and natural (plain) yogurt is added **sugar** (sucrose) and hence **energy** (Calorie) contents; although yogurt made from whole milk contains the same amount of fat as milk and sometimes more – as in strained Greek yogurt.

Yogurt is made by adding a culture of special bacteria to boiled milk which is kept warm for several hours. The bacteria multiply and convert milk sugar (lactose) into lactic acid, which suppresses the growth of harmful bacteria and partially curdles the milk. The milk is preserved (it keeps for about two weeks under refrigeration) and thickened. Originally the culture was naturally present in the milk and varied in different areas: some other cultures (for instance in kumiss) contain yeasts which produce alcohol.

Commercial yogurts contain two bacteria (*Lactobacillus bulgaricus* and *Streptococcus thermophilus*) which complement each other's growth. Any bought yogurt can be used for home made yogurt, but fresh pasteurised milk must be boiled before incubating it, otherwise harmful bacteria may become established before sufficient acid is formed to inhibit their multiplication. Dried skimmed milk can be added for a firmer, less acid, curd. All (except pasteurised) commercial yogurts contain living lactic acid bacteria, and are therefore 'live'.

The reputed health giving qualities of yogurt stem partly from the Russian scientist Metchnikoff about eighty years ago. He proposed that lactic acid producing bacteria would colonise the large bowel, thus inhibiting other, possibly undesirable ones. He himself ate yogurt regularly and established a fashion for it in many European cities for prolonging life. However, lactic acid producing bacteria are one of the major groups inhabiting a healthy large bowel – no matter whether or not yogurt is eaten. They are most likely to thrive in an acid environment, for example when the diet contains plenty of **fibre** for other bacteria to produce other acids, chiefly **acetic acid**.

Some bacteria in yogurt do survive digestion, particularly when taken as a pharmaceutical preparation of *Lactobacillus acidophilus*. These may help to check the diarrhoea which sometimes follows sterilisation of the intestines with antibiotics. Acidophilus milk contains *L. acidophilus*. Yogurt is also better tolerated than fresh milk in people with a deficiency of an **enzyme** necessary to split milk sugar (**lactose**), probably because the thicker curd is held in the stomach for longer than fresh milk.

Average nutrients in 100 grams (3½ oz) Yogurt

	natural	fruit		natural	fruit
Energy kilojoules	216	405	Iron milligrams	0.09	0.24
kilocalories	52	95	Copper milligrams	0.04	0.07
Protein grams	5.0	4.8	Zinc milligrams	0.60	0.63
Total fat grams	1.0	1.0	Vitamin A micrograms	9	13
Saturated fat grams	–	–	Vitamin D micrograms	0	0
Polyunsaturated fat grams	–	–	Vitamin C milligrams	0.4	1.8
			Vitamin E milligrams	0.03	0.07
Cholesterol milligrams	7	6	B vitamins:		
Milk sugars grams	6.2	4.9	Thiamin (B$_1$) milligrams	0.05	0.05
Added sucrose grams	0	13.0	Riboflavin (B$_2$) milligrams	0.26	0.23
Dietary fibre grams	0	0	Nicotinic acid milligrams	1.16	1.12
Sodium milligrams	76	64	Pyridoxine (B$_6$) milligrams	0.04	0.04
			Vitamin B$_{12}$ micrograms	0	0
Potassium milligrams	240	220	Folic acid micrograms	2	3
Calcium milligrams	180	160	Pantothenic acid milligrams	–	–
Magnesium milligrams	17	17	Biotin micrograms	–	–

(–) No information available   (0) Contains zero or trace amounts

Zinc

Zinc is a **trace element** necessary for growth, sexual maturity, wound healing, and taste and flavour perception.

Milk, **meat**, **cheese**, **yogurt**, **eggs** and **fish** are the best sources of zinc. Other foods such as nuts, vegetables, wholegrains and pulses contain zinc but it appears to be less well digested from plant foods. **Amino acids** in animal proteins may enhance its absorption into the blood stream. Wholegrain cereals and pulses are apparently good sources, but they contain **phytic acid** which interferes with absorption. More zinc is thought to be available from wholemeal bread leavened with yeast, which partially degrades phytic acid during proving. White flour is a poor source, but is also low in phytic acid. Fruits are also poor.

Most adults probably require about 10 milligrams of zinc daily – an amount contained in average British diets – but there is too little available information to set reliable recommended intakes. Adolescents and pregnant and breast feeding mothers have the highest requirements – the increased needs should be met with extra meat, milk and fish.

Less than 40% of zinc in the diet is thought to be transferred to the blood stream during **digestion**. Only 10% may be absorbed from strict vegetarian diets. Adults contain 2 to 3 grams of zinc, but most is retained in the skeleton and there appear to be no large stores that can be drawn upon when zinc is in short supply. The remainder is inside cells, where it is essential for the action of up to 100 **enzymes** – including those concerned with the formation of new body **proteins** for growth and repair, and with cell division and multiplication. Extra zinc is therefore needed for growth and wound healing. The young born to female animals fed a diet lacking in zinc during pregnancy are deformed – a finding that may be of importance to humans.

Zinc is lost from the body in urine and sweat. In parts of the Middle East, adolescents are known to suffer from dwarfism and sexual immaturity which can be prevented by improvement in diet or zinc supplements. These children were eating very restricted diets – mainly wholemeal unleavened bread – and, in the hot climate, were losing excessive amounts of zinc in sweat. Deficiency is made worse by loss of blood (from hookworm infection) and probably too little protein. Such severe deficiency is unlikely in Britain, but mild deficiency, affecting taste and smell – which would impair appetite and growth, has been detected in some American children.

Malabsorption can also cause deficiency, and there are large losses from the body in alcoholism, artificial kidney machine treatment, fever, and after surgery or burns. Unless extra zinc is given recovery may be delayed by lack of appetite and wounds may not heal. In animals, excess **copper** or cadmium (see **poisons in food**) can displace zinc in the body, but it is not known if deficiency can occur in this way in man.

Supplements of zinc are inadvisable (except for the treatment of deficiency): in animals excess zinc can cause copper deficiency, and interfere with the utilisation of iron, causing anaemia. Very large intakes are toxic: foods and water contaminated with zinc from galvanised metal containers have caused outbreaks of vomiting. However, the formerly fatal disease acrodermatitis enteropathica is due to an **inborn error of metabolism** in the absorption of zinc which has recently been found to be treatable with large doses of zinc salts.

Age range(a) years	Occupational category	Energy(b) MJ	Kcal	Protein(d) g	Thiamin mg	Riboflavin mg	Nicotinic acid equivalents mg(f)	Ascorbic acid mg	Vitamin A retinol equivalents μg(g)	Vitamin D(h) cholecalciferol μg	Calcium mg	Iron mg
Women												
18–54	Most occupations	9.0	2150	54	0.9	1.3	15	30	750	(h)	500	12(j)
	Very active	10.5	2500	62	1.0	1.3	15	30	750		500	12(j)
55–74	Assuming a	8.0	1900	47	0.8	1.3	15	30	750	(h)	500	10
75+	sedentary life	7.0	1680	42	0.7	1.3	15	30	750		500	10
Pregnancy		10.0	2400	60	1.0	1.6	18	60	750	10	1200(i)	13
Lactation		11.5	2750	69	1.1	1.8	21	60	1200	10	1200	15

Notes to Table 1
(a) Since the recommendations are average amounts, the figures for each age represent the amounts recommended at the middle of the range. Within each age range, younger children will need less, and older children more, than the amount recommended.
(b) Megajoules (10⁶ joules). Calculated from the relation 1 kilocalorie = 4.184 kilojoules, that is to say, 1 megajoule = 240 kilocalories.
(c) See Table 2.
(d) Recommended amounts have been calculated as 10% of the recommendations for energy (paragraph 44).
(e) See Table 2.

(f) 1 nicotinic acid equivalent = 1 mg available nicotinic acid or 60 mg tryptophan.
(g) 1 retinol equivalent = 1μg retinol or 6 μgβ–carotene or 12 μg other biologically active carotenoids.
(h) No dietary sources may be necessary for children and adults who are sufficiently exposed to sunlight, but during the winter children and adolescents should receive 10 μg (400 i.u.) daily by supplementation. Adults with inadequate exposure to sunlight, for example those who are housebound, may also need a supplement of 10 μg daily (paragraph 60).
(i) For the third trimester only.
(j) This intake may not be sufficient for 10% of girls and women with large menstrual losses (paragraphs 63–70).

Table 2 Recommended daily amounts (RDA) of food energy and protein for infants

Age range months	Body weight kg Boys	Girls	RDA food energy MJ Boys	Girls	kcal Boys	Girls	RDA protein g Boys	Girls
0–3	4.6	4.4	2.2	2.1	530	500	13	12.5
3–6	7.1	6.6	3.0	2.8	720	670	18	17
6–9	8.8	8.2	3.7	3.4	880	810	22	20
9–12	9.8	9.0	4.1	3.8	980	910	24.5	23

Appendix II
Serial and E Numbers of Food Additives

KEY: Additives are discussed in more detail under different sections:

A   Antioxidants
B   Bread
C   Colours
E   Emulsifiers and stabilisers
M   Miscellaneous additives
MH   Mineral hydrocarbons
P   Preservatives
See also modified starch, sweeteners.

C	E100	Curcumin
C	E101	Riboflavin (**Lactoflavin**)
C	101(a)	Riboflavin-5-phosphate
C	E102	Tartrazine
C	E104	Quinoline Yellow
C	107	Yellow 2G
C	E110	Sunset Yellow FCF (**Orange Yellow S**)
C	E120	Cochineal (**Carmine of Cochineal or Carminic acid**)
C	E122	Carmoisine (**Azorubine**)
C	E123	Amaranth
C	E124	Ponceau 4R (**Cochineal Red A**)
C	E127	Erythrosine BS
C	128	Red 2G
C	E131	Patent Blue V
C	E132	Indigo Carmine (**Indigotine**)
C	133	Brilliant Blue FCF
C	E140	Chlorophyll
C	E141	Copper complexes of chlorophyll and chlorophyllins
C	E142	Green S (**Acid Brilliant Green BS or Lissamine Green**)
C	E150	Caramel
C	E151	Black PN (**Brilliant Black BN**)
C	E153	Carbon Black (**Vegetable Carbon**)
C	154	Brown FK
C	155	Brown HT (**Chocolate Brown HT**)
C	E160(a)	alpha-carotene, beta-carotene, gamma-carotene
C	E160(b)	annatto, bixin, norbixin
C	E160(c)	capsanthin (**Capsorubin**)
C	E160(d)	lycopene
C	E160(e)	beta-apo-8-carotenal (C_{30})
C	E160(f)	ethyl ester of beta-apo-8-carotenoic acid (C_{30})
C	E161(a)	Flavoxanthin
C	E161(b)	Lutein
C	E161(c)	Cryptoxanthin
C	E161(d)	Rubixanthin
C	E161(e)	Violaxanthin
C	E161(f)	Rhodoxanthin
C	E161(g)	Canthaxanthin
C	E162	Beetroot Red (**Betanin**)
C	E163	Anthocyanins
C	E170	Calcium carbonate
C	E171	Titanium dioxide
C	E172	Iron oxides, iron hydroxides
C	E173	Aluminium
C	E174	Silver
C	E175	Gold
C	E180	Pigment Rubine (**Lithol Rubine BK**)
P	E200	Sorbic acid
P	E201	Sodium sorbate

P E202   Potassium sorbate
P E203   Calcium sorbate
P E210   Benzoic acid
P E211   Sodium benzoate
P E212   Potassium benzoate
P E213   Calcium benzoate
P E214   Ethyl-4-hydroxybenzoate (**Ethyl** *para*-**hydroxybenzoate**)
P E215   Ethyl 4-hydroxybenzoate, sodium salt (**Sodium ethyl** *para*-**hydroxybenzoate**)
P E216   Propyl 4-hydroxybenzoate (**Propyl** *para*-**hydroxybenzoate**)
P E217   Propyl 4-hydroxybenzoate, sodium salt (**Sodium propyl** *para*-**hydroxybenzoate**)
P E218   Methyl 4-hydroxybenzoate (**Methyl** *para*-**hydroxybenzoate**)
P E219   Methyl 4-hydroxybenzoate, sodium salt (**Sodium methyl** *para*-**hydroxybenzoate**)
P E220   Sulphur dioxide
P E221   Sodium sulphite
P E222   Sodium hydrogen sulphite (**Sodium bisulphite**)
P E223   Sodium metabisulphite
P E224   Potassium metabisulphite
P E226   Calcium sulphite
P E227   Calcium hydrogen sulphite (**Calcium bisulphite**)
P E230   Biphenyl (**Diphenyl**)
P E231   2-Hydroxybiphenyl (**Orthophenylphenol**)
P E232   Sodium biphenyl-2-yl oxide (**Sodium orthophenylphenate**)
P E233   2-(Thiazol-4-yl) benzimidazole (**Thiabendazole**)
P 234   Nisin
P E239   Hexamine (**Hexamethylenetetramine**)
P E249   Potassium nitrite
P E250   Sodium nitrite
P E251   Sodium nitrate
P E252   Potassium nitrate
M E260   Acetic acid
M E261   Potassium acetate
M E262   Sodium hydrogen diacetate
M 262   Sodium acetate
M E263   Calcium acetate
M E270   Lactic acid
P E280   Propionic acid
P E281   Sodium propionate
P E282   Calcium propionate
P E283   Potassium propionate
M E290   Carbon dioxide
M 296   DL-Malic acid, L-Malic acid
M 297   Fumaric acid
A E300   L-Ascorbic acid
A E301   Sodium L-ascorbate
A E302   Calcium L-ascorbate
A E304   6-O-Palmitoyl-L-ascorbic acid (**Ascorbyl palmitate**)
A E306   Extracts of natural origin rich in tocopherols
A E307   Synthetic *alpha*-tocopherol
A E308   Synthetic *gamma*-tocopherol
A E309   Synthetic *delta*-tocopherol
A E310   Propyl gallate
A E311   Octyl gallate
A E312   Dodecyl gallate
A E320   Butylated hydroxyanisole (**BHA**)
A E321   Butylated hydroxytoluene (**BHT**)
E E322   Lecithins
M E325   Sodium lactate
M E326   Potassium lactate
M E327   Calcium lactate
M E330   Citric acid
M E331   Sodium dihydrogen citrate (*mono***Sodium citrate**), *di*Sodium citrate, *tri*Sodium citrate

M	E332	Potassium dihydrogen citrate (*mono*Potassium citrate), *tri*Potassium citrate
M	E333	*mono*Calcium citrate, *di*Calcium citrate, *tri*Calcium citrate
M	E334	L-(+)-Tartaric acid
M	E335	*mono*Sodium L-(+)-tartrate, *di*Sodium L-(+)-tartrate
M	E336	*mono*Potassium L-(+)-tartrate (Cream of tartar), *di*Potassium L-(+)-tartrate
M	E337	Potassium sodium L-(+)-tartrate
M	E338	Orthophosphoric acid (Phosphoric acid)
M	E339	Sodium dihydrogen orthophosphate, *di*Sodium hydrogen orthophosphate, *tri*Sodium orthophosphate
M	E340	Potassium dihydrogen orthophosphate, *di*Potassium hydrogen orthophosphate, *tri*Potassium orthophosphate
M	E341	Calcium tetrahydrogen diorthophosphate, Calcium hydrogen orthophosphate, *tri*Calcium diorthophosphate
M	350	Sodium malate, sodium hydrogen malate
M	351	Potassium malate
M	352	Calcium malate, calcium hydrogen malate
M	353	Metatartaric acid
M	355	Adipic acid
M	363	Succinic acid
M	370	I,4–Heptonolactone
M	375	Nicotinic acid
M	380	*tri*Ammonium citrate
M	381	Ammonium ferric citrate
M	385	Calcium disodium ethylenediamine–NNN'N' tetra-acetate (Calcium disodium EDTA)
E	E400	Alginic acid
E	E401	Sodium alginate
E	E402	Potassium alginate
E	E403	Ammonium alginate
E	E404	Calcium alginate
E	E405	Propane-1,2-diol alginate (Propylene glycol alginate)
E	E406	Agar
E	E407	Carrageenan
E	E410	Locust bean gum (Carob gum)
E	E412	Guar Gum
E	E413	Tragacanth
E	E414	Gum arabic (Acacia)
E	E415	Xanthan gum
E	416	Karaya gum
S	E420	Sorbitol, sorbitol syrup
S	E421	Mannitol
M	E422	Glycerol
E	430	Polyoxyethylene (8) stearate
E	431	Polyoxyethylene (40) stearate
E	432	Polyoxyethylene (20) sorbitan (Polysorbate 20)
E	433	Polyoxyethylene (20) sorbitan mono-oleate (Polysorbate 80)
E	434	Polyoxyethylene (20) sorbitan monopalmitate (Polysorbate 40)
E	435	Polyoxyethylene (20) sorbitan monostearate (Polysorbate 60)
E	436	Polyoxyethylene (20) sorbitan tristearate (Polysorbate 65)
E	E440(a)	Pectin
E	E440(b)	Amidated pectin
M	442	Ammonium phosphatides
M	E450(a)	*di*Sodium dihydrogen diphosphate, *tri*Sodium diphosphate, *tetra*Sodium diphosphate, *tetra*Potassium diphosphate
M	E450(b)	*penta*Sodium triphosphate, *penta*Potassium triphosphate
M	E450(c)	Sodium polyphosphates, Potassium polyphosphates
E	E460	Microcrystalline cellulose, *Alpha*-cellulose (Powdered cellulose)
E	E461	Methylcellulose
E	E463	Hydroxypropylcellulose
E	E464	Hydroxypropylmethylcellulose
E	E465	Ethylmethylcellulose
E	E466	Carboxymethylcellulose, sodium salt (CMC)

E	E470	Sodium, potassium and calcium salts of fatty acids
E	E471	Mono- and di-glycerides of fatty acids
E	E472(a)	Acetic acid esters of mono- and di-glycerides of fatty acids
E	E472(b)	Lactic acid esters of mono- and di-glycerides of fatty acids (**Lactoglycerides**)
E	E472(c)	Citric acid esters of mono- and di-glycerides of fatty acids (**Citroglycerides**)
E	E472(e)	Mono- and diacetyltartaric acid esters of mono- and di-glycerides of fatty acids
E	E473	Sucrose esters of fatty acids
E	E474	Sucroglycerides
E	E475	Polyglycerol esters of fatty acids
E	476	Polyglycerol esters of polycondensed fatty acids of castor oil (**Polyglycerol polyricinoleate**)
E	E477	Propane-1,2-diol esters of fatty acids
E	478	Lactylated fatty acid esters of glycerol and propane-1,2-diol
E	E481	Sodium stearoyl-2-lactylate
E	E482	Calcium stearoyl-2-lactylate
E	E483	Stearyl tartrate
E	491	Sorbitan monostearate
E	492	Sorbitan tristearate
E	493	Sorbitan monolaurate
E	494	Sorbitan mono-oleate
E	495	Sorbitan monopalmitate
M	500	Sodium carbonate, Sodium hydrogen carbonate (**Bicarbonate of soda**), Sodium sesquicarbonate
M	501	Potassium carbonate, Potassium hydrogen carbonate
M	503	Ammonium carbonate, Ammonium hydrogen carbonate
M	504	Magnesium carbonate
M	507	Hydrochloric acid
M	508	Potassium chloride
M	509	Calcium chloride
M	510	Ammonium chloride
M	513	Sulphuric acid
M	514	Sodium sulphate
M	515	Potassium sulphate
M	516	Calcium sulphate
M	518	Magnesium sulphate
M	524	Sodium hydroxide
M	525	Potassium hydroxide
M	526	Calcium hydroxide
M	527	Ammonium hydroxide
M	528	Magnesium hydroxide
M	529	Calcium oxide
M	530	Magnesium oxide
M	535	Sodium ferrocyanide (**Sodium hexacyanoferrate (II)**)
M	536	Potassium ferrocyanide (**Potassium hexacyanoferrate (II)**)
M	540	*di*Calcium diphosphate
M	541	Sodium aluminium phosphate
M	542	Edible bone phosphate
M	544	Calcium polyphosphates
M	545	Ammonium polyphosphates
M	551	Silicon dioxide (**Silica**)
M	552	Calcium silicate
M	553(a)	Magnesium silicate synthetic, Magnesium trisilicate
M	553(b)	Talc
M	554	Aluminium sodium silicate
M	556	Aluminium calcium silicate
M	558	Bentonite
M	559	Kaolin
M	570	Stearic acid
M	572	Magnesium stearate
M	575	D-Glucono-1,5-lactone (**Glucono *delta*-lactone**)
M	576	Sodium gluconate
M	577	Potassium gluconate

M	578	Calcium gluconate
M	620	L-glutamic acid
M	621	Sodium hydrogen L-glutamate (*mono*Sodium glutamate or MSG)
M	622	Potassium hydrogen L-glutamate (*mono*Potassium glutamate)
M	623	Calcium dihydrogen di-L-glutamate (Calcium glutamate)
M	627	Guanosine 5'-(disodium phosphate) (Sodium guanylate)
M	631	Inosine 5'-(disodium phosphate) (Sodium inosinate)
M	635	Sodium 5'-ribonucleotide
M	636	Maltol
M	637	Ethyl maltol
M	900	Dimethylpolysiloxane
M	901	Beeswax
M	903	Carnauba wax
M	904	Shellac
MH	905	Mineral hydrocarbons
M	907	Refined microcrystalline wax
B	920	L-cysteine hydrochloride
B	924	Potassium bromate
B	925	Chlorine
B	926	Chlorine dioxide
B	927	Azodicarbonamide (Azoformamide)

BIBLIOGRAPHY

Bingham, S., (1977), *The Dictionary of Nutrition*, Barrie and Jenkins, London

Brothwell, D., Brothwell, P., (1969), *Food in Antiquity*, Thames and Hudson, London

Conning, D.M., Lansdown, A.B.G., (eds.) (1983), *Toxic Hazards in Food*, Croom Helm Ltd, Beckenham, Kent

Coultate, T.P., (1984), *Food, The Chemistry of its Components*, Royal Society of Chemistry, London

Department of Health and Social Security (1981), *Nutritional Aspects of Bread and Flour*, Rep. Health and Soc. Subj. 23, HMSO, London

Department of Health and Social Security (1984), *Diet and Cardiovascular Disease*, Rep. Health and Soc. Subj., HMSO, London

Durrant, P.J., (1964), *General and Inorganic Chemistry*, Longman, London

Masefield, G.B., Wallis, M., Harris, S.G., Nicholson, B.E., (1969), *The Oxford Book of Food Plants*, Oxford University Press, London

Miller, M., (1985) *A Report on Food Additives*, London Food Commission, London

Ministry of Agriculture, Fisheries and Foods (1985), *Approved Products for Farmers and Growers*, HMSO, London

Montagne, P., (1961), *Larousse Gastronomique*, Hamlyn, Feltham, Middlesex

Paul, A.A., Southgate, D.A.T. (1978), *McCance and Widdowson's The Composition of Foods*, HMSO, London

Paul, A.A., Southgate, D.A.T., Russell, C., (1980), *First Supplement to McCance and Widdowson's The Composition of Foods*, HMSO, London

National Research Council (1982), *Diet, Nutrition and Cancer*, National Academy Press, Washington, D.C.

Oddy, D.J., Miller, D.S. (Eds.) (1976), *The Making of the Modern British Diet*, Croom Helm, London

Painter, A.A. (Ed.) (1985), *Butterworth's Law of Food and Drugs*, Butterworths, London

Passmore, R., Eastwood, M.A., (1986), *Davidson and Passmore's Human Nutrition and Dietetics*, Churchill Livingstone, Edinburgh

Royal College of Physicians (1980), *Medical Aspects of Dietary Fibre*, Pitman Medical, London

Royal College of Physicians and British Nutrition Foundation (1984), *Food Intolerance and Food Aversion*, J. Roy. Coll. Phys. **18**, no. 2

Tann, S., Wenlock, R., Buss. D., (1985) *Immigrant Foods*, HMSO, London

World Health Organisation (1985), *Energy and Protein Requirements*, Tech. Rep. Ser. 724, W.H.O., Geneva

Reference has also been made to various scientific periodicals including: The American Journal of Clinical Nutrition; The British Medical Journal; British Nutrition Foundation Bulletins; The British Journal of Nutrition; Journal of the American Dietetic Association; Human Nutrition; Applied Nutrition; The Lancet; Nature; Nutrition and Food Science; Nutrition Reviews; and The Proceedings of the Nutrition Society.